Prefaces,

A sustained explanation of

CW01095142

Translation, Subjectivity, and Culture
in France and England, 1600–1800

Translation, Subjectivity, and Culture in France and England, 1600–1800

Julie Candler Hayes

STANFORD UNIVERSITY PRESS

STANFORD, CALIFORNIA

Stanford University Press
Stanford, California

Publication assistance for this book was provided by the College of Humanities and Fine Arts and the Vice Provost for Research at the University of Massachusetts Amherst.

Printed in the United States of America on acid-free, archival-quality paper

Library of Congress Cataloging-in-Publication Data

Hayes, Julie Candler, 1955–
    Translation, subjectivity, and culture in France and England, 1600–1800 / Julie Candler Hayes.
        p. cm.
    Includes bibliographical references and index.
    ISBN 978-0-8047-5944-1 (cloth : alk. paper)
    1. Translating and interpreting—France—History. 2. Translating and interpreting—England—History.   3. Classical literature—Translations into French.   4. Classical literature—Translations into English.   5. Literature—History and criticism.   6. Literature and society—France—History.   7. Literature and society—England—History.   I. Title.
    PN241.5.F7H39 2009
    418'.020944—dc22

                                    2008018843

Typeset by Bruce Lundquist in 11/14 Adobe Garamond

For Claude and Daniel
dans nos deux langues

Contents

Acknowledgments

This book was many years in the making, and I have incurred numerous debts along the way. It is a pleasure to acknowledge friends and colleagues whose moral support and comments on the work in progress have meant so much over the years: Dan Brewer, Lorna Clymer, Patrick Coleman, Tom Kavanagh, Marilyn Gaddis Rose, David Lee Rubin, Sherry Simon, and Janie Vanpée. The chapter on women translators would be much the poorer without the bibliographic suggestions of Linda Bree, Marie-Pascale Pieretti, Toni Sol, Aurora Wolfgang, and Judith Zinsser. The members of the 2004–2005 Literary Studies Discussion Group at the National Humanities Center provided invaluable feedback at a critical time. I have been helped by the comments and queries of anonymous readers for *Restoration*, *Early-Modern France*, and Stanford University Press, and by audience members at meetings of the American Society for Eighteenth-Century Studies, IAPL, MLA, and the Five College Translation Studies Seminar and at conferences at the Clark Library / Center for Seventeenth and Eighteenth-Century Studies at UCLA. I thank Emily-Jane Cohen of Stanford University Press for her wonderful responsiveness and guidance.

I am grateful to those institutions that made it possible for me to spend extended periods of time in rare-book collections in North America and France. I benefited from short-term fellowships at the Mills Memorial Library at McMaster University in 1996, the William Andrews Clark Library of UCLA in 1997, and the Huntington Library in 2004. The Faculty Research Committee of the University of Richmond funded summers in the Bibliothèque Nationale in Paris in 1995, 2000, 2001, 2002, and 2003. A research fellowship from the National Endowment for the Humanities, along with a Jessie Ball duPont fellowship at the National Humanities Center, enabled me to take a year-long sabbatical, during which my scattered notes, articles, and conference papers gradually came together.

I thank my former colleagues at the University of Richmond, whose friendship remains with me always, and my new colleagues and friends at the University of Massachusetts Amherst, whose welcome has warmed our first New England winters.

The book is dedicated to my husband and son. Their unstinting love and loyalty make all things possible.

A Note on the Texts

Considerations of space prevent me from offering extended quotations of many original texts. Fortunately, the vast majority of the English imprints are available via the Early English Books Online (EEBO) and Eighteenth-Century Collections Online (ECCO) databases. The original French texts not available in modern editions can be found online at http://scholarworks .umass.edu/french_translators/.

In quoting from seventeenth- and eighteenth-century editions, I have retained original spelling and punctuation. For texts with numbered signatures instead of page numbers (a common practice for seventeenth-century prefaces), I have retained the numbering system used for the specific volume rather than attempting to rationalize all such references into a common system.

All French translations are mine unless otherwise noted.

Translation, Subjectivity, and Culture
in France and England, 1600–1800

Introduction

Rethinking Neoclassical Translation

In 1638, Paris publisher Jean Camusat created a stir by bringing out a handsome quarto volume that was immediately understood to be an anonymous manifesto for the literary and cultural ambitions of the recently formed Académie française. The work, *Huit oraisons de Ciceron*, was a set of translations from Cicero; the translators were known to be four young intellectuals attached to Valentin Conrart, the "father" of the Académie. Chief contributor to the enterprise was Nicolas Perrot d'Ablancourt; educated at the Collège de Sedan and, like Conrart, a Protestant, he went on to become the leading translator of the day. The *Huit oraisons* volume proposed a French style of eloquence equal to that of the great Roman orator; it signaled a national project dedicated to promoting the preeminence of the French language. The *Huit oraisons* also opened a chapter in the history of translation in the West. By emphasizing both the literary values of their audience and the freedom of their approach, d'Ablancourt and his colleagues reshaped "ancienne Eloquence" to modern sensibilities and struck a profound chord with readers.[1] Such "neoclassical" translations would become one of the principal vectors not just for the understanding of the classics but also for the development of a national literature in both France and Britain, providing the basis for an ongoing series of debates on translation, authorship, language, and culture for over a century to come.

TRANSLATION AND TRANSLATORS

Translation is one of the key means by which the singularity of the literary event becomes absorbed into cultural practice. Translation makes language visible, reminding us that the bridges between cultures can never be taken for granted, but instead require patient probing and an openness to otherness and difference. The history of translation helps us to put contemporary issues within a larger perspective, to enlarge our experience, and to understand our alternatives. In recent decades, the rise of translation studies as an independent discipline at the confluence of philosophy, historical linguistics, and literary studies, as well as the calls for "global awareness" in popular culture and public life, have produced a vibrant, interdisciplinary, and timely field of inquiry. Through translation studies we examine our place within language, culture, and history, and our ability to communicate that reality and to understand the realities of others.

These are the broader concerns animating my study of the work of translators in France and Britain throughout the seventeenth and eighteenth centuries, a period of intense intercultural dialogue between the two countries, during which translation and the critical reflection inspired by it provided a framework for crucial features of the transition to modernity. Among the questions confronted by translators are the shifting relation to the classical past and the working-through of the loss of that past, the consolidation of national identity as represented in the national language, the construction of multiple approaches to authorial identity as well as a variety of techniques for expressing individual subjectivities in writing, and the creation of new conceptual spaces for imagining otherness, dialogue, and cultural change. These themes emerge across several spheres of activity. Translations from the Greek and Latin classics afforded sources of inspiration and emulation that enabled the vernacular literature to develop its own voice; translations from the Christian scriptures (and sacred writings from other traditions) provided new ways of experiencing one's faith and new avenues for exploring the relationship between language, truth, and meaning; and translations from recent and contemporary works in the modern languages have broadened cross-cultural communication and expanded the republic of letters.

While vernacular translations played a significant role throughout Europe from the Middle Ages onward, I focus on seventeenth- and eighteenth-century France and England not only because of the significant place each country had in the other's political and social imagination, creating a cross-channel dialogue that would become a crucial feature of the European Enlightenment, but also because during this period translators in the two countries were extremely aware of each other's practice. An implicit conversation on *how* and *why* to translate mirrored the exchange of ideas in the literary, philosophical, and scientific communities.[2] Beginning in the 1640s, exiled English royalist men of letters at the court of France, such as John Denham and Abraham Cowley, came into contact with the work of d'Ablancourt and his circle. The neoclassical translators were best known for translations characterized by strong literary values and highly adaptive or "localizing" translation strategies aimed at making the original author "speak French" according to the standards of taste of the day. While not without controversy, such translations—dubbed *les belles infidèles* (lovely unfaithful ones)—proved extremely popular in both countries and set the standard for literary translation. The intensity of the cross-channel dialogue continued to increase throughout the eighteenth century. Not only did the French and British translate each other's works extensively, but French and British translators also read each other's work, commenting on it—and sometimes borrowing from it. The mutual translations and commentaries bespeak a broad and extremely complex pattern of identity and difference, emulation and rivalry, *anglomanie* and *anglophobie*, Francophilia and Francophobia throughout the period.[3]

Why did the translations of d'Ablancourt and his friends constitute such an important shift in translation theory and practice? To answer this question, let us turn briefly to the background and immediate context of their work. In some accounts of the *longue durée* of the history of translation in Europe, little happens between Cicero's announcement in *De optimo genere oratorum* that he has endeavored to translate "not as an interpreter, but as an orator" and the advent of Romanticism.[4] Certainly there were important continuities over the centuries in the practice of, and especially in the critical reflection on, translation: discussions on the separability and relative importance of word and meaning, or *verba* and *res*; on the translator's degree of "freedom" or "servitude"; on the relative roles of grammar and rhetoric;

on the relationship between translation and hermeneutics. The recurrence of familiar topoi and classical references—Cicero, Horace, Jerome—reinforces the sense of a continuous conversation. Thus, it has been argued, we can trace an unwavering line from Cicero's presumed recommendation not to translate word for word (*non verbum pro verbo*) through certain key lines from Horace's *Ars poetica* to Saint Jerome, who quotes from both predecessors in his Epistle 57 when claiming to translate "not word for word, but sense for sense" (*non verbum e verbo, sed sensum exprimere de sensu*). Words and meaning, freely detached from one another, can be exchanged, "weighted," and made to compensate for one another. This configuration is only strengthened by an overlay of platonizing Christianity, in which "meaning" is cast as immaterial and spiritualized, while "words" remain corporeal, material, earthbound.[5]

While it is undeniable that these notions run through much of the discussion of translation from antiquity to early modernity, the discussion itself is far more complex. Saint Jerome's respectful citations notwithstanding, his reading of Cicero, like that of other patristic figures, downplays or even erases the Roman orator's emphasis on translation as invention and resignification.[6] Horace's role in early modern translation theory is even more complicated, given the long history of contradictory readings of the words from *Ars poetica*, "nec verbo verbum curabis reddere fidus / interpres." As cited in this fragmentary manner, Horace could appear to be suggesting that the "faithful translator" should *not* render word for word; in context, however, the passage is an injunction to poets. It is they who are enjoined not to imitate "in the manner of the faithful translator," suggesting that faithful translators, for their part, *should* adhere closely to their texts. Throughout the Renaissance, in particular, such "corrective Horatianism" among the Humanists emphasized the importance of literalist practice.[7] D'Ablancourt and his friends broke with this tendency. Horace's lines appear on the final page of the *Huit oraisons* to underscore the work's function as a polemical statement on translation. But by citing the verses out of context and taking advantage of the ambiguities of Latin syntax, the translators claimed Horace for their side and condemned a word-for-word approach. Their citational strategy was thus as free as their versions of Cicero—and would offer a target for later critics such as Pierre-Daniel Huet.[8]

During the Renaissance, translation had often been caught up in debates concerning the nature of imitation—its appropriateness in different contexts, its potential for either enriching the national culture or sapping it of authenticity. For Joachim Du Bellay, translation played a key role in the advancement of learning, but it could not ultimately infuse new riches into the vernacular. Other forms of imitation are required, he argued, "to lift our vernacular to be the equal and Paragon of more celebrated Languages."[9] Throughout the period, the terms *imitation* and *translation*, and the etymological variants *translater* and *traduire*, suggest a variety of understandings of the links among words, things, and ideas.[10] As the word *traduction* replaced *translation* as the primary term in French, emphasizing the translator's active intervention rather than the neutral circulation of texts, translation emerged as an increasingly autonomous activity, susceptible to theorization and separate from interpretation and imitation. Etienne Dolet's short treatise *La Maniere de bien traduire d'une langue en autre* (1540) offers not simply a set of procedures for producing correct translations but a more thorough intellectual grounding of the translator's work.[11] The rise of theoretical reflection, as well as the increased attention to the development of vernacular culture, contributes to enhancing the status of translation and, as Luce Guillerm has argued, to endowing the translator with a new authority. The translator's authority is not the authority of the author (to which the distinction between author and translator contributes), but the authority conferred on those who, like the sovereign, augment the national treasure and enhance the national language.[12]

Several elements that spurred the development of neoclassical translation were thus in place by the early decades of the seventeenth century: a new prominence for translators in the world of letters; an attentiveness to the enrichment and development of the vernacular; a significant body of critical reflection, with classical antecedents, situating translation with respect to language, imitation, and poetic creation. These factors alone, however, did not render subsequent developments automatic. Three years before the publication of the *Huit oraisons*, Claude Favre de Vaugelas, the arbiter of elegant French, read aloud a treatise by an absent colleague at one of the earliest meetings of the Académie française. The work, Claude-Gaspar Bachet de Meziriac's *De la traduction*, has been called the earliest rigorously systematic analysis of translation practice; it was also a blistering critique of one of the acknowledged masterpieces of Renaissance translation, Jacques Amyot's version of Plutarch (1559), long regarded as a model of style. For Meziriac, however, "the beauty of the language alone cannot suffice to render a translation estimable. . . . [Rather,] the essential quality in a translation is fidelity."[13] Meziriac died soon after the reading, however, and his treatise would not be published for nearly a century. Vaugelas would model his own translation practice not on Meziriac's recommendations but on the work of d'Ablancourt.

D'Ablancourt produced half of the translations in the *Huit oraisons*; he was joined by Pierre Du Ryer, better known to literary history as a dramatist, but also one of the most prolific translators of the day; Louis Giry, best known for translations of religious texts; and Olivier Patru, a close friend of d'Ablancourt's and a model of eloquence and *l'usage* as respected as Vaugelas. (Du Ryer produced two of the Cicero translations; Giry and Patru, one apiece.) Critics, particularly Antoine Furetière, would cast d'Ablancourt as the "captain" of the group that he himself referred to simply as "somewhat free" (*un peu libres*) translators.[14] The movement received a more telling name in a quip by Gilles Ménage, who affected innocent surprise both at the term's popularity and at its negative acceptation, and the translations have been known as "les belles infidèles" ever since.[15] At the moment of the publication of the *Huit oraisons*, d'Ablancourt and his friends were poised— by personal connections and talent, as well as by the confluence of political, institutional, and aesthetic developments bound up in the founding of the Academy—to play a key role in the making of French classical taste.[16]

The "belles infidèles" occasioned considerable debate in their day. Neoclassical translation practice actually involved a range of approaches to issues of freedom versus fidelity, the relation of past to present, and the capacity of language to represent other cultural realities. Nevertheless, beginning with Germaine de Staël and the Romantics, there has been a tendency to lump all the seventeenth and eighteenth centuries' translators together and to condemn translation "in the French manner" as overly restricted to the confines of local taste and unavailable to authentic cultural dialogue.[17] This critique has been amplified in the work of recent theorists such as Antoine Berman and Lawrence Venuti, who qualify French and English neoclassical translation practice as "ethnocentric" and "hegemonizing." While I believe that such critiques have provoked useful discussion of the norms appropriate for translators today, I also believe that we need a clearer, more nuanced understanding of the past. Certainly, inasmuch as the work of neoclassical translators subtends broader cultural projects such as the centralization and purification of the national language to the exclusion of regional variants and other local languages, it too has its darker side, its affiliation with nationalism and internal colonization.[18] Bible translation, to cite another example, can be viewed in relation to expansionism and the rise of imperialism during the period studied here. My principal aim, however, is to sort out the multiple agendas and projects that compose the "neoclassical school," through a careful reading of the translators' own words.

By "the translators' own words," I mean, quite literally, their statements on the meaning and methods of their projects, contained for the most part in their prefaces. Although I do examine certain individual translations, I am primarily concerned with the ways in which the translators conceived their projects and presented them to the world. My study takes into account bibliographic research on translation and follows the careers of a number of individual translators, but it is first and foremost an attempt to come to terms with these often quite complex texts through sustained close reading. Sometimes polemical, sometimes philosophical, sometimes deeply personal, prefaces and related materials provide us with a "translation theory" that is deeply contextualized, situated variously in terms of the work of other translators, the patronage system, the literary marketplace, and the world of ideas.

QUESTIONS OF METHOD

Reading Prefaces

If the relation of a translation to its source text slices across frames of reference that include linguistic choices, critical hermeneutics, and differing modes of literary reception, the relationship of the translator's preface to the translated text (and to its original) adds an additional layer of complexity. As a genre, the critical preface—often, indeed, a translator's preface—arose in Italy and France in the Renaissance and became popular in England in the course of the seventeenth century. The freedom of the translator's preface is surely one of the genre's most appealing qualities: content and tone may vary from elegy to political satire, from autobiography to *explication de texte*. Gérard Genette's typology of literary prefaces in *Seuils* (authentic or fictive, authorial or "allographic," and so on) does not capture the peculiar position of the preface written by a translator, who both is and is not the author of the text being presented; whose motives for translating may be pedagogical, spiritual, commercial, or oppositional; who may aim to influence the standard of taste, to shock—*épater le bourgeois!*—or to warn of a perceived danger.[19] As in other prefaces, the writer/translator offers a pact to the reader; unlike other prefaces, that pact includes a relationship with a third party, the original author, and frequently others, such as patrons and other translators (past, present, or future). The preface is furthermore the site of a transaction that is difficult to locate in time. It represents a completed reading of a work that we as readers have yet to encounter; it dislocates original authors from their place in history. One of the most commonly recurring topoi in neoclassical prefaces is the translator's desire to "make the author speak" as if he or she were alive before us, sharing our language. As Glyn Norton notes in his perspicacious study of Renaissance translators' prefaces, the translator "embarks on an act of deconstruction," setting forth the historical and personal contexts of reading and interpretation, the problems of meaning, interpretation, and cultural equivalency.[20]

It is tempting to sketch the outlines of a typology of translators' prefaces. Leaving aside fictive translators' prefaces to many a novel, one would need to take into account the function of the preface in different genres and disciplines—such as literature, history, philosophy, science, and travel writing—and the different functions performed by the preface: historical background, explanation, justification, and what Genette calls the "lightning rod" (ranging from the topos of modesty to apparent condemnation, as in the prefaces to the 1647 French version and the 1649 English version of the Qur'ān). The preface may discuss the origins of the source text (Pierre Le Tourneur's eighteenth-century prefaces to Young and Shakespeare) or those of the translation (William Gifford's Juvenal [1802]); anti-prefaces lampoon the genre (numerous prefaces of Roger L'Estrange); dueling prefaces attack one another (Silhouette's and Resnel's prefaces to their rival translations of Pope's *Essay on Man* in the 1730s). A translator's preface can also become juxtaposed to a translated author's preface (Aphra Behn's Fontenelle of 1688) or metamorphose into an editor's preface (Pierre Du Ryer's 1653 preface to Vaugelas's *Quinte-Curce*). And of course many of these texts involve sustained reflections on aesthetics, the relative merits of prose and verse, questions of language and meaning, national character, and so on.

Only recently have these densely textured, nuanced texts been fully recognized as significant contributions to the history of reading and criticism. George Steiner, for example, characterized all statements by translators prior to Schleiermacher as having only an "immediate empirical focus," in contrast to a "second stage . . . of theory and hermeneutic inquiry" arising after 1800.[21] More recently, critics such as Michel Ballard and Lieven d'Hulst have argued that the juxtaposition of "empirical" prefaces and "theoretical" treatises is faulty and anachronistic, and a growing number of anthologies of prefaces points toward a new appreciation for their place in literary history.[22] While I hope that the readings that follow will bear out the theoretical significance of many of these pieces, I also hope to show that they contain moments of beauty and drama as well.

So, focus on translators' preface.

Constructing a Corpus

We lack a complete bibliography of translations into English and French during this period, although there are a number of useful bibliographic studies of specific genres or of individual writers in translation. The two best-known bibliographic tools, by J.-A.-R. Séguin and Charles Rochedieu, survey translations from French to English and from English to French, respectively, but they are organized by completely different principles and are impossible to compare for the purpose of estimating the relative flow of translations back and forth across the Channel.[23] Nor can such studies tell us a great deal about the literary marketplace for translation (from the classics or from other modern languages) in general. Working with selected years from the English Short Title Catalogue (ESTC), Mary Helen McMurran estimates that French novels and romances accounted for 15–30 percent on average, and rising as high as 36 percent, of the prose fiction published in Britain between 1660 and 1770.[24] Séguin's bibliography of works translated from French to English shows a general rise, with some fluctuations, from an average of 30–40 titles per year in the 1730s to more than twice that number in the 1750s. Although there was a slight decline during the politically tense years of the 1760s, 1766 yielded the highest number of translations of any year surveyed, with 108 titles; then 60–80 titles continued to appear each year till the onset of the Revolution. Such figures correspond to what is generally known about the importance of French-English intellectual and cultural exchange during the Enlightenment.[25] One can also glean some sense of the relative presence of other national literatures through period compilations such as the abbé Goujet's *Bibliothèque françoise* (1740), but much work remains to be done to complete the picture. While one can imagine, given the availability of online library catalogues, databases such as ESTC or Research Libraries Information Network, the Centre d'études de la traduction database at Metz, and so on, that a "technical solution" to the question could be realized, we are far from possessing a tool that would allow a statistical study of the place of translations from both modern and classical languages in the literary marketplace, an "atlas of translation" along the lines of Franco Moretti's work on the transnational evolution of the novel.

I have been less ambitious than these data-driven projects in some ways and more ambitious in others. My basic corpus consists of 450–500 works, not all of which, ultimately, are cited, but whose existence often guided my readings and research. The texts include primarily translators' prefaces, but also polemical writings, treatises, pedagogical manuals, and other relevant documents from the end of the sixteenth century through the 1790s. The corpus is about equally distributed between French and English imprints and writers/translators, including approximately ninety French individual figures and the same number of English figures. Women make up 10 percent of both groups. The corpus also includes a dozen or so anonymous translations in each language. Given the thousands of works, not only in belles lettres but also in philosophy, religion, natural science, and political science, that were translated during this period into English and French, not only from each other but from other modern and classical languages, my corpus lays no claim to statistical representativeness.

Instead, I have been concerned with finding prefaces (and other texts that take up translation-related issues) that go beyond a schematic rehearsal of the matter at hand; that offer some form of self-reflexive, critical gesture; that point toward larger philosophical and cultural goals intersecting the act of translation. I soon realized that such critical reflections were often to be found beyond the obvious list, usually occurring toward the end of the translator's preface, of the "difficulties encountered" by the translator or the "rules of translation" offered in a treatise. Other questions—historical, philosophical, literary-critical, or even autobiographical—were often woven in as well, and these threads contributed to the density of the argument.

One corollary of this approach is that the corpus is weighted heavily toward translations from Greek and Latin. Latin, of course, was part of the intellectual equipment of all educated men, so many translations from the Latin classics are aimed at readers who can read the original and appreciate the translator's choices. With Greek and especially Hebrew, however, we enter the realm of "erudition." Such translations more often appear with prefatory remarks and notes. In both France and England, the cultural prestige of translations from the ancient languages may explain in part why such works are more often accompanied by a full-fledged critical apparatus than translations from the modern languages; I will also be suggesting that classicists found themselves forced to come to terms with matters of historical and cultural "difference" and linguistic undecidability that were not as immediately apparent to translators from modern languages. Certainly these are crucial issues in biblical criticism and translation, hotly debated during the period examined here. Revealingly, even though his *Bibliothèque françoise* includes discussions of works from English, Spanish, and Italian, the abbé Goujet understands the word *traduction* as pertaining to translation from Greek and Latin; he feels compelled to justify his use of the term with respect to the modern European languages, whose temporal proximity would appear to render them to some degree "transparent" in his perception. Over the course of the eighteenth century, especially in France, we will see an increasing number of writers' works accorded the status of "modern classics," with full formal treatment in elegant editions with critical prefaces: Jonathan Swift, Alexander Pope, Samuel Richardson, and Edward Young.

The predominance of classicists in the corpus explains in part the smaller *women* number of women, despite the importance of translation as a road to print for women writers and intellectuals and, indeed, the significant place women translators occupied in the literary marketplace. Classical scholar Anne Dacier, a powerful figure both institutionally and intellectually in England as much as in France, is an exception. Works produced in response to the "marketplace"—translations of modern novels, for example—do not, as a rule, receive the formal treatment. Eliza Haywood, though a prolific translator of French novels, rarely offers extensive prefaces. To the extent that the discourse on translation throughout the period is informed primarily by theoretical reflection rather than by observations on practice, translations appearing without a critical apparatus do not play as large a role in this book as they did in the publishing world. (Writing at the end of the eighteenth century, Alexander Tytler structures a significant part of his treatise on translation in terms of examples drawn from actual translations, but even so, much of his discussion remains a dialogue with critical writing.) Yet the numbers of women translators and the importance of gender as a category informing their self-presentation and discussion of translation merit particular study.

So far I have emphasized some of the limitations of the corpus and the ways in which it does not "represent" certain aspects of translation during this period. Other limitations are built into the nature of academic work, with its multiple demands of teaching, scholarship, advising, and administration. One can only spend so much time in research libraries and rare-book

Pressures of current academic employment

CHOICE
of TEXTS

*

rooms, or even checking the online resources of Early English Books Online (EEBO) and Eighteenth-Century Collections Online (ECCO). It would be physically impossible (for this working academic parent, in any event) to call up and examine all of the translations from Greek and Latin published in French and English over the seventeenth and eighteenth centuries. It is somewhat easier to come to terms with translations of individual texts, especially those by modern authors. One can, without too much difficulty, examine all the early French and English translations of *Don Quijote*, for example. Much valuable work on the reception of individual writers has been carried out in this manner. But the "brute force" approach, calling up all the Virgil translations in the Bibliothèque nationale, is not necessarily the most productive, if we are seeking to give an account of what was at stake—culturally, aesthetically, politically, and personally—for those men and women who found themselves poised at the edge of one linguistic and cultural experience, contemplating another.

CITATION
networks.

Instead, I have relied to a great extent on the translators themselves for my direction. Implicit in much of the text to follow are what I call "citation networks": translators who refer to other translators, books that refer to other books. While Dryden, Pope, and d'Alembert have ever been clearly present to literary and intellectual history, others, like Anne Dacier, Roger L'Estrange, or the abbé Desfontaines, are more the province of period specialists. The more one reads of prefaces, critical commentaries, or pedagogical reflection, however, the more one encounters their names, or those of figures such as Jacques de Tourreil, the abbé Delille, or George Campbell, major figures in their own day without whom the picture could not be complete. Citations and other references help remind us of the importance of networks and affiliations among translators: d'Ablancourt's followers, English royalists, Ancients and Moderns, Huguenot exiles.[26] The collective translations produced at the Jansenist retreat at Port-Royal are a vivid example of a tightly knit network, but the Port-Royal translators were also in dialogue with other men of letters and biblical scholars. "Completeness," in the sense of some Borgesian Total Library, or a map as large as its country, or, most tellingly, the perfect translation-as-replication (which is always different from itself) of Pierre Menard, is not to be found, and probably not to be wished for. But there is a compelling and necessary story to be told through a careful reading of these related texts. I would be remiss, however, if I did not give credit to earlier literary historians and scholars whose reception studies, histories of translation, and anthologies of writings on translation often guided my search, as my bibliography shows. For every profoundly interesting preface or dedicatory epistle that I rejoiced in finding on my own, I was pointed to numerous others through the work of colleagues past and present.

At the heart of this collection of texts, the works to which I will be attending the most closely, is a set of substantial reflections on language and literary traditions, poetics, semiotics, national cultures, readerships, writing and reading, and, frequently, other translators: either previous translators of a particular text whose work now appears insufficient to the needs of the present or translators whose own critical statements inspire or serve to justify the present translator's enterprise. The critical canon undergoes a radical change: for centuries, translators had justified their choices through references to particular passages in Cicero, Horace, and Jerome; many continue to do so, but now they also refer to recent and contemporary authorities such as Anne Dacier, Jacques de Tourreil, and Jean Bouhier in France, and John Denham, John Dryden, and the Earl of Roscommon in England. Roscommon's *Essay on Translated Verse* crosses the Channel and is cited on both sides of the debate over French translations of Pope. Translation is a prime site for discussion of the historicity of language and the evolution of literary traditions—and, indeed, the historicity of translation practice itself. In other words, we have before us a key component in the emergence of literary criticism and literary theory as a discourse, if not yet a discipline. The emergence of the word *literature* in both English and French as referring to something more specific than all writing and as distinct from belles lettres is coterminous with this shift.

Writing the History of Translation

In a lively and thought-provoking discussion of methodological issues in translation history, Anthony Pym argues that "even if everything that has preceded us were absolute rubbish . . . we should be able to say why what has been done is rubbish, according to what methodological faults, and how our future non-rubbish is going to correct those faults."[27] Contemporary translation studies is too vast a field for me to give more than the briefest summary of those threads—rubbish or not—that have the most bearing on the present project. My intellectual debts are apparent from the bibliography. As I have already indicated, however, while scholars of translation history such as George Steiner, Louis Kelly, or Frederick Rener have the great virtue of recognizing the rich interconnections among older statements on translation, their tendency to conflate the *longue durée* into a single moment or set of issues erases their historicity. I have already mentioned Steiner's decision to designate nearly all writing on translation before Schleiermacher as "pre-hermeneutic." All three tend to organize their analyses along structural or thematic lines, as if historical moment had no bearing on the question. Kelly's discussion of the topos of the translator's "struggle" cites within a single paragraph Henri Meschonnic, Saint Jerome, Cecil Day Lewis, Yves Bonnefoy, Philo Judaeus, Roger Bacon, Vladimir Nabokov, and Walter Benjamin (132); Rener refers to the eighteen hundred years from Cicero to Alexander Tytler as a single "period" with a single "theory of language" (13). Of course, translation theory has its continuities, both temporal and transnational—but it is also situated in time and place. Etienne Dolet was burned at the stake and Perrot d'Ablancourt elevated to the Académie française within a century of each other.

A great deal has been written on "polysystem theory" in translation studies, a movement that is geographically scattered but still most closely associated with the work of Gideon Toury, Itamar Even-Zohar, and the Porter Institute for Poetics and Semiotics at Tel Aviv University and its journal *Poetics Today*.[28] Toury's best-known work emphasizes the need to determine the "norms" according to which a translation (or other literary work) functions within a literary system: What is linguistically or culturally acceptable? What function does the presence or absence of the author's or translator's name have in the publication and reception of the work? While Toury's interest in "universals of translational behavior" encompasses transhistorical questions, others have offered interesting accounts of specific, historically situated literary systems as well as of systems changing over time. Descriptivist translation studies dovetails with other sociologically oriented approaches in literary studies, such as the examinations of the "literary field" inspired by the work of Pierre Bourdieu. Thus historians such as Alain Viala and Gregory Brown have examined the categories by which works were judged and literary careers were made in the Ancien Régime.[29] The fact that "strategies for success" for writers and translators were very different in 1630 and 1790 should warn us from too easy a conflation of similar-sounding translation theories from those years. (Is that not indeed the lesson learned from Pierre Menard?) Who our translators were by birth, where they were educated, what faith they professed, what other forms of writing they engaged in, what sources of income and what forms of patronage they benefited from, what salons, academies, epistolary networks, and political activities they participated in—all of these elements infuse and have a bearing on the meaning of their work.

For Bourdieu and other literary sociologists, as for the polysystems theorists, the aim is to understand the cultural reality of a moment in terms of "success": how does the system operate so that certain works meet with approval, certain attitudes and positions achieve recognition and capital (whether cultural or real), while others do not? In such a view, the literary field is a "force-field" in which "position-takings (works, political manifestos or demonstrations, and so on), which one may and should treat for analytical purposes as a 'system' of oppositions, are not the result of some kind of objective collusion, but rather the product and the stake of a permanent conflict."[30] While I have endeavored to keep aspects of this agonistic literary "system" and of translators' socioeconomic status, relative prestige, and so forth in mind in the readings ahead, it will quickly become clear that my main purpose lies not in determining what produced "success" in the field of translation. Here the aims and methods of a literary scholarship infused by philosophy and the history of ideas part ways with a more sociological approach. Hence I will be less concerned with describing the translation practices that best appealed to the reading publics—who won or lost the *Querelle d'Homère* or even the English Civil War, and who achieved or lost status thereby—than with exploring the texture of the ideas voiced, the sometimes surprising connections and disjunctions with each other and with ongoing debates in our own day. Instead of a demystifying "history of the present" laying bare the origins of contemporary practices, my focus here is the reconsideration of roads not taken, possibilities left unfulfilled. The past, like a text waiting to be translated, offers alternative readings, re-translations, that may stimulate new questions for the present.

Although the "history of translation" cannot be undertaken without attention to its location in time and place, it nevertheless continues to pose questions that remain urgent for us today. Recognition of the historicity of these texts does not therefore preclude engaging them on our own contemporary intellectual terrain. Indeed, such dialogue between past and present is not only inevitable but desirable. And this leads me to the third moment in my rapid methodological overview, the role neoclassical translation theory and practice have played in what could be termed the "ethical turn" in recent histories of translation.

Ethics and Otherness

As mentioned earlier, the "neoclassical" approach associated with translators and theorists from d'Ablancourt to Tytler fell under severe censure during the nineteenth century, beginning with Staël and the Romantics.[31] In his seminal study of German Romantic translation theory, *L'Epreuve de l'étranger*, Antoine Berman called for historical studies of translating practice that would show "how in each period or in each given historical setting the practice of translation is articulated in relation to the practice of literature, of languages, of the several intercultural and interlinguistic exchanges."[32] Clearly there is much to be gained, both for the history of ideas and for our own contemporary understanding of the issues, in examining the relations between translation and the philosophy of language, literary expression, the book trade, and national and cultural politics in a given context. Berman, however, then went on to make a case for what he called the "ethical aim," or *visée éthique*, of translation—"to open up in writing a certain relation with the Other, to fertilize what is one's Own through the mediation of what is Foreign" (4)—and to which he opposed "bad" or "ethnocentric" translations that carry out "a systematic negation of the strangeness of the foreign work" (5).[33] Already, there is a tension in Berman's manifesto between the descriptive and the normative, and a potential danger, which Berman himself acknowledged, that historical translation studies might simply degenerate into a sieve for separating out "good" versus "bad" translations, thereby effacing their historical locatedness. In more recent years, Lawrence Venuti has offered a similar critique, decrying neoclassical practice as "hegemonizing" and arguing that adaptive or "fluent" translation strategies have an "exclusionary impact on foreign cultural values," maintaining the prerogatives of cultural elites and "closing off thinking about cultural and social alternatives." Like Berman, he argues in favor of an ethical approach to translation that, instead of adapting foreign works to national taste, would "foreignize" the national language, bringing it in closer contact with the linguistic realities of other cultures.[34]

However valuable these arguments might be as we reflect on the place of translation in the world today—and I believe that they are quite valuable—they are a highly reductive account of neoclassical translation. Like Venuti, I take translators' statements seriously as "texts," susceptible to careful analysis and revealing multiple or unintended meanings, but I believe that a more flexible approach is needed, one that is more sensitive to the complexities of the period and to the complexities of "otherness," a concept that cannot be limited to people who speak languages other than mine. Otherness inheres within the inescapable slipperiness of language that is foregrounded by translation; within the conflicting claims of ownership of the author, translator, and reader; and within the translation's ties to both past and present. The situation cannot adequately be captured by a simple binary alternative such as Friedrich Schleiermacher's: "The translator either disturbs the writer as little as possible and moves the reader in his direction, or disturbs the reader as little as possible and moves the writer in his direction. The two approaches are so absolutely different that no mixture of the two is to be trusted."[35] As Arno Renken argues in a recent philosophical account of translation as representation, the reader's basic experience of a translation is one of "rupture," in that we are constantly aware of another text, the original, that is both present and absent. To reduce this complex situation to a stark opposition between alterity and assimilation is inadequate.[36] There are further ruptures within what appears to be a uniform field of adaptative (or "domesticating," as some would have it) translation practice: divergences that become clearer as we study the translators' own accounts of their projects. Thus, while it is useful to refer to "neoclassical theory" for economy's sake, it is important that the individual voices of individual translators not be melded into one, as if each were simply a manifestation of an ideal whole. Rather, they are participants in a debate, or series of debates, that evolves over time—and extends, with further variations, into our own day.

What we see over the course of the two centuries during which neoclassical translation remained—not without contestation—the norm is not a shift from "ethnocentrism" to "openness" but are instead constant and multiple reformulations of the very concept of otherness. Translators find themselves in many networks of relationships that are reshaped and reconfigured over time, with contemporaries, friends, critics, readers, patrons, authority figures, authors dead or living, fellow translators past and present, speakers of other languages, citizens of neighboring or distant countries, coreligionists, infidels, dissenters, ancestors, posterity, and God. Within these networks, translators enact *relations*. Hence the recurrent evocations of interpersonal relations—as in Roscommon's oft-cited line, "Chuse an *Author* as you chuse a *Friend*"—and of the many shapes that these relationships can take, variously structured in terms of compensation, negotiation, debt, gift, reciprocity, servility, authority, responsibility, love, struggle, and mourning. The creativity of the translator and the indebtedness of the author undergo questioning and reshaping as modern print culture takes on a recognizable form and opportunities for public speech are both created and repressed. Even as the modern notion of individual, autonomous authorship comes to the fore, the translator both puts that autonomy into question and asks us to consider a form of disenchanted agency, a "middle voice," a subjectivity that cannot dissociate itself from dialogue.

middle voice

Many are the examples of men and women who translate controversial, dangerous, or somehow "unsuitable" texts as a form of oblique speech; there are many complex variations of intersubjective relations as well. To anticipate momentarily some of the readings to come: Vaugelas consults friends on his choices, multiplying alternative versions, ultimately leaving the unresolved choices for his friends to edit after his death. One member of the Port-Royal group, perhaps Pierre Nicole, publishes a Virgil translation by other members of the group, perhaps Le Maistre de Sacy and Arnauld d'Andilly, without their permission, in a spirit of friendly connivance. John Dryden enters the late stage of his career thinking and writing not only through Virgil, but also through an earlier translator, Jean de Segrais. Denis Diderot reflects that "clever foreigners" (*des étrangers habiles en notre langue*) produce radically new insights through their unidiomatic approach to the language, suggesting that more could be found, than lost, in translation. For Anne Dacier, translation transforms the act of reading itself: "When we read only for ourselves, we're often content with a slight, superficial idea; but when we read for others, we are obliged to give them clear and distinct ideas; hence we pause to study the text in depth. Our thinking thus stimulated of necessity, we discover greater beauties and meanings than a rapid reading would have let us see."[37] "Reading for others" bears its own constraints or "obligation," but more important, it becomes a stimulant and a key to personal discovery.

historicizing viewpoint

Thus far, I have been arguing for a historicizing viewpoint, insisting on the need to acknowledge the cultural specificity of each text, its contexts and concerns. Those concerns inevitably take on a new sheen in the light of our own, however. We are not the public most immediately conceived by the creators of the texts; no amount of research will allow us total access to the palimpsest of allusion that constitutes each utterance. I am talking as much about reading, about literary criticism, as about translation. No reader today, however erudite, can replicate a seventeenth-century reader's response to d'Ablancourt's work, any more than d'Ablancourt could be perfectly sure that he had produced in readers of his *Tacite* the same effect that Tacitus had on the Romans of his day. Which is not to say that he was wrong to imagine doing so. The recurring prosopopoeia of so many translators' prefaces—to make Virgil (or Homer, or Cervantes) speak as though he had been a compatriot of the translator—is an impossible speech act, but a compelling one. Others felt differently: as Etienne de Silhouette observed in the 1730s, if Alexander Pope had written *The Essay on Man* in French, he probably would have written something quite different.

It comes down to a question of tact. Not merely the polite forms of ‘ tact’ self-censorship that we sometimes associate with the term but the scarcely perceptible touch, the caress or brush with the fingers, somewhere between the extremes of brutal appropriation and *Noli me tangere*: a subtle form of contact that avoids intrusion and remains poised at the edge of interdiction, following what Derrida calls "a law of tact" in his commentary on Jean-Luc Nancy.[38] Tact enables a truly ethical relation of response, communication, and change. As Derek Attridge puts it, "If I succeed in responding adequately to the otherness and singularity of the other, it is the other *in its relating to me*—always in a specific time and place—to which I am responding, in creatively changing myself and perhaps a little of the world as well."[39] Such encounters, Attridge goes on to say, allow writers "to realize a new possibility in a poem or an argument"—and I would argue that the same thing occurs in translation. Thus translators, whatever their commitments may be to "fidelity," are inevitably embarked on the production of something new, some further realization of a text's potential, what Walter Benjamin called the "afterlife" of the text. Even as we treat the texts of other cultures, other times, with the appropriate tact, we also engage them on our own intellectual ground, come to understand them in our own conceptual vocabulary. The point is not necessarily to make d'Ablancourt speak as though he had been born a postmodernist but to avoid foreclosing the advent of a new understanding of the past, or of the present, that might result from that encounter. By reminding us of languages and affective worlds beyond our immediate sphere, translation asks us to come to terms with our own contingent place in the order of things. Translation poses questions of agency, of originality. What is an author? Who writes? Who speaks with my voice? How many voices combine to produce the words I read, the words I write? The perennial quality of these questions becomes the common ground for a critical conversation between past and present.[40]

Certainly these questions resonate deeply in the world of contemporary philosophy. While no single figure or group of figures offers a total blueprint for the readings ahead, there are three in particular to whom my thinking often returned in the course of writing this book: Emmanuel Lévinas, Jean-Luc Nancy, and Jacques Derrida. I turn to them briefly now in order to evoke three ways in which "otherness" comes into a text that will echo in the readings ahead. For Lévinas, the self's radical openness, or "exposure," to the other is paramount. Presented in terms of "responsibility" and "substitution," exposure signals the disarticulation of the self and its implication in the other.[41] Exposure is further conceived as the distinction between language as a structured, finite set of propositions—the Said, *le Dit*—and language that is prior to expression and in which the subject's radical exposure to the other is taking place—the Saying, *le Dire*. Lévinas's account is valuable in helping us conceptualize a sort of complete dispossession that is neither abjection nor alienation, and an untethered form of otherness that disrupts the confines of language and prevents it from becoming rigidified, or "thematized." Although in some ways Lévinas appears to offer a model for the translator's complete abnegation, the more critical point is the unsettling of all discourse, domesticating or foreignizing, as it is "interrupted" by alterity. Even in the most reified language, Lévinas tells us, the reference to an interlocutor opens up and "permanently breaks through the text that the discourse claims to weave in thematizing and enveloping all things" (170). The interruption occurs on multiple levels, immediately and concretely, by the insertion of *je* and the sudden shift of gears that casts the philosophical analysis into a dialogue, pulling us into the text and illustrating the point. This move is reinforced by the reference to an unlocatable—uncanny—present, "the discussion I am elaborating at this very moment." Language is opened up, exposed, "pierced" by the interlocutor, whose unavoidable participation in the construction of meaning guarantees an infusion of change and unpredictability. Lévinas pursues this notion into the domain of print. The printed book appears fixed, unavailable to interruption. And yet "books have their fate; they belong to a world they do not include, but recognize by being written and printed, and by being prefaced and getting themselves preceded with forewords. They are interrupted, and call for other books and in the end are interpreted in a saying distinct from the said" (171). The point about the printed text—and prefaces—in general is especially true of translations, which call out beyond themselves in the crisscrossing of cultures and literary traditions. Another language shadows the translation, interpellating and opening up its seeming fixity. A complex set of relations, mediated by language, among translators, texts, readers, and many others, prevents any reduction into distinct, neatly paired terms of self and other. There is no fundamental reason to see "modernizing" neo-classical translation as a form of usurpation, not when both translator and text are in perpetual movement, and when the evocation of the *tiers*, reader or other translator (reader), shares in the general responsibility. It is also the case that the complete self-dispossession of the translator before texts, traditions, social environments, relationships, or language itself is not the only imaginable "place." Even the self-effacing translators of Port-Royal, working collectively and often under a variety of pseudonyms, sensitive and answerable to a God hidden within the literality of the letter, do not present themselves as empty conduits of meaning; rather, they must make choices within the boundaries of a specific time and place.

The translator's exposure is perhaps better understood as a careful attune-ment to those pulses of meaning, language, audience, and temporality that converge in the act of turning words from one language into another, an act of writing that is always and foremost an act of "writing-with." I am think-ing here of the "tact" I mentioned earlier, as well as of Jean-Luc Nancy's account of being as not merely coexistence but co-essence, co-being.[42] If Lévinas's hyperbolic language suggests that there is "no middle ground be-tween an enclosed self and an intrusive other," as one commentator has put it, Nancy imagines plural selves, permanently[43] exposed and disclosed in the condition of the "singular plural" that he sees as common to all. Translation, I would argue, is a practice that enables a particular awareness of such "with-ness" with regard to language. In language, Nancy tells us, beings are "exposed" to one another in their most fundamental relationship, and meaning circulates in a "dialogue or polylogue" between past and pres-ent. In a typical pluralizing gesture, Nancy claims that "there is no ultimate language, but instead languages, words, voices," without which there could never be any "voice" at all (85).

Derrida, too, reminds us that there is "always more than one language" as he engages throughout his career with the complex relations inherent in translation, variously evoked as debt, contract, double-bind, and, ulti-mately, promise. The importance of Derrida's work to translation theorists was underscored with the appearance in the mid-1980s of a collection of es-says by a number of prominent critics edited by Joseph Graham, *Difference in Translation*, which also marks the first publication in both English and French of Derrida's influential essay on Benjamin, "Des tours de Babel."[44] Much has been written since. For now, let a section of *Politiques de l'amitié*

Friendship | translation | Churchyard

suggest the multiple forms of "otherness" in the passage between languages and affective relations, in Derrida's explication of certain words attributed to Aristotle, filtered through Montaigne, and oft repeated ever since: "O my friends, there is no friend." In the course of the examination of these words in classical and modern discussions of friendship, we encounter a translation problem: it appears that there is good reason to understand the Greek phrase from Diogenes Laertius not in the canonical apostrophizing—and paradoxical—form just cited but rather as a pedestrian third-person observation: "He who has friends can have no true friend."[45] Thus, rather than a troubling, self-contradictory address that casts doubt on the possibility of friendship's existence, we have instead a question of number: how many friends is too many? Even these apparently opposed readings have their common chords: the third-person observation is ineluctably addressed "to someone," yet its "destiny or 'destinerrancy'" prevents it or any other enunciation from being addressed to a single interlocutor. Ultimately, both readings cause us to realize that just as there is always more than one language, so too there is never "one single friend" (215). As the multiple translations of the phrase in French, English, German, Italian, and Latin call out, cross over, and reverberate, they cannot efface the desire for the unique translation any more than they can either guarantee or deny the perfect friendship: "The desire for a unique friendship, an indivisible bond, an 'I love you' one time, one single eternal time, one time for all time(s), will never cease. But I do not want it" (215). Like friendship, translation takes place in a context that can never be closed, determined, or saturated. Both are caught between reciprocity, asymmetry, and vulnerability; each bespeaks a promise, the time of a promise, and the paradoxical structure of the condition of possibility (218). One friend, no friend, or more than one friend? A relation based on utility, pleasure, or virtue? Should friendship take the form of reciprocity that models itself on brotherhood? Or does it betoken asymmetrical relations? To what extent does friendship imply gendered relations? All these questions speak to translation as much as to the contradictions of friendship, which remains for Derrida (echoing his friend Lévinas) a "speech gesture" that "will never allow itself to be neutralized, and its saying cannot be reduced to the said" (217).

Each of these philosophical moments can be seen in some sense as an allegory of translation, a variation on the interrelations of self and others, affect and language. I am mindful that I have shifted the focus from the cultural and social "other" usually evoked by translation theorists to the "completely other" of philosophy.[46] The web of language—languages in their multiplicity—holds these together. Translation is "another name for the impossible," Derrida tells us in another place, yet nothing compels us more deeply.[47] The profound "work" of translation I find best described by Lévinas in his account of the inexorable unsettling of the most reified discourse. Nancy's modes of with-ness—being-with, writing-with—emphasize both language's intrinsic "excentricity" and its relation to bodies, to corporality: words touch.[48] Exposure, the mutual implication of self and other, and the manifold, open-ended possibilities of languages and communities are among the topics I will explore in the readings ahead.

During the period from Galileo's recantation to the French revolution, the world in which the neoclassical translators lived and worked underwent dramatic changes; the changes in the regime of translation are subtler but critical. Within the context of a given set of problems and practices, we see an increased probing of the foundations of language, selfhood, and the cultural environment; an awareness of change; a growing appreciation for the specificities of language and its embeddedness in time and place. Thus, while emphasizing certain topics and trends in various chapters, I shall maintain a roughly chronological order. The initial two chapters each offer a broad survey of seventeenth-century translators' reflections in France and Britain. In the first, I examine d'Ablancourt's circle as well as the Jansenist translators at Port-Royal in order to look at the place of translation in the constitution of French neoclassicism, which it both subtends and disrupts, and at the rise of the notion of the French language as "clear" and "universal," but also subject to change. Turning to the English context, I focus on translation's role for the Carolinian exiles, the interplay of translation and politics, and conflicting efforts to shape collective memory in the aftermath of the Civil War. These chapters are followed by individual studies of two pivotal turn-of-the-century figures whose influence was felt throughout the eighteenth century, John Dryden and Anne Dacier, both of whom crystallize tensions of the previous generation and open doors to the future in a pair of prefaces that are major theoretical and artistic statements. Dryden's *Dedication of the Aeneis* (1697) reaches not only back to Virgil but to his previous translators John Denham and Jean de Segrais in a reflection that confronts time, change, and the contradictory status of the translator-author. In her preface to the *Iliad* (1711) and contributions to the ensuing polemical exchange, Dacier examines historical distance, the legacy of past to present, and the materiality of language in ways that frequently appear more "modern" than her adversaries *les Modernes*.

As we move into the eighteenth century, certain underlying issues take on more prominence; the availability of translation as a tool for *l'esprit philosophique* becomes more pronounced, and translation intersects with the primary threads in Enlightenment epistemology and social thought. The discourse on translation is a key site for the development of national consciousness; both French and English translators aim at defining and identifying with the national language, construing national identity in terms of the cross-Channel other. While translation and language theory can contribute to ethnocentrism and cultural stereotyping, what emerges in some quarters is an awareness of cultural specificity and of language as such. The remaining chapters thus look at questions that involve both French and English translators. Chapter 5, "Gender, Signature, Authority," examines the work of women translators, their multiple strategies for being in the text, and their assumption of indirect authority/authorship. Chapter 6 discusses the ways in which Enlightenment thought intersected with tradition in the translation of ancient texts. Chapter 7, "'Adventurers in Print,'" turns to translation from the modern languages, with special attention to the practice of conferring formal critical prefaces and notes on modern works, a phenomenon particularly prevalent in the French treatment of English writers such as Pope, Shakespeare, Richardson, and Young. In conclusion, I examine the ways in which the history of translation was presented during the eighteenth century as a further means of setting the present study in historical perspective.

Every translation is at some level an act of faith, a hermeneutic leap, a gesture of reconciliation. And yet each translation occurs at a particular time and place, between two (or more) languages at particular moments in their development, within a specific confluence of social, political, and cultural values. For us, the need to translate, to find bridges between different cultures and modes of thought, speaks directly to our own political and ethical concerns, just as translation's questioning of language, rhetoric, and meaning resonates deeply within contemporary literary studies, history, and philosophy. I believe that our study of the past can both be true to the past and have something to say to the present. It should be clear that I am not advocating in any sense a return to the translating norms of the seventeenth century, but I contend that we should bring the same openness and desire for understanding to the cultures of the past as we do to other cultures today. In terms of the particular period under study, the sensitivities and questions of the neoclassical translators, being different from our own, reveal connections and modes of apprehending their materials that are worth considering now, as is their contribution to the intellectual and cultural revolution that was the Enlightenment.

CHAPTER I

From the Academy to Port-Royal

Secular   Sacred.

There are two important centers for translation, two major networks of translators, in seventeenth-century France: d'Ablancourt and the others associated with the *Huit oraisons* volume, and the *Messieurs*, the solitary Gentlemen of the Jansenist retreat at Port-Royal. Both groups left their mark on French language and culture—the academicians through their efforts to perfect and purify the language, and the *Solitaires* both as the theoreticians of general grammar ("Cartesian linguistics") and as proponents of a "tragic vision" permeating the century's final decades.[1] These two groups— the urbane, well-connected academicians on the one hand, and the austere theologians on the other—are often seen in contrast to one another. As late seventeenth-century critic Adrien Baillet shows in his compilation of contemporary commentaries, however, the Messieurs were as respected for the "purity and beauty of their discourse" as were any of the assayers of linguistic purity in the Academy.[2]

Derrida once qualified the quest for purity in French as a form of "resistance"—resistance to other languages, to its own internal forms of otherness, and to translation.[3] As we have seen, numerous are the commentators for whom the closure of French and its resistance to heterogeneity are nowhere more evident than in neoclassical translation itself. Translation played a major role in the constitution of the matrix of linguistic purity, *le goût classique*; academicians explicitly used their translations to forge a new ideal of clarity in French prose and to criticize the defective taste of previous generations. Both Vaugelas and Malherbe, the arbiters of the new elegance, saw their translations as central to their legacy.

As an avatar of limpid intelligibility, translation appears to heighten the contrast between neoclassical culture and the earlier, more freely experimental and irregular forms of the baroque that dominate the early decades of the seventeenth century. To the extent that translation foregrounds textuality, distancing, and a cognitive apprehension of meaning, as opposed to baroque spectacle, fusion, and revelation, the two remain antithetical.[4] Distinctions are rarely so clear, however. As we shall see, the discourse on translation offers its own forms of theatricalization, of persuasion, conversion, and allegory. Chief among these are its reliance on collaboration and intertextuality, rather than individual authorship and personal identity; on explicit, rather than transparent, modes of representation; on a concept of the sign that ultimately privileges embodiment over abstraction; and on affect and eloquence, rather than discursive reason.

I'll begin by examining prefaces and related pieces by d'Ablancourt and his friends, then turn to the work of the Port-Royal translators, in particular the Bible translation project led by Isaac-Louis Le Maistre de Sacy. If on the stylistic level these texts bespeak the rigorous transparency of neoclassical aesthetics, this stylistic clarity should not make us lose sight of the profound complexity, even obscurity, in the translators' understanding of their texts' internal functioning and location in culture. The academicians foreground the entwinement of translated texts with personal affective relationships, as well as with larger systems of cultural transmission. A translation may be a gift to one's friend, but it is also a legacy to posterity. Throughout, the translator's overriding concern is the task of replicating that which cannot be fully articulated: the eloquence of the text. In the second half of this chapter, we'll see this dynamic replayed on a philosophical and theological level.

FRIENDSHIP AND GRATITUDE

Louis Giry, Dedicatory Letter, and Antoine Godeau,
Preface, Des Causes de la corruption de l'eloquence, dialogue *(1630)*

Louis Giry's translation of the *Dialogue on Orators* by Tacitus is one of the earliest examples of the new style of translation that was discussed among Conrart's circle, and it would be regarded as one of Giry's most successful translations.[5] Giry dedicated the translation to Conrart, known as "Philandre" to his circle; another friend, Antoine Godeau, wrote the preface. Giry's translation and Godeau's preface would attract little attention upon publication in 1630, but the volume was reissued in 1636 to considerably more acclaim as they and their colleagues became better known.[6]

Giry's dedicatory epistle begins by situating the translation within the context of a friendship that is also a relationship of patronage, and it exemplifies the reciprocal obligations of both parties:

> To Philandre,
>   I am sending you the version that you obliged me to undertake, and that our friendship would not allow me to refuse. My desire to please you enabled me to overcome difficulties that would have prevented me from beginning this work, had I been free to follow my own inclination. Indeed it seems to me that I could never express in our language the beauties that are written in this remarkable piece without robbing them of their dignity, and in having to make the greatest Orators of Quintilian's day speak, I feared that what should be proof of my affection would instead be evidence of my weakness. (ã2r–ã3r)

Giry "obliges" his friend, who desired the translation and who has "given" him the necessary encouragement to complete the project. The work is "proof of my affection" but also an indication of Conrart's power, or *puissance*. This initial double transaction (request → translation; encouragement → affection) incites another, since Conrart, as possessor of the translation, will bear the responsibility of "protecting" the text and deciding whether or not it should be published. Giry demurs from publication ("your satisfaction is my only aim"). To the extent that Conrart is "satisfied," however, publication becomes the next logical step, and so the translator reminds him that "all your eloquence" may be required to defend it. The existence of the published book thus testifies both to the translator's work and to his friend's approbation; the work is offered to the reader ("au jugement des hommes") with the support of their shared responsibility. Giry gives only the briefest indication of his approach to translation, when he evokes the chief difficulty of the project: "to make the greatest Orators of Quintilian's day speak" without stripping them of their beauty and dignity. The call to Conrart to make use of his own eloquence underscores the importance of rhetoric, persuasion, and forceful speech.

Rhetoric, translation, and their social and linguistic environment are central to Giry's friend Antoine Godeau, whose preface follows the dedicatory epistle. Godeau's best-known reflections on translation were his *Discours sur les oeuvres de M. de Malherbe*, published in the same year as his contribution to Giry's volume.[7] In his preface to Giry's translation, Godeau expresses his admiration for Giry and speaks in his place ("Since humility is not the least of his virtues, I must inform his readers on his behalf," ĩ1v), underscoring their shared responsibility for the volume. Godeau's preface is one of the period's most thorough statements on the art of translation and its social function. He bases his arguments on a view of language as inflected by climate and corporeal disposition:

> Every language has its own graces, and there is no less difference among men's opinions regarding beauty than among their tastes in stylistic graces and the ornaments of eloquence. . . . For if we concede that the soul makes use of bodily organs in order to function, and that it functions more or less well according to the good or bad disposition of those organs, then it should come as no surprise that those who live under a climate that gives them a certain temperament do not reason in the same way, and hence do not express their ideas in the same way, as those who receive completely different influences from birth. (ē1r–ē1v)

Godeau develops this notion to suggest a confluence of language and national character that leads to different forms of intellectual production. Although he holds that scientific truths ("les maximes des sciences") are universal, he nevertheless wonders whether "the manner of treating a subject" might alter its "beauty" or even "its very nature" (ē2r). Languages in their local specificity, or *le génie des langues*, are a powerful link between the physical environment and all levels of culture, and rhetoric is not mere form or ornament but is constitutive of ideas. Hence the difficulty of appreciating foreign cultures: "One should not be surprised if what foreigners admire as incomparable finds little approbation here, and if that which appears divine to us in our language scarcely seems to them the product of an ordinary reasonable being" (ē3r). All in all, translation is an enterprise suggesting "more temerity than wisdom" (ē3r).

A century later, the notion of the génie de langue as fundamentally untranslatable would become linked to a desire for greater literality, but for Godeau this is precisely why a translator must strive to recreate not the foreign culture, which in his view cannot be separated from its material linguistic base, but rather a local equivalent founded in the local language, the local rhetoric. For Godeau, acknowledgment of cultural otherness and of the linguistic specificity of the foreign text are entirely compatible with Giry's decision to make radical stylistic revisions in translation: "Realizing that good translation is not word for word and that one must take the ears of those for whom one works into account, [Giry] boldly changed the linkages among the clauses in order to improve the sequences, and sometimes adjusted a line in order to explain something that might appear obscure. He employed circumlocution in order to avoid terms which would not be understood outside their culture, or to soften metaphors that might seem absurd (ī2r)." The purpose of the translation, after all, is to intervene in the present day, in the translator's own culture. An examination of eloquence and its relation to the political context, as well as a critique of fallen, imperial eloquence in the name of a republican past, the *Dialogue on Orators* underscores the link between language and culture and—as Giry's title announces—enables the translator and his colleagues to criticize their own "decadent" post-Tridentine present: "It seems to have been composed for our century" (ō3v).[8] A sudden excursus on "translations of so many abominable books" and the manner in which international commercial and cultural exchange "contributed to a fall from our formerly virtuous state" (ī3r) suggests a darker side to translation and a further reason for strongly adaptative rewriting. That said, to dismiss the project as xenophobic is clearly insufficient. The return to eloquence, the *imitatio ciceroniana*, is a considerably broader international project, and both the critique of present decadence and the underlying concept of linguistic embodiment drive home the importance of the call for reform. Godeau's overriding concern is not the danger of "bad books," nor is he demanding a return to antiquity. Rather, he points to the great humanist translator Jacques Amyot, whose Plutarch remains a model of style: "Who knows whether . . . Plutarch, had he spoken French, would have expressed himself any differently?" (ē3v).[9] He furthermore notes the excellence of many contemporaries (ū1r). Principally, he insists that the translation of the dialogue on eloquence must itself be eloquent. In a work where "eloquence speaks for herself," the translator's first task must be to render the beauty of the text—"which he could never have done, had he taken a different approach in his translation" (ĩ2r–ĩ2v).

D'Ablancourt, Preface to Minucius Felix, Octavius (1637)

In 1637, the year of his reception into the new Académie française and one year before the appearance of the *Huit oraisons*, Perrot d'Ablancourt published his translation of Minucius Felix. Like Giry, d'Ablancourt dedicated his work to Conrart, addressing him as "Philandre," with the familiar *tu* and a lighthearted tone of confidence and friendship. Also like Giry, d'Ablancourt foregrounds the reciprocal responsibility incurred by the dedication: "Know that in rendering you the honor that is your due, I am also burdening you with all my errors. Although I may have committed them, it wasn't I who published them."[10] The letter stages the principal gestures of the dedicatory epistle without taking them too seriously, refusing to offer a "panegyric": "Why should you care if others know the virtues of Philandre, if they know not who Philandre is?" (106). The closing quip pokes gentle fun at the use of pseudonyms in public discourse but also emphasizes the intimacy of the circle of friends, the former Illustres Bergers (now academicians).

In the oft-cited preface that follows the dedication, d'Ablancourt makes an even more strongly worded plea than Godeau's for the centrality of "eloquence" in translation: "I believe that two works resemble one another more when both are eloquent than when one is eloquent and the other is not. I do not claim that my work is eloquent but that I have always kept the force of the argument and the beauty of the discourse before me as my goal. It would be a Judaic superstition to attach oneself to the words and forget the purpose for which they are used. . . . After all, we only render an Author in part, if we rob him of his eloquence" (110–11). "Force" and "beauty": d'Ablancourt does not seek to render word for word, or even necessarily sense for sense; rather, he hopes to capture the aesthetic and affective power of speech, to represent his author in a particularly intense manner that is more suggestive of reenactment than imitation as conventionally understood.[11] This approach is hardly "infidelity" become "system," as a nineteenth-century critic would have it, or "imprecision become rule," as Henri Meschonnic has more recently claimed.[12] Although like nearly every French translator since the Renaissance, d'Ablancourt claims to reject the notion of "la superstition Judaïque" infusing language with mystery, he and his colleagues have replaced it with a concept of eloquence that is both equally metaphysical and equally attached to linguistic embodiment. Furthermore, references to the "Judaic superstition" (or the Pauline phrase "the letter that killeth") bespeak a half-conscious awareness of midrashic exegetical practices, thus creating an opening within the text, a gesture toward an alternative understanding of language, that automatically displaces "classical representation" as the sole norm.[13]

It is thus not the case that d'Ablancourt and his peers have, by eschewing literality, embraced what Lawrence Venuti calls "a translation ethics of sameness" (rather than difference).[14] Although Venuti, like Antoine Berman, ultimately came to recognize a serious textual work in d'Ablancourt's explicit adjustments to his source texts, the fuller context and broader implications of these adaptative translations have not been fully appreciated.[15] Like Godeau, d'Ablancourt does not ignore cultural and linguistic difference but rather sees such differences as providing the justification for his practice: "Insofar as the beauties and graces [of the language] are different, we should not fear to give the author those of our country" (111). Rather than falling back on an ethic of sameness, neoclassical translation represents a step toward the creation of something new, the language of *nostre pays* that d'Ablancourt and his circle saw as only beginning to come into its own. The key is to look at *le siècle classique* not as the "monument" that it would seem to later generations but as very much a work in progress.[16]

D'Ablancourt ends with an admission that he has raised more issues than he can adequately deal with, followed by a final evocation of the extraordinary power of speech, couched in an allusion to the conversion scene that concludes the *Octavius*, a moment of supreme eloquence "that converted a Philosopher and led him to desert the religion of his Ancestors" (112). As Zuber points out, there would appear to be an autobiographical reminiscence here, as d'Ablancourt had himself abjured his family's Protestantism in his early twenties, only to return to it some six years later—a move that almost certainly harmed his chances for advancement.[17] The translator aims, however hopelessly, for true eloquence, the eloquence that induces nothing less than conversion, transformation, change.

Pierre Du Ryer, Preface to Le Quinte-Curce de Vaugelas *(1653)*

The key text in the world of seventeeth-century translation was the life and deeds of Alexander the Great by Quintus Curtius, *De gestis Alexandri Magni, regis Macedonum*, translated by Claude Favre de Vaugelas and first published in 1653, three years after the translator's death, with a preface by Pierre Du Ryer. The volume's importance within the literary world of its day ensured that the issues foregrounded in the preface would have been present in the minds of many. Pierre Du Ryer had been identified with the neoclassical school of translation from the beginning but had written primarily for the theatre in the 1630s and 1640s, returning to translation as a solution to financial difficulties.[18] At the behest of Conrart and Jean Chapelain, he translated sections of the Quintus Curtius text untouched by Vaugelas and produced a preface for the posthumous edition. Du Ryer's preface is less a theoretical reflection on language than a description of the process by which the translation came to be published; his account vividly foregrounds the complex interweaving of voices, texts, and influences that enter into the process of translation, as well as opening up questions on what it means to call a text "complete."

The preface begins with a theatrical conceit that would have been natural enough to the dramatist Du Ryer: "Here is the celebrated Quintus Curtius, appearing in all his pomp and with every advantage on the Stage of France."[19] In addition to leading up to an exceptionally elaborate flourish ("everything is worthy of Alexander"), it sets the course for a narrative that reveals the theatre within the theatre, the complicated process of textual production. Du Ryer relates how Vaugelas spent more than thirty years on his translation: "a sufficient accomplishment for a lifetime, if by one's work one becomes immortal" (*2r–*2v). As the story unfolds, it becomes clear that what prevented Vaugelas from completing his project even after thirty years was not simply its length and complexity, or the need to attend to *ses affaires*, but a restless search for the proper style, a long march in the bewildering realm of synonyms and possibilities. Initially, we are told, Vaugelas took his inspiration from a friend, the historian and translator Nicolas Coëffeteau, "but when Monsieur d'Ablancourt's first versions appeared, he found them so delightful that he resolved to rewrite his own work on this new model" (*2v–*3r). Du Ryer cites a note left by Vaugelas praising d'Ablancourt's "clear and unencumbered, elegant and concise" style. By abandoning Coëffeteau's "diffuse" style for d'Ablancourt's lean, disciplined prose, Vaugelas strove to produce a translation as timeless as the original.

The search for the perfect style did not stop with the discovery of the perfect model. Du Ryer describes a manuscript that had become a garden of forking paths, filled with marginal annotations, variants, queries: "There was not a single page in all his books where there were not two or three glosses on each phrase, such scruples and doubts he had as to the expressions; he sought always the clearest, the simplest, and altogether the most concise and French" (*3v). Unable to decide among the possibilities, he consulted his friends, annotating the text in light of their responses. What emerges is a portrait of a man obsessed with the search for the final, perfect, ideal "façon de parler." It is not entirely surprising that the man best known for the rulings on "bon usage" in his influential *Remarques sur la langue française* should have been hypersensitive to the vicissitudes of *l'usage* to the point of paralysis. Adrien Baillet's discussion of translation in the *Jugemens des savans* is filled with references to translators whose style betrays the passage of time, including Du Ryer and d'Ablancourt.[20] Du Ryer relates that even as he readied his manuscript for publication, Vaugelas remained torn between the multiple versions written in the margins of his manuscript (*3v). Conscientious work begins to sound like avoidance when we are told that even during his final review of the text, the translator requested comments from his friends; when their remarks did not concur, he proposed the resulting questions to the Academy (*5v–*6r). Their opinions too were included in the margins of the heavily annotated work in progress.[21]

Translation terminable or interminable? As Du Ryer describes how the problem of establishing an accurate source text joined the translation problems, how the translator felt the need for additional "observations," and so on, it becomes clear that Vaugelas could have kept his public waiting much, much longer. We are told that had he been granted more time, his translation "would have been even more polished" (*8r), stretching the act of "finishing" into a process of indefinite duration. Inevitably, perhaps, the task of publication fell to his friends Conrart and Chapelain, who made what sense they could of the labyrinthine manuscript, in which each word had to be painstakingly deciphered (*4r). Elsewhere Du Ryer describes the copy as chaotic ("un chaos," *8v). He himself had been charged with translating the parts of the text left untouched—after consulting with "les amis de M. de Vaugelas," needless to say. While clearly the activity of the editor-friends was inspired by the desire to create a monument to the deceased (*4r), ultimately what the work represents is not Vaugelas at all, nor Quintus Curtius, nor Alexander. Instead, we are to read it as "a remarkable example of the fidelity that friends owe one another" (*8r). The final emphasis is not on the thirty years of work that went into the translation but rather on the tremendous efforts required to bring it to print:

> A most ardent affection was required to undertake so laborious and difficult a task, and uncommon insight, to discern unerringly what was best, when

everything was excellent; since whether we examined the words or manners of speech, or considered the variously translated passages, we found nothing that was not worthy of being preserved. . . . Judge thereby what you owe these two illustrious personnages who have labored no less for your satisfaction than for the honor of a friend who is no longer able to express gratitude; and confess that we are no less obliged to those who allow us to enjoy a thing, than to those who left it for us. (*8v)

Perhaps some of the celebrity of this translation was due to these final words and their imposing image of the ultimate translation, with its explosion of variants, all equally meritorious, equally compelling. The true *Quinte-Curce* is unreadable, overwhelming, glorious. In presenting the work, Du Ryer reminds us of the complexity and irreducible plurality of the act of reading we call translation; with his final injunction to the reader, he includes us as beneficiaries of the editors' labors on a level with their late friend, and inserts us within their circuit of gift and obligation.

The story does not stop there, however. Beginning with the third edition (1655) of the work, a note informs us that a new, considerably cleaner manuscript has been found and edited by Olivier Patru ("Everyone knows the esteem in which Monsieur de Vaugelas held this excellent man"), so that, at last, "the translation is in the state that its Author would have wished." Even as the anonymous editor—perhaps Du Ryer, perhaps another—strives to reassure us that previous difficulties have been resolved and that what we are about to read is indeed at last what Vaugelas, tellingly referred to as the "author," would have wished, the story repeats itself. There yet remain "a few places" where Vaugelas had been unable to determine the best possible word choice, and once again it falls to one of his friends to decide. Friendship and zeal for another's posthumous *gloire* are inextricably linked to the act of translation. Thus what is foregrounded is not translation's act of cultural appropriation but rather its inherent instability, its reliance on choices that are as impossible as they are ineluctable.

What can we learn from this story? Most striking is the paradox contained therein. As we have seen, for Vaugelas and the first generation of academicians, translation is mobilized in an explicit project of bringing the French language to a point of perfection from which it need never decline. And yet the work undertaken by many to exemplify that goal bespeaks even more clearly the transience of language, its inability to remain immune from the passage of time. That realization is prevalent throughout reflections on translation, particularly during the second half of the seventeenth century. Charles Sorel observes that retranslation is inevitably "reiterated every century" until "our Language is more stable [*plus fixe*] than it is now."[22] In the preface to his translation of Saint Jerome's letters, Jean Petit writes of the uselessness of earlier versions. Unlike the planks of an old ship, which might serve to construct a new one, words are subject to fashion, *la mode*, and "if we expressed ourselves with older terms, we would resemble people who run through the streets at Carnival time, disguised in antique clothing."[23]

Even the great Port-Royal theologian Antoine Arnauld linked translation to the state of the language, observing that French had evolved from a "brutish" state, "as we can see from the translations that have come down to us from those times."[24] It is perhaps not so striking to find translators of biblical or Patristic texts concerned with contemporary usage as the key to reaching a contemporary audience (one has only to think of the work of Eugene Nida for the American Bible Society), but it may be more surprising to find this awareness in Antoine Arnauld, who, as coauthor of the Port-Royal *Grammaire raisonnée* and *Logique*, is usually associated with an emphasis on the atemporal structures of language rather than the irregularities of custom. As we shall see in the second part of this chapter, however, Port-Royal language theory takes on a different sheen when viewed through the lens of translation.[25]

Vaugelas himself participated in one of the earliest moments of this awakening of consciousness. In December 1635, he read aloud to the newly founded Académie française Meziriac's systematic critique of the much-revered translation of Plutarch by the great Renaissance translator Jacques Amyot. Meziriac catalogued more than two thousand errors by Amyot and classified them in such a way as to produce a grid for the analysis of translation, and an implicit model for translations to come.[26] Although Amyot would continue to be regarded by many as a model of style, the notion that a "monument" of translation would require retranslation less than a century later was already linked to the notion of language change. After paying tribute to Amyot for his erudition and for having "brought our language out of its infancy," Meziriac nevertheless observes that his style is imperfect, "far removed from the purity of language that we find in the works of those who are considered excellent writers today."[27] Already in the midst of his multiple revisions of the *Quinte-Curce*, Vaugelas in reading this document would have been forcefully reminded of the limited life span of a translation, even one that had been regarded as a masterpiece.

His own attempt to produce a timeless translation was, needless to say, unsuccessful. After being regarded for decades as one of the exemplary translations of the age and a model of style (the circumstances of its posthumous publication could only enhance its aura), the *Quinte-Curce* was reviewed by the Academy in the early eighteenth century and found to be dated and defective.[28]

Historically, then, Du Ryer's preface suggests an alternative account of the seventeenth century's major preoccupations—and new questions for us. In addition to the reminder of the transience of language, the evocation of the editorial process from unreadable "chaos" to a book remarkable for the "correctness" of its printing foregrounds its materiality (*4r). Du Ryer's narrative abolishes any notion the reader might have harbored as to the naturalness or transparency of translation, the unimpeded progress of an "idea" in the source text through the translator's mind and onto the printed page. Just as the revelation of the editorial interventions of Conrart, Chapelain, and Patru unsettles any idea of a unified, finished translation, so too are the concepts of a unitary source text and individual translator rendered problematic, since Vaugelas worked from an early version lacking the additions discovered by German scholar Johann Freinsheims, which later had to be translated by Du Ryer and folded into Vaugelas's version. Vaugelas, furthermore, suspected his source text of containing errors—"he believed that his author had been mistaken"—thus adding to the confusion (*6r). The apparently seamless, limpid prose of the *Quinte-Curce* points toward a complicated textual genealogy in which the material trajectory of words over time displaces idealizing concepts of cultural transmission.

Translation would thus appear to perform a function analogous to that of allegory in Paul de Man's pivotal essay "The Rhetoric of Temporality." For de Man, it is time, rather than meaning, that subtends allegoresis. The allegorical sign is defined by its reference to an earlier sign, with which it can never coincide. Allegory "designates primarily a distance in relation to its own origin, and, renouncing the nostalgia and the desire to coincide, it establishes its language in the void of this temporal difference."[29] My claim is not that we should read disillusioned Romantic irony as fully present or articulated in the noonday of French neoclassicism, but rather that we should appreciate the degree to which reflection on translation enables a destabilizing temporal awareness. If for Renaissance writer Joachim Du Bellay translation was merely an expedient vehicle for the transmission of knowledge, unable to promote stylistic elegance or enhance *la langue* in any way, a century later it had become not only a force in the shaping of literary language but also a leading indicator of language change. The "allegory" of translation, writ large in Du Ryer's preface, consists in the foregrounding of its artifice, the inability to fuse translation and original, and the shifting of authorship in the form of textual responsibility (and redirection of the reader's gratitude) from the original author to the translator, who becomes "Autheur" in the second *avertissement*. As Du Ryer emphasizes in his closing words, we should be no less grateful to "those who allow us to enjoy a thing"—from the context, it is clear that he refers not to the translator but to his editors, who are even further removed from the author of the source text—than to "those who left it for us." Allegory is, after all, part of the traditional art of memory.[30] Far from reflecting "illusory identification" with the past, the adaptative translation strategies and literary ambitions of Vaugelas, Du Ryer, d'Ablancourt, and others point to an awareness of their historical solitude, as well as a means for coming to terms with it.

Du Ryer's invocation of "gratitude" underscores another aspect of the *Quinte-Curce*: the place of translation in a network of affective relationships and its role in a system of duties and obligations, as we've seen in the earlier prefaces. Maurice Blanchot makes the connection between translation and modes of friendship: "Even if we are grateful for those who enter bravely into the enigma of the translator's task, if we salute them as the hidden masters of our culture . . . our gratitude remains mute, somewhat disdainful—from humility moreover, for we are hardly fit to be grateful to them."[31] Both Du Ryer and Blanchot leave the public's gratitude toward translators as something of an open question. "Judge thereby what you owe," says Du Ryer, but the reader thus addressed remains beyond the text. At best such recognition would come from afar, *de loin*, as Blanchot observes.

What forms of obligation does Du Ryer envisage in his reflections on translation? Many— the preface is crisscrossed with references to merit, justice, duty, and especially friendship. In the first place, Quintus Curtius "deserved that Alexander, who wished for a Homer to describe his exploits, had wished to have him as his historian"—a complicated homage that wishes for a reversal of the temporal sequence in which the past is able to "wish for" the present, not as an abstract, longed-for "posterity" but in concrete, personal terms, by name. Beautiful things "cost," Du Ryer continues, and Vaugelas devoted thirty years to his project because it is impossible to "give too much" to perfection. If one cannot give "too much," then one might conceivably give forever, never reaching a limit. Like the temporal reversal of the opening lines, we have again come upon an opening onto the impossible—that is, unrealizable in practical material terms, and hence unbound by those terms and potentially infinite. Vaugelas was not possessed of limitless time; he gave to his translation what he "stole" ("ce qu'il pouvoit dérober") from his other concerns—and, of course, he was mortal. The imperative to give translation one's "all"—one's time—remains.

"Très-indulgent" with others but strict with himself, the arbiter of l'usage restricts self-expression by refusing to cultivate a personal style, imitating first Coëffeteau, then d'Ablancourt. The *Quinte-Curce* is thus a double translation, both of the Latin original and of the stylistic "models." The endless process involves the constant consultation of yet more *amis*. The friends Conrart and Chapelain reciprocate, as we have seen, and Du Ryer too both consults Vaugelas's friends and counts himself among their number (*5v). The editorial work, we realize, mirrors and replicates the work of translation. The final gesture of the preface is to extend the network of relationships to the reader and hence indefinitely.

"Judge thereby what you owe." To what degree do acts of generosity, such as this translation, place us in debt? Have we, as readers, additionally assumed the debt of Vaugelas ("who is no longer able to express gratitude")? It may well appear that the debt is endless, something no amount of gratitude will ever be able to compensate for, and if so, it could only be a burden. As Derrida has pointed out, to the extent that a gift imposes the oppressive burden of debt, it enters into a system of exchange and restitution and can no longer be considered a "gift." It cancels itself out.[32] The gift can only be preserved by interrupting the system of exchange in some manner (22) or by losing any and all grounding in "nature" (162). To the extent that our gratitude is motivated, it seems to render a gift impossible. Or must gratitude remain "mute," as Blanchot put it? For Derrida, the impossibility of the gift does not remain trapped at this juncture; he points instead toward the world of unsettling, open-ended exchange of the Aristotelian *khrema* (158–60). Other contemporary thinkers have sought to break the impasse and maintain the possibility of giving as well.[33]

Descartes pondered similar questions in *Les Passions de l'âme*, published only four years before the *Quinte-Curce*. Gratitude, or *reconnaissance*, is there likened to *faveur*, or the approbation of another's good actions and disinterested wish for that person's well-being.[34] Descartes compares faveur to pity, underscoring the importance of the sympathetic identifications implied in both; he observes of gratitude that it possesses the same "content" ("elle contient tout le mesme") as faveur but is specifically inspired by "an action that touches us and that we desire to return [*nous revancher*]." The problem arises again: the "action that touches us" would appear to obviate the disinterested benevolence of faveur, and, furthermore, "return" implies an attempt to evade the relationship by paying off the debt. Rather than stopping at this impasse, however, Descartes suggests that the "force" of gratitude is commensurate with one's degree of generosity.

Generosity, which Descartes defines as legitimate, measured self-esteem and a willingness to assume that others are as reasonable and as well intentioned as oneself, is founded on free will, or *libre arbitre* (*Passions* §153, *Oeuvres* 11:445–46). By associating generosity, and hence gratitude, with freedom, Descartes dissolves indebtedness and instead inaugurates a relationship based not on exchange but rather, ultimately, on *admiration*, "une subite surprise de l'âme," or the pyschophysiological state of openness to the world (*Passions* §70, *Oeuvres* 11:380). As an expression of libre arbitre and openness, the relationship remains unsutured, unbound, like the "generous struggles" of Corneille's plays, spiraling without resolution, and the limitless desire of Vaugelas and his friends for the perfect translation.

In his essay on translation and friendship, Blanchot teases out the analogy between *amitié* and Walter Benjamin's notion of the "reconciliation" between languages; Blanchot proposes a view of translation *as* friendship, as the "space between." But, as the reference to Hölderlin in Benjamin's essay suggests, it may be dangerous to navigate this space, this "constant, dangerous, admirable intimacy," as Blanchot calls it (73). One danger lies in the bottomless chasm of Hölderlin's madness, another in the labyrinth of Vaugelas's consultations and deferrals: two versions of the abyss. But the abyss is not the only issue (in the sense of exit). For Du Ryer and his colleagues, translation is bound up with the most radical form of the gift, the work of mourning. Death, writes Du Ryer, does not "dispense" us from "the fidelity that friends owe one another" (*8r), but translation (or its avatar, editing) transforms infinite debt into a working-through. Its open structure obviates return, exchange, and restitution: it is an act of generosity, a gift. It does not "compensate" for the loss of the friend, but (despite being a monument of sorts) it prevents the loss from being incorporated, enclosed, or silenced in a frozen crypt.[35] Instead, the translation is a process, an ongoing modification of the environment we live in, a reconciliation between the present and the past. "Reconciliation" is not "coincidence" but is instead an acceptance of difference and change.

Thus, while on one level Vaugelas failed—inevitably—in his ambition to create a "timeless" translation, one that would remain immune to language change or that might even prevent language change from occurring, on another level, thanks to the work of his friends, his work succeeds in coming to terms with its own location in time. In de Man's terms, "it establishes its language in the void of this temporal difference" between itself and its origin, resulting in a gesture that bespeaks openness, otherness, and generosity. This quintessential neoclassical translation affords its readers a means of reimagining themselves and their relationship to both past and future.

Looking back over these prefaces, we see a number of common threads. Prominent among them is the visibility and specificity of language. As we saw in Derrida, the insistence on neoclassical French "purity," its historical "resistance" to otherness (and a certain understanding of translation), accompanies an awareness of its own character, its *génie*, "the singular event of the original" that cannot allow for such clean-cut distinctions as that between *verbum verbo* and *sensum sensu*, word for word and sense for sense.[36] Hence, neoclassical translation contains within itself a significant alternative to what is usually presented as the representational paradigm, shearing apart words and meaning, of *la pensée classique.* This linguistic specificity and concreteness appear in Godeau's reflections on language's conditioning by the physical environment, and in another form in the various reminders of editorial choices, indications of the instability of the source text. A further source of instability occurs in the complication of authorship, or ownership, as responsibility is shared to some extent among author, translator(s), editor, dedicatee, prefacer—a circle of participants that includes the reader as well. Like the editorial questions, the multiplication of voices foregrounds textuality while blurring univocity. Yet all these texts set eloquence—the capacity of language to move, to persuade, to transform, rather than to signify—as their ultimate goal, and as the quality of the original to which they are most faithful. The emphasis on eloquence, embodiment, and instability suggests an ongoing "baroque" subtext, even at neoclassicism's apogee.[37] The baroque predilection for *figures de détour* (parable, allegoresis) finds a curious echo or survival in translation, seen not as an abstract set of cognitive procedures but rather as a means of approaching the ineffable.

TRANSLATION AS TRANSUBSTANTIATION

If d'Ablancourt and his fellow academicians formed one closely connected network of translators during the seventeenth century, the group of intellectuals associated with the convent Port-Royal were another. We tend to associate Port-Royal with language theory and philosophy—the *Grammaire raisonnée* (1660) of Arnauld and Lancelot, the *Logique de Port-Royal* (1662) of Arnauld and Nicole—and of course it is considered a center for the diffusion of the austere and controversial theology of Cornélius Jansen. In his *Jugemens des savans*, however, Adrien Baillet discusses the "Messieurs de Port-Royal" at length in the chapter on French translators; he expresses admiration for their piety and credits them with having "enriched and embellished" the French language.[38] Baillet underscores the contributions of Robert Arnauld d'Andilly (1589–1674); his younger brother, the theologian Antoine Arnauld (1612–94); and his nephew Isaac-Louis Le Maistre de Sacy (1613–84), the principal figure in the Port-Royal Bible translation project. The Arnauld family was closely connected to the history of the Jansenist movement, a history marked by the polemics of Arnauld and Pascal, condemnations from both Rome and the French monarchy, and an enduring influence in French intellectual and cultural life.[39] Arnauld d'Andilly and Antoine Arnauld were siblings of the reforming abbess of Port-Royal, Mère Angélique (1591–1661), whose decision in 1634 to invite Jean Du Vergier de Hauranne, the abbé de Saint-Cyran, to be the convent's spiritual director oriented the community definitively toward Jansenism. While a complete analysis of the confluence of translation, theology, and linguistics at Port-Royal falls beyond the scope of this book, the Messieurs' prefaces—one might almost call them meditations—offer a version of "Port-Royal language theory" that differs from accounts derived from the *Logique* or the *Grammaire* and offer a different basis for thinking about translation in the decades that followed.

As Baillet's remarks indicate, the Port-Royal translators were deeply admired in their day, and their influence was felt throughout the discussion of translation in the second half of the century. For Roger Zuber, they were responsible for a shift away from the *Belles infidèles* conceived as literary productions, toward a new focus on rigor and "rules of translation."[40] But despite their stated rejection of "worldly" styles of translation, as well as a theoretical program that clearly distinguishes them from d'Ablancourt and his circle, the Port-Royal translators were more given to adaptative techniques than their programmatic statements suggest. In an important article published in the 1950s, Basil Munteano examined a number of manuscripts by Arnauld d'Andilly, Le Maistre de Sacy, and their circle and concluded that the Messieurs engaged in an extended debate or "differend" in the early 1640s on issues of style and literalness in the translation of sacred texts, and that Sacy ultimately pulled away from the others toward a position of stricter literalness. Sacy's correspondence with his spiritual advisor, Saint-Cyran's successor Martin de Barcos, indicates considerable soul searching on his part as he sought to reconcile literary and spiritual sensibilities.[41]

Arnauld d'Andilly too appears to have accepted criticism from his family and associates and withheld his translation of Augustine for years until he arrived at a suitably sober version.[42] His contribution to the "differend," his *Remarques sur la traduction françoise*, were written in response to the *Règles de la traduction françoise* composed around 1647 by Antoine Le Maistre, his nephew (and Sacy's brother). Arnauld d'Andilly incorporates all ten of Le Maistre's rules into his *Remarques*, expanding on them and adding one; overall the *Remarques* suggest a high tolerance for adaptative translations. Le Maistre returned to the schematic *règles* as well, to produce a revised, more fully developed version of his own.[43] The question of biblical translation poses issues of faith, meaning, and expression in a particularly intense and complex way in Sacy's numerous prefaces and correspondence with Barcos. Arnauld d'Andilly's more self-contained preface to Augustine, however, offers as part of its programmatic statement on translation a pointed reflection on language's force and its effect on the reader.

Robert Arnauld d'Andilly, "Avis au lecteur," Les Confessions de S. Augustin *(1649)*

Arnauld d'Andilly's relatively short "Avis" opens on a note of epistolary intimacy ("My dear Reader") and explicitly eschews one of the habitual topoi of prefaces, "a long discourse on the excellence and utility of the work I present here" (ã4r). Instead, his emphasis will be on the "personal" qualities of the *Confessions*, seen less as introspection than as "testimony," or *tesmoignage*, and on Augustine's relationship to his readers.

For Arnauld d'Andilly, the sole aim of the devotional text should be "to lift the hearts and minds of its readers to God," with an emphasis on "hearts rather than minds" (ã4r). Augustine's *Confessions* fulfills this purpose better than any other by infusing the reader's soul with light and heat ("une lumiere plus pure & une chaleur plus vive & plus penetrante," ã4v). The emphasis on affect (*coeur, amour, charité*) and its privileging over mind (*esprit*), and the association of *lumière*, light, with *chaleur* rather than *clarté*, heat rather than light, offer a far more emotional, and less intellectual or cognitive, view of devotional practice than is often associated with Port-Royal. Arnauld d'Andilly returns again and again to an image of the saint, "burning with divine love," and to the communicative force of his work (ã4v–ã5r). The radiant heat of the *Confessions* acts first on their author, who becomes a model for all the faithful, not only through his exemplary life but through his exemplary engagement with the text, "abandoning himself entirely to the ravishment of his love" (ã5v).

Heart and soul, light and fire, continue to inspire Arnauld d'Andilly's account of the text, which despite brief marginal references to specific books, remains global and synchronic in its perspective. The *Confessions* are, to a great extent, a series of portraits of their author as reader—a schoolboy shedding misguided tears for Dido, an arrogant intellectual stumbling upon Cicero's *Hortensius*, a fully illumined convert able to produce the allegorical reading of Genesis in the final sections. The supreme moment of conversion is a scene of reading as well: *Tolle, lege.* But at the end of his evocation of the text, Arnauld d'Andilly lets the written word become breath: "So impressed [*imprime*—also "to print"] is he by the spirit of love and charity that is the soul of the new law, that love itself appears to speak through his mouth" (ã6v). This progression—from the evocation of the saint as reader, as writer, as written text, to divinely inspired love speaking "through his mouth"—becomes the transition for a brief reflection on translation: "The greater the merit of this book, the greater the difficulty in preserving its beauties and graces while changing its language. . . . I have done my utmost to be at least very faithful, if not always very eloquent; and to avoid both a low servility that, by remaining overly attached to words and to the letter, produces deformed, monstrous copies of fine originals . . . and the opposite and no less condemnable extreme, which is to give oneself the freedom to add and remove the authors' meanings under the pretext of making them speak more elegantly" (ã6v–ã7r). We could be reading d'Ablancourt. Here, too, "fidelity" is linked to "eloquence"; the preceding account of Augustine's transformative words becomes the justification for avoiding literality, conserving *beautez*. Arnauld d'Andilly rejects any change to "meaning" in the name of "elegance," but having split *sens* from the "servitude" of literality, he is well within the mainstream of his day.

What distinguishes Arnauld d'Andilly and others of his generation from the theoretical tradition going back to Cicero and Saint Jerome is their insistence on force, persuasion, and eloquence, their evocation of orality in the ostentatiously textual practice of translation. For example, in his *Remarques*, Arnauld d'Andilly states that the chief aim in translation is "to be extremely faithful and literal," which he promptly glosses as meaning that "if Cicero had spoken our language, he would have spoken just as we speak in our translation."[44] For us, there exists a tension between the demand for fidelity and that for beauty; for Arnauld d'Andilly and for many others, however, they appear to be reconciled in the impossible speech act ("if Cicero had spoken our language") repeated in so many prefaces! Another such moment occurs in the "Approbation des Docteurs" appended to Arnauld d'Andilly's preface. After noting the long history of French translations of the *Confessions*, the approbation concludes that this version offers the text "just as the incomparable Doctor [i.e., Augustine] would have given it if he had written in our language and in our time" (ã9r).

The differences between translation and speech are brought to mind when Arnauld d'Andilly recognizes the help of his associates ("mes amis") in checking his translation; he calls the reader's attention to his own editorial work on the Latin text. Textuality, unlike orality, opens up questions of multiple authorship and multiple versions. And yet, the written, translated text thus aims to produce the same effect on the reader as the living words of the saint on his listeners. The final words of the preface return us to the imagery of verbal/affective engagement evoked throughout the discussion of the *Confessions* and render it present, immediate: "I hope, my dear Reader, that the fire of divine love that enflamed the heart of St. Augustine and caused him to produce so excellent a work throws such lively sparks into yours that you become enflamed with the desire to renounce worldly affections and perishable pleasures . . . and I hope that out of charity you will not refuse my wish for you to pray God to grant me the same grace" (ã7r). Something is happening other than the familiar erasure of representation in the "pretense" of confronting us with an "original" through the window of transparent translation. To the contrary, the repeated evocations of eloquence, force, and conversion are here juxtaposed with reminders of the act of reading. They reach out beyond the depiction of the saint and his reading public at large to a sudden "discursive event," the dramatic staging of the I-you relationship in the apostrophe to the reader, since Arnauld d'Andilly can request the reader's prayers for his departed soul at any and every moment that his words are read.[45] An analogous event occurs at the end of Du Ryer's preface to Vaugelas, a preface already written in the name of the dead to readers whose gratitude for the editors' work similarly extends beyond the grave.

Isaac-Louis Le Maistre de Sacy, La Bible traduite en françois (1667–1696)

The Port-Royal Bible was hardly the first French translation of the Bible. More than a century had passed since the publication of the "Louvain Bible" by Catholic humanist Lefèvre d'Etaples, based on the Vulgate, and the Protestant translation by Pierre Robert Olivétan, based on the Hebrew and Greek versions. But within the aesthetics and ideology of the Counter-Reformation, with its emphasis on orality, mystery, participation, and the fusion of spectator and spectacle (whether in the theatre or in the Mass), translation, particularly the translation of scripture, is suspect. Translation is suspect first because it supposes an intellectual encounter with the text that precludes mystic fusion, and second because the Council of Trent, in declaring the Latin Vulgate Bible the "authentic" text of the Catholic Church, had severely restricted access to vernacular translations, in particular of the New Testament.[46] The council condemned the Louvain Bible, although its circulation in France continued to be tolerated—a sign of Gallican independence and the preeminence of print vernacular culture. The Calvinist Olivétan Bible was unacceptable to French Catholics, but by the mid-seventeenth century, the Renaissance French of the Louvain Bible seemed light-years from current usage. Several prominent translators, among them Amelot de la Houssaye and Michel de Marolles, offered versions of the New Testament, but Port-Royal produced what would be the standard French Catholic Bible for years to come.[47]

The Port-Royal Bible was a long-term project.[48] An initial translation of the four Gospels and the Book of Revelations, completed by Antoine Le Maistre in 1653 and reviewed by his brother Le Maistre de Sacy and their uncle Antoine Arnauld, became the starting point for a full translation of the New Testament by a group that included Le Maistre (who died in 1658), his brother, Arnauld, Pierre Nicole, and other members of the community, among them Blaise Pascal. The project took shape against a backdrop of the Jansenist controversy, marked by Saint-Cyran's arrest in 1638, papal condemnations, Arnauld's expulsion from the Faculty of Theology of the Sorbonne in 1656, and hostility from Mazarin and later Louis XIV. Forced into hiding, Sacy had just completed his New Testament preface when he was arrested and imprisoned in the Bastille in May 1666. There he remained until early 1669. Unable to publish their New Testament in France, his collaborators had it printed in Amsterdam by the Elseviers under the name of Gaspard Migeot, bookseller of Mons, in 1667. Liberated at the "Peace of the Church," Sacy began the long process of translating the books of the Old Testament, which began appearing individually in 1672. Each volume provides the translation alongside the text of the Vulgate, accompanied by a preface and extensive double commentary on the "literal meaning" and the "spiritual meaning." After his death in 1684, his colleagues oversaw the publication of his remaining manuscripts; the final volume appeared in 1694. The "Bible de Sacy" would become the standard French vernacular Bible, undergoing innumerable reprintings in many forms throughout the eighteenth century and into the nineteenth. It is unfortunate that Sacy's prefaces have never been reprinted, for they offer a rich series of reflections on the act of reading and interpreting scripture in addition to their discussions of the historical significance of the individual books. Following the initial programmatic preface to the New Testament, or "Bible de Mons," which outlines a number of critical points on language, meaning, and translation, later prefaces to individual books extend the discussion of figural interpretation so central to Jansenist thought, the function of Biblical prophecy, the spiritual development of the reader of Scripture, and the relation of language to truth.[49]

Let us first look briefly at Sacy's earlier, nonbiblical prefaces. These bespeak a concern for his audience, as in his 1647 translation of *Les Fables de Phèdre*, intended for students, and for l'usage. As we have seen, little differentiated the Port-Royal translators from the academicians in many of their public productions. As the director of the Port-Royal school put it in a book of translated epigrams, "one must translate just as one speaks one's language," arguing that a beautiful translation brings us closest to the author and, in a reversal of Cervantes's famous analogy, comparing it to the right side of a tapestry.[50] Sacy's extended discussion of translation norms in his 1667 translation of St. Prosper's *Poème contre les ingrats* turns on the specific difficulties of converting Latin to French syntax within the constraints of verse translation while nevertheless attempting to render "what the Saint would have done had he written in French."[51]

Although Sacy's principal concern would appear to be a clear, intelligible rendering of the author's meaning, he is sensitive to the fact that meaning itself is not always clearly intelligible. He defends the genre of the fable, for example, on the basis of its pedagogical utility. Not only do the fables contain explicit "instruction," but by their nature they also accustom readers to seek for hidden meanings, similar to "hieroglyphics full of mysteries."[52] On the linguistic level, he argues in the Saint Prosper preface, Latin "contains" more than French, rendering a verse-for-verse translation impossible; in a parallel fashion, poetry is better able than prose to gesture beyond language toward divine reality. The idea of language's capacity to gesture toward a reality it cannot discursively articulate stems from Sacy's Augustinian inheritance.[53] He had made a similar point in a work written around 1650, published posthumously, when he argued in the preface to his *Poëme contenant la tradition de l'Eglise sur le tres-saint Eucharistie* that poetry could "contain" (*renfermer*) in few words truths that require more extensive elaboration in other forms of writing. Poetic concision "strikes the mind and touches the heart" in a particularly intense way.[54] As we shall see, this notion of language's ability to "contain" more than it explicitly says is central to Sacy's understanding of his task.

Let us now turn to the preface to the "Bible de Mons." In the opening pages, Sacy moves from his discussion of the "excellence" of the New Testament to the problem of how a changing human language might "contain" the word of God. Using the analogy of the precious materials used for the instruments intended to contain Christ's body and blood, he asks whether it would be appropriate to leave God's word in language that would not "inspire reverence."[55] Such, he claims, is the problem with older translations such as the Louvain Bible: the features of their language "that are common to all living languages until they reach a point of perfection" have "disfigured" these earlier attempts at translation, now "strangely removed from our usage" (*4r). Sacy observes the distance between contemporary French and its earlier state in terms that echo other translators' efforts to "make the author speak" other languages: "If we had been of their time, we would have spoken like them; and were they of our time, they would speak like us" (*4v). The changing language is no longer a fitting vessel for divine meaning.

The most serious difficulty confronted by the translator, however, is that God's majesty and wisdom, "enclosed" (*renfermé*) within the text, remain hidden, "as though surrounded by a cloud and hidden by shadows and figures" (*6v). We know that Sacy struggled at length with the issue of scriptural "obscurity," a recurring motif in his correspondence with Barcos.

For the latter, only the most rigorous adherence to "the letter" can possibly approach reproduction of the *dépôt* of divine meaning. Accusing Sacy of having "made the Holy Ghost speak politely," Barcos argues that biblical obscurity is a manifestation of God's will; that humility, pain, and mortification are more important to understanding than cognition and learning, if we are to obtain eternal life "through the nourishment and light of his word."[56] Sacy tells his readers that he does not hope to explicate the deepest textual depths, but only "the meaning of the text and the force of the words" (*5v); the translation is thus said not to convey *le fond*, but only its linguistic container. Later, in the section of the preface specifically directed at translation technique, Sacy describes his own "pain and uncertainty" at being caught between *sens* and *lettre* (**3v). Saint Augustine ultimately provides guidance: first, by recognizing the benefits of multiple translations of the scriptures, which can "aid and enlighten one another" (**4r), and second, by acknowledging the preeminence of the Vulgate as a compromise between literality and clarity.

But Sacy cannot ignore the fact that the Vulgate, even if it had been proclaimed the "authentic" text of the church by the Council of Trent, is a translation and as such is itself a "representation" in which certain meanings have been privileged and others lost (**7r–v). Each successive translation reduces the multiplicity of meanings and stabilizes the fragile, indeterminate *sens suspendu*. In order to avoid the loss of any meanings potentially "enclosed" in the original, Sacy promises to provide notes: notes that explore the potential for a term's ambiguity, and notes comparing versions, particularly the Greek and Latin versions, in order to maintain the fragile "suspension" wherein meaning resides.[57] Emblematic of the difficulties is Sacy's evocation of the debates among the group of translators, who found that their own understanding of the text evolved over time (**8r). As Michel de Certeau once pointed out, if for textual critic Richard Simon the fragility of the scripture stemmed from the uncertainties of textual transmission, for Sacy its elusiveness and multiplicity have ontological significance, gesturing toward the ineffable.[58]

If the obscurity of scripture serves on the one hand to remind us of human imperfection, to humiliate us in our pride (*6v), it also has a profoundly transformative effect, through parallels with the sacrament of the Eucharist. Just as Christ is entirely present under the species and external appearance of the bread and wine, so too the Gospel, "under the simplest of words and under the mysterious veils of the parables, where nothing particularly grand or extraordinary seems apparent, nevertheless encloses all the treasures of God's wisdom and knowledge" (*8v). Text and Host are to be treated with the same reverence, but unlike the body of Christ, which should only be approached rarely and by someone in a state of grace, the scripture is available to those who remain in a state of sin as "the consolation of sinners, light for the blind, healing for the sick, and life for the dead" (**1r). Sacy completes his analogy: the Host contains the body of Christ, which as the bread of the soul can only be received under special circumstances, while scripture contains the word of Christ, which as the soul's "spiritual and divine" air may be breathed in at any moment, since our body needs constant air in order to live (**2r–v). As we shall see, Sacy explores the implications of this eucharistic conception of language throughout his writing.[59]

Sacy's translation of the Old Testament appeared over a number of years in separate books.[60] The first of these, *Les Proverbes de Salomon* (1672), features another significant theoretical preface in which one hears echoes of his exchange with Barcos in the late 1660s, particularly in the extended discussions of scripture's difficulty for both readers and translators. Biblical obscurity is "painful" to us, he says, because we always desire to know more things: "We want to satisfy our mind, and we forget that we are full of wounds."[61] Translation of scripture is especially difficult because it participates in the human desire to know and communicate as well as to "express in our language the very words of the Scriptures" and to "represent all of the meanings" (*7r) even though these meanings may be difficult to render in any language and beyond anything that we might conceive ("au dessus de nos pensées," *9v). The theme of "difficulty" or "obscurity" recurs in nearly all the prefaces. In the 1682 preface to *La Genèse*, it serves to remind us of the two infinities, "the smallness of the human mind and . . . the inexhaustible riches of God's wisdom"; in the 1685 preface to *Les Nombres*, it reminds us of "our nothingness [*neant*] and God's grandeur." Nearly all of the prefaces make references to the "hiddenness" of meaning (*le sens caché, renfermé*), but there are other kinds of difficulty as well—for example, the moral difficulty of coming to terms with apparently immoral behavior on the part of biblical figures such as Jacob or Judith or the seeming blasphemies of Job's counselors or Job himself in his despair, and the difficulty of confronting a text filled with lists and repetitions. Repetition can itself inculcate a moral lesson (*Deuteronome, Jérémie*), whereas genealogies and lists, whose spiritual meaning is among the most obscure, remind us that "all the elements of a painting contribute to its beauty" (*Paralipomenes*).[62] Borrowing an analogy from Saint Augustine, Sacy compares such passages to a musical instrument: "Just as all parts of a harp resonate together, but . . . only the strings, when touched by the artist, specifically produce the harmonious sound, so too in sacred history, not everything is a figure or a prophecy, and yet the slightest details provide the joins and connections for the major elements, which are themselves prophetic and mysterious."[63]

While in his preface to *Les Proverbes* Sacy ultimately decides that "fidelity" to the language is ultimately more important than "clarity," he offers the marginal notes as a sort of compromise between the obscurity of the text and the reader's quest for meaning (*Proverbes*, *10r–*11v). The notes and commentary are of two kinds, literal and figurative (*sens littéral* and *sens figuré*). The 1673 preface to *Isaïe*, the second of the Old Testament prefaces to appear, presents the two "meanings" with an allusion to Saint Paul: "Should we prefer the shadows of those carnal Jews who saw in the writings of the prophets only the letter that killed them, to the admirable light offered by the religion in which God gave us birth?"[64] The reference to "the letter that killeth" in 2 Corinthians 3:6 had been standard for translators since the Renaissance; we have seen it in d'Ablancourt and other contemporaries as well. Put simply, Sacy furnishes two sorts of commentary: on the one hand, explication of the literal meaning, the linguistic difficulties and alternative readings, as well as evidence from the historical record of the events recounted; on the other, the spiritual or moral meaning derived from the writings of the church fathers.[65] The preface to *Isaïe* clearly privileges the spiritual over the literal reading, giving as an analogy the interpretation of heraldic devices: if someone stopped at the literal interpretation of an emblem without considering its symbolic meanings, we would laugh at that person's ignorance. Thus, he concludes that "the spiritual meaning . . . is the soul, whose mere body is the literal meaning" (*Isaïe*, a6v). The later prefaces, however, complicate the situation. Sacy owes obedience to both la lettre and l'esprit, both of which are "enclosed" within the text (*Genese*, ***7r–***7v).[66]

A spiritual reading thus is also a figurative reading—and a figural reading. For Sacy, rhetorical figures are vivid instances of linguistic density or obscurity—"the obscurity of such deep meanings hidden beneath poetic and metaphorical expressions" (*Job*, c4v)—and as such they are valuable indices of hidden meaning, eliciting our interpretative attention or reminding us to adore "obscurity itself" (*Douze petits prophetes*, e2r). Thus the prophet Ezechiel, who speaks entirely through "enigmas" and "figurative expressions," rivets the attention of the reader "in suspense and admiration."[67] But if rhetorical figures are a source of mystery in the text, the figural tradition in biblical exegesis is one of the chief means for achieving clarity and understanding. Figural interpretation, based on Saint Paul's claim that all the Jews' sufferings were "figures" (*typikōs*; *figura* in the Vulgate; 1 Corinthians 10:6) of Christ's coming and the new covenant, enabled early interpreters, most notably Augustine, to postulate a close union between the Old and New Testaments, as well as complete conformity between "the figures contained in the former and the truth accomplished in the latter."[68] Figural interpretation, crucial to the Port-Royal understanding of scripture, would take on additional significance for eighteenth-century Jansenists, who saw a second, apocalyptic "figuration" of their own persecutions in the biblical texts.[69] Figures function like prophecy, according to Sacy; both are proofs of an eternal being for whom past and present are one (*Daniel*, a6v). As he observes in the preface to *Les Nombres*, "This history . . . encloses the past, the present, and the future" (a3r). Citing Augustine, Sacy underscores the mutual relationship between past and present, in which each reveals the other: "the new law hidden beneath the shadows of the old, . . . the old law discovered and made clear in the light of the new."[70]

The figural reading may thus be said to respond to the temporal "allegorical" dilemma we saw posed most dramatically in the case of Vaugelas's *Quinte-Curce*. In Du Ryer's account, translation is cast as varying inescapably not only from its original but also from itself and its own home in language. Du Ryer's "painful recognition" of the gulf between present and past, the sign and its referent, is palliated, or mediated, through an act of gratitude and remembering that finally compensates for the loss. Figuration is also a form of remembering, but its dynamic is more complex. Whereas the allegorical sign foregrounds repetition without coincidence, the figural sign precedes its referent, becoming visible in retrospect. The temporal dynamic is not purely symmetrical, because the second event both annuls and fulfills the first, or as Erich Auerbach notes in a classic essay, figural interpretation "establishes a connection between two events or persons, the first of which signifies not only itself but also the second, while the second encompasses or fulfills the first."[71]

This double relationship bears a striking resemblance to the structure of the linguistic sign as developed by Arnauld and Nicole in the *Logique de Port-Royal*. As they explain in their much-cited chapter 4, "The sign encloses [*enferme*] two ideas: one is the thing that represents; the other of the thing represented; its nature is to excite the latter by the former."[72] Signification is thus a form of representation operating on a dual relationship. Hence, if I look at a painting (to take the *Logique*'s example), I have both an idea of a "thing that represents" (the painting) and an idea of the "thing represented" (a landscape), or, as philosopher A. R. Ndiaye puts it, a relationship of both "presentation" and "representation" between the sign and its object, a dual movement of *doubling* (presentation and representation—"signifying not only itself but also the second") and *substitution* (of the idea of the landscape for the idea of the painting—"encompassing and fulfilling the first").[73] The analogy between the sign and the figuration are evident in the vocabulary—*chose figurante, chose figurée*—as well as in the examples of the different structural relations existing between signs and their referents. For example, there are signs "separate" from things, "such as the sacrifices of the old law, signs of Christ sacrificed"; there are also signs that both hide and reveal things, as when "Eucharistic symbols hide the body of Christ as a thing, and reveal it as a symbol" (81). As we have seen, the figural relation also both "hides" and "reveals."

Clearly these are not gratuitous examples (chapter 4 was added to the fifth edition of the *Logique* during controversies over the Eucharist).[74] The close association between figural interpretation and linguistic sign suggests that we should not underestimate either the subtext of mystical embodiment in Arnauld and Nicole or the linguistic relevance of Sacy's exegetics. As Auerbach points out regarding the two events in the figural relation, "both . . . have something provisional and incomplete about them; they point to one another and both point to something in the future, something still to come, which will be the actual, real, and definitive event" ("Figura," 58). The sign too points to something beyond itself; a "figural" understanding of this relation endows it with deeper significance.

The ultimate figure, incorporating past, present, and future, is the Eucharist. For Sacy, it is a double figure, incorporating Christ's body in the believer, and the believer within the body of the church: "Not only is the Eucharist, in its externals, the figure of the truth of Christ's body, which it contains, but the very body of Christ, clothed in these corporeal veils, is the figure of the same Savior's mystical body, which is composed of all the faithful, animated by his Spirit and participating in his Body" (*Poëme contenant la tradition de l'Eglise*, e2r). The transformation of the bread and wine prefigures our own transformation, consuming "everything in us that is terrestrial, carnal, corruptible" (f1r). The "veiled truths" of the Eucharist provide an intermediary between the "empty figures" of the old covenant and God's "naked truth" (c1r).

As we have already seen in Sacy's New Testament preface, scripture plays a similar intermediate role. The preface to *Les Nombres*, published in 1685, shortly after Sacy's death, develops this thought. Commenting that numerous chapters appear to contain "nothing edifying," Sacy reminds us of Augustine's teaching that the Word of God is no less worthy of veneration than the Body of the Son of God. Nevertheless, there is a difference, for if Christ is hidden from us in the Eucharist ("It is here that he is truly the hidden God, as he is called in the Scriptures, *Deus absconditus*"), God's Word offers both *obscurité* and *lumières* (a4r–a4v). Just as transubstantiation occurs beyond our perceptions, so we can experience the benefits of scripture without complete understanding:

> Thus occurs during our reading of these passages of the divine books of Scripture the same thing that occurs every day in holy communion. The truth of God's word is veiled from us and we cannot taste that sweetness that Saint Augustine calls the chaste delight of the soul; in like manner, Jesus Christ is hidden from us in his sacrament. But if he is sometimes hidden from us in Scripture, he is always hidden in the august mystery of our altars. Yet our faith in the certitude of Christ's word never wavers, but remains constant, even though the obscurity that covers this hidden God be impenetrable; and this obscurity causes neither lessening nor irritation in our faith, but instead its beatitude and its crown. (a6v)

Scripture is thus the site of a double participation in God's mystery: both the self-abdication in the "chaste delight" of eucharistic incorporation and the intellectual grasp of the Word's *lumières*.

What becomes clear in the course of these various writings is that what is true of the act of reading is also true of translation. Like the Eucharist, translation is an "intermediary" enabling access to that which is otherwise hidden, incomprehensible; translation "contains" (*renferme*) its original doubly, through attention to both l'esprit and la lettre. It has often been pointed out that Sacy represents a more "spiritual" side of Port-Royal thought, as opposed to the Cartesian rationalism of Arnauld and Nicole, but the parallel we have seen between the Bible prefaces and the *Logique* points toward what may be a spiritual subcurrent in Port-Royal language theory, or perhaps an alternative version of it. Words do not only point outward toward abstract meaning; they "enclose" meaning, which takes on the attributes of the Real

Presence, simultaneously hidden and revealed. As scripture is to the divine, so translation is to scripture. Note that in this view, language does not simply "veil" meaning, because the meaning is inaccessible without language. Language embodies meaning as the Host embodies the Real Presence; one cannot strip away the words in order to attain a pure Idea. At the same time, both language and Host gesture toward a greater reality beyond.[75]

The theological context inflects our understanding of Port-Royal linguistics and its central tenet that language is a representation of thought. In the eucharistic view of language, meaning is thus not sheared away, abstracted, or distanced, but linguistically (mystically) "embodied."[76] This realization complicates the usual view that Port-Royal linguistics and, by extension, all forms of general grammar see translation as unproblematical.[77] Certainly there is a transparent "ideal" of translation: if thought is universal and pre-exists language, and the variations among different languages are only local "accidents," then one could expect that, ultimately, all languages should be translatable into one another. Indeed, translation would be inherent in the structure of language itself.[78] To the extent that meaning inheres or is "enclosed" in language, however, translation becomes difficult, perhaps unintelligible. One could argue that the translation of scripture is a special case, since the divine Word is not knowable in the same way as human thought; scripture is a "full" utterance, a *parole pleine*, ontologically distinct from human linguistic production. Even if this is the case, the multiple readings and rereadings of the sentence "Ceci est mon Corps" throughout the 1683 additions to the *Logique* tell us that language is bound up with a need to come to terms with transubstantiation, which is another way of saying that no amount of reasoning will enable us to escape from the ineffable. As Jean-Luc Nancy puts it in his own meditation on language and embodiment, "*Hoc est enim corpus meum*: an impossible appropriation, the very impossibility of appropriation in general."[79]

TEMPORALITY, THEATRICALITY, AND THE FIGURE OF TRANSLATION

We have already seen in the case of the *Quinte-Curce* of Vaugelas how translation becomes a particularly vivid indicator of temporality, of the instability of language over time. Throughout the seventeenth century, the tremendous intellectual energies channeled into the reflection on language instill feelings both of pride in French as having "arrived," reached its perfection, and equaled the literary culture of the Ancients, and of tenuousness and enhanced sensitivity to shifts in usage. One way in which this deeper sense of temporality gains ground is in the realization that translations age over time and must be replaced. The "Approbation" to Arnauld d'Andilly's translation of the *Confessions* links the need for new translations directly to the recent "progress" of French: "Those who know how much our language has been enriched and perfected of late, and the degree to which the art of translation was neglected until now, can easily imagine what those older versions must be like" (ã8r).[80] Other translators comment on their relationship to other translators, especially predecessors. Louis Giry praises the earliest known translation of *De civitatis dei* in French (although he finds that more recent translations "leave something to be desired")[81]; Boileau hands out praise and blame in his preface to Longinus.[82] Jean Petit looks to his own author, Saint Jerome, the patron of translators, but also to his contemporaries at Port-Royal, for whom he has high praise (ĩ1r–ĩ1v). Jean Baillet's lengthy set of entries on translators into French, from Nicolas Oresme to Philippe Goibault Du Bois, testifies to the importance of translation and its history, as do significant chapters on translation in the "bibliothèques" of Charles Sorel and Claude-Pierre Goujet, in which translation is seen as a prime indicator of teleological change toward greater *pureté*.[83] Morvan de Bellegarde explicitly links adaptive, modernizing translation techniques (such as giving gallicized proper names, titles, and currency equivalents) to the evolution of the language: "Daring new words are preferable to old worn-out words, for our language is living and may be enriched by new manners of speaking."[84]

The concern with new usage returns in an essay written by Antoine Arnauld in 1694, the last year of his life, but published in 1707. In his *Regles pour discerner les bonnes et les mauvaises critiques des traductions de l'Ecriture-Sainte en François* (Rules for Discerning between Good and Bad Criticisms of French Translations of the Holy Scripture), Arnauld takes on the critics of the Port-Royal biblical translations (Dominique Bouhours and Richard Simon, among others). Although his first rule explicitly denies that translations of scripture should pursue the same "delicacy and politeness" of expression as in a work of "eloquence," many of his rules and observations concern the propriety of concessions made to l'usage and contemporary norms in translation, such as the avoidance of repetition.[85] The work reflects an author who was exiled and ailing but still feisty, and it contains a rich set of reflections on l'usage.[86] Arnauld tells us that he does not intend to combat Vaugelas's maxim "that Usage is the rule and tyrant of living language," but he probes its implications, suggests several correctives (noting for example that many exemplars of usage—such as Patru, Le Maistre, and Pascal—were never exposed to court life, supposedly the seat of le bon usage), and poses the question of language change. How can neologisms and new expressions come into the language if people are paralyzed by fear of seeming ridiculous, or if certain self-styled arbiters decry their usage? he asks, ultimately arguing for a more flexible understanding of usage and the realization that more than one usage may be acceptable.[87] In addition to the overarching concern with defending his colleagues' translation of the Bible, Arnauld frequently refers to translation as indicative of the state of the French language, and he cites a number of translations, such as Luther's, that are considered monuments of their national languages. Translation too provides a key argument against a single, exclusionary account of acceptable usage. In his Fifth Reflection, he denounces "certain Purists" who imagine that there is "only one correct manner of speaking." In order to demonstrate the absurdity of their position, he asks us to consider two translations of Augustine's *Confessions*, each produced by people "who have a reputation for writing well" (139–40).[88] Since no two translations are ever exactly the same (unless the second has plagiarized the first), we must assume that there are divergent, but equally valuable, means of expressing the same thing.

Arnauld's point about the noncoincidence of different translations rejoins the condemnations of "secondhand translation," or producing a translation based not on the original but on another translation, by many commentators.[89] Whether one sees in such critiques the rejection of "a copy of a copy" or instead the conferring of a special status upon translation (akin to Benjamin's assertion that there can be no translation of a translation), they reinforce the reader's awareness of the complications of authorship wrought by translation and by the relations of texts to other texts—their repetitions, identities, and differences. Translation exemplifies our inability to assign an unwavering identity to language, be it based on words, meanings, speakers. What I am calling translation's "theatricality" is this exemplary, explicit manner of bringing to the fore or crystallizing issues that underlie much of the reflection on language in general. But there is another form of dramatization that characterizes neoclassical translation as well.

"Sire, here are two illustrious foreigners who have learned your language in order to have the honor of conversing with you."[90] So begins d'Ablancourt's dedication to Louis XIV of his translation of Thucydides and

Xenophon. The initial promise to let the dead speak is followed up in the preface, when the translator defends taking a few liberties in order to conserve "our Author's glory": "For this is less the portrait of Thucydides than it is Thucydides himself, who has passed into another body through a sort of metempsychosis, and thus from Greek has become French, without being able to complain of a lack of resemblance when he appears less defective, any more than a patient would complain of a doctor who by the strength of his remedies had given him health and vigor" (201–2). D'Ablancourt rejects the notion of translation as a form of mimesis in favor of "the impossible speech act" we observed on several earlier occasions. Thucydides lives, but reminders of his death persist ("death prevented him from giving the final touches to his work," 203). While the image of the author speaking French had been a feature of the discourse on translation since the mid-sixteenth century, it is clearly the hallmark of the neoclassical style.

The evocation of the author's voice, which we have observed in nearly every preface examined so far, and which will be seen in many more through the end of the eighteenth century, is linked to the evocation of the author's eloquence. The *Huit oraisons* make the claim, implicitly or explicitly, on every page, not only through the style and presentation of the translations but also through the choice of texts.[91] Both Antoine Le Maistre and Thomas Guyot (successor to Le Maistre de Sacy as director of the Port-Royal school) specify that translation belongs to the discipline of rhetoric and that it serves to teach eloquence, or "the strength [*force*] of words."[92] Even the Jesuit Dominique Bouhours feels called upon to present his translation of Pianezza's *La Vérité de la religion chrétienne* with a scene of transformative eloquence, the emperor Constantine's appearance before the Council of Nicea, telling the reader that the audience of pagan philosophers "were touched more by the Emperor's discourse on the divinity of Christ than they had been by all the writings of the early apologists of the faith."[93] Although initially Bouhours would appear to be claiming that spoken testimony is more powerful than written, his point is rather the suasive force of Constantine's own renown and personal merit—hence justifying the biography of Pianezza that follows. The implied parallel confers upon his translation, then, the same potential to bring about change as the emperor's commanding presence.

Discussions of translation are filled with metaphors and analogies suggesting complex forms of representation: clothing, portraiture, mirrors, the reverse side of a tapestry, and many others. But certainly, in this period, none recurs so often as the evocation of the author speaking, the "figure

of address." To make Cicero—or Plutarch, or Tacitus, or Demosthenes, or Homer, or Augustine, or Jerome—speak is not only a representation of eloquence but is one of the most powerful figures of classical rhetoric. As the Oratorian Bernard Lamy explained in his 1675 *La Rhétorique, ou L'Art de parler*, "When a passion is violent, it renders senseless those in its possession. In such a moment, we converse with the dead or with stones, as if with living people: we make them speak as if they were alive. For that reason this figure is called *prosopopoeia*, because we make a person where there is none."[94] Quintilian had advised the greatest discretion in the use of prosopopoeia, one of the "figures of thought" most closely linked to the expression of passion and grouped with other figures of feigned or dissimulated emotions.

Like its related form apostrophe, prosopopoeia is both familiar and strange; its unsettling quality, de Man once argued, stems from the fear that if death speaks, then "the living are struck dumb, frozen in their own death."[95] Indeed, no sooner has Antoine Le Maistre discussed the proper way to make a saint or father of the church speak (*faire parler*) then he falls prey to monstrous imaginings. Citing his brother Sacy's translation of Saint Prosper, he claims that a translation lacking "force" no more resembles its original "than a dead man resembles a living man."[96] Le Maistre continues,

> For meaning is the soul of discourse and words are its body. And thus a literal translation is a body without a soul, the body being from one language and the soul from another, a defect in its essence. For the discourse should have nothing but what is natural in either its soul or its body; otherwise, if with a natural body, that is, words appropriate in its language, it is animated by a foreign spirit, that is, the meaning enclosed within the original in another language, it would be a sort of monster in its composition and a prodigy of baseness in its irregularity and its obscurity.[97]

Whereas Sacy had suggested in his Saint Prosper preface that the translator might "enter the spirit" of the author, Le Maistre gives the familiar Augustinian body-mind/word-meaning analogy a curious turn that results in either a dead translation or a living monster.[98] The lack not just of meaning but of force renders all too apparent the disunity of fallen language. What could be less *naturel* than the figure of address, or the image of a dead saint speaking French? Translation opens up the possibility for language to be possessed by *un esprit estranger*, for which there is no exorcism.

Antoine Le Maistre's grim image is not the only option, however. The figure appears less in Sacy's work, since such a formula would clearly be presumptuous in the context of scripture. Nevertheless, Sacy seeks in the Saint

Prosper translation to produce "what the Saint would have done himself had he written in French" (ã4v); in his Bible commentaries he imposes silence on himself while "making speak" (*en faisant parler*) those whom Christ has chosen as his interpreters (*Genese*, ****8r). The figure of address appears most dramatically, however, in the preface to *Les Nombres*, where the translator imagines the speech of the human soul: "The humble and truly faithful soul . . . speaks from the depths of the heart to that sovereign truth who deigned to let his voice be heard in the Scriptures: 'It is enough for me to know, Lord, that you created me'" (ã6v). The translator is doubly silent here, both through stepping back to let the soul speak and through the "mask" (*prosopon*) of the soul, who seeks only to listen and magnify the divine Word, *parole*.[99] In the soul's final words, the figure shifts from prosopopoeia to apostrophe: "Grant me O God . . . that I may listen to you in your Scripture, not through reason, but through faith; not through the mind, but through the heart" (ē1r). Where are we, as listeners or witnesses? As critics have noted, prosopopoeia supposes and projects an intersubjective relation, whether "by engendering the figure of a reader" (Cynthia Chase) or, as Lorna Clymer argues in the case of epitaphic address, through a displacement "from the grave to the ongoing life of the community that remembers the dead."[100]

The blurring of the boundary between cognition and perception is part of translation's most intimate drama, in which the audience is explicitly called upon to participate, along with the author and translator. In this sense, the figure of address does not "naturalize" the scene of reading but instead calls attention to it, as does the foregrounding of representational strategies—the metaphors of clothing, tapestries, paintings. The implication of the reader takes many forms, but none so vivid as the prosopopoeia, which is, on the one hand, one of the rarest of figures and yet, on the other, commonplace among translators' prefaces. The shattering of textual unity created by evocation of the reader, the translator, and the unsettling return of the author prevents a convenient closure, a seamless mimetic whole. As Lévinas says, the reference to an interlocutor "permanently breaks through the text."[101]

❧

The space of translation thus opens up a disturbance, a sort of permanent revolution of multiplicity, movement, and change, within the structures of classical thought. Even as translators from d'Ablancourt to Arnauld discipline their prose into conformity with *le goût classique* by toning down metaphors, eliminating repetitions, and pursuing Cicero rather than Seneca as a model of style, the discursive space in which they formulated their projects remained ebulliently metaphorical, rife with citations, aware of its own temporality, and given to rhetorical extremes even while unveiling its stratagems. The translators require us to attend to the choices involved in every act of reading. The baroque figures de détour are subsumed by labyrinthine editorial projects, competing versions, intertextual relations. This is not to claim, however, that "neoclassical" translation is a nostalgic enterprise. It interpellates its readers in order to call attention to the here and now of l'usage, and makes the dead speak not in order to return to the past but in order to come to terms with it, to recuperate its loss, and to integrate it into the construction of modernity.

CHAPTER 2

Transmigration, Transmutation, and Exile

Like the world of Renaissance and post-Renaissance France, England in the early seventeenth century was rich in translations from the classics, many of which, like Chapman's Homer or Sandys's Ovid, would take on the aura of classics themselves. And yet, as in France, a particular group of men of letters turned to translation at a given moment and declared their approach to be something new: "A new and nobler way thou dost pursue / To make Translations and Translators too."[1] It was John Denham who made this claim for innovation in Richard Fanshawe's translation of Guarini's *Il Pastor Fido*, not Fanshawe himself, yet one may see Denham's verses as the seed crystal in a citational network that would play a powerful role in English literary history and the history of translation. John Denham was at the center of a group of Royalist supporters—Fanshawe, Edward Sherburne, Thomas Stanley, Edmund Waller, and Abraham Cowley, among others—who spent years of exile on the Continent during the Civil War and Interregnum. All made important verse translations, and most of them wrote significant critical pieces on translation. Indeed, translation became so central to their legacy that one scholar refers to it as "the characteristic literary activity of Royalists in defeat."[2] Since at one point or another these men all spent time—in Cowley's case, many years—at the court of Queen Henrietta Maria in France, it has long been assumed that their interest in free translation was spurred through contacts in the Parisian literary world. T. R. Steiner, who builds his case by noting the close timing of d'Ablancourt's most influential translations and those by Denham, Sherburne, and Cowley, and by tracing echoes of d'Ablancourt's prefaces in Cowley's seminal 1656 preface to his *Pindarique Odes*, must nevertheless concede that he found no specific evidence of direct contact between Cowley and d'Ablancourt's circle.[3] Yet the Royalists themselves certainly offer "markers of a group," as Steiner puts it: in addition to their shared political affiliation and ties of friendship, they exchanged ideas and supported one another's translations. (*group*)

There are clear reasons why the exiles might choose not to draw attention to French influence on their work. While nascent English literary criticism did not yet cast itself as a rival to French writing as explicitly as it would later in the century, the Royalists, especially those who spent time abroad, had a stake in presenting themselves as the representatives of an unambiguously English national literary culture. As we will see, English translators habitually manifested a keen awareness of French literary criticism and translation practice, often noting that they had compared their version of a classical text to existing French versions or, as in the case of Dryden's careful reading of Jean Segrais's translation of Virgil, responding point for point to the French critical preface. Maintaining the "Englishness" of their projects was an important goal, one that French references ultimately bolstered by allowing writers an interlocutor with whom to contrast themselves.[4] At the century's end, the publisher of a miscellany volume proclaimed English independence from French models ("We are pretty well recovered from the Servile way of following their Modes") and the superiority of English letters, governed not by French "Foppery" but by English "Solidity of Judgment."[5] In the eighteenth century the situation would reverse itself to some extent as French awareness of English cultural production both provoked programmatic statements about "Frenchness" and "Englishness" and opened up "Frenchness" to new possibilities in the complex, ongoing spiral of national identity.

What few scholars have noted is that the shared approaches and methods of the French and English neoclassical translators obscure the fact that they operated in radically different contexts. Adaptative translation responded to the needs and ambitions of the bright young men of the Académie française, intent on promoting French eloquence, as well as to those of the defeated veterans of Edgehill, Naseby, and Worcester, who had more immediate problems on their minds. It is not enough simply to say that Royalists were especially attracted to the idea of "freedom" (why not Parliamentarians?), as Lois Potter suggests, or that their approach can be entirely explained as a reflection of "aristocratic values," as Lawrence Venuti claims.[6] Interests, desires, and values of several sorts crisscross in Denham's and the others' writing, often as conflicted and complex as the period in which they lived.

Coming from the French context, one is immediately struck by the range of tone and overt politicization that characterizes their writing. The "force" of expression is less an object of analysis than an abiding quality of critical discourse itself. The French reliance on the drama of prosopopoeia here yields to translation figured as transmutation and transmigration: metaphors of translation, figures of figuration.

If we look to only a small sampling of English translators from the decades before the Civil War, we see that—as in France—a number of the features identified with neoclassical translation are already present. A preface by Joseph Webbe to his 1620 translation of Cicero's *Familiar Epistles* offers a familiar reference to Horace in support of free translation. Webbe illustrates his point with a joke about an Englishman mangling Italian and an Italian traveler mangling English. Both "English-Italian" and "Italian-English" are seen as equally "different from puritie of speech, in either language."[7] A decade later, a more prominent translator, John Vicars, similarly claims to have "facility or smoothness" as one of his chief aims in translating the *Aeneid*, again citing Horace to make his point.[8] Yet, in addition, the topos of the author "speaking," the dramatic prosopopoeia so prevalent among the French translators, emerges, though less often and less emphatically. Robert Stapylton introduces his translation of *Aeneid* IV to his dedicatee: "The Queene of CARTHAGE hath learned English to converse with you: be pleased now to esteeme her as a Native, but in the errours of her language, still remember she was borne a Forraigner."[9] I take this statement as an expression of the translator's modesty rather than any deliberate attempt to "foreignize" the language.

A variety of related analogies describe the translation process. Translation implies the transmigration of souls for writers of two commendatory poems published with Vicars's *Aeneid*. "The soule (*Pythagoras* did teach) doth go / From body unto body," writes Thomas Drant; and another proclaims that "On then, if poëtrie pythagorize, / *Virgil* in *Vicars* sacred breast survives."[10] Yet another commendatory text, this one from the translator's cousin, Thomas Vicars, praises his care "in transplanting this worthiest of latine poets, into a mellow & neat english soile." Stapylton, by contrast, speaks the language of science: "It is true that wit distilled in one language, cannot be transfused into another without losse of spirits." As Theo Hermans has pointed out, the "transmigration" topos is echoed in the "transfusion" topos; both bespeak a dawning sense of the creative power of the translator and the autonomy of the translation.[11] Stapylton's analogy will later be echoed by Denham in his influential 1656 preface to *The Destruction of Troy*: "Poesie is of so subtile a spirit, that in pouring out of one Language into another, it will all evaporate; and if a new spirit be not added in the transfusion, there will remain nothing but a *Caput mortuum*."[12] Denham, indeed, seems to respond to Stapylton's "loss" by promising something "added in the transfusion."

Just as Stapylton's concern with loss may subtend a fear lest his Dido speak English imperfectly, so too does one of the most celebrated translations of the century, George Sandys's version of Ovid's *Metamorphoses*, foreground its foreignness. Having recently returned from a stint in the Virginia colony, Sandys dedicates the work to Charles I, observing, "It needeth more than a single denization, being a double Stranger: Sprung from the Stocke of the ancient Romanes; but bred in the New-World, of the rudeness whereof it cannot but participate."[13] "Denization" is not full naturalization but an intermediate status; Sandys predicts that his Ovid will remain to some degree a foreigner. Recent commentators have called attention to a persistent "strangeness" in Sandys, stemming from his deliberately Latinate vocabulary and from references in his annotations that juxtapose physical realities of the Old and New Worlds.[14] Long treated as a literary monument, the work would be displaced at century's end by the translations of John Dryden, who would nevertheless remember Sandys as "the best versifier of the former age."[15] His words remind us that the later Augustan writers would feel themselves separated from Sandys's generation by more than the simple passage of a few decades; tectonic shifts in epistemology, combined with irrevocable political changes, would make the world of the 1620s and 1630s as distant, in many respects, as the first Augustan age.

TRANSLATION DURING THE CIVIL WAR
AND INTERREGNUM

As historian Kevin Sharpe has put it, the English Civil War "fractured the Elizabethan world-picture" by creating unresolvable tensions within what had previously appeared to be the "shared languages" that articulated the ideals and goals of the body politic.[16] The questions of what constitutes a shared language and how to proceed in the absence of a shared language are very much at the heart of the work of translation and its role in the determination of modes of reading and interpretation. One of the most distinctive differences between the intellectual terrain in France and England during this period is precisely the extraordinary politicization of all levels of discourse, including translation. Certainly throughout early modern Europe there existed a shared frame of reference according to which particular texts from classical antiquity might be invoked to imply a particular comment on the present, as we have seen in the case of Louis Giry's translation of Tacitus's *Dialogue on Orators*, which reflects a long tradition of humanist references to this work. D'Ablancourt's dedications of his Tacitus to Richelieu in 1640 and his Thucydides to Louis XIV in 1662 may have reflected subtle political associations, but not at a level to elicit commentary, let alone controversy.[17] In the England of the 1620s, however, Thomas May's translation of Lucan's *Pharsalia* (1627) was already marked as an "anti-absolutist" text, offering the image of Rome at "that unhappy height, in which shee could neither retaine her fredome without great troubles nor fall into a *Monarchy* but most heavy and distastfull."[18] May's point was sufficiently clear that either he or his dedicatees had the dedications removed from most copies of the work for fear of reprisals.[19] Two years later, Thomas Hobbes's translation of Thucydides provided a sort of cautionary response, suggesting that just as a contemporary of the Greek historian "might have added to his experience" by reading the work, so too might present-day readers through "attentive reading of the same."[20] The injunction to find lessons for the present through an "attentive reading" of the past is a traditional justification for the reading of history, but it is also an invitation to read between the lines. As Annabel Patterson, Lois Potter, and other scholars have shown, translation was one of numerous techniques by which oppositional viewpoints might be "encoded" for transmission to the public.[21]

Richard Fanshawe's dedicatory letter to the prince of Wales in his 1646 translation of *Il Pastor Fido* offers a lesson in reading. Fanshawe situates his work temporally between a past-tense service to (the future) Charles II and "a new and more fixt relation to you in the future"; the translation thus represents Fanshawe's "hours of vacancy" as the Royalists await the next turn of events.[22] Among those events was the earl of Strafford's trial, about which Fanshawe wrote a poem at the same time that he worked on his translation.[23] As Fanshawe explains, Guarini's intent was to instruct his own monarch by treating "principles of Vertue, and knowledge *Morall, Politicall, and Theologicall*" in pleasing form ("in their masking clothes," A3v). Before embarking on a dissection of the moral, political, and theological "masque" for his own prince, however, Fanshawe offers another interpretative model: "Your Highnesse may have seen at *Paris* a Picture (it is in the Cabinet of the *great Chancellor* there) so admirably design'd, that, presenting to the common beholders a multitude of little faces (the famous Ancestors of that Noble man); at the same time, to him that looks through a *Perspective* (kept there for that purpose) there appears onely a single portrait in great of the *Chancellor* himself" (A3v). Fanshawe provides two interpretations of the image: on the one hand, the Chancellor as inheritor of "the Vertues of all his Progenitors," and on the other ("by a more subtile Philosophy"), the imbrication of public and private in "the *Body Politick*" (A4r). Lois Potter correctly draws the connection from the portrait described to the composites of Jean-François Nicéron's 1638 treatise *La Perspective curieuse*, as well as to the overall absolutist interpretation that Fanshawe attributes to it. The reference to Chancellor Séguier, the powerful keeper of the seals under both Richelieu and Mazarin and a fierce enemy of the *frondeurs* and all who questioned royal authority, is also in keeping with Fanshawe's position. Yet the object described, the "curious" or anamorphic perspective, as we would call it today, is open to further interpretation.

Anamorphosis, with its "acceleration" and "deceleration" of perspective, had made its entry into European art a century earlier: Hans Holbein's 1533 painting *The Ambassadors* remains the most enduring example.[24] The diagonal streak near the bottom of Holbein's painting might almost be overlooked on first glance, but when the painting is viewed from the side, the rich interior and the objects representing the arts and sciences recede into confusion, leaving only the image of a skull, a reminder of the ultimate truth behind the proud appearances of human endeavor. Anamorphosis thus reinforces the *vanitas* tradition by unveiling a hidden spiritual reality. Nicéron's catoptric anamorphoses, which require the mediation of a mirror or prism (such as the object described by Fanshawe), suggest another form of complexity, however. Nicéron is a Cartesian—*La Perspective curieuse* contains a reference to Descartes's treatise on optics—and his creations remind us that perspective is mediated by instruments and no longer entirely or "naturally" our own. Nor is the perspective available to others—at least, not at the same time that we are engaged with it. As John Lyons comments, it "suggests the limitations . . . of our unaided, spontaneous perception."[25] At the same time, the vanitas tradition of anamorphosis infuses the scientific structure to remind us of error, misprision, and inconstancy.[26] Fanshawe's choice to read the chancellor's portrait "first and chiefest" as an emblem of the "great one" is subject to reversal, just as the portrait is subject to fragmentation into its constituent parts: "a head, an eye, or a hand." The metonymic relation between whole and parts is fundamentally unstable: even if the portrait of the chancellor is the painting's "truth," what value should be attributed to what we see with our unaided vision? The parts may combine to form the whole, but the whole is (only) the sum of its parts and can only be achieved through artifice.

I am not suggesting that Fanshawe deliberately undercuts his interpretation of Guarini's play, but that his emphasis on perspective gives it a double edge nonetheless. His explanation, which juxtaposes the "ordinary view," according to which the play is "an Enterlude of Shepherds, their loves, and other little concernments," and the "*perspective*" available to "his *Royall Spectators*," which reveals the catastrophes that may befall a state, reminds us that translation is also a "perspective," or representation, and often a faulty one: "A *Translation* at the best is but the *mock-Rainbow* in the clouds, faintly imitating the true one" (A4v).

Whatever questions Fanshawe's preface might appear to raise regarding the status of translation are answered, however, by the confident certainties of Denham's poem that follows it: "Such is our Pride, our Folly, or our Fate, / That few but such as cannot write, translate." Denham's emphasis is entirely on those "few": writers of genius, the truest translators. For all the emphasis that is placed on his rejection of the "servile path" and "cheap vulgar arts" in favor of a "new and nobler way"—that is, freely appropriating and modernizing the text—it is worth remarking that, for Denham, the translator is not simply equal but ultimately superior to the original writer: "Secure of Fame, thou justly dost esteem / Lesse honour to create, then to redeem." As I suggested earlier, Denham's commendatory poem inaugurates a tradition, or more precisely a certain understanding of a tradition. Fanshawe's dedication emphasizes perspectivism and loss; Denham's verses celebrate "redemption." As Fanshawe's modern editor notes, the lines tell us more about Denham's thoughts on translation than about Fanshawe's practice as a translator—or Denham's own practice, for that matter.[27] In Dryden's eyes, Denham "advis'd more Liberty than he took himself."[28] *Il Pastor Fido* thus assumes its place in the literary system independently of the translation itself.

That *Il Pastor Fido* constitutes a political statement is underscored by Fanshawe's decision to reissue a new edition in 1648, barely a year after the first appearance of the work, with "an Addition of divers other Poems: Concluding with a short Discourse of the Long Civil Wars of Rome" and with a Horatian epigraph, *Patiarque vel inconsultus haberi*, which, as Annabel Patterson notes, is pure "royalist bravado."[29] The topical references are more strongly inscribed through the addition of the new material, which includes Fanshawe's poem on Strafford's trial, two Horatian odes "Relating unto the Civil Wars of Rome," and a "Discourse" featuring excerpts from a number of Roman historians and poets, including Virgil. Surprisingly—and perhaps as a moving reminder of personal loss—the volume contains Fanshawe's Latin poem written for the Parliamentarian Thomas May's continuation of the *Pharsalia*. The formerly close friendship between the two men had been one of the casualties of the Civil War; May's just-published *History of the Parliament* (1647) may have inspired Fanshawe's second edition.[30]

Two aspects of *Il Pastor Fido* seem most relevant to its role in the foundation of English neoclassical translation: its political dimension and Denham's poem, with its emphasis on "newness" and "redemption" through translation. Fanshawe did not invent politicized translation or the politicizing reading of the classics, but his book, particularly in its second edition, sums up Royalist fears and hopes. In the following decade, the preface to his most ambitious translation, *The Lusiad* of Luis de Camões, would also meld literary criticism and politics in a discourse on epic style that rejects (republican) Lucan in favor of (Augustan) Virgil.[31]

Meanwhile, another important Royalist translator both reinforced the practice called for by Denham and set the stage for the mythologizing of Charles I. In 1648, Edward Sherburne turned from publishing political tracts to publishing two translations from Seneca, at a time when uncertainties regarding the king's fate were becoming grimly resolved.[32] Sherburne lays claim to Seneca, historically linked to the critical, anti-absolutist tradition, by insisting on his emblematic status as a moral philosopher standing firm against violent oppression. Half a century later, at the end of a very long life, Sherburne would issue a significant theoretical statement on translation; however, his publications of 1648 had already reinforced the direction that translation would take. The first publication, Seneca's tragedy *Medea*, is offered not as "a *Translation*, but a *Paraphrase* (although it may be with some it might finde the Favour to passe under the *first Title*)."[33] Sherburne's parenthetical remark makes it clear that "translation" is more highly esteemed than "paraphrase" and that—modesty aside—he hopes "some" will consider his work to be the former in spite of his free approach. Sherburne being a member of Denham's circle, the expectation seems justified. The accompanying poem by Thomas Stanley maintains the elevation of the translator's status that we saw in Denham's poem to Fanshawe:

> So shar'st a double Wreath; for all that We
> Unto the Author owe, he owes to thee.
>   Though change of Tongues stolne praise to some afford,
>   Thy Version hath not borrowed, but restor'd.

The meaning of the second publication, *Seneca's Answer*, a translation of Seneca's reflections on the sufferings of the virtuous, is revealed through its dedication to Charles I, whom Sherburne sees as "*personating* to the life that sad *Patterne* which from the *Archetype* of Royall Patience (the King of Heaven himself,) the *Penne* of your Great *Father* drew."[34] The text by James I to which Sherburne refers, *A Paterne for a Kings Inauguration*, is an extended meditation on Christ's Passion as the model, or "pattern," for kingship.[35] James dedicated the text to his son, the same who in 1648 was awaiting execution. Of such stuff are Royalist myths made. The two dedications, from Charles's father and from his faithful courtier, frame his life and imbue his destiny with metaphysical significance. Christ is the "archetype," but in a reversal of traditional figurist interpretations of the Bible, he precedes the figure Charles, who "personates" the archetype. In the final lines of the dedication, the relations are again reversed, underscoring figurism's fusion of present and past. Charles's "*Heavenly* Throne" is declared certain, a vision that Sherburne prays God will "be pleased (as in a *Type*) to shadow forth unto You in the *Happinesse* of a *speedy* and a *glorious Restauration* to *This of Your Majesties Kingdomes*" (A3v).

As a published text, *Seneca's Answer* invokes a wider audience beyond its dedicatee. Sherburne also includes a short preface to the reader in which he justifies his verse translation of a prose text by citing a precedent in Ralph Freeman's translation of Seneca's *Consolation to Marcia*.[36] The reference functions as a mise en abyme, inserting a consolatory Royalist translation of Seneca within a consolatory Royalist translation of Seneca. And why might a translation prove especially consolatory? Sherburne discreetly omits the final lines of Seneca's original text, warning us in a note that they contain a "Stoicall exhortation to the Anticipation of Death," thus allowing his text to end with words that might be self-referential:

> Fortune despise; whose Power I have confin'd
> *She hath no weapon that can wound the minde.*
> Nay Death it selfe; *which ends, or doth translate*
> *Your bad condition, to a better fate.*
>
> (30)

As we have seen in other analogies between translation and various forms of change—transmutation, transmigration—the conversion and displacement of words into "a better fate" holds out an inherent promise, a hope for something else.

Abraham Cowley also looks toward "something better" in his *Poems* of 1656. From the mid-1640s to the mid-1650s, Cowley was part of Henrietta Maria's entourage in France, entrusted with the enciphering and deciphering of clandestine Royalist correspondence. Like a number of other exiles, he returned to England following Cromwell's 1652 Act of Oblivion, but the motives for his return and the meaning of his release after a brief imprisonment in 1655 were seen as ambiguous. Recent critics have taken a keen interest in the *Poems*, "a complex and enigmatic volume," as one puts it.[37] In his general preface, Cowley offers not only the summation of his literary career but also a personal apologia.

Contemporary critics have underscored the political subtext of the *Poems*, in which, despite a controversial call to his fellows to "lay down our *Pens* as well as *Arms*," Cowley's affinity for cavalier lyric, his experimentation with the "unruly" form of the Pindaric, and the allegorical resonance of his unfinished religious epic *Davideis*, to say nothing of his abandoned epic on the Civil War, bespeak consistently Royalist values.[38] The announced intent in the preface to the *Poems* is dramatic: "For to make my self absolutely dead in a *Poetical* capacity, my resolution at present, is never to exercise any more that faculty" (A2r). Why should this author stage his own death? Cowley offers two different explanations, one personal and the other public. He suffers on the one hand from what we would call burnout, a kind of exhaustion that he compares to a failed marriage between people who married too young, and on the other hand from the "rough and troubled" times in which he lives: "a warlike, various, and a tragical age is best to *write of*, but worst to *write in*" (A2v). The opening paragraph of the preface suggests, however, another source of anxiety that has more to do with Cowley's experience of authorship than with his poetic vocation or the troubled times per se. He evokes a series of "literary crimes," some of which he has experienced, including having a spurious work (and a politically dangerous one) imputed to him and having works of his own published without his permission, which he sees as an act "almost in the same kinde" as the forgery. Plagiarism would have been "much less injurious" (A1r). Certainly, the attribution of a virulent anti-Puritan tract is something Cowley would want to avoid upon his return from exile; however, he denounces merely its "ill Verses." (Understatement is one of the guiding tropes of the preface, which begins with a passing allusion to "my return lately into *England*" as the sole reference to all the complexities attendant on his long absence.) The spurious attribution leads to other associations having to do with textual mishaps, both deliberate and inadvertent: Cowley's "concealment of my own writings," the "publication of some things of mine without my consent or knowledge" (especially in a "mangled and imperfect" state), the loss of a revised manuscript ("I have lost the *Copy*, and dare not think it deserves the pains to write it again"). These vicissitudes of writing, which he sums up in a series of images of adulteration, forgery, and disfigurement, lead him to attempt to produce what is in effect a "posthumous" edition: "And this will be the more excusable, when the *Reader* shall know in what respects he may look upon me as a *Dead*, or at least a *Dying Person*" (A2r). In addition to the lack of inspiration and the "rough and troubled" times, Cowley admits that "the present constitution of my Mind" is another factor. He chooses to describe at length "the *Clouds* of *Melancholy* and *Sorrow*," but not in his own words; instead he offers us a short essay on poetry and affect, quoting from Ovid and Horace as he announces his intention to "retire my self to some of our *American Plantations*" in search of an "obsure retreat" (A3r).

Cowley then shifts from his reasons for publishing the collection to describing its various parts. The recital turns into another attempt at self-justification, however, when, after claiming (falsely, as later editors would discover) to have destroyed the manuscripts of his poem on the Civil War, he lays down his pen "as well as Arms." Cowley would later disclaim this passage, and his literary executor, Thomas Sprat, would excise it from the posthumous edition and make excuses for it.[39] The confession of "political editing" thus had to be edited, an example of what Steven Zwicker calls "the civic force of the literary."[40] Pledging not to "revive the remembrance" of past conflict, Cowley urges the most radical form of excision: "Neither *We*, nor *They*, ought by the *Representation* of *Places* and *Images* to make a kind of *Artificial Memory* of those things wherein we are all bound to desire like *Themistocles*, the *Art* of *Oblivion*" (A4r). For a writer to forbid himself access to memory, to representation, is itself another form of death. The Act of Oblivion of 1652 was one in a series of such acts, the last of which was issued by Charles II in 1660; the official language resonated throughout public discourse.[41] The tradition of legislated oblivion, which goes back to the Athenian city-state and had been seen as the foundation of democracy, clearly has its raison d'être as society moves away from violent dissension—but not without cost.[42] In Cowley's case, the cost is self-censure and paralysis.

As he lays out the structure of the collected works, however, possibilities for moving beyond this bleak situation begin to appear. Although the first two parts—a *Miscellanie* of youthful works and a cycle of love poems called *The Mistress*—represent a recapitulation of Cowley's earlier career, the last two sections point beyond previous accomplishments. The *Pindarique Odes* promise a bold, free style, with "many, and sudden" digressions and "Numbers . . . various and irregular." But the poet seems to place his greatest hope in the model offered by his (unfinished) religious epic, *Davideis*. Here we find, for the first time in this bleak and valedictory preface, some hope for the future of poetry. Denouncing the "theft" and "usurpation" of poetry from God's service, Cowley declares, "It is time to recover it out of the *Tyrants* hands, and to restore it to the *Kingdom* of *God*, who is the *Father* of it" (b2r). Cowley seems to be placing his (political) hope in a metaphysical solution that is nevertheless of this world, that is in human language. After the "*Regeneration*" of poetry, "it will meet with wonderful variety of new, more beautiful, and more delightful *Objects*" (b2v): a profusion of potential subjects offers itself, in contrast to the warmed-over "*Cold-meats* of the *Antients*." Cowley's language brims over with suggestions for future works as he contemplates the worlds opening up before him, then abruptly reins itself in: "There is nothing yet in our *Language* (nor perhaps in *any*) that is in any degree answerable to the *Idea* that I conceive of it" (b3v). Regeneration remains an unrealized vision.[43]

Cowley's *Pindarique Odes* are not presented as an explicit solution to his dilemma, but they offer a way that—unlike the religious epic—will be taken up by others. A major reference point in the history of translation, the preface to the *Pindarique Odes* is an extended defense of a free approach, which Cowley dubs "this libertine way of rendring foreign Authors" (Aaa2v). As he sees it, no other method will enable the reader to make sense of the Greek poet: "If a man should undertake to translate *Pindar* word for word, it would be thought that *one Mad-man* had translated *another*" (Aaa2r). The analogy of a text that is viewed, like a painting, at a great distance and hence indecipherable is framed in terms of loss: "losses sustained by *Pindar*," "the lost Excellencies of another *Language*," and the Pindaric form itself as one of "the *lost Inventions* of *Antiquity*." Fully cognizant of the "thousand particularities" of language and culture that separate him from his source text, Cowley's hermeneutic is one of recovery, which is only possible through compensation.

Translation exists in a vexed relationship with mimesis: "I have seen *Originals* both in *Painting* and *Poesie*, much more beautiful then their *natural Objects*; but I never saw a *Copy* better than the *Original*." The intervening factor appears to be "exact Imitation," which forestalls creativity through mindless repetition ("a vile and unworthy kinde of *Servitude*"). Being of a different order of existence than their "natural Objects," painting and poetry are far enough removed from exact imitation to escape servitude and produce "originals," but the translation of verbal forms to other verbal forms cannot. Like Denham and the others, Cowley sometimes endows the two sides with class connotations: "vile . . . servitude" versus "any thing good or noble." What is striking is the polarization of alternatives and lack of any mediating term. Translation is either "word for word" (and associated with "Grammarians") or "libertine." There seems to be no possibility of a translation that might be faithful, yet flexible or creative, no enabling "middle way." Instead, Cowley singles out the most respected literary translator of the previous generation, Sandys, and lumps him in with the grammarians, who "have not sought to supply the lost Excellencies of another *Language* with new ones of their own."

For a fuller conceptual resolution to the problem, we will need to await Dryden. Here, it is that insistence on "newness" that comes through most clearly. Particularly when we consider the preface to *Pindarique Odes* in the context of the general preface to the *Poems*, we see an author at odds with authorship, estranged from his own texts (lost, corrupted, misattributed), obliged to renounce former literary ideals (it being "almost *ridiculous*, to make *Lawrels* for the *Conquered*")—in short, a dead author, in search of a new form, a new inspiration, a new way of being in a text: "It does not at all trouble me that the *Grammarians* perhaps will not suffer this libertine way of rendring foreign Authors, to be called *Translation*; for I am not so much enamoured of the *Name Translator*, as not to wish rather to be *Something Better*, though it want yet a *Name*" (Aaa2r–Aaa2v). By projecting himself into a "nameless" role, Cowley will avoid both the bitter disappointments of authorship and the constraints of translation. Neither translator nor author, he creatively writes through another poet: "I have . . . taken, left out, and added what I please; nor make it so much my aim to let the reader know precisely what he spoke, as what was his *way* and *manner* of speaking." The result is "something which has not been yet (that I know of) introduced into *English*." The familiar topos of the foreign text "in an *English* habit" should not distract us from the intensity of the writer's desire for something utterly new, utterly other. Like the general preface, which projects a renewal of literature through biblical epic, this text too ends with a vision of transformation—of both the writer and his world.

The year 1656 also saw the anonymous publication of John Denham's translation of the second book of the *Aeneid*, which he titled *The Destruction of Troy* and to which he gave a preface that, like his poem to Fanshawe of the previous decade, would become an influential piece of the critical canon of neoclassical translation. Denham makes points that we have come to expect: an oblique reference to Horace in support of free translation ("I conceive it a vulgar error in translating Poets, to affect being *Fidus Interpres*," 26), the notion of poetry as susceptible to "evaporation" and of translation as a form of "transfusion," the disjunction of meaning from linguistic embodiment in the familiar simile of "clothing" ("as speech is the apparel of our thoughts, so are there certain Garbs and Modes of speaking"), and the topos of "making the author speak": "If *Virgil* must needs speak English, it were fit he should speak not only as a man of this Nation, but as a man of this age; and if this disguise I have put upon him (I wish I could give it a better name) fit not naturally and easily on so grave a person, yet it may become him better than that Fools-Coat wherein the French and Italian have of late presented him" (28). Denham fuses the "translator's prosopopoeia" with the clothing topos, amplifying it with the reminder that, indeed, authors might "speak" variously or wear different styles of clothing, as in the parodic "burlesque" translations that had recently become popular on the Continent. Denham presents his translation in ways that certainly echo d'Ablancourt and other French contemporaries, but there are differences. As we saw in the previous chapter, the French translators' emphasis on eloquence, the need to move the reader, bespeaks a theory of language as *affect*, not disembodied spirit—

a subcurrent that we also find in the Port-Royal translators' association of meaning and Real Presence. French neoclassical translation as a literary movement is also very attached to the development of a prose style, or as Zuber calls it, *une prose d'art*; all the landmark translations by d'Ablancourt, Vaugelas, and even the poet Malherbe are prose translations. English neoclassical translation, to the contrary, is inextricably linked to the development of the heroic couplet, considered the lasting literary legacy of Denham and his fellow poets. While attempts have been made to link the closed couplet with aristocratic values, its sole use, as David Norbrook notes, was not a political marker, as couplets were becoming "the more-or-less inescapable form whatever one's affiliations."[44]

Similarly, the broader trend toward adaptive translation is hard to pinpoint on a political map. Lawrence Venuti is certainly right to call attention to the numerous ways in which Denham's *Destruction of Troy* is shot through with Royalist resonances, many of which are cast into relief through comparison with the 1636 draft version contained in Lucy Hutchinson's commonplace book.[45] But it is equally striking that our source for the draft should be Hutchinson, a dedicated Puritan, whose husband was among the signatories of Charles I's death sentence. Hutchinson not only preserved Denham's draft, but she also emulated his style in her own verse translation of Lucretius from the 1650s.[46] Hutchinson's commonplace book also contained the Waller-Godolphin translation of *Aeneid* IV, another pillar of neoclassical translation written by men whose politics she rejected.[47]

The attraction of adaptive translation to anti-Royalists may further be seen in James Harrington's translation of selected books of the *Aeneid*. One of the chief shapers of republican thought, Harrington sees close translation as akin to courtiers' flattery: "*Virgil*, my Soveraign in Poetry, / I never flatter'd Prince, nor will I thee."[48] He goes on to explain that even the Prince of Poets "never shalt perswade me" of the patently unbelievable. From scenes depicting fantastic or morally inappropriate events, Harrington demurs: "Liege Lord, / In these I may not give thee word for word." Despite the jocular tone of the preface, the translation does not fit the comic mold of the various "burlesque" Virgils that were circulating.[49] Harrington clearly rejects the smooth style of Denham's and Waller's couplets—and as such his translation has generally been seen as an aesthetic failure—but his approach is not more "faithful" than theirs, nor does it seek to be. The strategies and motivations of neoclassical translation are thus not of a piece, and they do not bespeak a consistent ideological project.[50]

TRANSLATORS OF THE RESTORATION

The Restoration did not diminish translation's role as a vehicle for political allegorizing or other forms of both direct and indirect critique, such as the verse satire. The polemical use of translation fosters the emergence of an intensified self-awareness and consciousness of language. This self-reflexive strain encouraged the rise of literary criticism—as we shall see, for example, in Roscommon's hugely influential *Essay on Translated Verse*—but it also contributed to a demoralizing "Babel effect" and nostalgia for a lost home in language.

The poetic achievements of Fanshawe, Cowley, Waller, and Denham and the role of translation in those achievements combined with their Royalist affiliation and the timing of events to lend a particular preeminence to their style of translating—to produce, in effect, a "canon" of translations. We have already seen the early stages of canon formation through Denham's and the others' mutual echoes, citations, and exchanged commendatory verses. Their names would continue to function as the standard for excellent translation after the Restoration. In 1661, John Boys would publish two explicitly Royalist translations from Virgil, *Aeneas His Errours* and *Aeneas His Descent into Hell*, setting himself in the wake of Royalist Virgil translators.[51] Several years later, Alexander Brome would include a number of translators in a collective Horace; in his dedicatory epistle he decries "a nice *Pedantical Translation*, which *Horace* could not abide" and hopes that someday Horace may benefit from translators as excellent as "those *Standard-bearers* of Wit and Judgment, *Denham* and *Waller*."[52]

Waller, however, did not contribute to the elaboration of critical discourse on translation. As for Cowley, following his death in 1667, he received a huge state funeral at Westminster Abbey. Denham remembered his friend's translation in his eulogy: "Old *Pindar*'s flights by him are reacht, / When on that gale his wings are stretcht."[53] Denham reissued *The Destruction of Troy*, with other poems and translations, in a 1668 edition dedicated to Charles II. His final translation, published in the last months of his life, was another verse translation of a prose work, Cicero's *De senectute*, a text in which "*Cicero* did not so much appear to write, as *Cato* to speak. . . . Therefore neither consider *Cicero*, nor Me, but *Cato* himself, who being then rais'd from the dead to speak the language of that Age and Place, neither the distance of place or time makes it less possible to raise him now to speak ours."[54] The "transmigration" topos is echoed in the preface, where

Denham assures us that Cato/Cicero provides sure evidence of the immortality of the soul, "which none of our Atheistical Sophisters can confute" (A2v). He is also more explicit about the place of his own voice in the translation: "I took the liberty, to leave out what was only necessary to that Age, and Place, and to take, or add what was proper to this present Age, and occasion" (A2r).

Politically charged translation is not necessarily tied to dissident political opinions: John Boys's two Virgil translations are a vivid example. Following the recital of the hero's wanderings in *Aeneid* III, he offers "Some few hasty Reflections" (52–[68]), which turn Virgil's narrative into "the full prospect of a well-order'd Common-wealth" and the kingly attributes of Aeneas into those of Charles II, whom Boys addresses directly in his conclusion. Boys's translation of *Aeneid* VI contains an elaborate set of "Annotations" (34–215), much of which is historical rather than overtly political, but which does take a topical turn in a discussion of Tarquin's expulsion from Rome, where Boys claims not to "make a formal dispute upon the case, but only propound there the following *Quaeries*." The queries are not subtle.[55] Boys further appends several of his own political tracts—"monuments of loyalty rather than wit" (217)—among them a speech he prepared for Charles II's landing at Dover.

Two decades later, in the wake of the Popish Plot, Caleb Calle would offer a translation of Sallust's account of Catiline's conspiracy that is as politically marked as either of Boys's translations. Caleb titles his work *Patriae Parricida*, gives it an epigraph taken from Dryden's *Absalom and Achitophel*, and in the dedication embarks on a wide-ranging denunciation of "ambition."[56] After first taking aim at Cromwell ("the great Giant of our Nation, one of their [that is, the Titans] Off-spring"), he then moves into the present: "And to this day what are the minds of many men infected with, but the same Disease? What mean else these Plots and Conspiracies (of which Catiline is but the Model)? And these flyings from Justice, but the cursed fruits of Ambition?" By contrast, another Sallust translation from only five years later, "Made English according to the present idiom of Speech," discusses only the difficulty of Sallust's Latin and argues against literal translation.[57] In the following century, Sallust would again provide political writer Thomas Gordon with the means to comment on a contemporary "Conspiracy among us."[58]

Translation continued to provide a means for promoting "dangerous" ideas without asserting ownership of them. In the late 1640s, the French translation of the Qu'rān and the English translation based on it featured similar "firewalls," lengthy prefaces denouncing the "absurdity" of Islam, but left the full text intact and offered positive images of Muslims interspersed throughout the seemingly negative commentary.[59] Throughout the period, translations of Lucretius and the Stoic philosophers allowed for the expression and dissemination of materialism and non-Christian beliefs. John Evelyn might shrug off critics of his translation of Book I of *De rerum natura* by reminding them that all pagan poets were by definition irreligious ("Plato was a Leveller"), but in his complete translation Thomas Creech carefully protected himself from confusion with his author through orthodox commentary and annotation.[60] Edward Sherburne's freethinking moment from a translation of Seneca offers another example:

> The Spirit which informs this Clay
> >   So fleets away.
> *Nothing is after Death*; and this
> >   Too, *Nothing* is:
> The Gaol or the extremest space
> >   Of a swift Race.[61]

In a note for the benefit of "the unwary Reader," Sherburne cites Christian denunciations of Seneca's skepticism; other notes, however, offer references and quotations from a host of other Roman philosophers who thoroughly expound the tenets of Stoicism. Translation thus continued to make oppositional or non-normative discourse available.[62]

The rise of verse satire during the period corresponds to the vogue for translations of Juvenal and other Roman satirists.[63] Many critics have called attention to the importance of translation in the development of English verse satire, but it is also true that satire furnishes arguments for adaptative translation, as translators comment on Juvenal's "difficulty" and the best means for overcoming it.[64] As Robert Stapylton points out, the poet's obscurity is a function of his distance from us: "In his time, his Country was exasperated by too great a CLEARNESSE of his stile. . . . Afterwards, to remoter parts, and strangers to the ROMANE Customes, he appeared OBSCURE."[65] Stapylton's approach, like that of Barten Holyday in a translation published in the following decade, would be to rely on annotations and illustrations to enlighten the reader.[66] In 1685, however, Henry Higden offered a translation "equipp'd . . . *Al-a-mode*" of Juvenal's thirteenth satire aimed at contemporary vices.[67] He chose to call his version "A Modern Essay" since "as a *Translation* I could not, and as a *Paraphrase* I would not own it." The following year he brought out a similar translation of Juvenal's tenth satire, prefaced with enthusiastic poems by fellow Tories Dryden, Elkanah Settle, and Aphra Behn:

> You Naturalize the Author you Translate,
> And *Classick Roman* dress in *Modern State.*
> (Settle)

> Great *Juvenal* in every Line
> True *Roman* still o're all does shine;
> But in the *Brittish* Garb appears most fine.
> (Behn)

Claiming not to have "rambled too far" from his author, Higden again justifies his approach on the basis of his genre: "All *Satyr* having a strong taste of the Humour and particular Hints of the Times wherein they were writ."[68] In his translation of Plautus, Laurence Echard explains his modernizing in terms of the distance that separates us from the author: "Several of his *Jests* and bits of *Satyr* are undoubtedly lost to us, not only in respect of our Language, but also our Knowledge, and this sometimes makes his *Sence* a little obscure."[69] And finally, at the dawn of the new century, John Ozell produced a highly successful translation of Boileau's *Le Lutrin* in which all the French references were converted to their "dynamic equivalents" into a "Set of *English* Authors of equal Degree and like kind of Dulness with those mention'd by M. *Boileau.*"[70]

Howard Weinbrot once pointed out the interrelations among later Augustan imitation and seventeenth-century free translation and parody ("burlesque" translation).[71] In his reading, parody plays a kind of intermediate role between the adaptative translations recommended by Denham and his peers and later "original" imitations; unlike free translation, both parody and imitation require knowledge of the original work in order to be fully appreciated. The distinction is an important one, reminding us that ultramodernizing translations do not necessarily mask their originals but instead gesture toward them. Charles Cotton's popular *Scarronides* includes footnotes with Virgil's Latin text for the most famous passages, so that the reader will be able to make the necessary comparisons. As we've seen, all of these genres mutually reinforce one another. The topicality of ancient satire makes it attractive to translators who want to rail against modern degeneracy without assuming full responsibility for their words (another important thread in translation), and that same topicality produces barriers to comprehension that suggest the need for modernizing to some, thus setting us on the slippery slope to parody.

The translations of Roger L'Estrange combine topical satire, literary ambition, and, some would argue, parody or something close to it. A leading Tory pamphleteer and the regulator of the press during the period of the Licensing Act (1662–79), L'Estrange was also a prolific translator.[72] Although his *Fables of Aesop* (1692) would often be reprinted throughout the eighteenth century and has been the object of recent scholarship, little has been written about his other translations.[73] A veteran of Newark and Edgehill, L'Estrange was sentenced to death for spying during the 1640s and spent several years abroad, returning to England and entering the fray of political journalism in the late 1650s. One of his first translations, of Quevedo's *Visions* (1667), would prove immensely popular and go through multiple reprintings. The satire of the text spills into a satirical preface, written "merely for *Fashion-sake*, to *fill* a *space*," and he confesses that "pure *Spite*" inspired him to undertake the translation: "For it is a *Satyre*, that taxes *Corruption of Manners*, in *all sorts* and *degrees* of people, without reflecting upon *particular States* or *Persons*" (A3r–A4r). While L'Estrange is not the only author of flippant prefaces in the period—Charles Cotton mocked prefacing conventions even in his "serious" translation of *The History of the Life of the Duke of Esperon*—in his hands the anti-preface becomes something of an art form. Written in a lively, conversational tone, the prefaces offer another venue for L'Estrange's polemical writing, in which translation plays an important role.

In the 1670s L'Estrange's translations ranged from Christian apologetics to Rapin's treatise on Aristotle to the *Lettres portugaises*; beginning in 1678, during the turmoil over the Popish Plot and the Exclusion Crisis, when L'Estrange was both attacking the Plot's instigators and defending himself against accusations of crypto-Catholicism, the translations took a decidedly polemical turn, particularly his 1678 translation of Seneca, which would be reissued with a polemical addition after the Glorious Revolution in 1688. The Plot also motivated the 1680 translation of Erasmus's *Colloquies*, offered, first, as a way of aligning the translator with an exemplary Protestant figure, rather than "a *Papist* in *Masquerade*"; second, to encourage readers "not to involve *All Papists* under the same *Condemnation*"; and third, "to turn some Part of the *Rage* and *Bitterness* that is now in Course, into *Pity* and *Laughter*" (A3r). His best-selling *Tully's Offices* appeared in the same year with a declaration of the work's timeliness: "I have now turned it into *English*, with regard to a *Place*, and *Season*, that extremely needs it" (A3r). The *Fables* appeared in the 1690s and his final translation, of Flavius Josephus, in 1702, two years before his death. In the last years of his life, he would also collaborate with Dryden and others on a translation of Tacitus with a clear Jacobite subtext.[74]

Beyond immediate topical concerns, however, L'Estrange's prefaces keep up a running critique of the genre itself: "*Prefacing* against *Prefaces*," as he puts it in the preface to *Tully's Offices*, where he terms prefaces "an Idle Deal of *Fiddle-Faddle* betwixt the *Writer* and the *Reader*" and dedications "*Fashionable Fopperies*" (A2v). He elects to spare his reader "twenty Fooleries of Apology, and Excuse" in his preface to Aesop (A4r), just as in his final translation of Flavius Josephus he decides to skip "All *unnecessary Niceties*; As the *Time* that has been spent upon It, the *Books* and *Friends* I have Consulted upon the *Text*, The Difficulties that *Frequent* Troubles and *Ill* Health have Thrown in my Way, and several more of the same Kind" ([i]). Humor aside, L'Estrange demonstrates that the conventions of the genre were already well set in place by his time—and that academic prefaces have changed very little from his day to ours. The humor should not distract us from noticing the writer's intense self-consciousness, his awareness of context and genre. L'Estrange's very first translator's preface, to Rapin's *Reflections on Aristotle's Treatise of Poesie*, contains, appropriately, a short history of the rise of literary criticism, a practice in which "our Neighbour Nations have got far the start of us" and that he traces from Aristotle to the Italian Renaissance and, finally, to France. L'Estrange's prefaces do not begin to offer the level of interpretative analysis or theoretical goals that we see in Dryden's, or even those of a lesser light like Laurence Echard, but they do show an intense engagement with the critical genre, just as their lively tone bespeaks the spirited polemicist who earned the name "Towser."

The most complex and interesting of these writings are undoubtedly the preface and "After-Thought" appended to *Seneca's Morals by Way of Abstract*. As I noted earlier, the translation first appeared during the initial uproar over the Popish Plot; the "After-Thought" was added ten years later at the time of the accession of William III. An embattled partisan during the Plot, L'Estrange was a bitter Stuart loyalist in 1688. His treatment of Seneca is highly topical, not surprisingly given what we have seen of the long-standing tradition of politically charged translations, but it is also a remarkable reflection on reading and writing, translation and "paraphrase."

The preface begins with a brief defense of the decision to offer an "abstract" rather than a "translation" of his author, averring, first, the prior existence of a complete translation (Thomas Lodge's 1614 translation of Seneca's works); second, the presence of material "that is wholly Foreign to my Business," such as Seneca's discussions of natural philosophy; and third, what L'Estrange finds to be his author's "frequent Repetitions of the same thing again in other Words" (A3r). Clearly, then, the translator's "Business" takes precedence over the text itself, whatever regrets he may offer that it is not "written up to the Spirit of the *Original*" (A3v). The purpose of the exercise is not slow in coming: "We are fallen into an Age of *vain Philosophy*; (as the Holy Apostle calls it) and so desperately over-run with *Drolls* and *Scepticks*, that there is hardly any thing so certain, or so Sacred, that is not exposed to *Question*, or *Contempt*" (A4r). L'Estrange tells us that in his excerpts he has emphasized "the Theme of *Benefits*, *Gratitude*, and *Ingratitude*" as "a Lecture expressly Calculated for the Unthankfulness of these Times" (A4v). But his tone becomes even more strident as he recalls recent English history:

> Have we not seen, even in our days, a most Pious, (and almost Faultless) Prince, brought to the Scaffold by his own Subjects? The most Glorious Constitution upon the Face of the Earth, both *Ecclesiastical* and *Civil*, torn to pieces, and dissolv'd? The happiest People under the Sun enslav'd? . . . And by whom, but by a Race of *Hypocrites*, who had nothing in their Mouths all this while, but, *The Purity of the Gospel*; the *Honour of the King*; and, *the Liberty of the People*? . . . It is a wonderful thing (I say) that these Engines and Engineers should ever find Credit enough in the World, to engage a Party: But, it would be still more wonderful, if the *same Trick* should pass twice upon the *same People*, in the *same Age*, and from the very *same* IMPOSTERS. (A5v)

L'Estrange's outrage is more potent than his political analysis, and twenty-first-century literary critics are unlikely to feel much sympathy for his idealizing of Charles I or his hostility toward "*Drolls* and *Scepticks*." The unease that fuels his explosion, however, bespeaks not only a particular conservative agenda but also the welter of profound and as-yet-unassimilated changes that were taking place in his world. L'Estrange breathes politics like air but cannot comprehend that his enemies might use the same moral vocabulary as he.

Ten years later, his "After-Thought" offers a strikingly different perspective at a time when "the World has not been altogether so kind of late, to my Politicks as to my Morals" (465). L'Estrange continues to reject what he sees as the moral relativism of his adversaries—"as if the Standard of Virtue were to be accommodated to the various Changes, and Vicissitudes of Times, Interests, and Contending Parties"—and states his confidence that "however Truth and Justice may suffer a Temporal Eclipse," they will ultimately be vindicated (466). Rather than engaging in new tirades against "IMPOSTERS," however, an older, more subdued translator undertakes to examine the work he did a decade earlier.

Most of the "After-Thought" seeks to justify the considerable editorial work that has gone into the *Abstract*, all the while claiming that the end product is nevertheless "a Just, and Genuine Representation" of Seneca's meaning. The question, finally, is to understand where that meaning lies. L'Estrange comments on the unsystematic nature of Seneca's philosophy: "Many of his Thoughts seem to Spring only like Sparks, upon a kind of Collision, or a striking of Fire within Himself, and with a very little Dependence sometimes one upon another" (468). On the one hand, then, the translator/editor's work appears to be simply to organize a confused text by understanding the implicit connections and mending broken links. But on the other hand, even though each reader "confesses in his own Heart, the Truth of his Doctrine," Seneca remains elusive and in need of "a Paraphrase," an explication or commentary.

So which is it? Can the individual reader, "in his own Heart," attain the meaning of the text, or must he rely on an outside authority? L'Estrange appears to be aware of the tension in his text, because at this point he imagines objections: first, "that a Paraphrase is but the Reading upon a Text . . . at the Will and Pleasure of the Interpreter"; and second, "that the Paraphrase is foreign to the Text, and that the Animadvertor may make the Author speak what he pleases" (469–70). He responds to these supposed objections by acknowledging that paraphrases, like other human actions, may be "Loose, Arbitrary, and Extravagant"—but are not necessarily so. The point is not the "possibility" of "an Unedifying Exposition" but the "need" for a good one. L'Estrange is seeking his own middle way between the naked, unaided, individual conscience of a solitary reader and the "foreign" commentary arbitrarily imposed by another. It is a question, he tells us, of doing "a Necessary Right both to the Dead . . . and to the living, and a Common Service to Mankind" (470).

In the end, Seneca's very fragmentariness offers a solution to the dilemma. L'Estrange describes the text as being "manifestly design'd for other People to Meditate, Read, and Speculate upon . . . So that the very manner of his Writings calls for a Paraphrase" (470)—that is, the text, being incomplete, calls out for completion via commentary. This solution may resemble an opportunistic excuse to impose oneself on the text, but I believe that L'Estrange is struggling to articulate a more complex relationship between text and reader. In this account, Seneca is "a Paraphrase upon himself" (471), in which the absences and gaps within the text are already in some sense filled with the potentiality of future discussions, "a Foundation for those to build upon, that shall come after him" (472). Significantly, L'Estrange does not pretend to have realized this ambition; his work remains an "abstract," not a "paraphrase." He tells us that his reticence is due to the inevitability of criticism ("to have every Coffee-House sit upon him like a Court of Justice," 473), but the logic of this argument also clearly suggests that a better commentary is always yet to come. Just as the traditional topos of translators' modesty constructs a sort of translational sublime— the never fully articulated, never present, perfect translation, whose evocation reminds us of both the gap between languages and their potential reconciliation—so here L'Estrange allows discussion and commentary to spin off without closure into the future, "a Paraphrase, I say, superadded by way of Supplement."

Roger L'Estrange has rarely been deemed a harbinger of the Enlightenment. Yet in his final paragraphs the former censor, despite his earlier quip about coffeehouse critics, offers a vision of an open intellectual sphere: "For what's all the Writing, Reading, Discoursing, Consulting, Disputing, Meditating, Compounding, and Dividing, from the first Quick'ning Breath of the Almighty into Reasonable Nature, to this very Moment; what is all this, I say, but the Lighting of one Candle at Another? . . . Reason works by Communication, and one Thought kindles another from Generation to Generation, as Naturally, as one Spark begets another, where the Matter is dispos'd for the Impression" (473–74). All ideas are admissible, and all are in the public domain. Text and reader are jointly "Incorporated into one common Stock," not in a hostile takeover of one by the other but in an understanding of reading—and hence writing, commentary, and translation—as a form of dialogue in which both participants are constantly changing.

ROSCOMMON'S ESSAY ON TRANSLATED VERSE

We have seen an increasing critical self-awareness in the discourse of trans-lation throughout the second half of the seventeenth century, an awareness that was reinforced by the consolidation of a canon of translation criti-cism as well as of translation practice. For the generations that followed, Dryden would represent the culmination of both, not only as a master poet but also as, in Johnson's words, "the father of English criticism."[75] I think it likely, however, that the single most widely cited English commen-tary on the art of translation is the 1684 *Essay on Translated Verse* by Went-worth Dillon, Earl of Roscommon. His various injunctions to translators and poets and his celebrated comparison of French and English poetry ("The weighty *Bullion* of *One Sterling Line*, / Drawn to *French Wire*, would through whole *Pages* shine") would be frequently repeated, almost always admiringly, on both sides of the Channel.[76] A close friend of Roscom-mon's, Dryden would claim in his preface to *Sylvae* that the *Essay* inspired him as a translator and challenged him to turn "speculation into prac-tice."[77] If there is a dissenting voice, it would be that of Samuel Johnson, who suggested that most of Roscommon's precepts were a matter of com-mon sense and that the *Essay* deserved praise not for the rules themselves, but for "the art with which they are introduced, and the decorations with which they are adorned."[78]

If the *Essay* spurred Dryden to be a better translator but appeared merely commonsensical to Johnson, it was because it so well captured the goals of one generation that had become commonplace for those that came after: that a translation should be "*Well-bred*" and "*purg'd* from *rank Pedantick Weeds*" (5), that texts chosen for translation should take "a Sub-ject, *proper* to Expound" (8), and that the translation's language should "suit *Our Genius*" and "our *Clime*" (14). Translation is closely associated with original composition through their common basis in inspiration, which figures throughout the *Essay* as a powerful external force, as "the Muse" or the divine possession of the Cumaean Sybil. Analogous to the force of inspiration is the compelling presence of "truth" when the transla-tor has grasped the essential meaning of a difficult passage: "*Truth* Stamps *Conviction* in your Ravisht Breast, / And *Peace*, and *Joy* attend the glorious Guest" (13). The ravishment of truth and the overwhelming by the Muse both point to a fundamental dispossession of the translator in his work, which is conceived of as a relationship not so much with a text as with its creator:

> Then, seek a *Poet* who *your* way do's bend,
> And chuse an *Author* as you chuse a *Friend*.
> United by this *Sympathetick Bond*,
> You grow *Familiar, Intimate* and *Fond*;
> Your *thoughts*, your *Words*, your *Stiles*, your *Souls* agree,
> No Longer his *Interpreter*, but *He*.
>
> (7)

Translation, like composition, thus bespeaks "Judgment" and cool rational assessment, as well as a measure of the irrational, the inspired, and the fusion of souls. Roscommon's formulation, to "chuse an *Author* as you chuse a *Friend*," has continued to appeal to recent commentators: T. R. Steiner sees it as heralding a distinctive strain in English translation theory, that of the translator as "secret sharer," and Lawrence Venuti folds it into his recommendation that translators develop a "simpatico" relationship with their authors.[79] If we take the recommendation seriously, however, particularly in the context of the various forms of poetic dispossession that Roscommon evokes, then the relationship is not one of sharing but instead of total "exposure," abnegation before the authorial other—"No longer his *Interpreter*, but *He*."

Despite its elegance and poise and its role as a common reference point, however, the *Essay* is a complex piece of writing. Translation is presented on the one hand as deeply personal, stemming from the translator's private inspiration and "Sympathetick Bond" with the author, and on the other as a public affair, part of a national project. Roscommon presents translation as one of "the few Vertues that we have" and goes on to situate English translators in terms of the *translatio studii et imperii*, or the conjoining of cultural and political hegemony as one nation cedes dominion to another. We see this first with respect to France—

> The choicest Books, that *Rome*, or *Greece* have known,
> Her excellent *Translators* made her own:
> And *Europe* still considerably gains,
> Both by their good *Example* and their *Pains*.
>
> (3)

—and ultimately in the broadest possible terms (*"Empire,* and *Poesy Together* rise,"* 23) as Britain inherits the place once held by the great civilizations of classical antiquity.

These public and private dimensions of translation have analogous structures that further develop the dichotomy. On the one hand, both public and private participate in a relationship of comparison and emulation, looking toward the outside world, and on the other hand, both look inward, preserving autonomy and independence from any comparison. Thus, when we consider the national, "public" aspect, we see that "Britain" enters into comparison and emulation with other nations and with the past, aiming to *"be,* what *Rome* or *Athens* were Before" (24) but also to remain independent, "True to her self" and refusing "barb'rous aid" from outside (26). But if Britain is to be the "New Rome," then it is perforce a copy, not an original. Similarly, the poet-translator is enjoined to seek total self-presence—"The first great work, (a Task perform'd by few) / Is, that *your self* may to *your self* be *True*" (5)—even though, as we have seen, the act of translation, like that of poetic creation, is one of self-dispossession, allowing oneself to be inhabited by another: author, muse, godhead.

The *Essay on Translated Verse* thus offers more than a list of precepts and rules; rather, it points toward a complicated negotiation between inner self and wider world, autonomy and relationality. As Dryden observes in his commendatory poem, Roscommon instructs via example as much or more than he does via precept: "Nor need those Rules, to give Translation light; / His own example is a flame so bright" (A2v). The example Dryden had in mind was Roscommon's translation of Horace's *Ars poetica*, published the same year as the *Essay*, but, as Johnson would later point out, the elegance of the poetry in the *Essay* makes its own statement.[80] There are yet other ways, however, in which the language of the *Essay* embodies a significant statement regarding translation: its use of pastiche and intertextual allusions.

Let us look first at the two pastiche sections, each of which is quite distinctive, to the point of startling the reader. (Indeed, Johnson would counter them as the poem's only formal flaws.) The first occurs directly following a sustained didactic passage containing a long series of rules for the translator and emphasizing the need for elegance, euphony, and unity. Rather unexpectedly (given that *"Excursions* are *inexpiably Bad"*), the poem breaks unity with a not particularly elegant anecdote:

> A *Quack* (too scandalously mean to Name)
> Had, by *Man-Midwifry,* got *Wealth,* and *Fame*;

As if *Lucina* had forgot her *Trade*,
The *Lab'ring wife* invok's *his surer Aid*.
                                        (16)

Although stories and scandals involving man-midwives (who were indeed taking over what had hitherto been a women's profession) were rampant in the 1680s, I am unable to determine whether Roscommon had specific figures in mind for his digression into medical mayhem when the Quack "From *saving Women* falls to *Killing Men*." Johnson observed of this passage that it was "borrowed from Boileau," commenting that it was "not worth the importation," but the apparent source in Boileau is very different from Roscommon's text, despite the presence of the quack doctor: "In Florence once lived a doctor—a clever boaster, it was said, and a celebrated murderer." Boileau's disastrously bad doctor has the good sense to take up another profession, providing a moral for would-be poets: "Better to be a mason, if that is your talent."[81] Roscommon reverses the charlatan's progress by having him ruined once he steps beyond his successful practice as man-midwife: "And There with *Basket-Alms* scarce kept *Alive*, / Shews how *Mistaken Talents* ought to *Thrive*." Roscommon's piquant transition and satirical tone call Boileau somewhat to mind, but the story is hardly "borrowed." Both offer a lesson on the error of pursuing a career, however noble, for which one is not gifted, but Roscommon's anecdote is at most a highly localized translation/adaptation of the French text. Aside from the plot reversal, Roscommon's is hardly a comforting vision. In the allegory of the translator/man-midwife who attempts to shine as an author/physician, there is no glory in the choice, only trickery and self-interest. Initially presented as "too scandalously mean to Name," and having usurped "Lucina's" profession, his initial fame turns on drunken gossip and "*Maudlin-Eloquence* of *trickling Eyes*." That he should be ruined by overstepping even these dubious boundaries would seem only just, unlike Boileau's "celebre assassin," who flees the angry families of his dead patients and productively reinvents himself in a new profession. For Roscommon's quack, "*Repentance* came too late, for *Grace*."

Just as Roscommon's precepts are bodied forth in the poetry itself, here too the lesson of the passage lies less in its allegorizing than in the way it enacts a delicate midpoint between imitation and authorship. The anecdote is sufficiently reminiscent of Boileau to call the earlier text to mind, but it is also wholly original. It is not a translation per se and not meant to serve as an example of one. Instead, the precept concerns the place of the translator himself, poised between texts, looking back toward another author without ceding his own creative powers. Roscommon may have chosen Boileau as he would "chuse a *Friend*," but he makes it clear that, precepts aside, he retains some rights of his own.

Even more explicit is the second pastiche, the "Miltonic" interpolation in blank verse occurring near the poem's end. Here too Roscommon appears to contradict his own aesthetic fundamentals. Despite his evident commitment to and mastery of the closed couplet, he criticizes the domination of rhyme in English verse and asks us to consider another model:

> Have we forgot how *Raphaels* Num'rous Prose
> Led our exalted Souls through heavenly Camps,
> And mark'd the ground where proud Apostate Thrones
> Defy'd *Jehovah*!
>
> (24)

The passage is not simply a stylistic pastiche, but contains a number of phrases lifted directly from *Paradise Lost* VI. It was not included in the first edition of the *Essay* but appeared instead the following year (1685), after Roscommon's death, and it is said to be the first praise of *Paradise Lost* to appear in print. (Johnson found the insertion "unwarrantably licentious.") Here, both the borrowing and the analogy are more explicit than in the "quack" passage. Having dismissed rhyme as a holdover from Celtic barbarism and inferior to unrhymed Greek and Latin metrics, Roscommon asserts that "Raphaels Num'rous Prose" defeats "th' old Original Rebels," which in the immediate context of the *Essay* brings to mind ancient Celts and their "Mossie Idol Oak" rather than Satan and his hordes.

The Boileau and Milton pastiches point toward the larger world of allusions with which the *Essay* is shot through. Roscommon's evocation of Virgil's Cumaean Sybil—"And panting, *Lo!* The *God*, the *God*, she cries"—is marked by the repetition as a translation from the Latin.[82] Roscommon's ecstatic Sybil represents translation in both senses, as a linguistic transposition and a displacement, a shift in meaning. Aeneas consults the Sybil not in order to be inspired but in order to learn the proper rituals before entering the underworld and to be recognized. So too do authors—and translators—seek to create a sense of self that remains identifiable, "recognizable," despite change. Pastiche, like translation, opens up the text to otherness, blurring the boundaries between original and copy, fidelity and infidelity.

Other forms of intertextuality maintain the openness of the *Essay*. Roscommon's poem is part of a conversation, having been written in response to an earlier poem, the earl of Mulgrave's *Essay on Poetry* of 1682. Furthermore, while the commendatory poems point toward Roscommon's circle of friends in an explicit way, the *Essay* also contains a number of tacit allusions to poems written by members of the circle.[83] Roscommon's "Academy" is remembered for its nonpartisan political orientation.[84] Recently, Greg Clingham has argued that the Academy, with its emphasis on literary translation, had a powerful influence in Augustan literary culture, especially through the translation projects of its most brilliant member, John Dryden.[85] Roscommon's 1682 poem on Dryden's "Religio Laici" emphasizes less the poem's theology than the significance of turning away from the painful politics of religious extremism:

> To what Stupidity are Zealots grown,
> Whose Inhumanity profusely shown
> In Damning Crowds of Souls, may Damn their own.[86]

An Anglo-Irish nobleman with a strong Protestant upbringing in England and France, Roscommon nevertheless sprang from a family that included Catholics and "lukewarm Protestants"; as the nephew and namesake of the executed earl of Strafford, he had additional reasons to eschew violent sectarian politics.[87] Two of the poems published with the *Essay* comment on his dual-national background. "W' are sent to Ireland, by reverse of fate," writes J. Amherst, while Dryden goes even further:

> How much in him may rising *Ireland* boast,
> How much in gaining him has *Britain* lost!
> Their Island in revenge has ours reclaim'd,
> The more instructed we, the more we still are sham'd.
>
>   (A2v)

As critics have observed, Dryden's moment of potential "national anxiety" is quickly recuperated by an invocation of Roscommon's English ancestry:

> 'Tis well for us his generous bloud did flow
> Deriv'd from *British* Channels long ago,
> That here his conquering Ancestors were nurst;
> And *Ireland* but translated *England* first.
>
>   (A2v)

Ireland's sudden relegation to secondariness as a "translator" of England in this passage persuades Michael Cronin that Dryden and the other members of the circle, including Roscommon himself, see translation as firmly linked to the English imperial project.[88] What I have been calling the *Essay*'s "openness," however—its refusal to align itself with a single identity or poetic voice, its availability to engage in intertextual dialogue and conversation—suggests a more mobile configuration than that of "conquest." The rejection of rhyme, while presented as a rejection of a "barb'rous" bardic past, is equally (if not predominantly) a rejection of contemporary standards of versification; the call to "*be* what *Rome* and *Athens* were *Before*," while gesturing toward the language of *Paradise Lost*, is still a vision of a day that has not yet dawned. Thus transported, "translated verse" might afford a means, a "middle way" (as Dryden would call it) between competing claims and conflicting identities.

THE TRANSLATION CANON

One of the several stories I have been relating in this chapter concerns the progressive consolidation of the English neoclassical translation canon, which could be said to attain its fully achieved form in Dryden's preface to *Ovid's Epistles* (1680). Offering his much-cited distinctions Metaphrase, Paraphrase, and Imitation, Dryden associates a name with each: Ben Jonson, representing past practice, now abandoned; Edmund Waller, the model for emulation; and Abraham Cowley, an admirable model, but difficult, if not dangerous, to follow. The injunction against word-for-word Metaphrase is doubly reinforced by Horace's *Nec verbum verbo*—cited both in Latin and in the earl of Roscommon's translation—and by a quotation from Denham's poem to Fanshawe. In the space of a single paragraph, Dryden has recapitulated the previous half-century's neoclassical turn in translation, down to its gesture of rejecting its immediate past.[89]

Dryden goes on to reflect on Cowley's and especially Denham's contributions in greater detail, developing his own approach in a manner that foreshadows his more widely ranging "transmutation" of critics and predecessors in the *Dedication of the Aeneis*, which I will focus on in the next chapter. As Tanya Caldwell points out, Dryden understates his indebtedness to Denham as poet and critic, and as a result, literary history has tended to do the same.[90] Dryden frames his discussion of his predecessors in terms of affective relations: first, between Denham and Cowley ("As they were

Friends, I suppose they Communicated their thoughts on this Subject to each other," 116), and later, between the two of them and Dryden himself ("for I both lov'd them living, and reverence them now they are dead," 119). Between these two passages stands Dryden's commentary on Denham's alchemical metaphor: "'Poetry is of so subtil a Spirit, that in pouring out of one Language into another, it will all Evaporate; and if a new Spirit be not added in the transfusion, there will remain nothing but a *Caput Mortuum*'" (as quoted by Dryden, 117–18). The *caput mortuum*, or "death's head," refers to the residue left over following distillation or sublimation, both dead matter and the emblem of death. Dryden cites the sentence purportedly in order to tighten the reins on free translation or "innovation," but while his appropriation emphasizes the care to be taken of the "Language only of the Poet" and the need for translators "to look into our selves, to conform our Genius to [the author's]," in the end his conclusions are those of Denham's: that with proper attention to language and meaning, "the Spirit of an Authour may be transfus'd, and yet not lost" (118). Like the metaphors of transmigration we saw earlier, "transfusion" implies not only a change of form and place, but the overcoming of death, breathing life into the death's head. So too may one critic contain the ghost of another.

Dryden's evocations of friendship among poet-critics parallel his emphasis on the intersubjective relation between translator and author; they foreshadow the injunction of Dryden's friend Roscommon to "chuse an *Author* as you chuse a *Friend*." Friendship-in-translation situates the relationships among texts and languages within a context of affectivity and dialogue: the *cogito* of friendship is "I think therefore I think the other," as Derrida says in *Politiques de l'amitié*.[91] The tightly interlaced network of citations, affect, and communication lends more weight and "presence" to the neoclassical translators than to any others and explains in part how their account of translation comes to dominate. After all, why this canon, in this form? As we have seen, neoclassical translation arises less from a rupture with previous practice than from the explicitly expressed desire for "a new and nobler way." Denham's poem on Fanshawe is a critical speech-act, calling something new into being, turning readers' attention to something that was already there, but asking them to see it differently, articulating and thereby mobilizing hitherto unfocused intellectual (and political) passions: it is, in effect, a critical "desiring machine."

The environment was ready for the crystallization process. The educated public was already bilingual, if not multilingual; translation played an important role in pedagogy. Because the audience for translations from the classics was presumably already versed in Latin, the purpose of such translations was not to make works available to those who had no access to them (although they played this role as well), but to offer a new "curious perspective" on familiar works.[92] The world of late Renaissance humanists was far more multilingual, of course. Milton knew ten languages, wrote in four, and translated from five; although he claimed he "could never delight . . . in whole traductions," he produced verse translations and let the echoes of other languages resonate through his own.[93] But although the critical reflection on translation would call forth both consideration of the foundations of language and passionate political polemics, neither aspect engaged Milton. Might this have been because translation—or, at any rate, the theoretical discourse of translation—was already marked po-litically as a Royalist discourse?

Possibly. Although clearly translation itself belonged to no single fac-tion—after all, as we have seen in the case of May's *Pharsalia*, classical trans-lations were already taking on political (and anti-absolutist) associations as early as the 1620s—the rise of translation theory was marked by "Royalist poetics." As in France, the reflection on language and meaning inspired by translation became one of the primary sources for the emergence of literary criticism as a genre. This genre, too, would be marked in the English con-text by party affiliation, to the point that David Womersley, in the preface to his anthology of Augustan literary criticism, speaks of a "Tory literary his-tory" that has marked subsequent critical judgments in much the same way, apparently, that "Whig history" shaped later historiography.[94] Womersley bases much of the distinction on the party affiliations of the writers and the tendency of Stuart loyalists and Tories to mythologize their version of Brit-ain as the New Rome; he cites Whig poet-translator Richard Blackmore's rejection of classical epic models in his *Paraphrase on the Book of Job*. But, as we shall see in subsequent chapters, there are many rooms in the man-sion of neoclassicism, and some of them are startlingly "modern." If there is something new in Blackmore, it lies not in his vision of a new English epic inspired by Biblical poetry—after all, Cowley proposed the same thing—but rather in his comments regarding the differences in languages and cul-tures that have become clear to him through translation, and in his refusal to condemn non-European style as "irregular": "All that can be said is that our Tastes are different, and if they are barbarous to us, we are so to them, some of which, especially the *Chinese*, are, or at least have been, very wise and polite Nations."[95] Although Blackmore's willingness to project himself imaginatively into another aesthetic and cultural norm does not suggest a need to *translate* differently than his contemporaries (he tells us that he will adapt the text to English standards), it points toward the modulation of neoclassical translation during the Enlightenment.

Meanwhile, translation had a different role to play in the final decades of the seventeenth century. It enabled a self-reinforcing group identity among defeated and dispirited loyalists, and it proved a highly useful tool in the melding of aesthetic and political discourse. And, as a number of scholars have pointed out, it lent itself to a pervasive malaise concerning the state of language, the sense among many that language had failed in its communicative function or its ability to sustain truth: the "Babel effect," as Nigel Smith calls it.[96] What can be viewed from afar as a positive legacy, "a public space in which all these languages could be debated," could only be perceived by those who underwent the experience as a deeply wounding trauma, a rip in the fabric of their existence. Unsurprisingly, the critical reflection on translation arises in the context of a widespread interrogation of language and an attempt to repair, or reform, its ills.[97] Thus John Wilkins offers his "philosophical language" as a means of resolving ambiguity and the pernicious effects of rhetoric: "Witness the present Age, especially the late times, wherein this grand imposture of Phrases hath almost eaten out solid Knowledge in all professions; such men generally being of most esteem who are skilled in these Canting forms of speech, though in nothing else."[98] Thomas Sprat, in his *History of the Royal Society*, is concerned with the vicissitudes of the language during the recent civil strife, which began, as he sees it, at a time when the language "was still fashioning, and beautifying itself": "In the Wars themselves . . . then I say, it receiv'd many fantastical terms, which were introduc'd by our *Religious Sects*; and many outlandish phrases, which several *Writers*, and *Translators*, in that great hurry, brought in, and made free as they pleas'd, and with all it was inlarg'd by many sound, and necessary Forms, and Idioms, which it before wanted."[99] Translation's brief appearance in Sprat's text underlines its ambivalent character, importing phrases that add to linguistic chaos, on the one hand, but are felt to be needed, on the other. Nevertheless, during a period when the language of truth, order, and unity seemed to have been irrevocably shattered, one can well sense the appeal of translation, with its utopic promise, however deferred, of communication, the reconciliation of differences, and that obscure something "new" that language "before wanted." Translation repairs language by reversing the "Babel effect," but it is also a reminder of Babel, both by its reference to another language and through its insistence on its untranslatable secrets. As poets, Cowley and Denham are sensitive to the untranslatable residue; as cryptographers, perhaps they are drawn to that secret untranslatable core. Dryden too, for as he says of Horace, "There is a Secret Happiness attends his choice."

In a reflection on the (wholly) other that is also a reflection on literature's untranslatable "secret," Derrida reminds us that there are two forms of secrecy: the "visible in-visible" and the "absolutely non-visible."[100] The first is the code breaker's toy: the perfectly adequate translation, the reliable referent. But language shifts and is not adequate to itself; translation gestures toward a meaning that it cannot fully articulate. As we saw in the last chapter, the Port-Royal translators had faith in an absolutely nonvisible meaning, *absconditus* but no less a Real Presence. Vaugelas, by contrast, spent half his life in pursuit of a perfect translation, one that would stop language in its flight through time in an atemporal, enduring moment. He appears to believe that such a translation could exist, thus denying the secret, yet surely his quest is also a confirmation of it, a knowledge that he prefers not to recognize: his own secret. For Denham, the secret is the alchemical residue, the caput mortuum, the resistant and apparently meaningless substrate of linguistic matter. Does translation offer us a curious perspective, an anamorphosis, that allows us to see the death's head in the meaningless blur? The secret is the otherness contained in language, which translation both conceals and—at moments, tantalizingly—reveals, with its gestures toward an ultimate reconciliation.

In like manner, translation conceals and reveals the past. By letting us imagine Virgil as "a man of this Nation" and "a man of this age," translation urges us to forget recent events and instead to reach into the distant past, creating a bridge to the present. Translation thus carries out the work of oblivion: reconciliation through forgetting. Acts of oblivion have their origin in the general amnesty declared in Athens in 403 BCE, following the Peloponnesian War and the violent rule of the Thirty Tyrants. As Nicole Loraux observes, amnesty/amnesia is constantly threatened with various forms of "not-forgetting" (*non-oubli*), not the least of which is the paradox that the oath to forget constitutes an ever-present reminder. Notforgetting can take the form of *alaston penthos*, "a mourning that will not forget," which is etymologically related to fury, thus vengeance; but violent remembrance is ultimately subsumed by a positive form of not-forgetting,

aletheia, or truth.[101] Present and distant past entwine in order to disarm the recent past of its capacity to wound; we can see parallels in the effort to promote a "new" mode of literary translation and the vision of Britain as New Rome, particularly after the Restoration. While translation may have provided some consolation to those who sought to "repair" the language, its continuing availability for polemical discourse keeps grievances in public view; this very ambivalence is doubtless a more apt image of the emerging public sphere than any universal language could be.

It is difficult for us to translate ourselves into the intellectual and affective space of these writers, most of whom ended up on the wrong side of Whig history. Their belief in the divine right of kings gathers little sympathy; their desire to make Virgil speak like an Englishman seems naive. Yet it's precisely those points that remind us of their foreignness and remind us to read attentively. When we least expect it, something unusual occurs, as when the former censor Roger L'Estrange exclaims that "Reason works by Communication." Thus appear fissures in a hegemonic framework, contributing to new discursive formations.

Although most of the figures I've discussed experienced exile, they do not manifest what we usually think of as the symptoms of "exilic consciousness." But as their world was different from ours, so too were their "symptoms." Descartes, after all, relates that during his years of vagabondage "here and there in the world," he arrived at what we call the "Cartesian subject," with its associations of universality, centrality, and autonomy, on a particular wintry afternoon in a particular warm room with a stove, as the lands outside were or would soon be devastated by the Thirty Years' War. Nowadays, we would be more inclined to reflect on the ways in which the experiences of exile, migrancy, and conflict contribute to the dismantling of the Cartesian subject—what Iain Chambers calls the "drama of the stranger": "Cut off from the homelands of tradition, experiencing a constantly challenged identity, the stranger is perpetually required to make herself a home in an interminable discussion between a scattered historical inheritance and a heterogeneous present."[102] Indeed, Descartes observes that "when one travels for too long a time, one becomes a stranger in one's own land."[103] Even more than Descartes, who usually traveled voluntarily, the translator-exiles had significant occasion "to encounter the languages of powerlessness," as Chambers puts it.

Just as John Wilkins sought a philosophical language immune to corruption, ambiguity, and falsehood, so too did the neoclassical translators make themselves a home in a language of beauty and harmony, a language that sought to recapture and appropriate a noble past. Such translations may be seen as nostalgic, even reactionary, but as we have seen, they operate on many levels and toward many ends and are not all easily subsumed under one roof.

More than half a century after his initial Seneca translations of the 1640s, Edward Sherburne gathered his translations of the tragedies and reissued them together with some related texts in a volume published at the dawn of the new century and dedicated to his young kinsman Richard Francis Sherburne—although, as he noted in the dedication, the little boy was doubtless "more delighted at present in bestriding and managing Your Reedy *Pegasus,* than encountering Bookish Chimera's."[104] Sherburne had outlived most of his fellow poet-translators, including Dryden, his junior of fifteen years; his final volume both reflects their achievements and sounds a different note. In his prefatory remarks, "A Brief Discourse concerning Translation," he takes aim squarely at the long-established tradition of citing Horace in support of free translation, which we have seen reaffirmed by Roscommon and Dryden. Sherburne cites the lines from *De arte poetica* in their context, translating them thus:

> No publick Matter, but a private Wit
> May make his own; if the vile Track he quit;
> Nor Word for Word be careful to transfer
> With the same Faith as an Interpreter.
> (xxxvii)

Following Pierre-Daniel Huet, whose 1683 treatise *De optimo genere inter-pretandi* he quotes in Latin and translates into English, Sherburne chides the "groundless Prejudice of these *Fastidious Brisks*" for claiming that Horace gave rules for translation ("For doubtless he thought it beneath him") or thought of translation as anything other than strictly literal. Commentators have tended to see in Sherburne's gesture a radical departure from neoclassical norms, but, despite his evident pride in correcting a long-standing error, his description of his own approach has much in common with his contemporaries, as he promises to give "the genuine Sense of *Seneca*" but also to adhere to the Latin words only "as far as the Propriety of Language may fairly admit" (xxxviii). And like L'Estrange and so many others, he does not forget to indicate a "Political Lesson" for his young dedicatee: "*That the hidden Malice of revengeful (though seemingly reconcil'd) Enemies, together with the flagitious, unbridled Lusts of dissolute Princes, have been the Ruin of most flourishing Kingdoms*" (A7r). In such manner, the discourse of neoclassical translation undergoes a new mutation, incorporating previously heterogeneous elements and combining them with elements both old and new.

CHAPTER 3

Temporality and Subjectivity

Dryden's "Dedication of the Aeneis"

[handwritten notes: Networks / Intertextuality / Recuperation of the past / overcoming loss. Self / otherwise complicated;]

"Long before I undertook this work," Dryden writes of his translation of Virgil, "I was no stranger to the Original."[1] The material time that Dryden spent reading and studying the Roman poet is a significant feature of the account he gives of the act of translation, as is the oblique reminder that he was a poet first, and only later a translator. The translation projects of Dryden's later years, from the collective translations of Ovid and Juvenal to his own versions of Persius, the complete works of Virgil, and the Fables, served multiple purposes. They enabled him to maintain a polemical and critical posture that would have been difficult or dangerous to present on his own behalf; they opened up possibilities for exploring and extending poetic subjectivity and melding other voices with his own; and, of course, they made money.[2] Not only did he leave his mark on the poetry, drama, satire, and criticism of his age, but his reflections on translation simultaneously synthesized earlier commentary and took it to a new level, just as his practice set a new standard for poetic translation.[3]

The "Dedication of the Aeneis" is an exceptionally rich text in which Dryden works through the complexities of his own role as a translator, a role situated within a network of relations that are simultaneously inter-subjective, textual, and temporal. In the "Dedication," translation is an act of remembering and an act of being with the Other that escapes both dependency and conquest. The "middle way" is achieved through a meditation on time, coded variously as historicity, priority, and originality, and by dialogue with other translators and predecessors. The "Dedication" bespeaks both identification and estrangement, unity and complexity, as the political allegories and personal identifications shift in and out of focus. The text attempts both to overcome temporal distances, by bringing Virgil into the present, and to maintain an awareness of them, by emphasizing its own "time of reading," which is anything but linear or straightforward. Just as the work of memory crisscrosses the present, knitting it to the past, so Dryden's digressions prevent a seamless amalgamation of past and present. In many ways this activity resembles the work of mourning, which too must maintain temporal distinctions even as it seeks to reconcile us to feelings of loss through identifications in the present. These multiple strands of time, memory, and otherness connect in a process of cultural and psychological mourning that provides a means for coming to terms with personal loss and historical change.

In speaking of "mourning" I am not suggesting that this text reveals an explicit thematic of nostalgia of the sort that would become popular in the later eighteenth century. Dryden's losses are "personal"—immediate, political, financial—but they are also intangible, diffused throughout a larger process of cultural change. Patrick Coleman has reminded us of the forms of loss attendant on the emergence of European modernity: "Emancipation from inherited religious and cultural values involved a struggle with norms experienced not just as external artifice but as guarantees of inner coherence. However justified—indeed vital—it might be to question those norms, doing so carried the risk . . . of aggravating the process of cultural disintegration to the point where it might become impossible to reconstitute any form of imaginative cohesion."[4] At the end of a tumultuous century and a no less tumultuous public career, the structural analogies between translation and mourning provide Dryden with the means to respond to both the personal and the intangible losses in "impersonal" terms, and to articulate a new poetic voice that is "of a piece" with earlier selves, yet newly capable of confronting present change.

The "Dedication" is best known for its political reading of the *Aeneid* and its implicit, but extended, parallels between Virgil's life and career and

Dryden's.[5] These parallels arise within the context of an extended discussion of epic "unity," which Dryden (revising Aristotle) casts in terms of action, character or "manners," and time. But despite the necessity of the unity of epic action ("one, entire, and great"), and even though Dryden will go to considerable lengths to demonstrate that both the hero Aeneas and the moral fabric of the *Aeneid* are "of a piece," the question of time refuses to fit so neatly into the scheme. The "Dedication" foregrounds this preoccupation both thematically and discursively. For instance, the discussion of the Aristotelian unities focuses primarily on the unity of time, to which Dryden takes a revisionary approach; there is also an extensive account of the chronology of the *Aeneid* and the literary debates sparked by Virgil's "anachronisms." Dryden's defense and explication of Virgil involves rehearsing several literary debates, among them the accusation of anachronism in the meeting of two (semi-)historical characters, Dido and Aeneas, who must have lived centuries apart. Dryden dismisses this objection as silly: "Chronology at best is but a Cobweb-Law, and he broke through it with his weight" (5:300). Even so, history, the relation of past to present, and the possibilities for understanding and commenting on the present by recourse to the past continue to foreground questions of time and temporality, particularly as the parallels between Virgil's and Dryden's careers become increasingly apparent.

parallels

Let us look more closely at the "unity of character" and Dryden's identification with Virgil. Just as epic action should be "one, entire, and great," so too must its moral effect be uniformly uplifting. To this end, it is important that the epic hero be a consistent exemplar. As the case of Homer's Achilles shows, the example may be negative: "It is not necessary that the Manners of the Heroe should be virtuous. They are Poetically good if they are of a Piece" (5:271). An important part of Dryden's apology for Virgil is thus the demonstration of consistency, to show that Aeneas is "of a piece." Even more important, the same must be shown of the poet. Dryden launches an extended discussion (interspersed with digressions) to show that Virgil's outlook was coherent, that his views were informed by his life and political context, and that his work "was as useful to the *Romans* of his Age, as *Homer*'s was to the *Grecians* of his" (5:277). The description of Virgil, while speaking specifically to his politics ("he was still of Republican principles in his Heart," 5:280) also underscores his unity of character. Consistency and coherence do not exclude complexity in either Virgil or his hero, Aeneas, and for Dryden, the two are closely related. Just as Virgil played "the part of a Wise and an Honest Man" in his relationships with both "Prince and People," so too "I shall continue still to speak my Thoughts like a free-born subject as I am; though such things, perhaps, as no *Dutch* Commentator cou'd, and I am sure no *French*-man durst" (5:283). The slide from Augustus/ Aeneas and Virgil to Dryden is clear and, indeed, "of a piece," given the aspersions that had been cast on Dryden's character throughout his public life and especially in the wake of his conversion to Catholicism. The unstated premise that a writer's character is intrinsically connected both to his literary production and to his environment deepens the nationalist comparison to Dutch and French commentators by suggesting further reasons that Dryden's commentary be distinguished from theirs, however much he may have relied on them.

The most difficult element of the *Aeneid* to portray as being "of a piece" is its hero, Aeneas, whose abandonment of Dido has been particularly "Arraign'd . . . by the Ladies," as Dryden puts it, adding, "And I cannot much blame them" (5:294). At this juncture, Dryden again turns over his discussion to Segrais, who had argued that all of Aeneas's actions, however they may appear to us today, make sense under the Roman idea of piety. Dryden lets Segrais's arguments stand, but he does not appear to find them wholly compelling. In the end, it is the internal logic of the *Aeneid* that prevails over our ability to relate to its hero: "Where I cannot clear the Heroe, I hope at least to bring off the Poet" (5:297). Dryden actually offers us three readings of book 4: a psychological account of the progress of love (297–98); a political reading taking into account historical relations between Rome and Carthage (298–99); and, last, a witty prose "translation" in which Aeneas bids farewell to Dido in the manner of a Restoration libertine: "I made no such Bargain with you at our Marriage, to live always drudging on at *Carthage*; my business was *Italy*, and I never made a secret of it. . . . This is the effect of what he says, when it is dishonour'd out of *Latin* Verse, into *English* Prose" (5:303). Dryden enjoys a bit of fun at Aeneas's expense, but he also maintains the multilayered unity of the *Aeneid*. He also both distances himself from a thread in the poem that he finds inimical and recuperates it for himself through rewriting it.

Critics have had a great deal to say about Dryden's modulation of his translation through his own poetic vision as well as about his discussion of Virgil's life and times as a means to reflect on his own career.[6] Certainly the recurring motif of "wholeness," especially with regard to "character," reinforces the importance of achieving some form of unified subjectivity within and despite temporality and ideological dissent. Aeneas and his creator are "of a piece"; so too, by extension, is Dryden himself. On a more personal level is the chronology of Virgil's own life span, and Dryden's. Both "wanted time" to complete their work: we are reminded that the Roman poet desired to destroy his work when he realized that he would not live long enough to complete it and that the aging Dryden is being pressed by his publisher and subscribers to get the translation into print before it is truly ready (5:320, 5:333, 5:339). The implicit parallels between Virgil and his translator become explicit when Dryden claims a special privilege in understanding his author: "But one Poet may judge of another by himself" (5:283). Indeed, in the next sentence the identification becomes complete: "The Vengeance we defer, is not forgotten." By referring to earlier essays of his, Dryden maintains a textual presence as a writer, not a "copier"; despite his deferrals to Virgil, Dryden's magisterial closing discussion of English versification puts him on an even footing and enables him to speak authoritatively, as a poet (5:319).[7] Translation has become a form of oblique authorship for Dryden; he may overtly deny himself the privilege of "Invention," but, as many critics have noted, he gives us a Virgil suffused with his own norms, political concerns, and affective modes. The "Dedication" bespeaks both identification and estrangement, unity and complexity, as the political allegories and personal identifications shift in and out of focus.

The evocations of Dryden's own living time amplify and are amplified by his frequent references to the "timing" and the order of his exposition and the physical time that it must take its addressee, the Earl of Mulgrave, to read it: "I have said already more than I intended"; "I have detain'd your Lordship longer than I intended"; "But to return from my long rambling." Not only is the "Dedication" long, but, as Dryden fully admits, it is also unstructured, digressive; the exposition gets sidetracked, doubles back and repeats itself. Dryden teases us with his rambles: is this or that passage a digression or not? Sometimes what appeared to be a digression was not (5:275); sometimes Dryden baldly identifies it as such (5:317); and sometimes he appears to resist the temptation to digress and then succumbs: "I will not make a digression here, though I am strangely tempted to it; but will only say . . ." (5:324). Dryden so often points out his own repetitions and diversions as to make them appear methodical. "I design not a Treatise of Heroick Poetry, but write in a loose Epistolary way" (5:275), he tells us, and underscores the point again a few pages later by calling attention to the contrast between his "Dedication" and Segrais's preface to his French translation: "His Preface is an exact Method; mine is loose, and, as I intended it, Epistolary" (5:287).

All these threads—sequence, priority, authorial unity—converge near the end of Dryden's "defense" of Virgil, in the discussion of "Invention." As a great artist, Virgil must be allowed his "Inventions," or divergences from historical fact. The discussion of "Invention," which is also part of a discussion of the relative merits of Virgil and his predecessor Homer, also becomes a critique of any simplistic notion of "firstness" or priority. Here aesthetics and personal history meet. Dryden comes after Virgil—and a host of other translators in English and other languages. Nevertheless, as the numerous implicit and explicit parallels between Virgil and himself suggest, his position is not entirely abject. Not surprisingly, the discussion of "invention" and "copy" leads straight into the question of translation: " 'Tis one thing to Copy, and another to imitate from Nature. The Copyer is that servile Imitator, to whom *Horace* gives no better a Name than that of Animal: He will not so much as allow him to be a Man. *Raphael* imitated Nature: They who Copy one of *Raphael*'s Pieces, imitate but him, for his Work is their Original. They Translate him as I do *Virgil*; and fall as short of him as I of *Virgil*" (5:305). What begins as a familiar and straightforward parallel between translators and the "servile Imitator" of a painting gradually becomes complex: "There is a kind of Invention in the imitation of *Raphael*; for though the thing was in Nature, yet the Idea of it was his own." The complexity stems from the equivocal nature of the term *imitation*, which on the one hand points to the imitation of nature, or mimesis, and on the other points to any number of different sorts of textual relationships ranging from plagiarism to extravagantly free, modernizing translation—and the recognition of literary achievement. Although in this passage "Raphael's imitation" would seem to refer to the mimetic act, the word certainly appears in Dryden's lexicon as a form of translation. "Nature" is never an unmediated reality but is always already the "idea" of nature. Hence, in Dryden's "simile," Apelles and Raphael paint the same subject, only to demonstrate that there can be no "same subject" when perceived by two artists of different backgrounds and temperaments. The same could be said of two readers' approaches to an "original" text—or a translator's contemplation of the meaning of the wanderings of Aeneas. In the end, artistic genius renders the question irrelevant: "*Virgil* cannot be said to copy *Homer*: The *Grecian* had only the advantage of writing first" (5:306). While Dryden will not go so far as to say that Virgil's only advantage over him is that of "writing first," his constant identification with the Roman poet puts him structurally in the same relation to him as Virgil to Homer.

Dryden then turns to the question of translation itself, acknowledging that he has written "against" himself: "For presuming to Copy, in my course *English*, the Thoughts and Beautiful Expressions of this inimitable Poet" (5:318). How to translate—to imitate—the inimitable? His remarks on the "best way" of translating have a familiar ring: "The way I have taken, is not so streight as Metaphrase, nor so loose as Paraphrase" (5:329). Dryden had offered reflections on translation in his earlier critical writings, in particular the preface to *Ovid's Epistles* (1680), in which he describes three sorts of translation: the strict word-for-word "metaphrase," the loose "imitation," and the intermediate "paraphrase," his own course. Dryden's other accounts of translating practice tend in a like manner to offer categories that range from the literal to the free and to describe his own practice as falling somewhere in the middle. For example, in the preface to his Juvenal translation, "Discourse Concerning the Original and Progress of Satire," he claims to be giving us "not a Literal Translation, but a kind of Paraphrase; or somewhat which is yet more loose, betwixt a Paraphrase and Imitation" (4:87). The implications for translating practice are not particularly novel.[8] Indeed, Dryden's remarks echo closely those of key predecessor Jean de Segrais, who offers in his own Virgil translation "neither a paraphrase, nor a literal translation" but rather "the middle course [*le milieu*] between them."[9] But Dryden's desire as translator to steer "betwixt the two Extreams," like other moments in his work where he strives to go between or reconcile opposites, reveals a key aspect of his authorial self-consciousness.[10]

Shortly after stating his allegiance to the "middle way," Dryden voices an ambition that might appear to lead in a rather different direction: "Yet I may presume to say, and I hope with as much reason as the *French* Translator, that taking all the Materials of this divine Author, I have endeavour'd to make *Virgil* speak such *English*, as he wou'd himself have spoken, if he had been born in *England*, and in the present Age" (5:330–31). Thoroughly Englishing—adapting, localizing—Virgil would hardly seem to be in keeping with a middle way. Rather, Dryden seems bent on bringing the poet entirely over to his side. What is at stake here? As we have seen, the idea of making the author speak the translator's language is hardly a new one. In the immediate context of the "Dedication," Dryden's assertion not only strengthens his identification with the Roman poet but also reaches out to the earlier commentators. Translation involves the art of speaking "otherwise." Virgil may speak like an Englishman, for Dryden speaks with another voice as well: "like a Frenchman." His reference to Segrais, "the *French* translator," marks the passage explicitly as a repetition or paraphrase of Segrais's own statement: "I wanted to give a French Aeneid as I imagine that he would have given it himself, had he been born a subject of our glorious monarch."[11] Dryden is also speaking like another Englishman, his significant predecessor John Denham: "If Virgil must needs speak English, it were fit he should speak not only as a man of this Nation, but as a man of this age."[12] Thus, the passage in Dryden's "Dedication" is a double quotation, a palimpsest. To explicate it fully, I would like to digress a bit myself: first on Denham's translation, then on Segrais's.

As we saw in the previous chapter, Denham completed his translation of the second book of the *Aeneid* before the Civil War, publishing it anonymously twenty years later, with the note "written in 1636" as an oblique reference to the political subtext. After the Restoration, however, he issued a new edition of the translation along with other poetical works, signed and dedicated to the king. Although many commentators have examined *The Destruction of Troy* and its preface, few have called attention to the 1668 "Epistle Dedicatory" to Charles II. Here, Denham relates a visit he made to Charles I at the queen's behest during the king's captivity. In one of their conversations, Charles mentions that he has just read Denham's lines on Fanshawe's *Il Pastor Fido* and asks when they were written: "I told him two or three years since; he was pleased to say, that having never seen them before, He was afraid I had written them since my return into *England*, and though he liked them well, he would advise me to write no more, alleging, that when men are young, and have little else to do, they might vent the overflowings of their Fancy that way, but when they were thought fit for more serious Employments, if they still persisted in that course, it would look, as if they minded not the way to any better."[13] The dedicatory epistle frames the poems and translations in a number of important ways, evoking both exile and return, fidelity and faithlessness. *The Destruction of Troy*, with its scenes of slaughter and searing final lines on the death of Priam—"A headless Carkass, and a nameless Thing" (64), the one line Dryden explicitly borrowed for his own translation—was of course eminently "readable" for royalist sympathizers. Unlike the anonymous 1656 edition, in which the political subtext was left implicit, the signed 1688 edition deliberately frames the work in terms of politics through its recollection of Charles I's delivery "into the hands of the Army," a reference that could only call to mind the subsequent regicide. By dedicating his work to the dead king's son and offering a remembered scene of a gracious, "smiling" Charles I, Denham underscores his role as faithful courtier and servant of the royal family. He goes on to relate his role in helping the king maintain a secret correspondence in England and abroad, and, when this role was discovered, his flight to the Caroline court in exile in France and Holland. With "these clouds being now happily blown over" (iii) by the Restoration, however, Denham confesses that he has fallen back "into the follies of youth" and decided to publish the volume of collected poems and translations. The anecdote about Charles's concern lest Denham be spending his time with verse rather than "more serious Employments" relegates poetry to an idle courtier's pursuit. His recollection of the exchange here suggests that even the "happy" Restoration is not without cost: he is now an old man, free once more to "vent the overflowings of Fancy" but no longer involved in matters of state. (Denham died the year following publication.) Both the anecdote and the careful dating of the Virgil translation, "written in 1636," point to exile, return, and a painful temporal hiatus.

There is a paradox in the association of the new freer, or "fluent," style of translation of John Denham and Abraham Cowley, translation that makes Virgil or Pindar "speak English," with their experience of exile abroad. Dryden sees Cowley's language as having been forever marked by the experience: "For through the Iniquity of the times, he was forc'd to Travel, at an Age, when, instead of Learning Foreign Languages, he shou'd have studied the Beauties of his Mother Tongue. . . . Thus by gaining abroad he lost at home" (5:331–32). Whether or not Dryden is correct in his assessment of a "continental" strain in Cowley (a remark that reminds us that despite however many French writers Dryden may have ingested, he himself has never left English soil), the drive to produce an English-sounding Greek or Latin poet thus appears linked to a desire to recuperate or compensate for a loss: a lost country, lost language, lost home. Similarly, Denham's dedicatory epistle to a living king becomes a site for the work of memory, for remembering the dead. The return to England, the return to poetry, and the restoration of the monarchy can all bring consolation, but they cannot undo the loss of "your Royal Father." Making Virgil "speak English" thus reflects much more than a nationalist project; it bespeaks a desire to reclaim the past and overcome loss.

Let us turn now to Jean de Segrais, whose literary career could hardly appear more different from either Denham's or Dryden's. Born in 1624, Segrais was the well-born and well-educated son of a destitute noble family. He enjoyed minor success as a poet and in 1648 entered the service of Mlle de Montpensier ("La Grande Mademoiselle") as a *gentilhomme ordinaire* and literary assistant.[14] The salons of Montpensier and her friends saw the development of new forms of extended prose fiction that gave rise to the modern novel; the salons were also the site for complex forms of collaborative authorship. Segrais's name appeared on the title page of a collection of tales, *Les Nouvelles françoises* (1657), which he explained as drawn from Montpensier's conversations; his name likewise appeared on the title page of the novel *Zayde, histoire espagnol* (1670), but this work, according to his later statements, was entirely the work of Mme de Lafayette, as was *La Princesse de Clèves*, which appeared anonymously in 1678.[15] Critics of the day, however, were wont to give him credit for a large share of both. Segrais thus represents a very different approach to authorship from that of the public poet Dryden. His reasons for undertaking the Virgil translation are also quite different. Whereas Dryden's Virgil project got its impetus from the precarious financial and social situation in which he found himself after losing the laureateship, Segrais tells us that he began his translation on a whim and continued from pleasure.[16]

In spite of these differences, the two actually coincide in many respects with regard to their translations, moving in and out of phase but ultimately coming to profound accords.[17] The attributed and unattributed borrowings run the full range of translation styles, from word for word to modernizing adaptation. Sometimes Dryden presents them openly (for example, "What follows is Translated literally from *Segrais*," 5:288; see also 5:309). On another occasion, Dryden is content to stand back and let Segrais take on the debate over the *Aeneid*'s chronology (for example, "the Ronsardians reply . . . ," "Segrais answers . . . ," 5:310–11). Sometimes the importation is more ambiguous, as when after a series of clearly marked observations by the French translator on Aeneas's character and a response from Dryden signaled by the I-you relation of the dedicatory letter to Mulgrave (5:290), we suddenly find ourselves in the following paragraph confronting an "I" who appears to be Dryden but is not: "In the first place, if Tears are Arguments of Cowardise, What shall I say of *Homer*'s Heroe? shall *Achilles* pass for timorous because he wept?" (5:291). Compare with Segrais's statement: "No one ever blamed Homer for making Achilles weep, despite his hard inexorable character" (1:40).

Early in the "Dedication," Dryden claims that he will make limited use of the French translator: "[I] take up Segrais where I left him: And shall

use him less often than I have occasion for him. For his Preface is a perfect
piece of Criticism, full and clear, and digested into an exact Method; mine is
loose, and, as I intended it, Epistolary. Yet I dwell on many things which he
durst not touch: For 'tis dangerous to offend an Arbitrary Master: And every
Patron who has the Power of Augustus, has not his Clemency. In short, my
Lord, I wou'd not Translate him, because I wou'd bring you somewhat of
my own" (5:287). Even so, as Dryden indicates himself (and as his editors
carefully point out), there is a substantial amount of Segrais in the "Dedication."[18] While some importations are literal, others are looser. On one
occasion Dryden updates (but does not Anglicize!) the original by substitut-
ing "Versailles" for Segrais's "Louvre" in an analogy between architecture
and literary inventiveness: "Is *Versailles* the less a New Building, because
the Architect of that Palace has imitated others which were built before it?"
(5:304). He also improves on the original by citing a reference that Segrais
"forgot to cite" (5:289). And in other instances, he gives us a free-wheeling,
thoroughly Anglicizing, "imitation."

Let us look at such an example in detail. Segrais opens his preface with
an analysis of the psychology of taste. Claiming that three components
("terms, figures, and discourse") are common to all "works of eloquence,"
he proceeds to describe the type of reader who focuses on each component
and the cast of mind of each type of reader (1:2). The "smallest" sort of mind
attends only to lexical features of a text and forms peremptory judgments
based on terms they find improper or new. The second, "more dangerous"
sort looks for *belles pensées* but fails to take in the text as a whole. Only
those who are capable of seeing a work in its entirety and appreciating the
order and configuration of its parts are excellent judges: "Their judgment
instructed by memory and enlightened by wit [*esprit*] discerns correctly"
(1:4). Segrais's text bespeaks not only the overarching structures of rational-
ist thought and its concern with method but also the intellectual debates of
his circle over the status of the Ancients. It is a different world indeed from
Dryden's version, although he purports to be giving us Segrais: "*Segrais* has
distinguish'd the Readers of Poetry, according to their capacity of judging,
into three Classes: (He might have said the same of Writers too if he had
pleas'd.) In the lowest Form he places those whom he calls *Les Petits Esprits*:
such things as are our Upper-Gallery Audience in a Play-House; who like
nothing but the Husk and Rhind of Wit; preferr a Quibble, a Conceit, an
Epigram, before solid Sense, and Elegant Expression: These are the Mobb-
Readers" (5:326). Segrais's careful quasi-Augustinian parallels between the

faculties of the mind, the components of a text, and the mentalities of critics quickly become a witty social comedy that ends up not being about
readers or critics at all.

Declaring that "the most Judicious" readers have a "magnetism in their
Judgment" that attracts others to their opinion, Dryden suddenly veers
away from the magnetism of the critic to that of the text itself, which "insinuates it self by insensible degrees into the liking of the Reader" (5:328).
For Segrais, memory serves only to "instruct" judgment and by itself is inferior to natural intelligence or esprit. Time functions quite differently for
Dryden, for whom the truest test of a literary work is its life or death. It
must exist in time for its "lustre" to be known with certainty. Segrais's interest in temporality takes a different form; for him, translation requires that
we abandon our rootedness in time: "One must . . . rid oneself of one's century in order to conform oneself entirely to the sentiments of our author"
(1:8). The passage comes in one of the introductory sections of his preface,
where it opens the way for a reading of Virgil that will constantly take into
account the "diversité des esprits" and the intersections between intellectual work and social behavior, within his own society as well as between
seventeenth-century France and Virgil's Rome.

It may surprise us that this same Segrais, in the discussion of his actual
practice of translating some fifty pages later, tells us that he wished to make
Virgil speak as if he had "been born a subject of our glorious monarch"
(1:65). The two strains, of entering into the thoughts of the author and of
making him speak like "us," come together in a reflection on the differences between languages. Justifying Gilles Ménage's "translation" (in Virgil's
Bucolics) of *corylos* (hazel tree) as *alisier* (mountain ash) on account of its
euphony rather than the correct, but unpoetic, *coudrier*, Segrais explains
that what matters is thus not the signification of *corylos* but its "effect," a
momentary phenomenon of individual experience (1:69). Segrais goes on to
make a distinction between "interpreter" (from Horace's *fidus interpres*) and
"traduire" (1:70). Whereas "translation" is word for word, "to interpret" requires attention to a "consideration of language" and *usage*. As we saw in the
first chapter, usage is a crucial concept for Segrais and his age, bespeaking
the temporality and transience of language, its embeddedness in the social
context, and opposing an independent and atemporal meaning. *L'usage* implies being in the present—a contingent present, one that is not an absolute
measure of all truth, all reality, but that is aware of its difference from the
past, just as it is aware of the "diversité d'esprits" within.

Both Dryden and Segrais, despite the differences in their presentation of the relationship between past and present, recognize in translation the awareness of temporality. If, as Dryden claims, the judicious reader finds "new Graces" in a text with each reading, or, as Segrais observes, the constant impetus of linguistic change pushes the text-in-translation into a constantly changing present, then translation offers us the means to reconcile past and present through a realization that the past is changing too, that it can be part of the process of becoming that is the present even as it retains its identity as other-than-the-present.

Within such a scheme, the translator is no "servile copyer." The more Dryden translates and cites Segrais, the more he recreates Segrais through emendation and imitation and yet, quite explicitly, undoes Segrais by dismantling the "exact Method" of Segrais's neatly structured treatise and presenting the pieces in a "loose Epistolary way" that pays no heed whatsoever to the original order or context of the passages absorbed into the "Dedication": "I trade with both the Living and the Dead, for the enrichment of our Native Language" (5:336). Certainly Dryden's many references to the "honour of my country" and the excellence of native English writers bespeak a dawning national spirit, but to reduce his or Segrais's approach to translation to "ethnocentrism" is clearly to miss much of what is going on here, just as it is shortsighted to see the "Dedication" as "unoriginal" because it is shot through with quotations.

The "Dedication" is thus a work that not only discourses on translation but also performs the work of translation: it is a text filled with other texts, other voices, and yet it cannot be reduced to them precisely because of its multiple voices, its intrinsic temporality. As we saw in the discussion of "Invention," the "advantage of writing first" does not preclude the originality of those who come after. Similarly, in his discussion of the difficulty in rendering the range and beauty of Virgil's Latin vocabulary, Dryden nuances the translator's traditionally subservient role: "Slaves we are; and labour on another Man's Plantation; we dress the Vine-yard, but the Wine is the Owners. . . . He who Invents is Master of his Thoughts and Words: He can turn and vary them as he pleases, 'till he renders them harmonious. But the wretched Translator has no such privilege: For being ty'd to the Thoughts, he must make what Musick he can in the Expression" (5:334). Like the rift between thoughts and expression, the difference between author and translator, master and slave, would at first glance appear to be absolute. The shift in imagery, however, is telling: we move from a view of the translator as a "slave" having no part in the author's "wine" to one of a translator-musician who possesses certain creative powers.[19] The "Dedication" as a whole destabilizes such rigid distinctions through a nuanced consideration of originality, invention, and otherness. As many critics have observed, Dryden is a writer deeply engaged in dialogue and debate with other writers, ancient and modern, defining himself in relation to others, and others in relation to himself, in a historically innovative form of subjectivity.[20]

This new form of subjectivity suggests a wider range of application for the familiar ambition to adhere to the "middle way"—not only between literalness and license but also between master and slave, original and copy, self and other, past and present. Dryden's preface to Virgil is important less for what it says about translation norms, categories, and techniques than for the way in which it embodies crucial features of what for lack of a better term I could call "translational," rather than authorial, self-consciousness, overcoming the dichotomy between translators as abject and dependent and authors as independent and original. It is a meditation on authorship-in-translation. At a time when the question "What is an author?" could have such radically different answers as those suggested by Dryden's and Segrais's careers in public life and private salons, the question "What is a translator?" is even more vexed. Consider the conclusion to Dryden's discussion of "Invention" in Homer and Virgil, in which he distinguishes between imitating a master like Raphael and "servile Copying": "For every common Reader to find me out at the first sight for a Plagiary: And cry, This I read before in Virgil, in a better Language, and in better Verse: This is like Merry-Andrew on the low Rope, copying lubberly the same Tricks, which his Master is so dextrously performing on the high" (5:307). The analogical leap from Raphael's school to the fairground is a deft one indeed, as is the shift from Virgil's originality to Dryden's. This passage implicitly distinguishes real "servility," or plagiarism—"Merry-Andrew on the low Rope"—from the qualitatively different work of translation, by pointing out how bereft of art the former is in contrast to the latter, whose complexity is amply spelled out throughout the "Dedication." The fear of failure ("This I read before in Virgil, in a better Language") is not entirely absent, but the possibility exists of learning from Virgil, "imitating his Invention," without succumbing to his authority. *Apuleus → Cross bds.*

In his allusions and quotations, Dryden demonstrates numerous forms of authorship and intertextuality. While Virgil, along with Spenser and Milton, functions as a model author, subject to imitation by others, he also provides the model of "oblique" authorship, in which communication or political commentary can be made indirectly. Variations of textual being also include the quotation and echoes of Segrais and other sources, as well as the nonchalant "non-citations" in which Dryden explicitly demurs from giving his source. One should also add the ghostly presence of the Earl of Lauderdale, whose posthumous manuscript translation Dryden admits to having "consulted" (5:336–37). And, of course, there are Dryden's readers, both the Earl of Mulgrave to whom the work is dedicated and the wider public whose presence he sometimes acknowledges, as when he seeks to vindicate Virgil "to your Lordship, and by you to the Reader" (5:286).

Translation is often conceived as a direct "personal" relation between the translator and the original author: as Roscommon advised, "Chuse an *Author* as you chuse a *Friend*."[21] But the "Dedication" shows the situation to be much more complicated. Even with an author less encumbered by previous translators, commentators, and critics than Virgil, the relation between translator and author is forcibly mediated by time, distance, cultural distinctiveness, or any combination of these. The audience further complicates the relation. Dryden is a poet speaking of a poet to a readership that already knows him; thus Virgil, as many critics have suggested, becomes a transparent mask through which Dryden can communicate something of himself. The traditional division between original authorship and translation with which we have seen Dryden struggling gradually becomes nuanced through the realization, first, that absolute "originality" is a figment ("The Poet, who borrows nothing from others, has yet to be Born," 5:304) and, furthermore, that there are different kinds of unoriginality, not only within "imitation" but within translation as well.

Dryden is at some pains to limit his indebtedness to Lauderdale's translation, just as in the following century John Ozell, Alexander Pope, and many others will deny or minimize their (greater) reliance on Anne Dacier's French prose translation of Homer in the preparation of their English verse versions. "Secondhand translation" will fall under considerable opprobrium, but translators' readings of one another will continue to haunt their texts. The apparently simple binary relation

Author : Translator (or Author : Public)

is in fact a ternary relation, one that may be construed in two versions:

Author/Text : [Translator] : Public

in which the "invisible" translator is thought to render the author in a "noiseless" transaction; or, more accurately,

Translator : Author/Text : Public

in which the translator communicates something of him or herself to the reader. Such schematization does not render, of course, the heterogeneity possible within each of the terms, or the feedback loops possible between them. And, as we have seen, the relation is almost inevitably further mediated by competing translations or other preexisting cultural interpretations. In addition, one must remember that no terms of the relation are ever fixed; rather, they are subject to time and change in relation to one another.

Operating through these multiple, shifting circuits, translation manipulates its source text, hiding it from view, however "true" it may seek to be. As Paul Hammond puts it, "Translation entails the management of loss."[22] Creation stemming from loss is of course a deeply Virgilian theme, emblematized again and again as Aeneas reaches out to apparitions and ghosts of those he has loved—his parents, Creusa, Dido—whose deaths must somehow be made bearable, given meaning, through the final success of his mission. Aeneas will ultimately achieve a form of "restoration" following the destruction of Troy, but in a new place and in changed circumstances. And such is Dryden's sense of the inadequacy of his English version that he refuses to set it alongside the Latin, lest the losses become too apparent.

Memory, too, entails loss and shapes its objects. In a perceptive essay, David B. Morris suggests that for Dryden, memory is "a conscious effort to reshape the past" in order to bring forth "a realm that is already lost."[23] Unlike classical theories of memory that emphasized mental "space" and its organization into topoi, or "places," modern notions underscore memory's relation to temporality.[24] For Thomas Hobbes, who also turned from explicitly political writing to translation late in life, memory is not simply a replacement for absence or loss; rather, it *is* loss, figured as materialist "decay."[25] Sense impressions produce mental images ("imagination") that fade over time. The unending trajectory of bodies in motion carries with it an implicit postulate of inertia, a slowing down or dissipation of energy and vivacity, conceived as either time or space, both of which produce "distance." Language, according to Hobbes, is invented because thoughts are "apt to slip out of memory."[26] Ultimately, then, it is language that must assume the responsibility of recollection. This understanding of writing as reparative is intensified in the process of translation, which surmounts time and distance, recuperating and making present a voice, a poet, a culture.

Just as memory is a vestige of an earlier state, so too is translation the "afterlife" or survival of a work, as Benjamin put it, surviving to tell us less about the "content" of the work than about the nature of language and the relations among languages.[27] The "Dedication" offers us a "contentless" account (insofar as it is emotionless and affectless) of loss and remembrance: a set of relationships between the "living and the dead" that bring us to a new understanding and a new authorial voice in the present. This understanding is achieved through a process analogous to that of mourning. Like the work of mourning, translation and memory maintain temporal distinctions even as they seek to reconcile us to loss through identifications in the present. Dryden's translation does not set itself in an explicit context of mourning, as Denham's does, but it is no less a consolatory, compensatory project. Indeed, by subsuming Denham's stated aims within his own, Dryden enables the process to move beyond mourning for a single death, however emblematic, to achieve a fuller experience of temporality in which new forms of consciousness become possible. We have seen in the example of Denham's dedicatory epistle to Charles II how a translation can come to stand as an emblem of exile, loss, and (partial) recovery, as well as the ways in which translation enables Segrais and Dryden to consider various forms of temporality. Being-a-translator, or being-in-translation, becomes a way to confront being-in-time.[28]

To understand what is potentially at stake here, let us reflect momentarily on the process of mourning itself, especially in relation to time and the process of identity formation. In "Mourning and Melancholia," Freud associates time and mourning by noting that "time is needed for the command of reality-testing to be carried out in detail"—that is, for the ego to assure itself that the lost love object is really and truly dead, gone.[29] In the essay, of course, Freud is only concerned with the regular workings of mourning inasmuch as they shed light on its more disturbing variants, "pathological mourning" (in which the mourner blames him- or herself for the death of the loved one) and, especially, "melancholia," or depression. His interest in the ego's identification with the object is thus largely limited to narcissistic identification that turns the loss of the object into a loss of self. Further forms of identification in mourning, and further aspects of temporality, are explored in the work of Nicolas Abraham and Maria Torok, for whom failed mourning, or "incorporation," has its own mark of temporality, its "commemorative monument," within the self.[30] Extending Freud's discussion of oral libidinal identifications in melancholia, they contrast incorporation with introjection, which is the model of a successful working-through achieved through a fully realized mourning (262). The time of incorporation is the time of a frozen moment, while the time of introjection is the time of a process. Incorporation oversees the constitution of a "crypt," a carefully compartmentalized, secluded, and excluded part of the ego in which the lost one is kept, enabling the ego to deny the loss.[31]

The ambiguity—and the power—of translation, however, lies in its availability to more than one program. If neoclassical translation practice is understood as an illusory presentism ("as if he had been born in the present age") that "swallows" or denies pastness and otherness, then one could perhaps read therein incorporation's "anti-metaphors" or "active destruction" of figuration/introjection.[32] Or if the translator's task is viewed as a compartmentalizing of self before the imaginary power of the Other, then it can only be perceived as abject and fraught with unresolved tensions.[33] But, as we have seen in the "Dedication," such compartmentalization is not the only option. In the "Dedication," "therapeutic" identification, a transferential process with Virgil and a host of poet/translator predecessors, provides Dryden with a poetic "restoration," which despite containing crypts, forgotten debts, and unredeemed losses, still succeeds in establishing a renewed poetic authority. The passage through translation ensures that this renewed authority does not suffer from "delusions of mastery" but instead has achieved its provisional, dialogic, temporally bound voice, a voice aware of its own contingency.[34]

If we consider, then, what is at stake for the neoclassical translators as they reflect on their own and others' projects, we find constantly recurring questions of identity, authorial identity, and perhaps to a certain degree personal identity. Translation projects are fueled by absence, time, and desire: desire to recreate past writers, to make them speak again in one's own voice, and also to recuperate one's own language, one's own voice. The object of conquest is not the Other but one's own native speech, which must be regained—hence the profound appeal of translation projects for royalist exiles Denham, Cowley, Sherburne, and others, and hence too their increased attraction for Dryden when he finds himself a political outcast in the 1690s. Although there doubtless are nuances to be drawn from the differing social and political situations of the French translators, it is significant that Dryden imagines Segrais as "having no voice" ("I dwell on many things which he durst not touch," 5:287); as we have seen, Segrais too is a practitioner of oblique authorship in his collaborative salon projects, an authorial ambivalence reinforced by his assumption of the role of translator. Translation enables writers to overcome a loss, to return from speechlessness to speech. The risk, of course, is the loss of identity, the loss of voice, the submersion of translator into original author.

We have seen this concern in numerous abject accounts of the translator's authorial being, such as Denham's lines to Fanshaw: "Such is our Pride, our Folly, or our Fate, / That few but such as cannot write, translate." Another example is Cowley's apparent ambivalence regarding the translator's role: "I am not so much enamoured of the *Name Translator*, as not to wish rather to be *Something Better*, though it want yet a *Name*." The same complaint had also appeared in France in Guillaume Colletet's 1637 verse *Discours contre la traduction*: "I've been subjected to enough, I'm tired of imitating, / Translating is tiresome if you're able to invent."[35] Colletet's seriocomic *Discours* points to the concept of translation prevalent just before the innovations of d'Ablancourt and his friends. And such complaints contain the potential for an ennobled understanding of the translator's role, as demonstrated by Denham's "few" and Cowley's wish for a new and better name to describe his poetic role. One could relate this theme to the omnipresent topos of translation as "struggle," between author and translator.[36] The psychological dimension of these alternatives—self lost, self regained—surely is part of what drives the constant recourse to formulations of the "middle way."

Dryden seeks a means of recovering a past and a language that does not lead to a loss of identity but instead offers a renewed, mutable form of subjectivity that escapes the dichotomy of self and other. Like introjection, his projects succeed in establishing the possibility for ongoing speech and dialogue based on the recognition and integration of the past (Virgil) or the other (Segrais). Indeed, although the integration of these two "others," Virgil and Segrais (and other critics and translators), poses some diverging questions, it is nevertheless very much part of the same process. Dryden *is* Virgil "translated," as he reads his career into that of the Roman poet; he can also cast himself as a "variant" or unrealized possibility of Segrais, a "Segrais" minus his rationalism, a Segrais born into a different political environment.

Like the texts it takes as its object, the activity of translating is itself lifted up and brought over in a provisional sort of *Aufhebung*, constantly carried on in time and in the process of becoming. To speak of translation in terms of mourning is to understand it as operating on multiple levels as a cultural and linguistic *process*. Translation bespeaks a particular need to take otherness and pastness into account, in all of their difference, as a means of coming to terms with the present. It is a fuller experience of the present that simultaneously allows room for the dimensionality of the nonpresent. An awareness of temporality actually saves us from loss by instigating a distance or depth that prevents everything from collapsing into the black hole of negation and absence. Of course, one may approach the experience in different ways, or it may function differently in different contexts. Dryden's historical project is not exactly that of d'Ablancourt or Denham, nor is it that of Segrais or Dacier. Together they reflect the complexity and diversity of investments in the neoclassical school.

Nicolas Abraham proposes the neologisms "anasemia" and "anasemic discourse" to describe a form of commentary or repetition that reveals or opens up a hitherto unrecognized preoriginary *récit*, or "fable," within a given discourse. This process of reading the language of psychoanalysis back onto itself led Abraham and Torok to give the title *Anasémies* to their collective enterprise and led Derrida to coin the phrase "anasemic translation" in his preface to *L'Ecorce et le noyau*.[37] Our project here is to read back the *récit* within translation theory, to consider its enabling conditions and constraints, its possibilities for both openness and closure.

One further illustration of the connections between translation, mourning, debt, and recognition can be found in William Gifford's preface to his translation of Juvenal, a remarkably engaging autobiography detailing Gifford's rise from charity case to university-educated tutor to the son of Lord Grosvenor. Gifford writes, "I began this unadorned narrative on the 15th of January, 1801: twenty years have therefore elapsed since I lost my benefactor and my friend. In the interval I have wept a thousand times at the recollection of his goodness."[38] The translation project was begun at the behest of the man who rescued Gifford from an apprenticeship and saw him sent down to Oxford, delayed after the benefactor's death, and returned to over two decades, and it is bound up in Gifford's mind with various relationships to people who have died: his benefactor, William Cookesley; his parents, who died too soon; his younger brother who died at sea before Gifford was in a position to help him. Additionally, there are more material debts on Gifford's mind, money "owed" to people who took out subscriptions to the Juvenal translation when Cookesley first proposed it as a source of revenue while at Oxford. Two weeks later, on January 15, 1781, Cookesley died, and Gifford realized he was not yet up to the task of producing the translation, but although he refunded as much of the subscription money as he could, some subscribers proved elusive and others refused reimbursement. Twenty years later, Gifford hopes to make good on those debts. Shortly after publication, Gifford finds himself denying other sorts of debts, however, as he defends himself against a reviewer who claimed that much of the Juvenal translation was "borrowed plumage" from Dryden; Gifford wants both to deny the charge and to assert his profound admiration for Dryden—a pair of alternatives in which, again, the translation itself becomes the "middle way."[39]

Published at the dawn of a new century, what is innovative about Gifford's translation is not—as the hostile reviewer noted—its style or its approach to Juvenal. Rather, what is striking is the ease and explicitness with which the translator situates the translation within the affective economy of his own life and the singular aptness of such a project for retiring so many unfulfilled desires and debts, whether intellectual, monetary, or personal. For Gifford, as for his predecessor Dryden and many others, the translation allows him to forgo the crypt and experience *le temps retrouvé*, with twenty years (and more) finally regained, made present, and resolved.

("affective economy of his own life")

CHAPTER 4

Meaning and Modernity

Anne Dacier and the Homer Debate

'Both difference and sameness resonate in the uncanny "otherness" of the translation' p. 134. Dacier's transl. of Homer's Iliad?

Arguably the foremost classical scholar of her generation, Anne Dacier produced a series of annotated translations of Greek and Latin literature for the Delphin series that set the standard for European translations of the classics.[1] In 1712, she brought out her long-awaited prose translation of the *Iliad*, followed by the *Odyssey* in 1716. With each she included copious notes and extended prefaces. These prefaces, along with other polemical pieces, mark her entry into the *Querelle d'Homère* or Homer debate, the "final phase" of the Quarrel of Ancients and Moderns, the literary-philosophical debate that traditional intellectual history sees as having heralded in the Enlightenment through the victory of the Moderns. Dacier, needless to say, supported Homer against what she saw as the contemporary decline in standards of taste. Yet, as a careful reading of Dacier and her "modern" interlocutors shows, there are issues at stake other than the usual "traditionalism vs. progressivism" divide. Their debate over translatability and meaning would continue to reverberate in Enlightenment linguistics and semiotics, and it appears that in some respects, at least, Dacier was more "modern" than the Moderns.[2] Although the Moderns examined here—Houdar de la Motte, Thémiseul de Saint-Hyacinthe, and the abbé de Pons—raise significant questions regarding the status of classical culture and our ability to gain access to it through reading, they are ultimately crippled by a monolingualism that is as much philosophical as linguistic. Dacier and her ally Etienne de Fourmont, however, bring a more nuanced sense of the materiality of language and its interaction with lived existence, as well as a greater appreciation for cultural otherness.

The Quarrel of Ancients and Moderns and the period of the Homer debate in particular have produced mixed reactions from literary historians. Traditional accounts tend to celebrate the victory of the Moderns as the rise of *l'esprit critique*, belief in progress, artistic innovation, and so on. Even nineteenth-century historian H. Rigault, whose sympathy with the Ancients leads him to respond point for point to Charles Perrault in his "analysis" of Perrault's *Parallèle des anciens et des modernes* (1688), and who concludes his study by expressing his regret for the decline of classical studies (which he blames on the Quarrel), nevertheless reaffirms his own place as a Modern: "I believe in progress."[3] In what remains the most thorough modern survey of the debate, Noémi Hepp analyzes the complexity of the classical heritage in the Enlightenment.[4] Recently, Joan DeJean has argued persuasively that we should see the debate in terms of the development of the "public" in Old Regime France; she also claims (less persuasively, in my view) that the Homer debate prefigures the Culture Wars in the late twentieth-century United States and, unlike Rigault, believes that ultimately the Ancients triumphed, to the detriment of progressive ideals.[5]

The decades-old Quarrel of Ancients and Moderns flared up anew when Antoine Houdar de la Motte published his modernizing verse translation of the *Iliad* in 1714. Later that year, Dacier attacked both La Motte's introductory "Discours sur Homere" and the translation itself in her line-by-line rebuttal, *Des Causes de la corruption du goust*. Also in 1714, Jean-François de Pons published a thirty-page pamphlet, *Lettre à Monsieur *** sur l'Iliade de M. de la Motte*, apparently intended to second La Motte's "Discours," since it makes no reference to *Des Causes*. Later, following the publication of Dacier's *Odyssey*, Pons wrote the more extensive *Dissertation sur le poeme epique, contre la doctrine de M. D. . . .* , published in the *Mercure* in January 1717. The debate reached its most intense moment in 1715, with the publication of Thémiseul de Saint-Hyacinthe's fifty-page *Lettre à Madame Dacier, Sur son livre des Causes de la Corruption du goust*; La Motte's own reply to Dacier in *Réflexions sur la critique*; and a number of works by other participants. Dacier and La Motte engaged in a public reconciliation in the spring of 1716, however, and the tone of the print debate calmed, with several works attempting to moderate the Quarrel, including Etienne de Fourmont's *Examen pacifique de la querelle de Madame Dacier et de Monsieur de la Motte sur Homère*. It is my purpose here not to give a strict summary of the debate but rather to call attention to the significant linguistic and epistemological issues that it raised. The prevalence of the exegetical or "point-counterpoint" approach in Dacier, La Motte, Fourmont, and others makes for strange reading, as passages echo and re-echo in the opposing camps. I will focus on several recurring issues: the relationship of language to thought, the accessibility of the past, and the forms of knowledge and aesthetic experience that are available through foreign languages, through one's own language, and through translation.

In addition to La Motte, Dacier levels her critique at an earlier participant in the Quarrel, Charles Perrault. Perrault's *Parallèle* of 1688, one of the first "assaults" in the Quarrel of Ancients and Moderns, is still witty and readable today, but alongside its well-known affirmation of progress in the sciences and the arts, it offers passages that would have trouble winning many twenty-first-century converts, particularly in the discussion of translation. One side of the argument is an extension of Perrault's view that "we are the Ancients"—that is, the "adult" culture that has matured over time and benefited from the lessons of history—whereas classical Greece and Rome represent cultural infancy.[6] The other side involves a particular view of the mental processes involved in speaking or possessing a language. Perrault's mouthpiece in the dialogue, the abbé, supposedly knows both Latin and Greek perfectly (which was *not* the case for Perrault), but on a couple of occasions, he proclaims not only that a good prose translation makes anyone qualified to pronounce judgment on classical texts but also that reading texts in translation offers *advantages* over reading them in the original.

The abbé argues that since Latin and Greek are dead languages, our ignorance of their authentic pronunciation is emblematic of our alienation from the true, lived experience that native speakers enjoy. He claims that we enjoy an advantage by reading in translation: when we read a foreign language, we devote part of our attention to silently "translating" the text, whereas when reading in our native tongue, we give undivided attention to the substance of the text (2:10–11). The belief that non-native readers of a language inevitably "translate" into their own tongues as they read (a practice common among beginning language students, perhaps, but who else?) is repeated by La Motte and others. The abbé goes on to distinguish between stylistic "elegance," which non-native speakers cannot ever truly judge, and substantive "eloquence," which a faithful prose translation can convey. Furthermore, he argues, the reader of a translation benefits from the translator's prolonged contact with the text and all previous commentary: "Just as a Translator understands a text better after having taken the trouble to translate it, we have the same advantage in reading his translation" (2:11–12).

It is noteworthy that here Perrault appears to recognize that a translation is, after all, an interpretation and not a "reproduction," but this insight does not deter him from holding that there must be one true interpretation, just as there is one true meaning, one verifiable "éloquence," which may be—must be—distinguished from the ornaments of style. He concedes that Homer may indeed be "mélodieux" (3:108), but stylistic effects remain superficial and in any event are not up to contemporary standards of diction (the epithets are line fillers, or *chevilles*; the variety of dialects and forms of speech represent a defect in the unity of tone). The abbé proposes a supposedly literal paraphrase to show that Homer is clumsy, vulgar, and frequently ridiculous.

Histories of translation theory often touch on the Homer debate as exemplifying the reign of classical taste over unruly originals. Where an original did not correspond to current moral or aesthetic standards, it had to be "improved." Such, at any rate, was the reputation of the belles infidèles. Nevertheless, it was a huge leap from the meticulous, if strongly localized, translations by d'Ablancourt and his followers to La Motte's 1714 verse translation (or adaptation) of the *Iliad*, in which he reduced the twenty-four books to twelve and cleaned up the action by deleting such "digressions" as the account of Achilles' shield. La Motte did not know Greek himself, and based his work on Latin versions and Dacier's French prose version. Although La Motte's proclamation in his prefatory "L'Ombre d'Homere" may strike us as fatuous—

Homer left me his Muse
And if pride does not delude me
I will do what he would have done.[7]

—this was precisely the claim made by the abbé de Pons in the ensuing quarrel with Dacier: "If Homer with his same genius and taste were born in our time," then doubtless he would have achieved as excellent a style in French as the real Homer achieved in Greek.[8]

Although the topos is familiar, the emphasis has shifted from prosopopoeia ("making the author speak") to hypothesis ("if Homer were French").

Homer would doubtless have said "something different" in French, and in La Motte's hands he proceeds to do just that. Even today, critics are divided on the meaning of La Motte's free approach: is it an example of naked ethnocentric aggression, or is it an important "modernizing" gesture that paves the way for Enlightenment critique?[9] Translation historian Edmond Cary once even argued that both La Motte and Dacier are guilty of domesticating their original (he slightly more than she).[10] Since the two translations appeared vastly different to their contemporary readers, however, Cary's claim casts into sharp relief our need to tune our latter-day hearing and sensitize ourselves to the issues that distinguished Dacier's and La Motte's versions in their day. Yet contemporary critiques of "ethnocentric" translation do have the merit of making us reflect on the intolerance of the Moderns. Decrying Homer's "disfigured" plot and "bizarre" characters, Pons expresses his satisfaction that La Motte's "great genius" has so "disguised the Greek monster that, far from shocking us, he is charming to our gaze."[11]

Joseph Levine argues that the Moderns' self-conscious decision to adapt and localize indicates that they at least were aware of the cultural distance that lay between them and the classical world, whereas the Ancients maintained an illusory identification with the past.[12] I would argue, though, that the writings of Fourmont and Dacier show a highly developed linguistic sensitivity—less an "identification with the past" than an awareness of the world-disclosing capacities of language. Arguments over the historical existence of Homer or the significance of Achilles' shield bespeak not so much the Ancients' misguided antiquarianism or naive "positivism" as a failure of the Moderns to imagine subjectivities different from their own.

In the end, the discussion between Dacier and her interlocutors hinges on the questions of whether one could authentically access the past and whether French or Greek is a better instrument. In a larger sense, the debaters are struggling with the relation of language—any language—to experience. Some of the most provocative and interesting passages occur in the discussions of "expression" and "diction," or the multiple ways in which languages can convey meaning. For example, Dacier stirred up a hornet's nest in her preface to the *Iliad* with her claim that any French translation, including her own, would appear "cold" compared to Homer's Greek, and that French was "always well-behaved, or rather always timid" and lacking any "freedom."[13] Dacier's observation that classical *bon usage* had rendered French a less-than-perfect instrument for rendering Homeric Greek was taken by the Moderns as an assault on the national language. "On what is founded this supposed disadvantage of our language?" sputtered La Motte in his *Discours sur Homere*. "Does it lack words? Just what is it not able to express?"[14] Pons took up the cause of French by recalling the literary glories of the past century: "Did French not well serve Corneille, Racine, Moliere, Boileau, la Fontaine?"[15]

Dacier simply treated La Motte's question as absurd in *Des Causes*, but he returned to the issue in his *Reflexions*, where he dismissed as an "illusion" the expressivity and "harmony" that for her rendered Greek so unlike French.[16] Going on the conventional linguistic wisdom of the day, according to which verbal harmony, and indeed words themselves, were completely distinct from meaning, or *sens*, La Motte claimed that if there were any worthwhile meaning in Homer, then it would be perfectly translatable: "Any rational meaning, regardless of the language in which it was conceived, can be transported into ours."[17] What is at stake for La Motte and others is no less than the fabled French *clarté* that for theoreticians throughout the seventeenth and eighteenth centuries assured the adequation of French to the structures of cognition.[18] He is thus skeptical to the point of derision when Dacier claims that the verb in a particular passage might have two different meanings: "I confess frankly that I do not believe it."[19]

Resistance to ambiguity and multiple meanings guides (and is guided by) La Motte's view of the French language as the limpid vehicle of rational thought, but he is hampered from exploring the relative merits of French and Greek by his ignorance of Greek. Undaunted, he asks in the *Réflexions* whether or not any living human being can truly understand Greek as it was understood by Homer. He points out that we learn our own language and other living languages "through habitual exchange with those who speak them," whereas we can only learn dead languages "by means of languages we already know"—in other words, via an intermediary that stands between us and the living voice of l'usage and prevents us from developing the exquisite tact, the feel for the language that alone permits us to judge on matters of taste. The normally civil La Motte states flatly that these considerations make clear "Madame Dacier's incompetence in precisely judging Homer's expression."[20]

What does it mean to *know* a second language, especially when we have no contact with living speakers? This is one of the most profound questions of the debate. The abbé de Pons too raised it when he returned to the question of language, expressiveness, and meaning in his "Dissertation on languages in general and French in particular," which took up a number of themes from the Homer debate. Like Perrault and La Motte, Pons is skeptical regarding our potential for truly being able to enter into and thoroughly understand dead languages. Pons wonders, Why do scholars claim that it is impossible to render the beauties of Greek or Latin in French? It cannot be any lack of richness in French. (Like La Motte, Pons tends to come to the defense of the French language even when it is not under attack.) Instead, he speculates, this sense of inadequacy has more to do with the translators' own lack of certainty of the "fixed expressions" in Greek and the more generalized problem of rendering private experience in language.

In a fascinating passage, Pons recapitulates what he imagines to be the mental state of a translator working through a passage in Latin or Greek. It is taken as a given that one cannot know "the true properties of each expression," and therefore the translator's imagination "fills up with all the vast range of meanings and accessory ideas of which he senses the basic expressed idea might be susceptible," leaving him in a "stunned, delirious" state.[21] Thus, although the original author must have had a specific meaning in mind as he wrote, the translator's lack of access to the living language prevents him from the certitude of knowing which of a range of similar expressions is the precise equivalent of the foreign term. Pons has no doubt that such a precise equivalent, "un sens unique," exists—the problem lies in our incapacity to identify it.

In the abbé's account, the translator is at last forced to choose among the "various confusing meanings that obsess him." Alas, since no single meaning can ever encompass the inebriating experience of contemplating all possibilities at once, the translator vents his frustration: "Wretched language! You will never reproduce in me the sentiments I felt" (182–84). In order to uphold the principle of linguistic clarity and univocity, Pons ascribes all ambiguity and confusion to the translator's own befuddlement. His epistemological narrative is not meant, presumably, to claim that linguistic expression is faulty in its translation of private experience—although I think that this skeptical view subtends his argument, given the translator's seeming inability to articulate or "translate" his own states of mind. He does, however, hold that language expresses the immediacy and specificity of lived historical moments; thus *vacher* means one thing to a peasant, something else to an educated city dweller (who furthermore knows the distinction between *vacher* and *berger*).[22] Pons argues that language holds a "fixed" meaning and that if we knew a language perfectly, we could accede to that meaning: "The text would offer the same meaning to everyone" (185).

The Moderns' view is contested at length in Etienne Fourmont's *Examen pacifique* (1716). Fourmont, who was professor of Arabic and Middle-Eastern languages at the Collège royal de France, member of the Académie des inscriptions, and one of the first serious scholars of Chinese in Europe, takes on the Moderns' account of language in his chapter "De l'expression."[23] Responding directly to La Motte's denial that a Greek verb could have two separate meanings, Fourmont recognizes that ultimately it comes down to one major question: "Do we know ancient languages?" (279). He thus proceeds to elaborate a theory of language acquisition, one that is inflected, like La Motte's, by the theories of the Port-Royal grammarians, but also by his own experience in working with non-European texts.

Basing his argument on primary language acquisition in early childhood, La Motte had contended that language acquisition inevitably passes through an intermediary, thus assuring that we possess "the same idea" as our model. He went on to argue that we, lacking a native informant (such as a parent or nurse) in acquiring a dead language, must pass through the intermediary of the first language, hence distancing ourselves from the second language's lived reality.[24] According to Fourmont, language involves three components: "terms," "phrases," and the resultant "feelings and sentiments." He argues that learning the individual terms of an ancient tongue is no different from learning any modern language, which can be accomplished without direct contact with native speakers. As for our ability to judge "phrases," Fourmont observes that we in fact do look to academicians (such as La Motte) to arbitrate matters of taste, not "just anyone." La Motte had proudly sided with those "who threw off the yoke of authority" in rejecting Homer—but Fourmont accuses him of misappropriating the discourse of Enlightenment. It is no slavish deferral to authority, he argues, to recognize the expertise of those who have studied something in depth (292). Fourmont goes on to underscore the importance of *reading* for the greater grasp of one's language and the improvement of one's style, noting that this is one of the key reasons why we read excellent writers—such as La Motte, for example (293). It is Fourmont who is "modern" here: in order to minimize or even deny an essential difference between "living" and "dead" languages, he has denied an older notion, exemplified in Vaugelas, that living speech is the primary determinant of l'usage. According to that older notion, the primacy of the spoken word ensured that only the court elite could be said to be the arbiters of the language; Fourmont, by contrast, extends the capacity to judge throughout the wider-ranging print culture, which remains the same and is available to all, whether the language is living or dead. What changes, he claims, is pronunciation, which has no effect on meaning (296–97).

Fourmont thus accepts the historicity and change of language without capitulating to the requirement of physical contact with living speakers. His primary insight is to point out that La Motte's and Pons's reasoning applies equally well to one's native tongue, which few people, if any, ever *know* in its entirety, in all of its moments and contexts, but which in order to be apprehended in all its nuances, must be approached through writing— and thus our knowledge of ancient languages can be as thorough as our (never entirely complete) knowledge of our native tongue. He concludes the chapter by suggesting that if La Motte were to study another language, he would see things differently and realize "that we know as little French as we know Latin or Greek and that . . . living languages have no advantage over dead ones" (315–16). Wide reading in different languages, argues Fourmont, and comparative reading in different genres, can further develop one's "ear" (295). Reading thus remains rooted in experience—a point that is also important to Dacier. Both Dacier and Fourmont display the linguistic awareness that comes from actual work with more than one language; linguistic difference, time, change, and the potential effects on "the ear" open up different zones of meaning.

Anne Le Fèvre Dacier had long been established as a prominent scholar when she published her translations of Homer. While she evidently possessed considerable social skills—numerous contemporary accounts attest to a widespread astonishment that the learned lady could actually be pleasant to chat with!—she was fully capable of mustering an impressive arsenal of irritation, biting irony, and scathing line-by-line close readings of her opponents in her polemical writings, especially her six-hundred-page reply to La Motte, *Des Causes de la corruption du goust* (1714). Her fierce polemical style, particularly when juxtaposed with La Motte's more worldly approach, has rendered readers uncomfortable in her day and our own. It is worth asking whether as a woman she was held to a stricter standard of civility in public debate than were men.[25] We also sometimes lose sight of the subtler forms of rudeness of her interlocutors. Consider the tactics of La Motte's defenders, Thémiseul de Saint-Hyacinthe and the abbé de Pons. Like Perrault earlier, Pons claims that her prose translation, far from enhancing Homer's reputation, instead makes us realize the extent to which his reputation has been inflated.[26] Saint-Hyacinthe declares that only a widespread ignorance of Greek has hitherto protected Homer from scrutiny and that by exposing

him "to broad daylight" she has inspired others to view him with a critical eye.[27] This strategy is particularly clever, allowing La Motte's defenders
to render homage to Dacier's scholarship even as they denigrate her poet,
and it paradoxically allows their misogyny free rein. For if Dacier is such a
good scholar-translator, it can only be by some weird female whim that she
bestows such disproportionate affection on Homer. Saint-Hyacinthe slyly
insinuates that she has a "weakness" (entêtement) for Homer (2) and expresses mock surprise that "a Lady who brings such honor to her sex and to
her country, lets herself be blinded by her preoccupation for a man who has
been dead for three thousand years" (10). Pons also feels that Dacier's critical faculty is not commensurate with her erudition, dismissing her for her
uncritical adoption of Aristotle's "dogmas."[28]

The text that has tended to get lost in the clamor is sadly one of the rich-
est: Dacier's 1712 preface to the *Iliad*. Although recognized by historians of
translation and excerpted in various anthologies, the seventy-page preface
has never been reprinted in full or produced in facsimile as have a number
of later pieces in the Querelle d'Homère.[29] The preface is not devoted, as
DeJean would have it, to "an extended diatribe against the values that novels
allegedly produce" but is a much more wide-ranging and nuanced piece.[30]
(The discussion of novels and affectivity takes up less than 10 percent of
the text.) And although it is clearly written with at least one adversary in
mind—Perrault—the distance in time between his *Parallèle* and her *Iliad*
allows for a less attack-oriented rhetoric than the inflammatory *Des Causes*.
Unlike *Des Causes* and most of the pieces in the later debate that are organized as line-by-line refutations of an interlocutor's texts, the *Iliad* preface is
structured in terms of Dacier's own concerns. The main divisions of the text
reflect what she terms the "difficulties" she encountered in the course of her
project. While analyzing Plato's criticisms of Homer and setting forth an
"ethico-allegorical" interpretation that aligns the *Iliad* with the teachings of
Christianity, she also succeeds in countering Perrault's portrayal of Homer.
The interpretive passages speak directly to his accusation that Homer's world
is primitive and ludicrous. She also offers an alternative to the skeptical view
that casts doubt on the expressive capacities of dead languages or even their
ability to communicate anything at all.

Dacier discusses five difficulties in the translation of Homer, most of
them having to do with the problem of bridging the cultural differences
between his world and early eighteenth-century France. They include the
French misunderstanding of the nature of the epic, lack of patience with

"allegories" and "fables," contempt for the apparent rusticity and simplicity of the "manners and characters" of Homeric Greece, and impatience with "fictions," supernatural events, and other infractions of verisimilitude, *vraisemblance*. The fifth and greatest difficulty concerns Homer's language, *la diction*. In a sense, the first difficulty subsumes the next three; Dacier's entire discussion and her notes are aimed at helping the reader enter into the epic genre and understand its conventions, rendering Homer more comprehensible if not less foreign. Thus the allegories, while running counter to contemporary taste ("Our age disdains these veils and shadows and esteems only what is simple and clear"), are compatible with Christian morality;[31] the supernatural "fictions" can be seen as *vraisemblables* inasmuch as they are part of a self-consistent universe (a more sophisticated treatment of vraisemblance than is usual in the period).

But if Dacier is concerned with building bridges and drawing parallels between Homer's world and ours, her discussions of *moeurs* and diction bespeak the need to respect the ongoing "foreignness" of the *Iliad*. Initially her view seems to be simply a nostalgia for an impossible past: "Nature as it was in its first simplicity and before it fell from its dignity and nobility . . . I confess that I have not sought to soften the force of his vision in order to bring it closer to our century" (xxi). The discussion turns, however, to a more nuanced examination of historical representation. Manners, or *moeurs*, determine the "character" of an age. Epic is intended to render moeurs—not necessarily to provide a literal depiction of reality itself—and actions stem from manners as their logical consequences (xxi). Appreciation of epic is bound up with fidelity to the pastness of the past, but it should not be construed as a simplistic or literal notion of representation. Unlike modern "historical" novels, whose period settings and historical personages are but transparent masks for the present day, Dacier argues both that the epic endeavors to be true to its subject and that in order to understand epic, we need to be willing to enter its world, rather than distorting it to fit ours: "Homer could not conform himself to the customs of later centuries; it is up to later centuries to make room for the customs of his age" (xxii).[32]

Should we embellish the past in order to mark our admiration for it? Hardly, says Dacier: "I find these ancient times all the more beautiful inasmuch as they do not resemble ours" (xxiii). The parallel between "manners" and "diction," between understanding and language, is borne out with a quotation from Aristotle: "That which comes from abroad appears admirable, and that which is admirable pleases and provides enjoyment" (xxiii).

Dacier's preface thus far, then, attempts to create schemas for understanding Homer, while continuing to respect his fundamental difference. These issues of interpretation are also issues of translation, as her following discussion of Homer's language shows.

The discussion of "diction" proves to be a dense and fertile discussion of language and aesthetics. While relying on Aristotle's distinctions between "ordinary" and "poetic" usage, Dacier gives her own account of what makes Homer's language powerful.[33] She speaks at length about the *sound* of Homer's verse, which she characterizes by a number of terms equating "sound" and "harmony" with "life," "animation," or "soul": "Let no one claim that it is an error to emphasize ideas and things by the choice, the sound, and the harmony of words" (xxviii). Harmony subtends a discourse of seduction and mastery; it provides a sensuous enhancement that enables ideas to "reign over the mind."

Dacier goes on to state that beauty has two aspects: clarity (*clarté*) and nobility (*noblesse*). The former stems from "proper words" and the latter from "borrowed words," or figurative terms. Homer's language is enriched— and not degraded, as Perrault had argued—by his attention to physical details as well as to heroic actions, his ability to muster *mots propres* (which "do not change") rather than *mots figurés*, and his ability to mix high and low terms by means of his harmonious style. This sort of "mixed composition" incorporating both figurative and proper, Dacier concedes, is "unknown in our language" (xxxii). French, according to Dacier, lacks the features of Greek syntax and harmony that would enable it to accommodate the mixed style, and it is thus "incapable of rendering most of the beauties that burst forth in this poetry" (xxxii). This argument would be deformed later in the debate as an indictment of French's expressive qualities in general.[34] Pons, as we have seen, insists on the historicity of language even as he claims that its meaning is invariable and fixed—and thus inaccessible over time. Dacier, by contrast, is less willing to divorce meaning from linguistic expression, signified from signifier. The sound/word allows us access to meaning, or "meaningfulness," meaning-effects. That link does not abolish aesthetic or cultural difference, but nevertheless gives us a possibility for establishing some sort of connection of understanding or empathy.

It may thus seem surprising that Dacier gives us a prose translation. In a much-cited passage, she compares her version to a mummified Helen of Troy: "You will not see those flashing eyes, that complexion animated by the most lively, natural colors, that charisma that gave rise to so much love . . .

but you will recognize the perfection and beauty of her features, her large eyes, her small mouth, the arc of her fair brow; you will discover her noble and majestic form" (xxxv). Helen—or rather Homer—is "structurally" recognizable. Perception of form enables the imagination to vivify the rest— and not imagination alone. Just as she indicated the evocative qualities of "harmony" in Greek, so here Dacier argues that certain utterances, while never truly able to reproduce the effects of the original, can nevertheless recapture them in subtle ways, or offer alternatives. Homer is recognizable as Homer because the translation is free from the conventions and constraints of French metrics. Dacier sums up her thinking with a paradox—"Poets translated into verse cease to be poets" (xxxvii)—and praises the suppleness of prose, which "can follow all the poet's ideas, preserve the beauty of his images, say all that he said" (xxxvii–xxxviii). Dacier's emphasis is on speaking (*dire*); French prose can "say what Homer said" even if French verse will never "do" what Homer "does." Prose has "precision, beauty, and force" that poetry cannot equal (xxxix). But this seemingly modest program ultimately lays a great deal of weight on the poetic capacity of prose, its abilities to suggest more than it "says" through rhythm and sound, enabling a prose version to become "a second original" (xl).

Indeed, Dacier's translation continues to be appreciated for its writerly qualities, the forthright verve and rhythm of the prose.[35] She does not attempt to render the formulaic style or the epithets, she occasionally cleans up "vulgarisms," and she is said not to understand Homer's humor. To this extent, perhaps, she may be seen as remaining within the confines of classical taste. In her theoretical writings, however, she clearly has moved beyond classicism. Her impatience with the tameness of her contemporaries' writing and her desire for "bold strokes" intimate an aesthetic sensibility that will not be fully articulated for another generation or more.

Like Dryden in his discussion of "Invention," Dacier abandons the notion of the translator as a copyist subject to a model; instead, the translator is like a sculptor whose work is based on that of a painter (lii). She takes the analogy a step further in imagining Virgil in the act of describing *Laocoön and His Sons*: the poet re-creates in words the three-dimensional representation of a non-existent event. Here the power of *ekphrasis*, the representation of the visual by verbal means (which is also the power of Achilles' shield), becomes the power of translation and accedes to the mimetic sublime: "The soul full of the beauties that it desires to imitate . . . lets itself be transported by this foreign enthusiasm that it makes its own, and thus it produces expressions and images that are quite different, and yet similar" (xl–xli). Later in the passage she considers another analogy, comparing the relation of translation to original with that of performance to musical composition. Dacier seeks ways to articulate links between what remain different objects, respecting the differences rather than subsuming or disguising one as another, ever in search of "something quite new in a familiar subject" (xli). She is bilingual in the fullest sense. Her long experience of working in and between languages has taught her that although Greek and French can be apprehended by the same mind, they do not provide the same experiences, and that although translation is in some sense always "impossible," it remains both necessary and productive of those expressions "très différentes, quoique semblables." Both difference and sameness resonate in the uncanny "otherness" of the translation.

I have only one language; it is not mine.

As Derrida explains in his quasi-autobiographical reflection on language, cultural belonging, and translation, *Le Monolinguisme de l'autre*, there's monolingualism and monolingualism.[36] However many languages I speak, however many shards, phrases, texts, new harmonies and associations I encounter, I shall never know anything beyond my own idiosyncratic network of phrases and meanings, my own portal into language. I may glide with "near-native fluency" between English and French, stammer a few phrases in Chinese, memorize street signs in Hungarian—all this constitutes my one language, my interface with the world. And yet clearly none of it is "mine"; I cannot lay claim to it or possess it. Derrida's own relationship with French may be unusual for the particularly sharp way in which these issues are cast into relief, but it is not necessary to have experienced colonization and occupation, secondhand citizenship and statelessness, in order to recognize the contingency and mutability that enter into the construction of one's own language, the language that possesses us and exceeds us. La Motte is not "monolingual" in the ordinary sense—he knows Latin—but for him Latin and French are transparent grids that should fit seamlessly together. To put it another way, for him, there is only one language: French. Anything that cannot be translated into French is meaningless and deserves to be forgotten.[37] Eighty years later, Rivarol would also suggest as much: "That which is not clear is not French."[38] Even Diderot would claim that Cicero "thought" in French before speaking Latin.[39] But Rivarol's account of the universality of French and its absolute connection with clarté recognized that the connection was historically produced and that all languages performed distinct cognitive functions. Diderot's speculation as to the inherent "Frenchness" of thought occurs in the context of a larger argument on the inherent idiosyncrasy and "foreignness" within any language.

La Motte himself is recognizably modern, not only for his ability to mobilize the discourse of public dialogue and enlightened exchange but also for his insistence on clarté and critical reason. And his emphatic adoption of the neoclassical translation style points to a form of cultural awareness (*via negativa*). There can be no "illusory identification" with the past here. La Motte may reject that past as barbarous or absurd, but in any event he has recognized it as distinct from the present. And it is in this respect that he and Dacier concur and that the entire Homer debate advances the cause of modernity. Tolerance for difference is another matter, however. And here perhaps Dacier is slightly more modern than the Moderns. True, she reserves her intolerance for the present day, many of whose features she finds distasteful and whose emphasis on affectivity seems to her misplaced.[40] She is not afraid to reveal her own affectivity, however, in the searingly painful postscript to her *Iliad* preface, when the death of her only daughter suddenly throws everything that she and her husband have lived for into question: "Everything is turned to bitterness for us, even literature" (lxix). Throughout, Dacier has shown herself capable of being moved by something quite foreign to her world, and she realizes that not every thread of experience can be automatically translated from one language to another. As we shall see, the next generation of intellectuals would pursue this reasoning and reflect that "French" was not a closed system but one that was permeable, mobile, and susceptible of growth through contact with other languages. Thus poet-translator Jacques Delille, who considered translations to broaden the mind in the same way as travel, would look back with dismay at the period when "Perrault condemned what he did not understand and La Motte disfigured Homer in order to correct him."[41]

The Homer debate derives much of its modernity from its strong emphasis on reading and on print. La Motte extols the virtues of polite conversation and exchange, but like other participants, he is much more dramatically involved in a print war, whose textuality is underscored by the practice of line-by-line refutations on both sides. Indeed, it is when the debate refers to actual conversation that it becomes the weakest: Here is what Boileau said to *me* regarding the Homeric gods, says La Motte; I knew him better than you, replies Dacier, and he would never have said that; Oh yes he did, says La Motte; and so on.[42] Reading and the transmission of meaning are at the heart of each stage of the debate—and never more so than in the lamentable misunderstanding, fueled by mistranslation, that prompted Dacier's late attack on Alexander Pope in a re-edition of her *Iliad*. The readings, rereadings, and misreadings produce odd effects, a sort of clamoring echo chamber in which stagnant repetition takes the place of sequenced, progressive replies. At the same time, the back-and-forth process of citations produces a peculiar textual density, a foregrounding of textuality, not unlike that of translation itself. Not surprisingly, many of the issues in the debate are primarily linguistic, and this too is a sign of modernity inasmuch as the examination of language throughout the Enlightenment involves a profound interrogation of the structures of thought.

I have tried to suggest that there are a host of linguistic, epistemological, and political questions that crisscross in the Querelle d'Homère and that are not easily subsumed under the too-familiar historical rubric of "Ancients vs. Moderns" or the overly general problematic of "fidelity vs. freedom." The relationship to the past of all the writers involved in this debate is complex. Although Perrault brusquely shoves antiquity from its honored place by claiming that "we are the Ancients," Pons complicates the relationship between the present and the past: first, by sounding what by 1715 was a well-worn but rhetorically and psychologically powerful topos, that if Homer had been born in modern France, he would have written as La Motte wrote; and second, by taking the conventional view of language as bound by l'usage a step further, arguing that past usage can neither be comprehended nor recuperated. Both Fourmont and Dacier deny this utter divorce from the past, but without falling into illusory identifications with the past. Fourmont underscores the importance of literacy and print culture in *la langue* (and even *la parole*), and Dacier elaborates a series of interpretive schemas that enable us to approach the past without losing our grounding in the present. Language is the central issue as the debaters examine its role in epistemology and aesthetics—hence La Motte's, Pons's, and Fourmont's concern with the process of language learning. The later generation of *philosophes* would, of course, delve deeply into the question of the origin of languages, but rarely would one find again as sustained a discussion of secondary language acquisition and cognition, issues that are foregrounded in the discussion of translation. Both the Moderns' skepticism and Dacier's and Fourmont's responses are significant in signaling a problematic—what do we know, in knowing a

second language?—and attempting to articulate the real experience of working with the problematic. For Dacier, that articulation must extend to the
ways in which language, in its phonetic and syntactic aspects, produces the
combination of meaning and affect that results in the aesthetic experience.
Here she is poles apart from the Moderns, whose "Cartesian" linguistics
presuppose a complete split between words and meaning.

These texts by Dacier, Fourmont, Pons, and La Motte remind one of the
richness and historical specificity of this exchange, which is shot through
with multiple discourses and anchored in several, often opposing ideolo-
gies. For example, various commentators have offhandedly identified La
Motte's approach to translation/adaptation with that of the belles infidèles
of the previous century. But his project has little in common with that of
d'Ablancourt and his circle. D'Ablancourt was a careful scholar and a lover
of the classics; his translations, while "somewhat free" (as he put it), were
carefully calculated and thoroughly documented infusions of contemporary
"eloquence" that aimed to provide the reader with an experience compa-
rable to that of the original.[43] Zuber argues that the importance of the belles
infidèles as a literary movement declined after 1660; he cites shifting tides
in the intellectual environment, such as a greater concern with rigor, exacti-
tude, and individual style (exemplified by Pierre-Daniel Huet) and a desire
to set forth "rules" for translation, particularly among the influential circle
of translators at Port-Royal.[44] The shift was, in some respects, from a model
based on eloquence and rhetoric to one based on codes and grammar. Neither La Motte nor Dacier entirely fits either model, however. La Motte retains only the most casual and superficial features of the earlier generation's
appeal to eloquence, and Dacier, trained as a scholar and "grammarian,"
is not really attuned to the universalizing abstractions of Port-Royal (general) grammar as it was understood by the successors of Arnauld, Nicole,
and Sacy after 1700, with their distinctions between language and thought,
word and meaning. In Dacier, we find a more nuanced recognition that
"eloquence" is not an abstraction, nor meaning entirely divorced from "expression," which inheres in sound, syntax, idiom, and other linguistically
specific elements.[45]

Questions appear in the Homer debate that will recur, with elaborations, in
the "inversion debate" over whether French (or Latin) follows the "natural
order" of thought. We already see the issues arising in the abbé de Pons and

Fourmont; later, and more visibly, it will engage Batteux, Beauzée, Diderot, and others. Dacier's most visible legacy, however, lies in the immense authority accorded her work on both sides of the Channel, throughout the eighteenth century. Echard's Plautus, Ozell's *Iliad*, Pope's *Iliad*, and many others would all contain acknowledgments of their indebtedness to her French versions and her annotations. Her quarrel with Pope at the end of her life, while providing ammunition for his enemies at home, seems not to have lessened her standing in English eyes.[46] Indeed, rumors later circulated of a reconciliation between them, but this was clearly wishful thinking— perhaps echoing accounts of her reconciliation with La Motte—since Dacier died before reading Pope's response to her harsh comments of 1719.[47]

By the time of her death, her name was synonymous with erudition; the advertising blurb for a 1723 translation of her father's pedagogical treatise, *Méthode courte et facile pour apprendre les humanités Grecques et Latines*, underscores the fact that "the Famous Madam DACIER, his Daughter," learned by this method.[48] Half a century later, James Beattie would cite her defense of Homer in his own essays "on the utility of classical learning"; and Edward Greene would also enlist her in defense of Apollonius as "a lady who made classical writers altogether her own." Even at the century's end, she would be held up as a model in John Burton's *Lectures on female education and manners*.[49] In France, although her scholarly reputation remained equally undimmed, one nevertheless finds less flattering references. The abbé Goujet mentions with dismay her "preference" for Greek, which he attributes to her "zeal" and her "ardent love of Homer," thus echoing certain misogynistic passages from the Homer debate.[50] Sixty years later, Mme de Genlis offers a distinctly mixed image: while holding her up to her children as an example of studiousness, she refuses to allow the children to read Dacier's *Iliad* without supervision because numerous annotations suggest approval of Homer's "cruelty." Genlis too finds that Dacier's "admiration for Homer" detracted from her ability to remain impartial. Emilie Du Châtelet, however, cites her as a model intellectual in the draft to her Mandeville translation.[51] In England, the dual-career marriage of Anne and André Dacier offers a positive image to one of Samuel Richardson's female characters: "May not two persons, having the same taste, improve each other? Was not this the case of Monsieur and Madame Dacier?"[52] To Maria Edgeworth, they represent the ideal couple: "Happy Madame Dacier! you found a husband suited to your taste!"[53]

One of Dacier's most important contributions as a woman of letters, one that reached beyond the domain of classical scholarship, is doubtless her participation in the emergence of literary criticism, where she lent new strength to the notion of the power of French prose. While France had no Dr. Johnson to proclaim her the "mother of French criticism"—in part perhaps because French criticism had no one parent, no Dryden, in an extended family including Corneille, Rapin, Boileau, Huet, and André Dacier—her name remains central to one influential citational network in particular, as the principal authority cited in the ongoing debate over whether poetry should be translated into verse or into prose. She made her position clear in her earliest translation, *Les Poésies d'Anacréon et de Sapho*, where she criticized the earlier translation of Pléiade poet Rémy Belleau because it was in verse "and consequently little faithful." A few decades later (but before her major statement on the subject in her *Iliad* preface) Antoine de la Fosse would contest this view by offering a verse translation of Anacreon.[54] While La Fosse's translation would be reprinted and referred to on both sides of the Channel, the most frequently cited critical reference point for the French proponents of verse would be academician and magistrate Jean Bouhier's preface to his translation of Petronius from 1737: "Let them decorate prose with whatever ornaments they like, it will only give a cold imperfect image of poetic fire."[55]

Bouhier's approach would have its partisans, but the century's only verse translations of any lasting influence would be those by poet Jacques Delille in the 1770s and 1780s, by which time the entire discussion of poetics would be taking a new direction. Unlike England, where verse translations could become literary models in their own right, Enlightenment France would invest its cultural capital in prose.[56] Educator Charles Rollin cites Dacier to argue that a prose translation need never be "servile" but should retain poetry's "fire, vivacity, and noble daring."[57] After Dacier, however, the most cited proponent of prose translation would be the abbé Desfontaines, renowned (and feared) as a critic, whose prose version of Virgil received much praise.[58] While in his preface he dismisses earlier French translators with his usual tact (for example, dubbing Marolles "ridiculous and barbarous," 1:i), his ensuing "Discours sur la traduction des poëtes" would be cited by friend and foe as a major critical statement. The "Discours" offers not just a defense of French prose but an attack on the conventions of French verse. Or as he would write elsewhere, "Prose, especially French prose, has its own harmony that is clearly the equal of verse."[59] Cultural conservative though he may be, Desfontaines has picked up and echoed Dacier's impatience with the hidebound rules of French verse.

Even though she rejects the belles infidèles and adaptative translation in general, Dacier's idea of a "generous and noble" prose furthers the aims of d'Ablancourt—an admirer of the work of her father, a fellow Protestant humanist—and all those who wished to elevate the literary language and forge a new *prose d'art*. Writing at the beginning of the new century, however, she comes to the task in a different spirit, rigorously critical, impatient with the unreflective anachronism of the Moderns. A partisan of the Ancients, she is inspired to "something new" by her sense of the incapacity of conventional poetic forms to capture the energy she experiences through texts from another time and place. The marquise de Lambert sums up Dacier's legacy well. While tending to side with her friend La Motte on the question of Homer's literary merit, her admiration for Dacier's achievement is unstinted: "Our sex owes her much: she protested against the common error that condemns us to ignorance. As much from disdain as from superiority, men forbade us learning; Madame Dacier's authority proves that women are capable of it. . . . She liberated our minds that had been held captive by prejudice; she alone gives us our rights."[60]

Gender, Signature, Authority

Literary historians and historians of translation have long taken an interest in the ways in which translation projects afforded women an apprenticeship in literary culture and textual production during periods when authorship was essentially an exclusive male domain.[1] By means of translation, women engaged in intellectual debate and literally determined the terms of the argument through their translating choices, from the early modern period to the present.[2] By the eighteenth century, female authorship was less of an oxymoron for the general public, but traditional constraints had hardly disappeared. Emilie Du Châtelet remarks that even if men more easily accept women translators than women authors because of the subservience associated with translation, "some may yet find that it is presumptuous for a woman to attempt it."[3] Even within the field of translation there are gender norms and divisions, notably in the divide between classical and modern languages. "The *dead languages* are ingrossed by men; these are their peculiar privileges, and they are up in arms when we invade their provinces," notes Elizabeth Griffith, translating from the French.[4] Women classicists, such as Anne Dacier in France and Elizabeth Carter in England, were exceptional.

As an entry into the literary marketplace, translation from contemporary texts, especially novels, could be profitable but was hardly as prestigious an enterprise, or one that called as frequently on the translator to make elaborate prefaces, theoretical statements, or extensive annotations.

Despite the constraints and ambiguities of their relation to the world of print, women translators succeeded in creating a number of different roles for themselves vis-à-vis the texts they translated and their public. At a time when *authorship* was itself a mutable term, the practice of translation operated on even more contested and rapidly evolving grounds. (There is still no translator's term equivalent to the English *authorship*.) Translation offers to women a range of strategies for being—or not being—in the text, through prefaces, dedicatory letters, or in the choice of texts themselves. In addition to looking at a variety of gendered prefacing gestures by Aphra Behn, Anne Dacier, Marie-Jeanne Riccoboni, Frances Brooke, and others, I will also give an extended close reading of the 1771 English translation, attributed to Elizabeth Griffith, of the "memoirs" and (apocryphal) letters of Ninon de l'Enclos.

It seems appropriate to complete our transition from the seventeenth to the eighteenth century with an examination of women translators, given the ways in which women's gradual accession to public writing marks this period. Women take advantage of the generic flexibility of the translator's preface to reflect on their position as gendered readers, writers, and transmitters of texts. The group of translators referred to here is relatively small, approximately twenty, and is evenly divided between English-speaking and French-speaking writers. Of the French women, most translate from English into French (Du Châtelet, Du Boccage, Keralio, Riccoboni, Belot, Thiroux d'Arconville, and Guizot); two reside in England and translate from French to English (Aubin and Montolieu; Montolieu also translates from English to French); and only two translate from classical languages (Dacier and Du Châtelet). Of the English women, nearly all translate from French to English (Philips, Behn, Aubin, Collyer, Floyd, Haywood, Lennox, Griffith, and Brooke); of those working with classical languages, Lucy Hutchinson translates from Latin and Elizabeth Carter and Sarah Fielding from Greek (Carter also translates from Italian).

Much has been written in recent years about anonymity and female authorship, but nearly all of these women published their translations under their own names. Some identify themselves through references to other works by which they are known, as when the title page of Charlotte Lennox's translation of the life of Mme de Maintenon bears the indication,

"By the Author of the Female Quixote." Lennox then goes on to sign the dedicatory epistle. Frances Brooke's early translations of Marie-Jeanne de Riccoboni are anonymous (Riccoboni's name does not appear either), but she does sign her 1770 translation of a novel by Nicolas Etienne Framery, which further includes a publisher's reference to earlier books "published, by the Translator" (Riccoboni's name still absent). Elizabeth Griffith, who indicates that her translation of Ninon de l'Enclos is "by a Lady," advertises her later translation of the memoirs of Mme de Caylus as being "by the Translator of the Life and Writings of Ninon de l'Enclos." Sarah Fielding, who published her novels anonymously, or "By the Author of David Simple," nevertheless signed her translation of Xenophon (1762). Elizabeth Carter did not sign her 1739 translation of Algarotti's *Il Newtonianismo per le dame* (*Sir Isaac Newton's Philosophy Explain'd for the use of the Ladies*), but her later Epictetus (1758) does appear under her name. Although we tend to lend translation a subservient role with respect to authorship, author's names, men's as well as women's, seem more likely to vanish from sight than those of translators. The distinction between translator and author can also be completely blurred, as when Haywood's version of Mouhy's *La Paysanne Parvenue* is said to be "Translated from the Original, by the Author [i.e., translator] of *La Belle Assemblée*" (by Marie de Gomez). Haywood goes on to sign the dedicatory letter in her own name.

Recent scholarship on the history of authorship and publishing reminds us that anonymity is perfectly compatible with the "author-function," as when we consider the distinction between "thoroughly anonymous" and "anonymous female" translations: Du Boccage, Belot, Griffith, Guizot, and Montolieu carefully left indications of their gender, whether on a title page designation ("By a Lady," "par Madame B***," and so on) or in their prefaces. Such designations are not necessarily indications of constraints on female authorship but may reveal "an authorial strategist" seeking to position her (and sometimes his) text with respect to an audience.[5] An often overlooked indication of the translator's importance is the assumption that translators have a form of literary property in the authors they translate; Haywood asks her readers not to consider her retranslation of Mouhy (another version having appeared the previous year) as "a kind of Invasion on the Property of the first," on the grounds that she had begun her translation "long before the *Country-Maid* was advertised" and that the main character (whom she treats as real) had personally asked her to improve on the earlier translation.[6] This sense of literary property, or propriety, is not confined only to women: Philippe-Florent de Puisieux voices a similar reluctance to retranslate Fielding's *Amelia* out of respect for Mme Riccoboni's translation, and also given that such famous translators as the abbé de Prévost and Pierre-Antoine de la Place were already "in possession of" works by Fielding.[7] Such reservations, however fleeting (since both Haywood and Puisieux proceed with their retranslations), further disengage the traditional association between the emergence of a strong concept of individual authorship and that of legal responsibility, or copyright, in texts.[8]

Translation was thus a zone of the literary marketplace where not only a female presence but also many women's names were quite visible. It has been said that translation was a form of authorship that may have been more readily available to early modern women, one that would enable them to write, circulate their writing, and even appear in print without presuming to lay claim to original authorship. This assertion appears to be unexceptionable, although we should keep in mind that the concept of "original authorship" was by no means as reified as it would become by the end of the eighteenth century.[9] Certainly, part of what stimulates the French-inspired school of free translation of Cowley and Denham in the mid-seventeenth century is the perception that translation is a secondary, subservient art— but their solution is not to abandon translation for "original composition" but rather to translate in a new manner. Over the course of the eighteenth century, the relative roles of the translator and author evolve and the concept of writing itself changes as "originality" becomes a highly prized commodity, even as the commodification of writing calls on writers to perform "vanishing acts," as Catherine Gallagher has put it, as a condition of entry into the marketplace.[10] While an analysis of women in the reading public lies beyond the purview of this book, their presence is felt, sometimes quite dramatically, as in Alexander Pope's "appeals to the ladies" in the notes to his Homer, as well as in the strong association between women (as readers and writers) and the new genre, the novel.[11]

From earliest times, women translators made use of traditional topoi of modesty and courtly behavior in order to assert their writerly presence in their prefaces.[12] Several commentators have called attention to sixteenth-century translator Margaret Tyler's revision of the usual relation between (male) writers and (female) dedicatees, in which she asks that if men "bestow" their work on ladies, may not women read the work—"and if wee may read them, why not farther wade in them to the search of a truth?"[13] As Douglas Robinson has pointed out, Tyler's sly conflation of the roles of patroness and author ("it is all one for a woman to pen a storie, as for a man to addresse his storie to a woman") may gesture to a questioning of the "author-function." That move, however, is ultimately less incisive than her earlier question: "Why not wade farther in them?" A century later, Lucy Hutchinson provides an example of women's "wading" in her preface to the unpublished translation of Lucretius that she presented to the earl of Anglesey in 1675, in which she portrays herself working on the translation while her children studied with their tutors in the same room.[14] Although Hutchinson decries the "wickd pernitious doctrines" in Lucretius, she clearly thought well enough of her work to present it to the keeper of the privy seal. As we saw in Chapter 3, even male translators of Lucretius—John Evelyn, who published his translation of book 1 in 1656, and Thomas Creech, whose complete translation of Lucretius did not appear in print until 1682—would similarly need to preserve their "deniability" by distancing themselves from the dangerous philosophy of the Roman poet and by emphasizing the parts of his philosophy that were amenable to Christianity. As the trend of politicizing translations in seventeenth-century England amply demonstrates, the possibilities of "indirect writing" through translation were critical to men as well as women. Nevertheless, for the reasons we have seen, women might well have been particularly interested in the safety of translation as "a simultaneous claiming and disclaiming of authorship," as Laura Rosenthal writes of Katherine Philips.[15]

By the eighteenth century, too, more and more women were in print. Published translations also remind us that women are "in print" at more than one level of the text. Although the scope of this book does not allow an extensive analysis of women's role as readers of translations, women readers are frequently invoked in prefaces. They are implicated as audience based on the assumption that most eighteenth-century women did not know foreign, especially classical, languages. Anne Dacier says of her Anacreon that she wished to give the pleasure of reading the poet "to the ladies."[16] Aphra Behn thanks Creech for making Lucretius available to her:

> Till now I curst my Sex and Education
> And more the scanted Customs of the Nation
> Permitting not the Female Sex to tread
> The Mighty Paths of Learned Heroes Dead.[17]

Haywood, too, underscores the fact that *La Belle assemblée* is by a woman and notes that, although she dedicates the translation to the French ambassador to Great Britain, she destines her translation specifically to "the Ladies of my Country."[18] Two highly visible works of scientific vulgarization aimed at women are also translated by women: Aphra Behn translates Fontenelle's dialogues between a philosopher and an inquisitive marquise, and Elizabeth Carter takes on Algarotti's book on Newton "for the use of the ladies." As we will see, both translators take advantage of their role to promote the advancement of women's knowledge, as well as to critique male assumptions. Among the reasons that prompted her to do the Fontenelle translation, Behn notes the role of the central female character: "I thought an English Woman might adventure to translate any thing, a French Woman may be supposed to have spoken."[19] Women also translate other women's works, as when Anne Floyd translates Lafayette, Eliza Haywood translates Gomez, Elizabeth Griffith translates l'Enclos, Frances Brooke translates Riccoboni, or Pauline Guizot translates Hays. Furthermore, two of these translations of women by women are dedicated to women. Charlotte Lennox offers her *Memoirs for the History of Madame de Maintenon and of the Last Age* (1757) to the countess of Northumberland, underscoring the theme of a woman's rise to power and influence and comparing the countess and Maintenon.[20] Elizabeth Griffith dedicates *The Memoirs of Ninon de l'Enclos* to the duchess of Bedford and her later translation of Marmontel to Elizabeth Montagu, the "queen of the bluestockings." Gender cements the connection between translator, dedicatee, and frequently author, strengthening the female literary tradition. Susanne de Lotbinière-Harwood underscores the importance of such textual connections for "creating solid woman-ground."[21]

Many of these prefaces and dedicatory epistles draw on familiar topoi, in particular those of "idleness" and "morality," both of which maintain a certain distance between the translator and her text. The "idleness" topos is certainly a familiar one in women's writing, but it may still come as something of a shock to find it in the writing of Anne Dacier, given her scholarly prominence. Yet the dedicatory letter of one of her early translations of Anacreon and Sappho, addressed to the duc de Montausier, begins by referring to her translations as "little pastimes" that she would never have thought to make public until Montausier, by order of the king, requested them for the education of the dauphin.[22] The young Dacier proffers her work well buttressed by the strongest possible forms of male authority. The preface, however, gives a rather different view, first by suggesting that the translation was written not for the dauphin but for "les Dames" and next by acknowledging and then gently disengaging herself from a male authority possibly more powerful than the king, her own father: "My father once made some

Remarks on this author that were so well received that I need not speak of them here. Nevertheless, however much veneration I have for his memory, I must say that I am not always in agreement with him" (iii).

Numerous are the examples of such initially self-deprecating gestures on the part of women translators, who often present their work as the fruit of "leisure Hours" or "amusement." Male writers can also present themselves in this manner, as when Jean de Segrais tells us that he undertook his translation of Virgil on something of a whim. Such demurrals have the effect of distancing translators from the marketplace where translations are sold and returning them to a leisured courtly or domestic life. Penelope Aubin contrasts her leisure with her dedicatee Dr. Smithson's "more useful studies," Marie-Ange du Boccage emphasizes the "littleness" of her translation of Milton in contrast with the "great and sublime" original, and Pauline Guizot tells us that "le hasard" brought her project to her.[23] Each of these diminutions of the translator's work, however, has its counterbalance. Aubin remarks that she would like to offer something more substantial than the novel *Les Illustres françaises*, but she is still waiting for "an Augustus, or at least Maecenas, to assist me"—observing indirectly that Dr. Smithson is neither, and incidentally comparing herself to Virgil, "or at least" Horace. Du Boccage recommends Dupré de Saint-Maur's Milton for those who want "a more precise knowledge" of the text: in other words, we should read her version for the poetry and for her own vision. As much might be said of Guizot's version of Mary Hays's *Emma Courtney*, which grows from a two-volume English novel to a five-volume French one through her efforts. Given the transformation, her observation that the project at least started as a translation ("it's not entirely mine; I wish to rob no one") underscores her intellectual honesty and her own creative powers.[24]

Octavie Belot's preface to her 1763 translation of Hume's *History of England under the House of Tudor* presents a striking contrast to the topos of (apparent) facility and modesty by emphasizing that the difficulty of the project attracted her to it.[25] She also sets herself in direct opposition to conventional images of leisured women of letters, describing her "natural penchant" for serious subjects and her need for intellectual activity. Emilie Du Châtelet redefines her leisure as a retreat, beginning her 1735 preface to Mandeville with an evocation of the transient nature of worldly preoccupations and her search for a project that would focus her energies: "I am amazed to have been so preoccupied with my teeth and my hair, and to have neglected my mind and my understanding."[26] But whereas Belot's preface bespeaks confidence in challenges met, Du Châtelet's text diverges along paths that set up unresolved tensions: on the one hand, she puts a positive spin on the role of translation, which she considers secondary, praising translators as "merchants of the republic of letters"; on the other, she denounces the sorry state of women's education and "the weight of the prejudice that excludes us so universally from the sciences" (135). Women's idleness is an imposed state and a trap; Du Châtelet's program of self-education and projects such as the Mandeville translation are the means by which she resists. Why, she asks, do women seem barred "by an invisible force" from excelling (135)? The bitterness of the question suggests why Du Châtelet would have abandoned the Mandeville project for a task that further blurs the distinction between originality and "secondariness," her *Institutions de physique*.[27] When she returned to translation a few years later, it would be to take up a far more imposing task, and one closer to her own interests, the translation of Newton's *Principia*.[28]

We have a particularly strong example of the translator simultaneously making use of and distancing herself from her text in Aphra Behn's translation of Fontenelle. While most scholars assume that Behn turned to prose translation late in her career because of financial difficulties, it nevertheless seems clear that in translating Tallement, La Rochefoucauld, and Fontenelle she was choosing sources "consistent with her own views and temperament."[29] To the translation of Fontenelle's *Entretiens sur la pluralité des mondes* she attached her most extended reflections on the practice of translation, "A Preface, by way of Essay on Translated Prose."[30] As we saw earlier, Behn justified her translation of Fontenelle partly on the presence of a female character in the philosophic dialogue. In her commentary, however, she is less than enthusiastic about the role given to the marquise, just as she has considerable reservations regarding the work as a whole, finding that Fontenelle pushes his speculations regarding other worlds to the "height of Extravagancy." And as for his female character, "he makes her say a great many very silly things, tho' she sometimes makes Observations so learned, that the greatest Philosophers in *Europe* could make no better."[31] (Indeed, Fontenelle's invention of the marquise was well meaning; he had intended her as an example of women's potential.) Behn proceeds with a discussion of the theological implications of Copernican astronomy. Offering her remarks with a modest disclaimer—"I cannot but take his part as far as a Woman's Reasoning can go" (4:78)—she is in effect taking over and revising the role of Fontenelle's marquise, that of an "untutored" woman who can read and reason for herself with considerably more cogency and force than the fictional marquise, a passive recipient of knowledge. Behn's essay thus corrects what she sees as an unsuitably condescending portrayal of the woman as learner.

A generation later, Elizabeth Carter translated Francesco Algarotti's *Il Newtonianismo per le dame*, a work that explicitly followed in Fontenelle's footsteps by staging an "instructive" conversation between a philosopher and "a lady." Here, too, the sexualized depiction of the woman learner struck at least some thinking women as offensive. Du Châtelet, who maintained a friendship with Algarotti and received him at Cirey, privately expressed misgivings about the work and feared to be taken for the real-life model of its heroine.[32] Carter, while refraining from a critique as explicit as Behn's of Fontenelle, quietly revised and elided troublesome passages, presenting a text of considerably more feminist import than the original.[33]

Thus, we have begun to see how women translators made use of prefaces and dedicatory epistles to comment on their situation as writers and to assert subtle forms of authority. Their attitudes toward the texts they translate are also revealing, for here the translator most explicitly speaks in the voice of the critic. In the next group of texts, I am interested in looking at the different modulations of the discourse of morality within textual commentary. "Moralizing," as Douglas Robinson points out, is one of the traditional topoi by which women excuse their public writing even while asserting cultural power. In the period of this study, however, it can take a number of forms. Some assertions on behalf of translations simply repeat arguments for the morally instructive effects of fiction, as when Mary Collyer introduces her 1743 translation of Marivaux's *Vie de Marianne* as "a useful piece of instruction, a lesson of nature, a true and lively picture of the human heart."[34] Certainly, the stern condemnation of "wickd pernitious doctrines" that we saw in Hutchinson can be found in eighteenth-century examples. In her translation of the abbé de Sade's biography of Petrarch, Susannah Dobson avers that the Italian poet's life is worth reading as a negative exemplar of the unhappiness brought on by an adulterous inclination: "What a striking lesson for youth! What an awful lesson for all human beings!"[35] Frances Brooke takes it upon herself to "correct" Framery's portrayal of one of his characters, a "fallen" woman:

> The picture of Henrietta appears . . . to be drawn with too careless and too coarse a hand. . . . A well-educated woman, and such Henrietta is represented

to be, might possibly have felt the passion of love to the degree, but not in
the manner, our author describes. . . .

Perhaps, but this idea is offered with diffidence, woman alone can paint
with perfect exactness the sentiments of woman.[36]

For all its flaws, the novel offers Brooke the opportunity to make a strong
statement—however "offered with diffidence"—regarding women's writing
about women.

The prefaces of moralizing translators carry out a program similar to that
described by Catherine Gallagher for female novelists, who stressed the "chas-
tity and the moral seriousness of their works" in order to counterbalance the
"scandalmongers of the previous generation."[37] The situations in England
and France are, of course, somewhat different. In France, there were fewer
"scandalous women" whose personal lives generated as much titillating interest as their writings—Mme de Villedieu comes to mind—but simply *being*
in print might be considered scandal enough.[38] Yet the English writers could
gesture toward what was perceived as greater freedom of manners in France
as a means of reinforcing a modest self-presentation—a move that is particularly important for Elizabeth Griffith in her translation of the memoirs of a
scandalous French woman of the previous century, Ninon de l'Enclos. It is
perhaps noteworthy that while nearly all my examples of "thoroughly anonymous" translations are by English women (their anonymity perhaps owing as
much to arrangements with booksellers as to moral or social concerns), all of
the "anonymous female" translations save Griffith's (a special case, as we shall
see) are by French women, even though most are of "high" literary works—
Milton, Hume, Delille—for whom no apology need be made.

"Moralizing" discourse is the most complex of the topoi, as we have
seen in the Hutchinson example, where the woman's intellectual advancement and the "wickd pernitious doctrines" are inextricably linked. A certain
amount of distance is required whenever the text is not in perfect conformity with social or moral standards. Translators have on many occasions deliberately chosen such dissident texts, taking advantage of their nonauthorial
status to introduce heterodox ideas into their culture. Lucretius appears to
function in this way for many, as does Ninon de l'Enclos for Griffith. The
task of simultaneously presenting and distancing is a delicate one, especially
for women, and especially when the translator's stake in the text is greater
than, say, Brooke's in the Framery novel. Thus, although Elizabeth Carter
says of the "heathen philosophy" of Epictetus that it may remind us "of the
extreme Need of a divine Assistance, to rectify the Mistakes of depraved Rea-

son," this does not prevent her from giving a thorough account of its major tenets or from arguing that nothing in Stoicism, "equitably interpreted," is strongly in contradiction with Christianity.[39] My purpose is not to suggest that Carter is attempting to subvert the established order as such, but rather to underscore the degree to which translation allows her a space for speaking out on philosophy and theology and offering what Claudia Thomas terms "a distinctly feminine, Christian critique of her culture" by pointing out the limitations of Stoicism and, by extension, of her freethinking contemporaries.[40] Even so, Carter ends her introduction by recommending Epictetus both for his "improving" qualities and because "his good Sense is enlivened by such a Keenness of Wit, and Gaiety of Humour, as render the Study of him, a most delightful as well as profitable Entertainment" (xxxiii). Carter thus takes a tack quite different from Dacier, who sought to demonstrate Homer's compatibility with Christian teaching, but their aims are similar: to create links to an ancient text while preserving its strangeness; to reverse unreflective received notions (on the moral absurdity of Homer, on the moral viability of Stoicism) through a thoughtful, sympathetic, and "pretty strictly literal" (xxxiv)—Carter's expression—translation.

For one more example of the contingencies of "distance," let us turn again to Octavie Belot's translation of Hume, whose criticisms of Roman Catholicism pose a dilemma: should she repeat what is effectively a blasphemous text or censure it?[41] For Belot, who prefers to remain as close as possible to the text, gender becomes the unexpected solution to the problem: "I would have gone beyond the limits prescribed for my sex, had I risked combatting these false opinions in a dogmatic tone in an area removed from my competence." The point is not "subversion," but rather Belot's awareness of textual danger and her neat use of gender to escape the limitations on her translated discourse.

There is a final, more loosely constructed category of prefacing gestures that I would like to call, simply, "relationships." Here the translator situates herself with respect to a textual addressee, who may be the reading public at large, a patron or dedicatee, or a group of subscribers. Some of the liveliest prefaces are by women writers who have their own literary stock to consider in undertaking their translations, Eliza Haywood and Marie-Jeanne Riccoboni. Haywood was a prolific translator of French texts, and we can see interesting shifts in her approach by comparing two prefaces written twenty years apart. In 1721, at the beginning of her career, Haywood publishes a translation of Boursault's *Lettres d'une dame à un cavalier* as *Letters from a Lady of Quality to a Chevalier*. Haywood's name appears; Boursault's does not. Her preface begins by suggesting that the translator's "insignificant Lowness" will protect her from the "Rush of Winds" of criticism, then goes on to imply that she has made substantial alterations to the text: "If those few I wish to please are satisfy'd, I shall not ask the Question, whether it be with *mine* or the *French Author's* part of the Performance."[42] She then promises an upcoming novel "on the danger of giving way to passion." Boursault's novel has become the springboard for her own literary projects. Two decades later, when Haywood brings out *The Virtuous Villager*, a translation of Mouhy's *La Paysanne Parvenue*, her situation has changed: she is now a best-selling novelist in her own right, and she has to contend with the presence of a rival translation, a highly successful 1741 version called *The Fortunate Country Maid*. Here Haywood, rather than trumpeting her improvement of the work, instead elects to extend its fiction, claiming that her version, a "slavish Adherence to the Letter," is based on a fuller set of original documents than the 1741 version or even Mouhy's novel itself. According to Haywood, Mouhy's text was based on an insufficient attention to the originals, so that "he was obliged to make up the Deficiency by the help of his Memory, and where that failed by his Invention."[43] Haywood's *Virtuous Villager* thus trumps not only its rival but the original as well, promising further revelations and clarifications. She further claims that she, unlike the previous translator, possesses the "Capacity of en-tring into the soul of the Author" (who is of course male, but who assumes a female identity as the letter-writing marchioness), an artfully contrived moment of gender switching. Of interest too is Haywood's insistence on the marchioness's desire to see her letters published. The origin of the text is presumed to be not only a writing woman but one who wants to see her private messages in print. Haywood's preface has given birth to a new fiction.

Marie-Jeanne Riccoboni gives us not a preface but a letter to her publisher. (I am immediately reminded of a story regarding a colleague whose voice-mail message reputedly ended, "If this is my publisher calling, please ring me at home," a message that could not fail to arrive at its destination, whoever the listener might be!) Riccoboni is a hot literary property, and her *libraire* is banging on the door for a new book. Sorry, she replies, I don't have anything new—the novel is stalled. But when the publisher promises to print anything at all that bears her name, she proposes "une folie." She has been trying to teach herself English by translating Henry Fielding's *Amelia*: "Whatever was difficult, I left it out; if I didn't understand, I assumed it was badly written and moved on." In the end, she has "a very unfaithful translation of Mr. Fielding's novel. . . . Print it anyway, and let it become what it may. If it's a flop, too bad for the author; we'll claim that it's a literal translation. If it sells, we'll boast of the infinite care with which we added, cut, corrected, and embellished the original. But since paper costs money, I recommend the first two volumes only."[44]

Riccoboni's "preface" to her English exercise is a witty tour de force that overturns all the conventions, beginning with the most sacred rule, that the translator should master the foreign language. Fielding does keep his name, but *l'auteur Anglois* is relegated to a minor role indeed in the staging of Riccoboni's fame and success, right down to her concern with the price of paper. Like Haywood, she leaves the question of final textual responsibility, author-ity, up for grabs: let us see the sales figures first, please. The market-place is fully present and brilliantly illuminated.

As noted earlier, Riccoboni's unabashed presentation sparked a rejoinder from Philippe-Florent de Puisieux in the preface to his own translation of *Amelia*, who claims to have withheld his version upon hearing that Riccoboni's was about to appear.[45] He goes on, however, to relate his dismay at the casual approach described in her preface, and at the "formless, very free" results (vi). Puisieux puts the reason for his retranslation on the title page: "Amélie, Histoire angloise, Traduite *fidélement* de l'Anglois de M. Fielding" (emphasis added). The contretemps is less lively than it appears. Puisieux's version came out in 1762, nearly twenty years after the publication of Riccoboni's 1743 translation; its main effect seems to have been to spur a re-edition of Riccoboni's translation, which went though several reprints well into the nineteenth century. Puisieux's *Amélie, histoire angloise* appears to have enjoyed a single reprint, in 1784. The name of one of the century's most popular writers continues to trump any complaints about the accuracy of her version.

Other translators' texts stress more immediate, more personal relations. Marie-Geneviève-Charlotte Thiroux d'Arconville began her extensive trans-lating career with her anonymous *Avis d'un Père à sa Fille, par M. le marquis d'Hallifax*, which she dedicated to her niece. The dedication, as well as the "Avertissement" that follows it, situates Thiroux d'Arconville in a way that reveals her identity to those who are closest to her but conceals it from the public. Not only does her name not appear, but neither does any marker of her gender; adjectives referring to the translator are masculine. The father-daughter relation of the text might even suggest a similar gendering of the dedication, especially given that the translator slips into the father's role: "My tenderness for you, dear Niece, gives you the place of a daughter in my heart."[46] Her later translation of James Hervey, *Méditations sur les tombeaux*, offers the same situation: the dedicatee, "Madame de ******," who is referred to as "Adélaïde" in the text, presumably knows who her translating friend is, yet the outside reader knows nothing of this translator who speaks of sincere friendship yet remains concealed by the gender-neutral pronoun *on*.[47] As Marie-Pascale Pieretti has argued, however, anonymity does not prevent Thiroux d'Arconville from producing a coherent body of work, through references to other works ("by the author of the *Traité de l'amitié*") and, more profoundly, by consistently investing her texts with a didactic mission.[48]

Thiroux d'Arconville's translation projects, which range from poetry to history to scientific texts, link to one another and to her work as a *moraliste*, a philosopher of human conduct, which she pursues most systematically in her two moral treatises *De l'amitié* and *Des passions*. Here, too, she writes anonymously, using *on* and masculine adjectives. Already the dedication and preface to her Halifax translation contain the elements of social analysis. Addressing a young lady about to enter the world, Thiroux d'Arconville warns her to beware of "ces femmes dangereuses" who, having lost their own virtue, seek to seduce others: "They are constantly told that they can best employ their minds to dissimulate their taste, their desires, and their aversions, the better to be able to rule over those around them."[49] Such a warning seems to offer intimations of Mme de Merteuil, a quarter century before the publication of *Les Liaisons dangereuses*. Thiroux d'Arconville's view, later to be amplified in her philosophical works, is bleak: true friendship, although possible, is rare, and caught between virtue and "des passions," our best recourse is simply to acknowledge our own weakness and flee (iii–iv). The effacement of the author/translator is thus the symptom of a more generalized retreat.

In a marked contrast to Thiroux d'Arconville's disengagement from the reader, both Ann Floyd and Marie-Françoise Abeille de Keralio infuse gender into their dedications through the language of flirtation and sociability. Floyd dedicates *Fatal Gallantry* (1722), a translation of Mme de Lafayette's *Histoire d'Henriette d'Angleterre*, to John Law, praising his restoration of the French economy, and offering herself as a model for other women: "If they use the same Caution in their Gallantries, and Passion, that I have done in my Dedication, by making choice of a Person of real Worth, Generosity and Honour, they will have less Reason to repent of their Conduct."[50] Given that more than a year had passed since Law fled France for his life following the catastrophic failure of his fiscal policies, Floyd's encomium seems ill timed, but as a dedicatory strategy, it is a shrewd gesture, clearing Floyd of flirting with a public figure yet allowing the relationship between translator and dedicatee to be drawn into the sphere of social and even passionate relations between women and men. Lighthearted sociability informs Mme de Keralio's 1759 translation of Gay's *Fables*, although she dedicates the work to "Monsieur P.D.V.C.D.J.D.L.R.M.," who remains anonymous in the dedication. His anonymity will extend no further than print, she assures us: "For although you forbade me to name you . . . who could know me and hear me speak for a moment without piercing the modest veil that you wished to hide behind?"[51] The usual roles are reversed as Keralio teasingly promises to tear aside the veil of masculine modesty.

Sarah Fielding does not dedicate her 1762 translation of Xenophon to any particular person, but she begins her preface with an expression of appreciation to those who subscribed to the book.[52] Here we see not just the shift toward a modern literary marketplace in the substitution of a subscriber list or collective patron for the individual patron but also an extension, and perhaps further complication, of the affective system created in the act of dedication. The usual dedication expresses the writer's gratitude for favors past (and perhaps future), which the dedication repays. Here, the favor is tangible and quantifiable, operating within the contractual expectations of the subscription, which might lead one to expect that it could be more easily repaid, as in a commercial transaction. Fielding would appear to be free from the kinds of debt we have seen evoked by Pierre Du Ryer or even William Gifford. Yet she finds "nobler Motives" in the subscribers' participation, and these place her under "an additional Obligation." It is the logic of this gift that it cannot every truly be repaid, only "somewhat," and here merge the demands of the gift, of moral obligation, and of the translator's need to render justice to the text—another impossible demand. Fielding's sense of the unmet and unmeetable demands of translation echoes a page or so later in her discussion of the utter distance that lies between modern readers and ancient texts. Quoting an earlier (unnamed) translator, she argues that there will always be something we do not understand in texts from a culture so far removed from our own, but that when we do not understand, we ought to assume a meaning: "We ought to take it for granted, that there is a Justness in the Connexion, which we cannot trace; and a Cogency in the Reasoning, which we cannot understand" (iv). Thus, modern readers enter into a sort of moral subscription agreement with ancient texts, giving them the benefit of the doubt in the expectation of meaning.

Finally, I would like to signal a small, but distinct, trend of what I call "gynocentric translation": translations by women of women's writing, especially those dedicated to women—as when Charlotte Lennox dedicates her translation of Mme de Maintenon's memoirs to the countess of Northumberland, or when Elizabeth Griffith dedicates her Ninon de l'Enclos to the duchess of Bedford—in terms that emphasize the significance of women as role models for one another.[53] The present corpus, emphasizing prefaces and critical writing, cannot fully represent this phenomenon, which remains an object for future study. A related matter is the interest of women translators—and, eventually, other female commentators—in determining the sex of anonymous writers. In her introduction to a translation of *La Princesse de Clèves*, for example, Elizabeth Griffith speculates that the author must have been a woman: "Men are not apt to imagine such refinements; and even, perhaps, less to impute them to the sex."[54] Isabelle de Montolieu makes a similar observation regarding *Sense and Sensibility*: "A man would never have been able to seize the nuances, develop the feelings, or penetrate women's hearts in such detail or with such truth."[55] As we saw, Frances Brooke claims that "woman alone can paint with perfect exactness the sentiments of woman."[56] Such comments belong more, perhaps, to the history of the construction of the female voice in fiction than to that of translation, but I speculate that they also play a role in the evolution of women translators' sense of themselves and of their work.

In reflecting on the importance of translation in the careers of writing women over the centuries, Sherry Simon underscores its function as "an intensely *relational* act, one which establishes connections between text and culture, between author and reader."[57] Because the "positionality" of translation so closely doubles the positionality of women with respect to writing, it is not surprising that translation has often been gendered as "feminine" or that women have played a significant role as translators. As this brief survey has shown, the translator's authority is far more flexible than the author's, and enables multiple forms of engagement and disengagement with texts, with ideas, with people. Certainly some of this freedom is available to practitioners of other kinds of textual criticism, to biographers, to philosophers—affective investments are an expanding universe, and there is no limit they cannot reach, however "impersonal" the writing—but one of the odd beauties of translation is the degree to which the space for freeplay is visible to all. Is it me or is it Fielding? asks Riccoboni. Let's see how it sells.

THE "REGULATED PASSION"
OF ELIZABETH GRIFFITH

[handwritten: "paratextual (configuration)"]

I now turn to one of the most extraordinary interactions between translator and text from the period, Elizabeth Griffith's *Memoirs of Ninon de l'Enclos, with her Letters to M. de St-Evremond and to the Marquis de Sévigné, Collected and Translated from the French, by a Lady* (1761). What makes this translation unusual is its significant paratextual apparatus. The work appears in two volumes. Following the dedicatory letter and introduction, we have Ninon de l'Enclos's correspondence with Saint-Evremond, about forty pages long. The rest of the volume is composed of a six-page essay, "The Translator to the Reader"; a sixty-page text, "The Life and Character of Ninon de l'Enclos," culled from French sources; and a second essay titled "The Translator to the Reader," nearly fifty pages long, which ends by introducing the letters to the marquis de Sévigné. Most of the second volume is taken up by the remainder of the letters, followed by a third brief essay, "The Conclusion. The Translator to the Reader" (2:243–47).

The question of the authorship of the *Memoirs* is at least as complicated as its paratextual configuration. The apocryphal letters from L'Enclos to Sévigné had been published in 1750 in France under a fictitious London imprint; they have been attributed to Louis Damours (d.1788) as well as to the well-known novelist Crébillon fils. An anonymous English translation, presumably the one that Griffith criticizes (1:148–51), appeared in 1751. Griffith cites a French serial publication, the *Petit réservoir*, as the source for the letters to Saint-Evremond and the (also apocryphal) "memoirs."[58] The *Petit réservoir* publication would appear to be a reprint or pirated edition of *Mémoires et lettres pour servir à l'histoire de la vie de Mademoiselle de l'Enclos* (1751), attributed to Douxménil (d. 1777 or 1778). Multiple authorial voices and veils of anonymity swirl around this translation "By a Lady." In addition to the texts that Griffith translates, there are other named and unnamed sources. She includes an anonymous commendatory poem at the head of the work; several interpolated texts in the longest of her critical essays, the second "Translator to the Reader" piece; a philosophical dialogue between Ninon de l'Enclos and Mme de Maintenon that she attributes to Voltaire (1:117–26);[59] an "editor's letter" to an anonymous woman concerning the letters to Sévigné (presumably by Louis Damours, who furthermore quotes at length from the abbé Chateauneuf regarding L'Enclos's epistolary skill, 1:127–31); and an "Essay on Classical Translation" by an unnamed gentleman friend (1:142–46).

In what originally appears to be a triply gynocentric translation (by a woman, of a woman, and dedicated to a woman), the text itself turns out to be a collection of pieces by female impersonators, only one of whom, Voltaire, is recognized or named. The insistence on the duchess of Bedford's name in the dedicatory epistle takes on a deeper meaning. The translator explicitly refuses to name herself and recognizes that she has breached protocol by giving the recipient no warning of the appearance of the book— "stealing this address upon you." The text is compared both to a "nameless foundling" and to a coin about to be newly stamped, to "render it current, and cover its allay" (1:iv). The duchess alone must stand for the text, and her identification renders it unassailable: "I do not imagine there is any thing in these writings that can offend the most reserved ear, when I venture to present them first, to a person whose character and station so justly intitle her to the highest and nicest respect" (1:vi).

The commendatory poem, however, directs our attention not to the text's inoffensiveness but to the translator's role in rendering it so:

> Whilst Ninon's spirit kindles all love's fire,
> Thy moral chastens every loose desire.
> Thy regulated passion, void of blame,
> Warms without scorching, like the vestal flame.
>
> (1:vii)

From this point on, although the translator may remain anonymous, she is anything but "invisible." It little matters, ultimately, who wrote the "letters and memoirs": under the duchess's ("stolen") protection, the translator embarks on an exploration of gender roles and language. Having erected a barrier of deniability, she allows herself a racy anecdote from Ninon's life, commenting with perfect aplomb, "This extract naturally raised my curiosity to inquire a little farther after so extraordinary a woman" (1:xi).[60] She claims equal freedom in what she calls her "method of translating, quite new": "Not being perfect *mistress* of the French idiom, I was obliged to read the letters frequently over, in order to catch the spirit of the writers; which I have endeavoured to convey to the readers, in such a free manner as one tells a story or repeats a conversation; by imitating the humour, or expressing the sentiment, though not in the same literal way they received it" (1:xii). The word "mistress" resonates ambiguously here. Literally, Griffiths is telling us that she is no "master" of the French language—but like so many gendered pairs, this one is asymmetrical, all the more so given the context, a discussion of a courtesan's life. The translator has it both ways: by translating freely, she abdicates "mastery" (for lack of a corresponding feminine term) but also eludes being "the mistress" of French, being dominated by her source text. Instead, she likens translation to conversation—specifically, to *remembered* conversation, a making-present of some past interaction rather than some agonistic striving with the "original."[61]

These two threads—the gender politics of L'Enclos's life, which is both extraordinary and exemplary, and the translator's relationship with her text—weave their way throughout the work. Of correspondence between L'Enclos and Saint-Evremond, "that charming old couple," the translator remarks, "May these excellent examples serve to rouse up the supineness of all who are *declining in the vale of years*, and inspirit them to exert some effort to preserve their intellectual faculties from a lethargy!" (1:46). In the "Life and Character" section, although the translator punctuates the text with occasional moralizing footnotes, the presentation focuses on the seeming paradox of Ninon's "two characters": sexual libertinism versus philosophical intelligence, goodness, and generosity. Griffith's footnotes sometimes question and sometimes defend Ninon's beliefs as related in the main text, the dialogic aspect becoming concretized when she includes the L'Enclos-Maintenon dialogue in the longest of the "Translator to the Reader" essays. In Voltaire's dialogue, the sexually emancipated woman and the pious wife of Louis XIV share a moment in remembering their old friendship, a bittersweet recollection for Maintenon, who is unhappy in her "supreme grandeur." Ever since her ascension, she tells Ninon, "my heart became a void; my mind was under constraint" (1:121). Ninon's final advice—"by the helps of friends, liberty, and philosophy, one may be sufficiently happy for our stage in life"—is interrupted by the arrival of two "ministers of state" (1:126). Griffith responds more forcefully to Ninon in her commentary but defends her as well, noting the cultural differences between England and France, and the relative "usefulness" for women to have a fuller understanding of the stakes in the *lutte des sexes* (1:133–37).

In her remarks on "galantry" Griffith advocates a pleasant "social intercourse of the sexes" of a studiously nonpurposive nature (in which "polite men may often exert galantry toward women, without the least thought of them either as mistresses or wives; and women generally receive and return such addresses with at least as innocent designs," 1:138). Such relationships,

Griffith tells us, are like "ancient writings" and "must be referred intirely to *taste*; for the pleasures of both arise from certain inexpressible graces, which refined sentiment or accomplished education only, can render us sensible of" (1:139).

The sexual politics of the *Memoirs* are spliced with the textual politics. As I have already suggested, the "freedom" of the translation, the proliferation of more or less anonymous or misattributed texts, and the "namelessness" of the "foundling" book all combine to open up a world in which texts circulate as freely as Ninon de l'Enclos herself and the translator's freedom is the greatest of all. A striking example of this disembodied freedom can be found in the interpolated "Essay on Classic Translation" attributed to a "gentleman of taste," who purportedly gave it to her to read when she complained that all the classical works she had read in translation were "insipid." The essay, which has less to do with the Greek and Roman classics than with translation in general, argues that translation (like the "inexpressible graces" required to appreciate "galantry") requires genius, taste, and something other than a "faithful" or grammatically correct rendering. (This position will later enable Griffith to criticize the previous translator of the L'Enclos letters as the "dictionary-bound" "usher" of a "boarding-school," 1:147.) All this is good grist for Griffith's mill, but the manner of presentation speaks loudly as well. The arguments are hardly original, and much of the essay turns on the seemingly inevitable recycling of words, phrases, and images as a feature of intellectual life. It cites well-worn phrases from Denham and Horace, and manages to trot out a number of commonplace similes for translation (comparing it to painting, to the wrong side of a tapestry, to the process of evaporation "in chemistry," and so on). In a note, Griffith underscores the close resemblance of one of the author's observations to a line in Samuel Butler's posthumous works—supposedly published "long after these notes were written"—but leading her to the conclusion that "Good wits jump" and the same ideas may arise spontaneously in different writers (1:143n).

Words and ideas "jump" or are carried, *translated*, from place to place. What no author can ever lay claim to, the translator/freethinker makes her own by assuring that it is "nobody's." At the end of her concluding essay "to the Reader," Griffith returns to Ninon's world, the world of "the greatest male wits of France, *La Bruyere, Rochefoucault, St. Evremond, Fontaine,* &c.," and contests, one last time, their view that pleasure is the "end" of virtue. In Griffith's modified Epicureanism, pleasure and virtue are inseparable, but virtue cannot be "reduced to sensuality" (2:245). And here she offers a notion of subjectivity that, like the ineffable something of gender relations and of source texts, is unreachable, unfettered, and yet remains within her sphere of conscious moral decision: "It is a received opinion, that the bulk of mankind do not know the real motives from which they act. It is possible indeed, that I, for instance, may be guided by principles, which I may be ignorant of. But then, in the name of common sense, how come these presumptuous reasoners to be better acquainted with them, than I am myself?" (2:246). Griffith accepts the *moralistes'* view that many of our "real motives" may be unavailable to consciousness, but she refuses to relinquish responsibility for moral action, which is "determined by the *consciousness* of the agent" (2:247), or to see pleasure as inherently vicious. She thus steers between the horns of a familiar dilemma. The translation project, with its multiple voices, circulating texts, and overarching dialogic structure, has afforded her the middle ground from which such a position can be articulated.

THE TRANSLATOR'S MIDDLE VOICE

In his well-known essay "La Différance," Jacques Derrida draws on an analogy from linguistics to explain his key concept. The middle voice, "a certain nontransitivity," offers him a way to articulate something "between" active and passive: that is, something that is neither active nor passive, neither subject nor object. Secondarily, he wants to claim that Western philosophy has founded itself on just this split, a claim that has not only logical but also ontological and ethical ramifications.[62] Vincent Pecora called into question the proposal for a poststructuralist ethics based on the middle voice, arguing with respect to this passage in Derrida that the apparent source text for the analogy, Emile Benveniste's essay "Actif et moyen dans le verbe," does not bear out the claim that the middle voice was ever "repressed" by "Western" thought.[63] While Pecora is probably right to say that "repression" is not really at issue in Benveniste's essay, he nevertheless leaves intact Derrida's primary point that, like *différance*, the middle voice is a useful concept for helping us think outside of conventional categories.

What can a rereading of Benveniste's essay offer us? As Benveniste points out, when we attempt to comprehend within our own linguistic habits the notion of a middle voice, our notions of active and passive must also change.

Benveniste focuses on how there can be two modalities of agency (active and middle); he is less concerned with the passive voice, where action simply originates outside the subject and takes place in or with it. Nevertheless, as he points out, each member of the system must derive its meaning from the set of oppositions, and together the three terms must determine "the positional field of the subject" (1:174).

The active-passive dichotomy has long been present in discussions of translation and authorship. Translators are praised (or condemned) for "slavish fidelity" to their texts, whereas authors are considered agents who direct the text as they will. Those asymmetrical relations in turn have given rise to the persistent gendering of translation as female, subservient.[64] Let us take a moment, however, to consider the parallels with Benveniste's scheme. The active voice, where the subject initiates a process that goes on beyond it, corresponds to the view of the writer as autonomous originator of texts that, once produced, circulate in the world. The passive voice, in which the action taking place in the subject is initiated outside, finds a reflection in the view of the translator as passive recipient and transmitter. Neither formulation is quite adequate, of course, since both translation and original authorship are informed by a complex dialectic of conscious and unconscious decisions and intuitions. It is the explicit "positionality" of translation, however, that casts the inadequacy of the dichotomy into sharpest relief. It is thus not surprising that the history of writing on translation should so regularly ask the question of agency or express dissatisfaction with the idea of the translator as passive: Cowley's search for "a better name" and Dryden's endless recasting of the "middle way" come to mind. It is furthermore not surprising that women writers, who must constantly confront their positionality with regard to textual production and social relations (in ways that males, naturalized as agents and producers, may not), should have found in translation a stimulating and creative environment in which to work.

For Benveniste, as he looks over a dozen or more examples from Latin, Greek, and Sanskrit, the middle bespeaks a process "located within the subject," a form of agency that necessitates restructuring both active and passive, which are conventionally opposed to one another in modern Western thinking. Analogously, let us consider a text not as a message initiated and released to the world in a fixed form, nor as an entirely foreign entity external to the subject, but rather as something that is ongoing and bound up with the subject, a process in which the subject is implicated. There are implications for all forms of textual production here, of course, but it is translation that most insistently denaturalizes and demythologizes the conventional representations of autonomous texts and autonomous selves, just as the question of gender most insistently focuses our attention on the involvement of translation in hierarchies of power.

That demythologizing is not, historically speaking, a constant. Writing at the dawn of the Romantic age, successful translator and writer Isabelle de Montolieu defends her recourse to translation in a curiously abject manner in the preface to the third edition of her novel *Caroline de Litchfield*, claiming that "I lack the gift of genius, of creative imagination."[65] Even her novel, she notes, is based on "a little German tale." Original authorship is a fraught subject for Montolieu, who elsewhere in the preface explains that, whereas she had always published her translations under her own name, *Caroline* initially appeared in print with neither her permission nor her name, being attributed solely to "le traducteur de Werther" (v). The self-deprecation of her lack of "originality" suggests that Montolieu has fallen prey to what Berenice Carroll called the "class system of the intellect," the emphasis on "newness" and ex nihilo creation that has informed the concept of originality since the advent of Romanticism and from which women are generally excluded.[66] Unlike our earlier translators, male and female, who found forms of authorial agency within translation, Montolieu regards the clearest example of her authorial agency as contaminated by translation. The problem lies not in her assessment of authorship—ineluctably bound up in dialogue with earlier texts—but in her willingness to assign a second-class status to writing that does not measure up to the mythic ideal of "newness." In such a scheme, anything less than "original" is relegated to the "passive voice."

Let us return to Elizabeth Griffith for a last example of the complex ways in which gender, translation, and signature intersect. Having published earlier translations "by a Lady," Griffith signs her 1770 translation of Mme de Caylus's memoirs as "The Translator of the Life and Writings of Ninon de l'Enclos." Here, too, Griffith seems drawn to a striking female figure, "distinguished equally for her wit and beauty," whose pleasingly disordered prose style has "the free, easy, and engaging air of a correspondence, or a conversation, rather than the dull regularity, and stiff restraint of narrative."[67] Griffith also seems drawn in a more complex way to her heroine's aunt, Mme de Maintenon, who as we saw also plays a role in the l'Enclos texts and to whom Griffith returns in a brief closing note. Her judgment of the "*factitiousness* of Madame de Maintenon's character" is not flattering but bespeaks a wish to come to terms with this figure of undeniable power.

A power for whom she has less sympathy, however, is none other than Voltaire. The volume of memoirs ends with an "Appendix by the Translator," in which Griffith tells us that just as the book was complete, a new edition of the original work with notes and a preface attributed to Voltaire made her stop the press in order to satisfy the public's interest in the philosophe (2:172–73). The deferential gesture quickly becomes two-edged, however, as Griffith interrupts the text with ironic footnotes ("What a fond partiality Monsieur de Voltaire seems to have here for his own works," she comments, regarding a reference to Le Siècle de Louis XIV, 2:177), ultimately breaking off altogether to conclude with her own reflections on the writing and the reading of history, novels, and memoirs. Noting that although the French are said to "excel in writings of mere amusement," their works "are notwith-standing full of sentiment and deduction" (2:185). This thought leads her to acknowledge that she has in fact interspersed her own "sentiments and observations" throughout her translation of the Caylus memoirs (2:187). What might appear as effrontery she codes as feminine modesty: "I hope, therefore, that such a reserve as this, may help to class me, in the favour of Monsieur de Voltaire, among the small number of those women he hints at . . . who *affect not a display of parts, upon every occasion*" (2:187–88).

Having had her fun with Voltaire, Griffith turns briefly, as I have noted, to Mme de Maintenon, whom she presents as a mixture of visibility and impenetrability. Griffith condemns her for her ostentation in the one mat-ter that should be most private: her charitable acts. Regretting the pre-ponderance of "ostentatious, rather than concealed, charity, in the world," Griffith closes with a quotation, her final words for the volume: "I wish, however, as Henry says, in the Series, 'that there were more of such char-acters in the world—persons who can give alms without charity; and be liberal without generosity—for *the outward and visible sign* is sufficient to all the purposes of this life—*the inward and spiritual grace* is the business of the other'" (2:189–90). The "Series" (from which Griffith cites exact volume and page number) is *A Series of Genuine Letters, Between Henry and Fran-ces*, first published in 1757.[68] Unlike so many letter novels of the day that merely purported to be authentic, the letters of the *Series* actually were real letters exchanged by Griffith and her fiancé (and later husband), Richard. By citing the words of Henry/Richard, rather than Frances's/her own, she adds a further layer to the mystifications of the text's voice—and, certainly, expresses affection for her partner, with private words spoken in public.

The quotation is a secret signature, a "stamp" on the anonymous text. Griffith speaks "as another" on multiple levels: as Henry, not Frances; as translator, not author; as Mme de Caylus, not herself—and as an independent-minded reader of Voltaire, not a slavish epigone. Thus Griffith proves herself master and mistress of her art—through the middle voice.

CHAPTER 6

From "A Light in Antiquity" to Enlightened Antiquity

Modern Classicists

Taking his distance from "those modern Criticks" such as La Motte, Alexander Pope emphasizes his attachment to "that ancient World" and extols the pleasures that readers will find there: "Let them think they are growing acquainted with Nations and People that are now no more; that they are stepping almost three thousand Years back into the remotest Antiquity, and entertaining themselves with a clear and surprizing Vision of Things no where else to be found, the only true mirror of that ancient World."[1] The vividness of the "surprizing Vision" makes us forget the temporal abyss and focus on a world with which one might, indeed, become "acquainted." In this chapter, I will be examining this "worlding" of antiquity in the reflections of eighteenth-century translators of Greek, Latin, and Hebrew texts. For Dryden and to a certain extent for Dacier, the classical world is unalterably gone; translation becomes a means for dealing with that loss, incorporating traces of the past into one's present project, which is cast as poetic ambition for Dryden and as the furtherance of knowledge for Dacier. For later translators, the pastness of the past is conceived as cultural, rather than temporal, distance.

This shift marks one of two major changes in the status of classical learning in the intellectual hierarchy of the republic of letters. Although translators continue to assume that the classics have something powerful to teach us and that they represent the foundation on which we stand, the texts come closer to us, in effect, by being recoded as "foreign" rather than unimaginably ancient. The second change in the cultural capital accorded to ancient texts occurs through the increasing prominence and respect accorded to works in the modern languages and to their translations, the topic of the next chapter. As we shall see, modern poets, dramatists, and even novelists gradually stake their claim to the same sorts of editorial presentation and methodological punctilio as the works of Virgil. As in any period, hegemonic structures, such as the preeminence of classical learning, are not airtight but are instead paratactic, segmented, permeable, their seeming unity of structure and purpose an illusion.

In this chapter, I will look at some of the ways in which "newness enters the world" within the traditional practice of classical translation. Because of the central location of such scholarship within the world of letters, echoes of larger debates can be heard in our body of translators' prefaces. This is particularly the case in France, home of the *grammairiens-philosophes*. One of the major philosophical debates of the period, the "inversion" debate, over the relationship of language to the structures of thought, is touched off by questions of translation between Latin and French. In England, as Murray Cohen has pointed out, there is a greater division of labor between grammarians and philosophers.[2] Translators' interest in the structural proprieties of language corresponds more closely to grammarians' concerns than to those of such philosophers as James Harris who were investigating the philosophical status of language itself. Yet, as we shall see, translation also falls under the province of such rhetoricians as Bible translator George Campbell, a member of the Aberdeen Philosophical Society and an interlocutor of David Hume. In Britain as well as France, then, the echoes of eighteenth-century philosophical linguistics and epistemology—What do we know when we know a foreign language? What form of knowledge is language itself?—can frequently be heard, even if the main forum of those debates lies elsewhere.

Trevor Ross has argued that the literary value traditionally invested in the "inaccessibility" of classical texts becomes recoded through Dryden and others as a privileged understanding of the text's poetry and access to the author's subjectivity—as well as one's own. Access to the other was not a function of resemblance; to the contrary, the "author . . . was perceived as significantly and perhaps immeasurably different from oneself."[3] Such "difference," however, is a function not only of an enhanced notion of authorial subjectivity and originality, of individual "genius," as Ross argues, but of a growing sense of the cultural and historical otherness, the "genius," or *génie*, of language. Such perception means that while ancient languages may begin to lose their centrality, the question of otherness in language is more powerful than ever, and that while literary translation may no longer be a key activity for writers and intellectuals, it becomes one of the principal means for thinking about cultural differences. Languages, whether Latin, Greek, or Spanish, are "foreign" in a way they previously were not: they bespeak other manners, customs, and habits of thought. The question for the grammairiens-philosophes becomes, To what extent are these habits of thought conditioned by, if not constructed from, language, rather than being simply reflected or represented by language? *Génie* is the term enabling the articulation of historicism, ethnography, and psychology that infuses discussion of language and culture. When seventeenth-century translators talked about linguistic génie, they were referring to the characteristic turns of phrase, idioms, and syntactic structures that posed problems in the conversion of one language into another. For the eighteenth century, the ramifications of génie extend much further.

WORLDING IN BRITAIN: LANGUAGE AND TIME

Alexander Pope's *Iliad* and *Odyssey*, published in stages from 1715 to 1726, would set a new standard for poetic translation. As Johnson would remark, he "wrote for his own age and his own nation."[4] Pope's Homer, like Dryden's Virgil, would stand as a daunting model, so that even at the century's end, William Cowper might criticize the "fetters" of Pope's heroic couplets but not the "immortal honour" of his writing.[5] In our day, Pope's preface to the *Iliad* has been termed "one of his ablest pieces of criticism."[6] As numerous critics have observed, the preface is as much a poetic manifesto for Pope himself as it is a commentary on Homer. In this respect, Pope's presence in this preface is quite different from Dryden's in the "Dedication." Both are self-conscious writers intent on making a statement on their craft, but whereas Dryden's reflections lead him toward literary criticism and surreptitious autobiography, or at least *apologia*, Pope offers insights into his own

poetic project. As Douglas Knight's study of Pope's manuscript revisions
shows, he deliberately de-emphasized the critical debates of the day, the better to foreground the *Iliad* and to forge a bond with readers.

From the first sentence proclaiming Homer "to have had the greatest
Invention of any Writer whatever" (3), the preface is a call for an energized
understanding of poetry. Invention and Imagination infuse a wild exuber-
ance into the "order'd Garden" of polite letters and serve as a poetic credo
that privileges the visual and the immediate.[7] Initially describing Homer's
work in luxuriant organic terms (the "wild Paradise" that caused him grief
with Dacier), Pope's discussion of "invention" quickly shifts to images of
heat and light: "Fire and Rapture" (4), "Fire from Heaven" (5), "a powerful
Star" (5), "the bright imagination of *Homer* shining out . . . the strongest
and most glowing imaginable" (9). "Like Glass in the Furnace" (10), Pope's
own genius of invention shone forth for his readers.

Pope is also saying something about language. While his comments on
the translation—his promise to deliver Homer "entire and unmaim'd" and
to steer between the extremes of "a servile dull Adherence to the Letter"
and "a chimerical insolent Hope of raising and improving [the] Author"
(17)—have a familiar ring, the imagery manifests a desire to express a power
that inheres in language but cannot be described by it. Greek is "a superior
Language," Pope tells us, hence hard to render in English. That difficulty
should be taken as all the more reason to adhere closely to the text: "If there
be sometimes a *Darkness*, there is often a *Light* in Antiquity, which nothing
better preserves than a Version almost literal" (17). The light of antiquity,
like the fire of the poem, suggests a world of passions and experiences accessible in Greek. If they are accessible in English, it is to the extent that
the poet has managed "to keep alive that Spirit and Fire" animating Homer
(22). Language thus compensates for temporal distance and makes vivid
that which is estranged from us.

Peter Connelly has argued that the underlying theory of translation in
Pope's preface is closely constructed from picture theory, "ut pictura translatio," leading to a concentration on color, visuality, and design.[8] Given
the prominence of Pope's translation, however, it is striking that for other
translators the achievement consists in the poem itself, rather than in the
accompanying notes and reflections for what they might reveal on the art
of translation. It is not that the translation was less "visible" as a translation—all those notes would prevent one from thinking otherwise—but
for Johnson, "the notes of others are read to clear difficulties, those of

Pope to vary entertainment." Translators would cite Pope as a dazzling poet, a model, rather than as a critic. The immediacy of the relation he establishes with readers, bridging time and distance to bring them as much in contact with the translator as with the author, is unlike any other. As we consider other, admittedly less brilliant eighteenth-century translators of the classics, we will continue to see both the search for the immediacy of Pope's "clear and surprising Vision" and the deepening sense that other language contains "the only true Mirror" of other worlds.

The desire to vivify the past appears in a fanciful and unintentionally comic mode in Thomas Francklin's 1753 poem "Translation." Here, however, the perfect confluence of author and translator seems to take place primarily within the realm of fantasy. Francklin recasts Roscommon's injunction to "chuse an *Author* as you chuse a *Friend*" in terms of "the more lively passion":[9] "Unless an author like a mistress warms, / How shall we hide his faults, or taste his charms . . . ?" (9). From this sexualized evocation of the translator's task, Francklin proceeds to imagine perfect translator-author "couples" (Plautus and Vanbrugh, Lucian and Swift, Johnson and Juvenal) between whom he senses a "secret sympathy" (10n), another rejection of erudition in favor of feeling. Whether united by "sympathy" or "lively passion," Francklin's ideal homoerotic unions seem remote from the real world—just as they are relegated to footnotes and kept separate from the main text. The poem asks whether British men of letters ("you sons of fame") will "join with Warton and with Me" (a reference to Joseph Warton's Virgil) but ends with the as-yet-unfulfilled hope that Francklin himself will be able to do justice to the classics in his own work. Past and present appear as close, potentially, as partners in a love affair, but their relationship remains unconsummated.

The long-standing English tradition of politicizing translation continued to provide an important means of connecting past to present; the eighteenth century saw an increasing emphasis on historically grounded linguistic differences that nuance the connections suggested by topicality. Thus Thomas Gordon suggests in his book on Cataline's conspiracy that "our Circumstances may be like those of old *Rome*, when this Plot of *Cataline* was set on Foot."[10] To assert the relevance—or the "cogency"—of the ancient text is not to conflate past and present but rather to set two separate realities in relation to each other. For Gordon, the state of the language reflects the state of a nation's political institutions and "the taste and stile of the Court"; thus he argues that L'Estrange put forward "doctrines of servitude and a defence of Tyranny" in his Aesop (31). A political motivation is foremost in his decision to translate Tacitus—"I have vindicated the principles of civil Liberty," he tells us of his project (33)—but a linguistic motivation, the "strengthening" of English through an infusion of terse Tacitean style, is the secondary goal that underlies his decision to produce as literal and Latinizing a translation as possible.[11]

Although his translation strategy is completely different from Gordon's, William Guthrie also believes that "true Eloquence," in which the Ancients were unsurpassed, "is built upon the *Love of Liberty*."[12] True eloquence being the offspring of a deliberative body "where Freedom of Debate is the principal Privilege," he turns to the most powerful exemplars from the contemporary English context to render Cicero, asserting that "such a Language is used in the two Houses of Parliament, as might become a *Roman* Senate," and that certain contemporary English orators would fill Cicero himself "with Delight and Jealousy" (xv–xvi). It's important to see Guthrie's modernizing not as a failure to recognize cultural distinctions between past and present but, to the contrary, as part of an awareness of the growing autonomy of English. Guthrie discusses at length the differences between English and Latin eloquence; it is a common appreciation to a republican tradition that makes such a rhetorical translation possible. For Guthrie, "*Living Manners* alone can communicate the Spirit of the Original" in a way that mere "competent Knowledge" cannot (xix–xx).

While few translators would espouse as thoroughly Latinizing an approach as Gordon, fewer still would advocate a full-fledged "modernizing" of classical texts. As George Colman argues in the preface to his translation of Terence, adaptative translation "deprives the modern reader of the pleasure of directly comparing the manners and customs of another age and country with those of his own"; also, the conjunction of "antient cast" and "modernizing spirit" produces "a fantastical medley, which represents the manners of no age or country at all."[13] It is this sense that language and style represent the vast range of attitudes, beliefs, and behaviors covered by the term "manners," as opposed to representing ideas, that is at work throughout the translators' statements of this period. When style becomes as important as meaning in conveying the truth of a writer, especially a poet, a uniform style is clearly inadequate to convey poetic variety. "Style is Genius," claims Philip Francis, translator of Horace. "But the Misfortune of our Translators is, that they have only one Style, and that consequently all their Authors, Homer, Virgil, Horace, Ovid, are compelled to speak in the same Numbers, and the same unvaried Expression."[14] Francis's call for a departure from the confines of rhyming couplets is echoed by Alexander Strahan, who sets himself under the banner of Roscommon and Dryden but also revisits the Horatian injunction *Nec verbum verbo*, citing multiple scholarly sources, including Huet, to argue for "the strict manner of translating."[15] Cowper's comments on Pope underscore the extent to which changes in taste and language combine: "Accustomed always to rhime, he had formed to himself an ear which probably could not be much gratified by verse that wanted it."[16] That even the greatest poet of an earlier generation could not "hear" blank verse speaks to major changes in the literary language.

Not only style but also linguistic register becomes a vector infusing difference into language. Joseph Warton observes of his *Georgics* that although "the meanness of the terms of husbandry is concealed and lost in a dead language," many of the words that appear in his translation, such as "*plough and sow, wheat, dung, ashes, horse and cow*, &c. will, I fear, unconquerably disgust many a delicate reader."[17] Translation historians have typically looked askance on such comments as indicative of the low tolerance for anything falling outside the well-guarded boundaries of polite culture. We should not, however, overlook the fact that such utterances also bespeak writers' very real awareness of the historical dimension of their utterances. As Cowper puts it, "It is difficult to kill a sheep with dignity in a modern language."[18]

For Joseph Priestley the gulf between past and present is understood in terms of the mechanisms of language change even in the context of the presumably ahistorical structures of universal grammar. Priestley comes to the conclusion that the contrast between the constant flux and minute distinctions of living languages and the stasis of the ancient languages is such that translation is "absolutely impossible."[19] While few translators would make so categorical a statement, many find themselves reflecting on the genius and present state of English. William Smith prefaces his midcentury translation of Thucydides with a critique of Thomas Hobbes's 1629 version, partly on the basis of Hobbes's errors (and politics) but partly because "the English language hath gone through a great variation, hath been highly polished, since Mr. *Hobbes* wrote."[20] As early as 1705, Martin Bladen calls attention in the preface to his translation of Caesar's *Commentaries* to the "many Improvements" that English has received since the last translation a century earlier. In the first half of the eighteenth century, the sense of linguistic progress was as strong in England as in France. Bladen takes heart at the "degree of politeness" brought to English by such "Incomparable Masters" as Thomas Sprat and Roger L'Estrange and rejoices that they have "sav'd the Kingdom the Expence of an Academy." While L'Estrange would not long be cited as a stylistic model, the self-consciousness with respect to French is shared with many; as we have seen, Roscommon and others in his circle wished to form an English Academy on the French model. William Guthrie, in his translation of Cicero, argues for "an Academy for the Perfection and Purity of the English Language."[21] Awareness of the temporality of language is bound up with awareness of the worlds inherent within language—and the capacity of language to body forth the national character, as we shall see in the next chapter.

Like their French counterparts, the English translators have become aware of the distances that separate their language and "manners" not only from antiquity but from their own history. Despite his confidence that English has progressed, Martin Bladen finds a "melancholy Thought" in the notion that unlike the French or Italians, who can still see a connection between medieval and modern forms of their tongues, his compatriots cannot recognize older forms of English: "*Petrarch* still speaks good Italian, tho' *Chaucer*, who dy'd Sixty Six Years after him, must have a *Saxon* or *Scotch* Commentator to make him intelligible."[22] It is significant that Bladen associates Scots with older forms of English. Within a few decades, and unlike the French, some eighteenth-century British writers would begin to attach a value to the earlier state of the English language, and while they may generally have regarded English as having "improved," the connection to a literary and linguistic *longue durée* was an important element in the development of British nationalism. Thus the critic Thomas Warton (Joseph's brother) speaks of Spenser as having drunk from "the well of English undefiled" in his reading of Chaucer.[23] In the later eighteenth century, Ossianism is of course the primary locus for the idealization of older cultural forms.[24] Thus any sense of loss attendant on awareness of the temporality of the national language is recuperated and refigured as an enhancement of the national myth.

THE WORLD OF HEBREW

Few forms of translation evoke as sharply the combination of connection and estrangement from another tongue as translations from the Hebrew Bible; accounts of the Hebraic language reflect ongoing debates among both Catholics and Protestants on language, history, and meaning. Because scholars had dismissed the notion that Hebrew was the God-given Adamic language, its obscurity and "difference" were perceived as defects.[25] In Richard Simon's highly influential account, the obscurity of the Bible stems not only from the problem of irregular transmission and textual corruptions but from the Hebrew language itself, being "so concise and elliptical, that it is difficult to find a complete meaning."[26] Not only does the substance (*la matière*) pose massive problems of interpretation, but much of the language has been forgotten over time by Jews and Christians alike. In his equally influential response, Protestant Jean Le Clerc denied that Hebrew was as rife with ambiguity as Simon claimed; his argument was not that the more poetic books of the Old Testament did not contain obscure passages and awkward sentences, but that it was nevertheless possible to distinguish between truly equivocal passages and those with "a known meaning."[27] While recognizing that the differences in syntax made a literal translation between Hebrew and Latin, or the modern languages, impossible, he maintains the hope that the "value" of particular terms might be maintained even in ambiguous passages, translating ambiguity for ambiguity (347). Le Clerc's keen sense of linguistic value has a temporal dimension, as when he warns against using a word in an older sense, even were it to furnish a close equivalent, because of the potential for confusion as the semantic field of a given term expands or contracts over time (348). Several years later, in the dissertations prefacing his Latin translation of Genesis, he would strive to preserve the obscurity of the original without overwhelming the reader. Like so many others, Le Clerc argues for a "middle way" and cites Cicero's lost translation of Demosthenes as his ideal. Given, however, that "Languages do not answer one another . . . exactly," a perfectly transparent literal translation is impossible, and, ultimately, "no Translation can be in all respects compleat."[28]

Hebrew thus remained on the horizon as an intractable, obscure language, skewing optimistic notions of the potential harmony among languages, even as the text of the Old Testament was held up as an example of "sublimity" in Boileau's widely read translation of Longinus. Thus Richard Blackmore, whose relative openness to foreign literary norms we observed earlier (see Chapter 2), expresses his wonder that we should be affected by the "Beauty and Majesty" of the book of Job, "considering the Obscurity of the Stile or manner of Expression in the Eastern parts of the World, their Eloquence, as well as their Customs and Habits, being very different from ours."[29] Joseph Priestley, having catalogued the potential for ambiguity of

Hebrew and the "poverty" of its lexicon, suggests that the "striking simplicity of style" of the Old Testament is due to the lack of "improvement" in the
language over time and the widespread illiteracy of its speakers.[30]

It was Robert Lowth who shifted the direction of commentary on Hebrew from an emphasis on its obscurity and defects to an appreciation
for the formal qualities and the expressivity of its poetry. For Lowth, the
"genius" of Hebrew is "directly opposite" to Greek and Latin, hence to the
educated European's aesthetic ideals, with the result that "a Hebrew poem,
if translated into Greek or Latin verse, and having the conformation of the
sentences accommodated to the idiom of a foreign language, will appear
confused and mutilated; will scarcely retain a trace of its genuine elegance,
and peculiar beauty."[31] Whereas Blackmore sought to avoid repetition in
his translation of *Job*, Lowth saw it as fundamental to Hebrew poetics.
In his translation of Isaiah, he argues for the centrality of the literal as
the basis for all forms of interpretation, "Spiritual, Mystical, Allegorical,
Analogical, or the like."[32] He goes on to set an ideal standard of fidelity:
"It is incumbent on every Translator to study the manner of his Author; to
mark the peculiarities of his style, to imitate his features, his air, his gesture, and, as far as the difference of language will permit, even his voice;
in a word, to give a just and expressive resemblance of the Original. If he
does not carefully attend to this, he will sometimes fail of entering into his
meaning; he will always exhibit him unlike himself" (*Isaiah*, xxxv). "Expressivity" has become as key to the depiction of Hebrew as "obscurity,"
if not more so.

It was in this context that George Campbell published his new translation
of the gospels, with copious annotations and twelve prefatory dissertations,
in 1789. A biblical scholar and Church of Scotland minister, Campbell was
one of the original members of the Aberdeen Philosophical Society, whose
members included Common-Sense philosopher Thomas Reid. At the time
of the publication of the Gospel translation, he was already well known for
his published sermons, his *Philosophy of Rhetoric* (1776), and a *Dissertation
on Miracles* (1762) that aimed at rebutting David Hume's skeptical account
of miracles by offering the "common-sense" argument that unbiased testimony of eye-witnesses and indeed language itself could be relied upon.
Translation historians today are aware of Campbell primarily because the
dissertations accompanying his gospel translation are cited by Alexander
Tytler in his *Essay on the Principles of Translation*.[33] In the second edition of
his *Essay*, Tytler expresses his pleasure at his discovery of Campbell's work,

a feeling he describes as "that satisfaction which always arises from finding our opinions warranted by the concurring judgement of persons of distinguished ingenuity and taste."[34] The two offer very similar principles for translators to follow, particularly with regard to what Tytler refers to as "all the Ease of Original Composition" (209) and Campbell describes as the "quality of an original performance, as to appear natural and easy."[35]

Such "ease" and "naturalness" are the hallmarks of "fluent" or "domesticating" translation for Lawrence Venuti, who dismisses both Tytler and Campbell for their "bourgeois valorization of transparent discourse" and concealed "investment in domestic cultural values," such as, in Campbell's case, "a Christian dogmatism with anti-Semitic overtones."[36] Without trying to present him as some sort of closet deconstructionist, I would like to explore some of the depth and complexity of Campbell's work, which may valorize transparent discourse but also reflects transparency's discontents. Because of his commitment to certain axiomatic principles and canons of taste, not all the discontents can be articulated nor all the complexity resolved. Yet George Campbell is a careful enough translator, a serious enough scholar, and a thorough enough critic that the problems that stem from his presuppositions inevitably emerge. The most arresting issues arise not in the obvious places where a translation historian would automatically look, such as dissertation 10, "The chief Things to be attended to in translating," but throughout the volume, particularly in the early dissertations on questions of language, language change, and meaning.

The basic assumptions are set forth in the preface, where Campbell ridicules the current vogue for originality in literature that renders it like "every other commodity."[37] His own work, by definition, has no part in such dubious commerce: "A translator, if he do justice to his author and his subject, can lay no claim to originality" (xvii). Yet Campbell asserts his scholarly authority with regard to his apparatus, the dissertations and notes. The clean distinction between thoughts and ideas, or between the ideas of one writer and those of another, recurs in the distinction between the "sentiment" of the scriptures, which is divinely inspired, and the "expression" by the prophets and "sacred penmen," which is a function of time and place: "The truths implied in the sentiments, are essential, immutable, and have an intrinsic value: the words which compose the expression, are in their nature circumstantial, changeable, and have no other value than what they derive from the arbitrary conventions of men" (26). Unlike the Port-Royal translators, for whom divine meaning inhered in language as its "real presence," Campbell severs the connection by rendering it contingent, "language as well as dress being in fact no more than a species of mode" (14). He thus distinguishes between the inspiration of pagan oracles and that of the prophets:

> [The pagans] are reported to have uttered their predictions in what is called extasy or trance, that is, whilst they underwent a temporary suspension both of their reason and of their senses. Accordingly they are represented as mere machines, not acting but acted upon, and passive like the flute into which the musician blows. . . .
>
> Totally different was the method of the prophets of the true God. The matter, or all that concerned the thoughts, was given them: what concerned the manner, or enunciation, was left to themselves. (27–28)

The distinction here between "thoughts" and "enunciation" restates the distinction between "sentiment" and "expression." What is important, given the contingency of expression, is that human language, in all its range of accents, styles, and registers, be adequate to the task of expressing divine sentiment. That "sentiment" must furthermore be so perfectly clear as to allow its transposition into different styles, registers, and languages—just as "author's thoughts" and "translator's thoughts" are perfectly distinct, separable from one another, and capable of being represented in language. The adequacy of language to thought is for Campbell axiomatic.

The arbitrariness of language is also axiomatic: "Are words of any kind more than arbitrary signs? . . . Is there a natural fitness in one word or phrase more than in another, for denoting the thing signified? Is not the connexion between sounds and ideas merely artificial—the result of human, though tacit conventions?" (13). In the context of the argument, the arbitrariness of the sign functions to dematerialize signification to the greatest extent possible and to minimize the impact of translation on the divine Word. Language being unrooted in any necessary truth, its capacity to represent rests on an act of faith. At the same time, even though language's outward appearance presumably has no connection with inner meaning, Campbell must also account for the disparity between the ordinary speech of the prophets and apostles and the glory of the Word. Noting that the "external figure" of "poverty and ignorance" might fail to elicit interest or respect, he concludes that the "disadvantages or defects, both in speech and in outward figure" of the sacred writers are the "reasons of God's preference, whose thoughts are not our thoughts, nor are our ways his ways" (14). Strangeness and the refusal to adhere to the conventions of "good company" thus become markers of the divine rather than purely arbitrary signifiers.

The language of scripture is also shaped by what Campbell refers to as "idiom." Although he also uses the term in its conventional sense as an expression or arrangement of words peculiar to a given language, in the first dissertation he distinguishes it from "language." "Idiom" is eschatology in the sense that it incorporates God's message as revealed through history: "The knowledge of what is contained in that introductory revelation [i.e., the Old Testament], is always presumed in the readers of the New Testament, which claims to be the consummation of an economy of God for the salvation of man; of which economy the Old Testament acquaints us with the occasion, origin, and early progress. Both are therefore intimately connected. Accordingly, though the two Testaments are written in different languages, the same idiom prevails in both" (1–2). "Idiom" would thus appear to be another term for the nonlinguistic presence, "sentiment," or "thought" that lies beyond the external forms of language. At the same time, the term itself and Campbell's further use of it point us back to language. The overarching issue is the intelligibility of divine revelation: "If the words and phrases employed by the Apostles and Evangelists in delivering the revelation committed to them by the Holy Spirit, had not been agreeable to the received usage of the people to whom they spoke, their discourses being unintelligible, could have conveyed no information, and consequently would have been no revelation to the hearers" (1). "Intelligibility" relates to the continuity of divine revelation to the Jews, yet it is also deeply connected to Jewish history and culture and to the particular linguistic fate of the Hellenized Jews. In both the New Testament and the Septuagint, the "phraseology is Hebrew, and the words are Greek" (12)—returning us to the conventional linguistic understanding of the term "idiom." As far as the translators of the Septuagint are concerned, the hebraisms are partly intentional (because of the "scrupulous, I may even say superstitious, attachment of the Jews not only to the words, but to the letters and syllables, to every jot and tittle of the original," 12), but also partly accidental, as one language exercises a gravitational pull on another. "Idiom" thus reflects something deeper than echoing syntactic patterns, referring instead to culturally conditioned habits of thought and receptivity to the divine message. As he will later explain in his discussion of language change, "The idiom keeps a much firmer hold of the mind, than the words, which are mere sounds, do, and which, compared with the other, may be considered as but the body, the material part of a language whereof the idiom is the soul" (48–49).

Language may consist of arbitrary signs, but those signs are shaped by historical circumstances. Those differing circumstances explain language diversity and language change, which Campbell explores in his second dissertation. Here too we find him positing a distinction between the external "form" of language—its phonetic, syntactic, lexical, and morphological components—and its "spirit." The former can be "learnt from a tolerable grammar," whereas the latter requires an intimate knowledge of customs, history, institutions, and manners. Cultural phenomena operate on people's "sentiments"; those sentiments in turn "have a principal effect, first on the associations of ideas formed in their minds in relation to character and to whatever is an object of abstract reflection; secondly, on the formation of words, and the combination of phrases, by which these associations are expressed" (33). Both word formation and the association of ideas are hence the product of "sentiments," which are themselves the expression of historical and material circumstances. Those circumstances can thus be said to provide a ground for language—no longer completely arbitrary—and explain both linguistic diversity and change. Language change is directly related to historical change: "Indeed it is manifest, that if a nation should continue at the same precise degree of advancement in the sciences and arts both elegant and useful, should undergo no variation in their form of government, religion, and laws, and should have little or no intercourse with foreigners, their language and idiom would in all essential characters remain the same" (47–48). Campbell supports his argument by tracing a relationship between Jewish history and the evolution of Hebrew, which as we have seen he considers fundamental to the understanding of New Testament Greek.[38]

The shift to a more grounded notion of language and its imbrication in culture has important implications for translation, since vastly different circumstances between peoples and cultures complicate our ability to draw correspondences between languages. Campbell describes three categories of words, representing three degrees of correspondence. The first offer no difficulties to the translator. These are the "obvious productions of nature" for which all languages have perfectly equivalent terms, such as *sun, moon, bird,* and *tree* (33); elementary relations of kinship also fall into this category. The third category consists of terms that are completely untranslatable but not deeply problematic. These include names of objects, offices, institutions, or "weights, coins, and measures" that simply do not exist outside of their national and historical context (42). The second category of terms proves the most intractable. These include "most of the terms relating to morals, to the passions and matters of sentiment, or to the objects of the reflex and internal senses, in regard to which it is often impossible to find words in one language that are exactly equivalent to those of another" (36). Such incommensurability is in direct proportion to differences in the "constitution, religion, and laws" of nations, on which their "sentiments, manners, and customs" depend. These lead translators to rely on "approximation"—a term which Campbell notes is borrowed from the realm of mathematics, thus gesturing in passing to a linguistic weak spot in English. Misleading etymologies and false cognates not only represent traps for naive or inexperienced translators but also point to the deeper problem of language change over time (37).

Campbell cites d'Alembert's assessment of our defective understanding of the range of Latin synonyms but then focuses particularly on the Abbé Girard's influential work on synonyms—or "words that pass for synonyms"—to underscore a more important point.[39] For Girard and for many of the French *philosophes*, true synonymy, strictly speaking, does not exist; even the most closely related terms are distinguished by delicate shades of meaning, nuances, *idées accessoires*, variations in usage and register—a testimony, in Girard's view, to the precision and clarity of French. Campbell concludes that "it is impossible, in a consistency with either perspicuity or propriety, to translate them uniformly by the same terms. . . . For, as has been observed, they are such as do not perfectly correspond with the terms of a different tongue" (40). As we earlier saw in Le Clerc, Campbell is sketching the outlines of a quasi-Saussurian notion of linguistic "value," the shifting correspondences among different acceptations of terms, closely related to Saussure's key concept of differential meaning. Campbell is thus torn between arbitrary signifiers and motivated signifiers; between a language that is completely adequate to the task of conveying meaning and languages that can never completely correspond to one another.

In the final part of the second dissertation, Campbell takes up the question that has been implicit in much of the previous text, that of "the difficulties found in translating the Scriptures." These include the differences of "manners," whose implications he has already explored; the "penury of words in the ancient oriental languages," about which he will have more to say in later dissertations; the lack of extant texts in the ancient language; and the "nature of the prophetic style," to which I will now turn. Prophetic "style," as he terms it, is "highly figurative, or, as some critics have thought proper to denominate it, symbolical. The symbolic or typical is, in my apprehension, very much akin to what may be called the allegoric style" (55). The difference between symbol (or figure, or type) and allegory consists in the conventional aspect of the former, whereas the latter "is more at the discretion of the writer" (55). Consequently, figures (which Campbell likens to Egyptian hieroglyphs) need not closely resemble their referents, since their interpretation is a matter of "established use," whereas allegory requires resemblance in order to be decipherable. Figures are thus never truly "obscure"—and neither is scripture in general, as Campbell will later argue in a dissertation critiquing Richard Simon's biblical textual criticism.

Indeed, Campbell is at great pains to make the traditional stumbling block of Bible translators, the "obscurity" of the text, completely disappear in a blaze of textual perspicuity. The inherent difficulty of figures is eliminated through exegetical conventions; that of allegory, through resemblance. In any event, neither is a problem for the translator, who (unlike the "expounder" of the text) is concerned strictly with the literal meaning, not the figurative. Campbell's earlier distinctions between words and meanings here bear their fruit; correct understanding of the text is the responsibility not of the translator but of the individual believer: "*Whoso hath ears to hear*," he reminds us, "*let him hear*" (56). A correct translation of the densest allegory, parable, or even the Apocalypse may be achieved by "one who has no apprehension of the spiritual meaning" (56).

Campbell promptly undermines his own argument, however, by observing that it is more difficult to translate texts of "a mixed character, where the emblematic is blended with the historical" and for which therefore "some knowledge of the mystic applications is more essential, than for translating unmixed prophecy, allegory, or paradox" (57). Clearly, if translation conveys no more than the literal meaning, the "character" of the text should make no difference. Difficulty also resides within the reader, whose ability to "hear" the text may be impaired by habit, ill-formed ideas, lack of historical understanding, and "the amazing power of prejudice and prepossession" (59). Given that some of these impediments to understanding may be created by faulty translations, it becomes clear that the bare literal meaning of the text is no guarantee of true understanding, and that it cannot be rendered by one who has not already reached true understanding.[40]

There is an implicit theology of the Fall in Campbell's account. In the beginning was a perfectly clear text, remarkable for its "simplicity" (65). Drawing on the work of Robert Lowth and other scholars for whom the simple syntax, repetitive structures, and relatively narrow range of vocabulary of classical Hebrew were not defects but instead markers of beauty and sublimity, Campbell claims that the "poverty of the Hebrew tongue" does not in itself create ambiguity:

> Knowledge precedes, language follows. No people have names for things unknown and unimagined, about which they can have no conversation. If they be well supplied in signs for expressing those things with which they are, either in reality or in imagination, acquainted, their language, considered relatively to the needs of the people who use it, may be termed copious; though, compared with the languages of more intelligent and civilized nations, it be accounted scanty. . . . There is no defect of signs for all the things which they can speak or write about, and it can never affect the perspicuity of what they do say, that they have no signs for those things whereof they have nothing to say, because they know nothing about them. (75)

Whereas translation from an "advanced" language into a "simpler" one would entail obvious problems, the reverse should be possible, at least in theory. (Robert Lowth had warned that, given the different characters of the languages, a Hebrew poem translated into Greek or Latin verse might "appear confused and mutilated.")[41] Campbell dismisses one by one the arguments of Simon and others that the Hebrew text must remain to some degree essentially inaccessible to us.

Well before publishing his translation of the gospels, Campbell had explored the matter of linguistic perspicuity in his lectures for the Aberdeen Philosophical Society, published in *The Philosophy of Rhetoric*:

> Perspicuity originally and properly implies *transparency*, such as may be ascribed to air, glass, water, or any other medium, through which material objects may be viewed. From this original and proper sense it hath been metaphorically applied to language, this being, as it were, the medium, through which we perceive the notions and sentiments of a speaker. . . . [I]f there be any flaw in the medium, if we see through it but dimly, if the object be imperfectly represented, or if we know it to be misrepresented, our attention is immediately taken off the object, to the medium. . . . The case of language is precisely similar. A discourse, then, excels in perspicuity, when the subject engrosses the attention of the hearer, and the diction is so little minded by him, that he can scarce be said to be conscious, that it is through this medium he sees into the speaker's thoughts. On the contrary, the least obscurity, ambiguity, or confusion in the style, instantly removes the attention from the sentiment to the expression, and the hearer endeavours, by the aid of reflection, to correct the imperfections of the speaker's language.[42]

Campbell's lecture on perspicuity succeeds in reducing obscurity largely to questions of grammar, denying it any philosophical or ontological import. The dissertations, however, do not elude the issue so completely. The text is absolved of blame: Campbell dismisses the notion of the "obscurity and ambiguity" of scripture as a Catholic obsession, "the common plea of the Romanists."[43] Although the original Hebrew text of the Bible—including the Hebrew subtext or "idiom" of the New Testament—may be in essence perfectly perspicuous, our ability to perceive that clarity is lacking. Ignorance, prejudice, and unreflective habits of thought prevent us from seeing as clearly into the original meaning of scripture as into a speaker's "thoughts."

Translation adds to the confusion. Among the "difficulties" involved in understanding and interpreting scripture, Campbell mentions that our habit of reading in translation elides our historical sense, so that we consider "many ancient and oriental terms, as perfectly equivalent to certain words in modern use in our own language, by which the other have been commonly rendered" (57). True understanding is based on a temporal paradox: we must see directly into the original, pristine text; but we can never forget our distance from it. And despite the stricture in the *Philosophy of Rhetoric* that anything that draws our attention away from the "object" to the "medium" is a defect, the detour seems impossible to avoid, particularly when we remember that the text of the New Testament is already a kind of translation, a spiritual "idiom" from one language enclosed within the body of another, or that the "disadvantages or defects" of the sacred writers are a witness to their inspiration. And our understanding of any language at all is complicated, as we have seen, by incommensurability caused by cultural differences and by the labyrinths of imperfect synonymy.

One present-day commentator finds "a not inconsiderable amount of confusion" in Campbell's *Rhetoric*, attributing it to a profoundly Humean belief that all mental activity is ultimately derived from sensation.[44] Even though Campbell was widely considered Hume's most successful critic in his own day, following the appearance of his essay on miracles, we can sense the skeptical undercurrent, the mixed messages, in his reflections on language. Language should be a limpid vehicle for the divine ideas, but languages are a product of given historical environments. The "literal" meaning should be available to all who have ears to hear, but it is enmeshed within a culturally dependent language and interpreted by those who have culturally dependent "associations of ideas," if not worse forms of prejudice and prepossession.

Although the lack of true synonyms may point to a given language's richness and capacity to represent the complexity of an advanced civilization, it also suggests that no two terms (save, perhaps, those representing *sun, moon, bird,* and *tree*) from different languages, bespeaking different histories and different associations of ideas, could ever be truly adequate to one another.

With these ambiguities in mind, let us consider Campbell's brief remarks in dissertation 10 on "The chief Things to be attended to in translating." These are a "just representation of the sense of the original"; a conveyance of "the author's spirit and manner, and . . . the very character of his style" to the extent allowed by "the genius of the language" of the translator; and, finally, "the quality of an original performance, as to appear natural and easy."[45] Campbell immediately acknowledges that it is often "impossible to attain one, without sacrificing both the others," and notes that "ease" is frequently impossible to attain without grave damage to the first two criteria "when the two languages differ very much in their genius and structure" (446). Where sacrifices must be made, the criterion of "ease" is less important than the first two, although "this is by no means so unimportant as some would imagine," given the importance "in any language" of perspicuity and propriety.

What are we to make of this definition of the translator's task? The inevitability of sacrifice, the series of concessions, particularly the ambivalence surrounding the importance of "ease," bespeak the impossibility of any immediate, "perspicuous" transfer of "ideas" from one language to another. Campbell, like many another translator, speaks of steering between "two extremes in translating"; he also cannot help remarking on the frequency with which such language is used by commentators and what the "general sentiments" are on either side. He departs from that well-worn path, however, to observe the relativity of the terms: "For, I may consider a translation as close, which another would denominate free, or as free, which another would denominate close" (448). Similarly, he had observed earlier that what "may be perspicuous to one . . . is obscure to another" (73). Even the notion of a "literal" translation, he finds, contains "so many differences in degree, that, without specifying, it is in vain to argue, or to hope to lay down any principles that will prove entirely satisfactory" (448). In other words, whatever capacity for the clear conveyance of meaning Campbell may wish to attribute to language, that capacity is sorely tested, if not undermined, by his awareness of the slipperiness and complexity of language, the vagaries of human perception.

For Campbell, these tensions are contained within a capacious and reflective faith. Although a thorough study of the preface to the dissertations would take us beyond the scope of this book, it is worth pointing out that in that text he lays the groundwork for his project in terms of the complementary domains of faith and reason, and the viability of both human and divine testimony. In such a context, it would not be accounted a failure to observe that certain features of his argument, such as the ultimate knowability of truth, despite the imperfections of language, rely on faith. Indeed, the intractability of the epistemological and linguistic problems and the consequent proliferation of translations provide further proof: "The different translators are like so many different touchstones. Those truths which can stand such numerous trials, are rendered quite indubitable" (xxxvi).

WORLDING IN FRANCE: LANGUAGE AND THOUGHT

In France, the Latin classical writers remained key cultural referents, although with a shift away from Cicero and toward the more skeptical writers such as Juvenal and Tacitus.[46] As in England, Latin translation was central to the educational curriculum. In France, however, there was no sharp division of labor between pedagogical and philosophical linguistics. Educational reformer Charles Rollin includes a significant chapter on translation theory and technique in his influential pedagogical treatise *De la maniere d'enseigner et d'étudier les belles-lettres* (1726–28), in which he cites passages from both Anne Dacier and Jacques de Tourreil.[47] Rollin's discussion of translation comes as part of his longer chapter "De l'étude de la langue françoise," reminding us that, even if knowledge of other languages "makes us in some ways contemporaries of every age, and citizens of every realm" (1:65), a prime function of learning Latin is, as Desfontaines puts it, "to perfect us in the use of our own idiom, to form our taste, and to lead us to write a pure French."[48] Although he critiques Rollin's pedagogical recommendations, the same key assumptions are held by César Chesneau Du Marsais, encyclopedist and intellectual heir to the Port-Royal grammarians. Du Marsais recommends a specific technique of reconstituting Latin texts in accordance with French syntax in order to enable students to grasp certain fundamental structures, removing their "inversions," before presenting them with the original syntax intact.[49] Du Marsais's project would give rise

to a major philosophical debate about the nature of language and its relation to thought.

Before turning to the inversion debate, however, let us consider the changing stakes in discussions of the classics within the world of letters. Perhaps
because of the intensity of the Homer debates, the discussion of the relative
worth of the ancient writers is much less of an issue in translators' prefaces after 1730. In the preface to his popular anthology of Greek plays, Père
Brumoy expresses his regret that philosophical modernism has persuaded
the public that nothing matters beyond the boundaries of French, "that our
own treasures enable us to live without foreign riches, especially those which
come at the price of difficult voyages."[50] His solution, however, was not to
call for a renewal of classical scholarship but instead to offer lively translations of Greek plays as a means of reviving interest in ancient literature. Like
the British classicists, he is attuned to questions of *génie*, though with a particular emphasis on linguistic features: "Every language has its own way of
arranging ideas, its turns of phrase, its terms both noble and base, energetic
or weak, lively or slow-paced" (1:xvi). The differences between Greek and
French and the risk of transforming "a fine Greek word" into "a bad French
sentence" (1:xviii) impel him to provide a prose translation. Like Anne
Dacier, Brumoy sees a "poetic" prose as offering the most graceful solution
to the problem of suiting ancient verse to modern French metrics.

Brumoy's comments stem from the ongoing debate (discussed in Chapter 4) on the relative merits of prose and verse translation, which pursues
questions raised in the wake of the Querelle d'Homère regarding the possibilities and limits of the French language and the expressive possibilities of
prose. All participants concur on the material, linguistic grounding of the
génie of French, particularly with regard to word order, and a sense of its
incompatibility with other languages. Accompanying this heightened sense
of French specificity one also hears echoes of a sense of "constraint" as in
the Homer debates: the concern that as rich as French may be, there are
simply some effects that it cannot produce. La Motte's indignant assertion
that a "rational meaning" could be translated into French is undercut by the
persistent theme—present in d'Ablancourt, Sacy, Dacier, and others—that
language "embodies" a powerful nondiscursive dimension.

These conversations among translators—and philosophers—complicate
the generally accepted account of eighteenth-century language theory, or general grammar, in which language is a purely vehicular, transparent "representation" of things. In what remains the best account of what I'll call the "pure"

form of general grammar, Sylvain Auroux presents what he calls the Enlightenment's "language-translation hypothesis" (*hypothèse langue-traduction*), or LT, according to which all language is a "translation" of thought, just as thought is a "translation" of the experiential world. Language adds nothing to thought; every element of language corresponds to something in the speaker's mind.[51] A corollary to the LT holds that the absence of an idea results in the absence of a word. Auroux calls this the "correspondence of language to thought" (*correspondance de la langue à la pensée*), or CLP, and states categorically that it does *not* point toward anything resembling the Whorf-Sapir hypothesis, which gives language a causal influence on thought. Auroux refers to such a strongly causal view as the "correspondence of thought to language" (*correspondance de la pensée à la langue*), or CPL. While he admits various nuances to the CLP, he nevertheless firmly denies that any eighteenth-century writer ever assented to the CPL or "enclosed Reason within the contingent possibilities of expression" (112) in any way.

The discourse on translation, however, shows us that this is not entirely the case. Within the boundaries of general grammar as such, whether voiced by Arnauld and Nicole, by latter-day grammairiens-philosophes such as Du Marsais or his disciple Nicolas Beauzée, or in the mathematically inflected linguistics of Condillac and d'Alembert, the LT doubtless holds, at least as a postulate or an ideal. In the world of actual, literal translation, the picture is less clear. If the LT is true, then translation should be unproblematical, the different languages being no more than "accidental" renderings of a single idea. As we have seen, however, translators are haunted by the awareness that the different renderings are not "the same." Few are willing to state without a doubt that the génie of a given language has an influence on thought, yet the propounders of génie find themselves under increasing pressure to explain the differences among languages as meaningful.

We see both the power of the LT and its complicating factors in two very different texts by grammarians of the early part of the century, Père Buffier's *Examen des préjugez vulgaires* (1704) and the abbé Girard's immensely influential *treatiste La Justesse de la langue françoise* (1718). Buffier's *Examen* is a series of dialogues in which proto-philosophe Téandre boldly advances a series of propositions that his companions find outrageous and yet must ultimately concede.[52] Such are Téandre's contentions that all languages, even (gasp) Bas-Breton, are equally beautiful, that "harshness" and "sweetness" are relative, and that the current hegemony of French has nothing to do with its innate properties: "When you speak of a beautiful language, don't you really mean a popular language, a useful language?" Even the notion that French has a special "clarity" by virtue of its word order "has no substance" (211), according to Téandre, for whom all languages possess equal capacities for their own speakers (176). Unlike Maupertuis, who sees the differences in the material conditions of different human societies as fundamental, Buffier sets universal human experience at the origin of all utterances. Buffier's main point is not that the differences among languages are meaningless, but that our judgments of them are ineluctably bound to our own location in a particular language. Our embeddedness in our own language shades both our aesthetic judgments and our ability to learn other languages; when Timagène claims that Arabic is intrinsically harder than Italian, Téandre responds that it only appears so to a speaker of French (169–70). Timagène would like for French to be a transparent, neutral norm against which all other languages are more or less sonorous, commodious, or easy to learn: Téandre points out that his unreflective rootedness in his own language constitutes a form of *préjugé*.

For Buffier there is no place to stand, no meta-language, from which the LT might be said to be accurate. The abbé Girard's work on synonyms complicates the LT in another way. Girard is best known for his elaboration of the concept of the "accessory idea" (*idée accessoire*), the nuance distinguishing one particular word from another that refers to the same object.[53] Ultimately, true synonyms do not exist; hence Girard's reference in his subtitle to "words that pass for synonyms." Girard's concept would be reflected in the structure of the *Encyclopédie*, in the series of articles under the rubric "Grammaire: synonymes," each carefully pointing out the distinctions between pairs of similar terms. Taking the LT or something similar as a given, Girard suggests that the ability to distinguish the nuances in language indicates greater mental capacity: "If the use of speech is given us to represent mental ideas, the ability to diversify terms is given us in order to correspond to the diversity of ideas that our mind forms" (xlvi). Greater discernment among terms is a sign of greater mental capacity, or greater "taste," *distinction*. Non-synonymy is not itself an argument against the LT, since it says nothing about the origins of our ideas. Yet Girard makes translation appear dubious indeed: if no two words—like Leibniz's leaves—are absolutely synonymous within one language, then *a fortiori* words in different languages will have even less in common.

One writer who explicitly endorses the "extreme" view, taking linguistic difference to incommensurability, is Maupertuis. In his *Réflexions philoso-*

phiques sur l'origine des langues (1748), he comments that although some neighboring languages, such as English and French, are simple "translations" of one another, exotic languages offer a different situation entirely: "There are languages, especially among very distant peoples, that appear to have been constructed on conceptual schemes [*plans d'idées*] so different from ours that one can scarcely translate into our languages what is expressed in theirs."[54] Auroux and other historical linguists tend to dismiss Maupertuis's suggestion as a lone comment falling outside the mainstream, but Turgot's rebuttal suggests that the question was hardly unique to Maupertuis: "One hears a great deal of discussion of the influence of languages."[55] For Maupertuis, different languages structure thoughts differently. Even if "basic perceptions" are the same among all humans, he posits that if both Europeans and educated members of an exotic culture were to translate their ideas into a common language, "each side would find the other's reasoning very strange, or rather they would not understand each other at all." The failure to communicate stems from each side's language, which "assigns signs to perceptions" in an "arbitrary" way.[56] Turgot ripostes that all languages are based on perception and hence on universal human experience, and are thus ultimately translatable. Differences are reduced to "ornamental" rhetorical effects: "Less strange reasoning than strange expressions" (2:718). Even so, Turgot elsewhere agrees with Maupertuis that the study of exotic languages has much to teach us about other worldviews.[57] The "influence" of language, while rarely accepted, is nevertheless felt in any number of ways.

Neither Buffier nor Girard go as far as Maupertuis in arguing that language shapes thought per se—both make statements assuming the contrary—but both monolingual préjugé and non-synonymy are evidence that enclosure within one language, however self-aware, renders access to the "ideas" contained in or reflected by another language highly problematic. We are a long way from the chains of identical propositions that "translate" mathematically, noiselessly, from one to another in the well-made language of Condillac's *La Langue des calculs*. Presumably "strange expressions" denote thoughts that are unfamiliar to us, since our own thoughts have not produced similar expressions. Learning a new expression, a nuance, or a language, then, gives us access to something previously unfamiliar: newness comes into the world.

That newness is all the more apparent if one sees a feature of specific languages, such as syntax, as meaningful. This is one of the key issues in the inversion controversy. That debate has been extensively rehearsed else-where, so I will note only the most relevant points here.[58] At the center of the debate over whether Latin or French best represents "natural order" is a question of translation. As we saw earlier, Du Marsais had put the issue on the table by recommending that students who were translating from Latin to French do so initially from a Latin text rewritten to correspond to the more "natural" syntax of French. To this, sensationist philosopher Charles Batteux responded with his *Lettre sur la phrase française*, later incorporated in his *Cours de belles lettres* as "Principes de traduction." Like most of his contemporaries, Batteux takes the LT as given: "Expressions are to thoughts as thoughts are to ideas. There is among them a sort of generation that takes resemblance from one to the next, from the first to the last term."[59]

For Batteux, however, it is the flexible syntax of Latin, not French, that best responds to the variety of events. For even though human nature is uni-versal ("Men are essentially the same in all places and in every age," 4:309), their needs and desires are motivated and modified by their immediate circumstances. Although all languages correspond to their "ways of being" (*manieres d'être*, 4:311), it is also the case that the génie of diverse peoples varies according to environmental factors, especially climate and sociopoliti-cal system. Difference in génie is completely material: more or less strength, speed, and so on in the conjunction and articulation of ideas. But although Batteux regards languages themselves as secondary properties attached to a single human essence (4:335), he also argues that particular linguistic con-structions, being founded on the speaker's "interest" or "perspective," should be conserved and reproduced, to the greatest extent possible, in translation (4:336). Thus his rules for translation lay a heavy emphasis on the relation-ships among ideas as manifest in word order, investing syntax with meaning and anticipating the practice of contemporary translation theorists.[60]

Both translatability and untranslatability are key to very different views of language in the period. For Batteux's interlocutor Beauzée, "thought" is one and universal; language is the tool by which the simultaneity of experience is analyzed, rendered discursively, translated.[61] For Diderot, who critiques both Batteux and Beauzée in his *Lettre sur les sourds et les muets*, the ques-tion of "order" is entirely relative. Not only does the génie of each language render it apt for certain tasks—"French is made to instruct, enlighten, and convince; Greek, Latin, Italian, and English to persuade, to move, and to deceive"[62]—but certain poetic configurations of sound, syntax, and meaning produce "events" that themselves cannot be fully explicated or articulated.

Diderot calls these events "hieroglyphs," arguing that they can be replicated (in painting or music, for example) but never translated as such. Diderot's views on the nondiscursive "materiality" of language are startlingly original in many ways, but as we see here, they also draw on themes and intimations from the contemporary discourse on translation.[63]

Many of these threads come together in Jean le Rond d'Alembert's widely cited preface to his translation of Tacitus.[64] D'Alembert dismisses as absurd the view that all languages are fundamentally the same, going on to argue that even if, in the hands of a writer of genius, any language can lend itself to any style, it is still not the case that they are equally apt to express the same idea on account of the diversity of their génie (3:7–8). Italian is the most flexible language and thus best able to reproduce the effects of other languages; French is the most strict and thus least amenable to translation. For d'Alembert, however, a translator is not completely bound by the rules or the génie of his language. Génie cedes to the writer's genius in the production of the new. What is an expression of genius? he asks. "It is the necessary and adroit joining of several known terms in order to produce a new idea with energy" (3:18). Just as Diderot's hieroglyphs defied translation, so too d'Alembert sees as untranslatable writers whose "character" resides primarily in their style, in the turns and echoes of language itself. How does one come to know poetry written in another language? By learning the language (3:15).

According to d'Alembert, the writer of genius operates as if he were speaking a foreign language. He bases this claim on his observation that "clever foreigners" (des étrangers de beaucoup d'esprit) produce "energetic and singular" expressions in French by virtue of translations and transpositions from their native tongue. Such is the nature of a good translation: "The original should speak our language, not with the superstitious timidity that we have with our native language, but with a noble liberty that lets us borrow features from one language in order to subtly embellish another." A good translation should combine naturalness of expression with "a taste of the soil" (le goût de terroir) of the foreign text (3:19). Language—foreign language—does inflect thought, enabling new thoughts, new connections, new ways of seeing the world. D'Alembert's analogy between translations and clever foreigners is itself an echo, a reinterpretation of a passage from Diderot's Lettre sur les aveugles comparing clever foreigners and writers of genius: "The situations that they invent, the delicate nuances that they perceive in characters, the simplicity of their descriptions, remove them at every moment from the usual expressions and lead them to adopt turns of phrase that are truly admirable. We forget the license and are struck only by the truthfulness of the expression."[65] Both these passages appear to assume the LT: writers and clever foreigners speak from a position of lack, needing to invent expressions to represent their fertile ideas. What happens next, however, goes beyond the LT: writers and clever foreigners change the language. How does newness, energetic and singular, come into the world? In Diderot's and d'Alembert's accounts, it is prompted by innovative usage made possible through contact with another language. The real advantage of translations is not to perfect one's own style but to "enrich all languages" (3:19), extending the space of collective innovation rather than providing a model for individual imitation.

D'Alembert's privileging of the non-native speaker is worlds apart from the image presented in Buffier's *Examen des préjugez vulgaires*, where even if the enlightened Téandre will not go so far as his interlocutor Timagène in ridiculing the speech of foreigners, he hardly proposes them as any sort of model but rather observes with his usual detachment that "they have their habits, and we have ours."[66] From the midcentury on, even translators who do not approve of infusing their language with *le goût de terroir* of another assent to the notion that language, expression, and génie are inextricably linked. A translator of Pindar defends his loose "paraphrase" precisely because all forms of textual "order" are meaningful, and hence impossible to reproduce in French.[67] Critic and dramatist Jean-François de La Harpe, in his preface to Suetonius, argues that close translation is simply impossible because "a man of genius thinks and feels with his language . . . and a foreign language cannot render either his thoughts or feelings without stripping them of the colors of the native idiom."[68] A number of translators refer to a text that, although not specifically addressing translation, crystallizes the thinking of many regarding the génie of ancient and modern European languages, the abbé Arnaud's 1768 "Discours sur les langues." For Arnaud, great writers have enlarged and transformed the modern languages; yet each national language possesses its specific character and capacities. Anticipating Antoine de Rivarol's better-known work on the universality of French by more than a decade, Arnaud argues that French, by virtue of its clarity and methodical order, was destined to become "the dominant language of Europe."[69]

Thus, even if language is seen as an effect, rather than a cause, its own causes have become more complex and are no longer pure "thought." These notions cut across ideological lines. For the philosophe Arnaud, the national language guarantees that "the génie, the mind, and the character of peoples passed into their writings" (3); for the anti-philosophe Jean-Marie-Bernard Clément, a nation's language is also bound up with its *moeurs*, or manners.[70] Just as language and culture are inextricably linked, so too are a writer's thought and his "style"; the one cannot be conveniently sheared away from the other. For translator Dureau de la Malle, style is Seneca, and Seneca is style. The pleasure of Seneca's style derives from "the constant relationship of accessory ideas with the main idea, of the tone with the subject, of the word with the thought, the sound with the object."[71] Whether or not they choose to inflect their language with the sound of another, whether or not they regard close translation as possible or desirable, these translators harbor in their work a new understanding—sometimes quite explicit—of meaning as fundamentally inherent within language, not simply "represented" by it.

In the final sections of this chapter, I turn to two case studies of classical translators. Both were figures who, as significant as they may have been in their day—rubbing shoulders with literary giants, being cited with respect by some and contested by others, playing a role in the institutional politics and cultural debates of their time—are all but forgotten now. Yet, as we shall see, their work intersects powerfully with the Enlightenment's changing views on language, meaning, and culture.

JACQUES DE TOURREIL'S DEMOSTHENES

If Jacques de Tourreil is remembered at all, it is because of his prominent place in the citational network of French Enlightenment translators, especially Etienne de Silhouette, whose much-cited essay on his translation of Pope offered extensive quotations from Tourreil. He was not an especially prolific writer; his complete works comprise only two quarto volumes. Of particular note are his early Demosthenes translations of 1691, his *Essais de jurisprudence* of 1694, and his later revised and expanded Demosthenes versions of 1701 and (posthumously) 1721. He surfaces twice in the *Histoire de l'Académie française* begun by Paul Pellisson and completed by the abbé d'Olivet in the 1720s. In the first incident, he figures in an account of some backstage politicking to scuttle someone's nomination; the second is a more telling scene that d'Olivet claims to have witnessed.

The scene takes place in 1709. D'Olivet relates that following the death of Gilles Boileau, Nicolas Boileau asked Tourreil to complete the translation of

Aristotle's *Poetics* that his older brother had left unfinished. Given the circumstances, one might assume Boileau's confidence and respect for Tourreil to be significant. However, as soon as Tourreil leaves, the poet turns to the young d'Olivet, makes a slighting comment about Tourreil's "monstrously" inflated Demosthenes, and tells an unflattering anecdote: "One day when Racine was at my house in Auteuil, Tourreil came over to consult with us about a passage that he had translated five or six different ways, each less natural and more stilted than the last. *Ah the torturer!* whispered Racine to me. *At this rate he'll render Demosthenes witty!*"[72] D'Olivet's own role in relating this story is not without self-interest, as within a few years after the first appearance of the *Histoire* (1729), he would publish his own translation of Demosthenes with a preface critical of Tourreil's version (1736). But the Boileau anecdote and Racine's quip ("Ah le bourreau!") reveal the paradoxical status of translators: their privileged link with classical antiquity, coupled with mistrust and ridicule. (One is reminded of the numerous critics who praised Anne Dacier's erudition while mocking her "excessive" admiration of Homer.) The circumstances of the conversation also remind us of the ambiguous status of translation, which is both a text and a process, open-ended and subject to revision, editorial decisions, and multiple authorship. Nicolas Boileau's invitation to Tourreil to complete his brother's translation harks back to a celebrated example, the completion of Vaugelas's *Quinte-Curce* by his friends, and anticipates the fate of Tourreil's own manuscripts, posthumously edited and published by others. Another aspect of the same open-endedness, however, Tourreil's request for input from his friends, leaves him vulnerable to ridicule.

Fast-forward to another view of Tourreil. In 1782, Jean-Pierre Brissot de Warville included in his *Bibliothèque philosophique du Législateur* a reprint of one of Tourreil's *Essais de jurisprudence*, "Si la torture est une bonne voye, pour découvrir la vérité" (Whether Torture Is a Good Means to Discover Truth). Brissot offers the text as an example of moral bankruptcy. Noting that Tourreil referred to his essay as "a mental game" and that he ultimately found in favor of the question "because there is no law without injustice," Brissot expresses his horror: "Where was the philosophical spirit? Despotism strangled it."[73] It is impossible to know whether Racine had Tourreil's essay in mind when he whispered "Ah the torturer!" to Boileau, but the coincidental images of Tourreil as the apologist of torture and the torturer of Demosthenes offer an odd, ironic harmony. Ever since I first encountered these texts, I have wanted to understand the ways in which they might explicate one another, how the unenlightened position on judicial torture might relate to one of the most widely cited texts on translation of the Enlightenment.

Much like Vaugelas, Tourreil's career as a translator was marked by a turn. Having in his early translations aimed at making Demosthenes elegant or "witty," he later decided to attempt a stricter literalism. His shift would later be described admiringly by Etienne de Silhouette. According to Silhouette, Tourreil went from producing translations where one could "scarcely recognize the model" to painstakingly faithful versions that followed "the turns, the figures, the rhythm and cadence" of the original.[74] The abbé d'Olivet, however, accused him of "bloatedness" in these later versions.[75] The abbé Millot expressed disgust at Tourreil's efforts to render the effects of Greek syntax: "Who suspects Demosthenes of expressing himself poorly in Greek? If he expresses himself poorly in French, it's the translator's fault."[76] I have compared Tourreil's texts enough to ascertain that there are significant differences between his 1691 translation of the *First Philippic* and the later posthumous edition of the same text (1721). Let us focus, however, on the ways in which Tourreil discusses his work in the erudite and highly self-reflective prefaces that accompanied his translations.

Tourreil's first published volume of translations contained the *First Philippic*, the *Olynthiacs*, and *On the Peace*; the volume was dedicated to the king and featured a short preface that is notable for the translator's description of himself. In his self-portrait, Tourreil underscores his cheerfulness, humility, "docility," and willingness to accept corrections and "the truth" from others.[77] While requesting comments and corrections from "Messieurs les Critiques," Tourreil nonetheless offers two justifications for the degree of freedom that he has taken in the translations.

The first justification comes from the nature of Demosthenes' text, whose highly elliptical style requires that the translator fill in the blanks: "His language cannot suffice for his mind and his elliptical expressions [*paroles suspendues*] with all their energy offer only a draft of his thought. . . . Demosthenes makes no connections, he moves without warning from one argument to the next" ([iii–v]). Thus, Tourreil seems to be suggesting, a fuller style in French is necessary. Tourreil connects Demosthenes' use of ellipsis to his oral performance: whereas a listener can be "carried away" and "guess what is left unsaid," a reader experiences the text at a slower pace and requires more accommodation.

Tourreil's second justification comes in the form of another authority figure, his predecessor among translators of Demosthenes, Cicero. He proceeds to cite the famous passage from *De Optimo genere oratorum*—the primal scene of Western translation theory—in which the Roman tells us that he translated Demosthenes not "as an interpreter, but as an orator," and that rather than translating "word for word," he sought to preserve the original's "force."[78] Long cited by proponents of free translation, Cicero's passage has been viewed as the starting point of a "neoplatonic" approach to translation in which spiritualized meaning and eloquence could be divested of their material embodiment in words, an approach that would become central to the Christian tradition when Saint Jerome took up and extended Cicero's phrase by announcing that he translated "not word for word, but sense for sense." Tourreil's self-justification via this model nevertheless leads to a somewhat odd conclusion: "The judgment of the great men who excel in eloquence takes the place of argument, and one becomes lost gloriously [*s'égare glorieusement*] by following such guides" ([vii]). Having earlier distinguished himself with a declaration that he preferred to err on his own, Tourreil now intimates that error can also befall those who follow an authoritative guide.

Ten years later, in 1701, Tourreil published a translation of the complete *Philippics*, this time with an elaborate "Préface historique" of more than a hundred pages, which would be the source of much of his fame as a scholar for years to come.[79] In the opening lines of this preface, Tourreil's focus is less on himself as translator than on the reader's need for accurate historical understanding, without which "Demosthenes will continue to speak Greek, even if he is translated."[80] In the preface's final pages, Tourreil returns to the importance of contextual information by offering a theory of reading. In order fully to appreciate the text, he tells us, it is necessary to "transport ourselves in our imagination to Athens" (266) and to adopt the passions and sentiments of its citizens. And yet—here Tourreil appears to falter in his own argument—how can readers let themselves be so thoroughly persuaded? "How can we forget ourselves to the point of believing . . . that we have no more mortal enemy than Philip of Macedonia? The heart is not so easily fooled, and fiction cannot stir us as much as reality" (266–67).

This sobering reflection invites another: "When a foreigner speaks our language and says nothing that is not in our manners and customs, he insinuates himself in our thinking: we willingly naturalize him and his sentiments become ours." Yet, if instead of "coming to us, he wants us to go to him," then we reject him, because "we tend to disapprove of whatever does not appear intelligible to us" (267). Tourreil's comment on "naturalization" anticipates in the reverse Schleiermacher's famous dictum about the two ways of translating, either by "moving the reader toward the writer" or by "moving the writer toward the reader."[81] It's a curious turn in the argument, since presumably the preceding hundred pages of historical detail were aimed at creating readers' understanding and enlivening their interest, a project that now appears cast into doubt. Tourreil's "we" is also ambiguous. Is he describing an attitude that many were wont to ascribe to the French reading public, but distancing himself from it? Or is he recognizing that his enterprise must inevitably fail? Rather than clarifying his stance, he drops the matter and shifts to an evocation of Demosthenes' reputation among readers. This topic, too, leads him first to evoke an imaginative fusion ("rendering to these inanimate words a part of their soul," 277), then to abandon the idea as "a perpetual illusion" (278). Once again, at the moment when Tourreil seems at the point of nailing down his argument, he draws back, and skepticism replaces belief. It's impossible, he observes in the final lines of the "Préface historique," to make everyone happy: people are all different and there is no single standard. It is at this "Pyrrhonic" moment that I would like to turn to Tourreil's other major piece of writing from the same decade as his *Philippics* translations: his *Essais de jurisprudence* (1694), in particular the essay on torture.

Supposedly aimed at a young audience, Tourreil's essays offer legal analysis in "an easier and freer" style.[82] The pieces range from technical to broadly philosophical, from serious to whimsical, on topics including parental rights, the legal autonomy of women, theft, "ingratitude," judicial authority, and property. As Brissot observes, the eleventh essay, "Si la torture . . ." argues both sides and finishes with an affirmation of the status quo. What conclusion is actually reached, however, is another matter.

Tourreil begins by imagining a defensive interlocutor: "A fine question! you say."[83] In the opening lines, he refers to the necessity of judicial torture as self-evident and relegates any question the essay might raise to "mental games." Was he simply showing servile prudence in the face of despotism, as Brissot speculated? It is hard to say. In any event, the first half of the essay marshals a number of important arguments against the practice. Torture goes against the spirit of the laws, according to which punishment should be meted out only as a regretted final outcome, not as a step in the judicial process. Tourreil describes crime as a "wound" inflicted on society, but evokes the torture of potentially innocent suspects in the same terms (106). Furthermore, torture is simply not efficacious: "Truth rarely triumphs in torment." Tourreil argues that neither confession nor silence under torture reveals anything other than mental or physical strength or weakness, which do not correlate with guilt or innocence. Finally, he observes that even supposedly "barbarous" nations do not allow the practice.

The second half of the essay rejects these arguments without actually refuting them. Speaking now for the apologists of torture, Tourreil denies the equation of torture and punishment (*le supplice*), treating it instead as a tool to "uncover" (*lever les voiles*) crime and lead to certitude via "incorruptible witnesses"—presumably the physical signs of the suffering patient (108). But he immediately admits the possibility that these signs may deceive us. The innocent man who yields a false confession under duress "is to be pitied," we are told, but he himself can only blame "nature" and "education" for his weakness of body and mind. Having conceded the possibility of false confessions, Tourreil proceeds by fiat, rather than by argument, and claims that the punishment of crime is a public good that trumps all the others. Torture may be "inhuman," but it is only a reflection of "the weakness of our understanding." Tourreil further notes that a confession produced under torture can be retracted—which of course demonstrates the futility of the procedure—and concludes that torture is a necessary evil, "inseparable from the human condition" (109).

It is a strange exercise. As Brissot points out, Tourreil's logic is often muddled.[84] What is clear, however, is that whether or not the essay manages to justify torture, Tourreil's answer to the initial question—does torture provide a means for discovering truth?—is simply no, it does not. Ultimately, the justification relies not on the apologist's ability to prove that torture produces true knowledge but rather on the bald assertion that the state's need to exact punishment overrides all other considerations. There is no attempt to bolster this claim, just as there is no suggestion that there is anything particularly positive about a status quo in which laws aimed at preventing injustice in fact cause it. I would not argue that Tourreil is being deliberately subversive—it is impossible to decide what his views are, as Brissot realized to his intense irritation—but rather that the essay is fundamentally incoherent, that its viewpoints oppose one another without responding to one another, and that it bespeaks a desire for truth and certitude that can never be fulfilled but is instead constantly undercut and repressed. It is significant that in what Brissot reads as a "servile" introduction, Tourreil presents his essay not only as a "mental game" but also as an exercise of reason: "Wherever reason is permitted, I prefer reasoning to authority." Even more to the point, perhaps, is his claim to "show pyrrhonism's claims on the most widespread established truths" (105).

The explicit skepticism of "Si la torture . . ." can also be felt in the writings on translation, such as with Tourreil's repeated expressions of doubt in his own ability and willingness to receive the opinions of others and even, perhaps, in the capacity of any language to be adequate to thought. In spite of these doubts, we have seen the translator's willing assumption of responsibility for a free translation and his belief that the free translation will somehow succeed in transmitting the "force" of the original. In his final years, however, Tourreil abandoned that notion.

Like Vaugelas, who labored for thirty years on his translation of Quintus Curtius and ultimately left a nearly unreadable manuscript of labyrinthine alternatives, Tourreil refrained from publishing his translation of a text that must have held an almost talismanic significance for him, the disputations of Demosthenes and Aeschines on the crown—in other words, the same text that Cicero had translated into Latin and that inspired his comments on eloquence in translation. The editor of the posthumous edition of Tourreil's complete works draws the parallel with Vaugelas and observes that he left seven or eight versions of each sentence. The editor, very much in the manner of Tourreil himself, consulted with others and decided that Tourreil's own indications of preferences were sound, with a few exceptions where the editor chose otherwise—without indicating where they are, needless to say—offering a text that purports to give us the translator's work but then extends the process and underscores its inevitable incompleteness.[85]

Tourreil's "Préface sur les deux Harangues" begins at the primal scene of translation: "I attempt today that which Cicero once accomplished."[86] He goes on to cite the passage he has already quoted in each of his earlier major prefaces, expressing afterward his regret that Cicero's translation has not come down to us: "It would have taught us how to translate well" (3–4).[87] Cicero may be the ultimate authority, but the loss of his perfect example opens the door for all who follow. Tourreil proceeds to speak more authoritatively than in his past prefaces: he reviews previous translations of the orations on the crown and finds them lacking, then offers a separate chapter that is really a separate treatise on the "rules" of translation. This is the section that Silhouette and many others would cite at length.

In spite of the trappings of authority—the review of other translations, the treatise format, the production of "rules"—the role that Tourreil sketches for the translator is hardly endowed with autonomy or power: "To think nothing, to say nothing of one's own; to cease existing [*s'anéantir*] in order to reproduce oneself as another" (7). In the pages that follow, Tourreil outlines the familiar dilemma of the translator caught between fidelity and freedom; like many other theoreticians of his day and since, he seeks a middle course, "a wise liberty" that avoids both extremes. Of more interest is the account given of the translator's subjectivity: "To take on the genius and character of the author one wants to translate; transform oneself into him to the greatest extent possible; to clothe oneself in his sentiments and passions that he transmits to us; to repress in one's heart that interior complacency that tends to bring everything back to ourselves" (11). Tourreil does not claim to pursue a radically different, literalizing (or as contemporary critics would put it, "foreignizing") practice; he still argues that one should be allowed the freedom to determine "equivalents" (11), but his initial self-presentation as merely "modest" has deepened into a profounder form of self-abdication.

The same becomes true for the reader. In the following section—not so widely cited as the earlier one—Tourreil takes up the topic of readers' "injustice" and "false judgments" (13). Rather than responding to critics as the title suggests, he returns to the topic that interested him in the historical preface of 1701, the psychology of reading—the influence of passion on our judgments, our difficulty in fixing our attention, the unconscious bias that leads us to accept or reject the text before us, and the role of the imagination. He also returns to his theme (this time buttressed with a quotation from Quintilian) of the difference between the experience of hearing an oration and the experience of reading it. Again, Demosthenes' style exacerbates the problem, which leaves us with little hope: "Part of Demosthenes has disappeared when we read him instead of hearing him. He will not be found in entirety in my translation, because he is not wholly in the original" (20).

The abdication of the translator and disappearance of the author are followed by the surrender of the reader. Indeed, the text cannot be apprehended otherwise. Having in his earlier preface evinced doubts as to whether readers could sufficiently suspend their disbelief in order to enter the world of the text, he now calls on them to do just that: "We cannot let ourselves be put off by manners, customs, ceremonies, games, laws that are entirely different from ours. We must train ourselves to them, or risk losing all that one may gain through commerce with fair Antiquity. We can understand and appreciate ancient writers only to the extent that we transport ourselves onto their stage. We may say like Plautus in the prologue to one of his comedies: *The scene is at Epidamnus, a city in Macedonia. Go there, Sirs, and stay as long as the play lasts*" (21). The world of Jacques de Tourreil is a world of shadows and absences, of ellipses and simulacra. The ideal model, Cicero's translation, is lost; Demosthenes has "disappeared" from his text; the task of both translator and reader is to forget themselves, to be transported and transformed, to become other than they are. Tourreil's juridical essays underscore and perhaps contribute toward the deepening uncertainties that characterize his career. We have seen this most dramatically in the essay on torture, but it is also present elsewhere. Together, these writings offer a conceptual space for translation—and reading in general—that dissolves into doubts and questions. The authority of the classical scholar serves to reveal the gaps and empty spaces within all forms of authority and meaning.

Tourreil's example shows us that membership in *le parti des Anciens* hardly renders one insensitive to those forms of critical consciousness, self-reflexive thought, and skepticism regarding received structures of institutions and of truth that we associate with the Enlightenment. Like many of his contemporaries, he desires to enter into another world—in his case, as in Dacier's, the cities and towns of classical antiquity rather than the forests of the New World or the cities of Asia and Africa—and to "learn the language," with all that the phrase implies of projecting oneself imaginatively and emotionally into a new world: "Go there, Sirs."[88]

JACQUES DELILLE'S GEORGICS

A verse translation in an age of prose, Delille's version of the *Georgics* both incorporates and extends the notions of cultural immanence that we saw developing in French linguistic thought over the first half of the eighteenth century. His work is also noteworthy as the only French translation singled out for praise by Germaine de Staël in her essay "De l'esprit des traductions," a biting critique of the neoclassical school. Although the paragraph comparing translation and travel from his "Discours préliminaire" to the *Georgics* appears in many anthologies of historical prefaces, Delille himself appears to be all but forgotten by contemporary critics.[89] The entire "Discours" is worthy of attention, however, for its fusion of classical scholarship and Enlightenment thinking on language, culture, and commerce.

The "Discours" begins with an extended discussion of the contemporary relevance of the ancient Latin poem.[90] Delille's "Georgic modernity" shifts between genuine admiration for the new agricultural science, irony directed at "Agromania," and ambivalence regarding the relative importance of theory and practice (1).[91] The relevance of this section is more than purely topical, however, as political economy and social difference will play an important role in Delille's understanding of his project. The first half of the "Discours" thus looks at Virgil's text from a utilitarian standpoint, first commenting on the relevance of historical documents for modern agricultural research, then defending the poem for those stylistic features that clearly set it apart from practical or scientific texts, such as its seeming lack of "method" or clearly articulated transitions. Delille regrets the lack of public interest in any form of poetry not destined for the stage (14); throughout, he calls on his readers to open their minds to something new, whether in the idea that an ancient text might prove of contemporary use, or in an unconventional (by modern standards) means of effecting transitions, or in the untapped potential of didactic poetry, which offers the French language "a new world from which can be had countless riches" (15).

I'll return to the riches of this new world in a moment, but first let us consider the second half of the "Discours," where Delille sets out to comment on his translation and the "difficulties" he has encountered in the course of the project. This section, taking up some twenty pages in the 1770 edition, is complicated both visually and conceptually by a long footnote of some one thousand words, spread out over five pages below the main text, which occupies only a relatively small band along the top part of the page. In that top section, we are initially told that the chief difficulty in the translation was "the difference in the two languages," an expression that almost seems tautological but whose full explication launches the note that splits the text in two. Above, Delille continues the discussion by contrasting Roman republican virtue with a decadent present rife with class prejudice. Below, the footnote explores another contrast, this one between Leibniz's dream of a universal language and actual languages, multifarious and fragmented: "We ask how humans, with their common origin, could speak different languages. But the real question is how it is possible that any large group of humans ever spoke the same language" (21–22n). Here is "Babel revers'd" in an unusual way. A unified language being only a philosopher's project, this story of origins concerns difference rather than unity, and individual idiosyncrasy rather than collective practice. Language as a social phenomenon is an effect of chance and coincidence; as soon as people go their separate ways, "Nature reclaims her rights" (22n). Language's degree zero is utterly unique, "idiomatic" in the strongest sense. For Delille as for Rousseau, the natural state is thus one of incommunicable solitude; unlike Rousseau, for whom the passage into language and social life was irreversible, Delille sees language as entropic, ever prone to breaking down into private, individual idioms.

Delille's note proceeds to explore the multiple causes for language change and the variables confounded in the notion of génie: time, place, climate, social system, material conditions of production, political system, technological advances, "civilization." Lexicon is an important feature of génie as an indication of a society's principal preoccupations: "The Arabs have one hundred fifty words for lion and three hundred for serpent" (24n). Like contemporary urban legends of ever more numerous Eskimo words for snow, Delille's virtual vocabulary lists stir the imagination and evoke radically different environments with different needs. Lest we imagine that Delille only conceives of the expanded lexicon of foreign tongues in a one-to-one relationship with objects in the environment, consider his observation (in the top half of the text) that the Romans "had many words to describe the action of doing good; we have only the recent word *bien-faisance*" (26). Like the abbé Girard's (non)synonyms, the variety of terms indicates a fuller, more developed understanding of a concept. Génie is thus a function not only of the lexicon but also of the relationships among the terms, of "different combinations of words, their relations with the ideas they express" (23n). At the heart of génie lies physical experience, grounded in climate, which affects both the social system and the disposition of bodily organs that determine pronunciation. The "difference in the languages" comes perilously close to absolute difference.

Although Delille appears to see social life as a fragile contingency in a natural world filled with individuals and differences, the failings of his own society are a key concern. At the top of the same page where he comments in the footnote on the multiple terms for "lion" and "serpent," he draws conclusions from vocabulary and register: "Prejudice has debased words as it has people, so that there are noble words and common words" (24). Unlike Cowper's ironic observation that it was difficult to kill a sheep "with dignity" in a modern language, Delille expresses contempt for the polite euphemisms of his day, which he compares to impoverished noblemen who prefer indigence to derogation (26). Language (be)speaks culture, and historical linguistics becomes the grounds for cultural critique.

Despite the spectacle of contemporary moral and financial ruin, Delille imagines that the French language—and presumably France—might yet be renewed and made better. Having described an immense gulf between Latin and French that appears to be as much social and ethical as syntactic, lexical, and phonetic, Delille affirms his confidence in translatability, which is also the capacity of the genius of the great writer to overcome and shape the *génie de la langue*. If "climate, government, and manners" influence language, the writer of genius is no less effective: "He bends languages to his will, renews antique words, naturalizes new ones, transports the riches of one language into another, bridges their distance, forces them to sympathize" (32). The irresistible charisma of literary genius appears able to overcome the natural tendency toward singularity and fragmentation, transforming the "sterile" singular *idiôme* into a universal *langue*. The "riches" thus transported—that is, translated—consist in connectivity, innovation, and newness.

Delille is so sensitive to the implications of lexicon that one wonders to what extent the recurring references to riches and resources, in this passage and others, are deliberate, especially in this text whose opening pages celebrate the coming of the agricultural revolution. Turgot, who by 1770 had turned from translation to grain markets, also saw languages as a free-trade zone, arguing that the study of languages "overcome[s] the barriers that make each discipline a separate independent state."[92] Delille's decision to locate the *Georgics* in the context of *agromanie* was an early, explicit indication of the "economic" dimension of his thinking about Virgil; his text reveals the extent to which the contemporary discourse of political economy had filtered into other domains. While no Physiocrat himself, Delille shares in their vision of a stable natural order underlying the free circulation and increase of wealth. His understanding of Virgil's "method" is inflected by the same notions. Defending the Roman poet's lack of "transitions," Delille argues that Virgil refuses to be tied to the expository norms of science, preferring the "natural" sequence (*la suite naturelle*) of ideas, which he indicates in the most minimalist fashion possible, sometimes with a single word (7–9). Transition resides primarily in the mind of the reader (9). Reading requires participation in the text's construction of meaning. Unlike French syntax, which typically spells out connections and transitions, dictating the order of ideas, Latin enables active, constructive forms of thought that "enrich" us by encouraging new ideas.

Translation completes the process, converting the ongoing difference and differentiation of languages into tangible benefits. In an oft-cited passage that recapitulates and completes the previous thirty pages of argument,

Delille compares translation to travel: "I have always regarded translations as one of the best means of enriching a language. Differences in governments, climates, and manners tend to augment differences in speech. Translations, by familiarizing us with the ideas of other peoples, familiarize us with the signs that express them. Imperceptibly they bring into a language many turns of phrase, images, expressions that seem foreign to its génie, but that . . . are first tolerated and ultimately adopted" (35). Writing in our own language, we tend to use familiar, accepted expressions; when we translate, however, our language is transformed by the influence of the source text: "To translate is somehow to import into one's language, through a fortunate commerce, the treasures of other languages. In a word, translations are for a language what travel is for the mind" (35–36). The unproductive labor of writing in one's own language gives way to the riches of hitherto unknown thought processes spurred by "turns, images, and expressions." Delille's *commerce heureux*, which avoids dependency and inequality and in which all stand to enrich themselves, is utopian in inspiration and grounded in Enlightenment hope. It is also grounded in an Enlightenment view of language, not as the transparent vehicle of universal ideas but as the considerably more material site where particularity, idiom, is made available to others without losing its distinctiveness. Delille does not claim that the transaction results in perfect communication or clarity, only that it produces something new, contributing to progress. Impersonal factors—governments, climates, and manners—change language as well. But inasmuch as they simply subtend the processes of desocialization, they provide nothing new until one idiom comes into contact with another, enriching both and reversing the individuating trend.

Delille concludes his preface by reflecting on the necessary compromises inherent in translation, the need to prioritize, and the inevitability of debt. The topos of indebtedness and compensation sends us back through centuries of translators' remarks as far as Cicero, but here it also serves to remind us that Delille's economic policy stresses exchange. Unlike the abyssal debt of, say, Vaugelas, Delille's indebtedness is part of an ongoing system of credit, quittance, and compensation (45). The ultimate exchange, however, is between the role of the translator and that of the poet: "Translating is to a certain extent composing" (45). Taking his inspiration from the same sources as his author, the translator retreats to the countryside in order to appreciate the *Georgics*, only to realize that the text and its source of inspiration exist in a relationship of reciprocity and mutual enlightenment as well: "I never find nature so beautiful as when I read Virgil; I never find Virgil more admirable than when I observe nature" (46).

In a recent study, David B. Paxman argues that early modern advances in navigation and concomitantly evolving views of space shaped the period's understanding of language. For Paxman, static spatial concepts such as the topoi of rhetoric yield to dynamic, expanding, self-critical perspectives, culminating in Humboldt's account of language as "humanity's journey across a terrain."[93] Humboldt's journey, with its emphasis on the stages of cultural development, is not the same as Delille's euphoric voyage of commerce and discovery. Both, however, participate in the worlding of language, in the view that language contains as well as shapes subjectivity and its location in culture. Classical translation underscores this shift. Dryden conceived the distance of antiquity through a sense of temporality that infused even the recent past with loss. By the late eighteenth century, however, one might almost say that Latin had become a "modern" language, even as Latin poetry and prose were increasingly obliged to share the intellectual landscape with vernacular literature, because its distance was now construed in cultural, not temporal, terms. The discovery of the foreignness of Latin, Greek, and Hebrew offers a model for acknowledging the foreignness of English, Spanish, French, German, and all contemporary tongues. Locke, certainly, had raised the question of the role of language in the formation of our ideas. But in France the reflection on the relation of language to cognition, and of both to the construction of culture, comes via a reflection on the relation of a modern language, French, to Latin. Translation proves to be the intersection at which these questions become apparent. Thus classical translation, while continuing to offer models for literary emulation and access to the treasure troves of the past, is influenced by and participates in Enlightenment critical consciousness.

CHAPTER 7

"Adventurers in Print"

Modern Classics

The term *world literature* is an eighteenth-century invention, even if such notions of textual circulation as classical inheritance or the *translatio studii* had
been around for much longer.[1] As Europeans gradually came to reimagine
themselves as belonging to nation-states, rather than to communities of faith,
regions, social orders, or other sources of identification, earlier transnational
concepts such as the Republic of Letters would be reconfigured or understood
and experienced differently, in response to the newer forms of belonging and
situatedness. Hence the shift from the *republica litteraria* to Enlightenment
cosmopolitanism: citizens of the world know that theirs is citizenship in a
divided world. "World literature" circulates in a world aware of national differences, in which nation is associated with national language and specific
characteristics attributed to the various languages and to their speakers.

NATURALISATION AND NATURALIZATION

It is not surprising that the international circulation of texts is often conceived in the same manner as that of persons. The term *naturalisation*

comes into prominence as the passage from "foreign" to "native" takes on special significance in the course of the sixteenth century. The key term in French would not be *natif* (native) but *naturel* (*les naturels du pays*), and the key word for the transformation of foreign to native is, of course, *naturaliser*, to naturalize.[2] In both French and English, translation has long been spoken of as a form of, or an activity analogous to, naturalization, the legal process by which foreigners become citizens. In French, the verb *naturaliser*, in its legal sense, is attested as early as 1471, but the process it refers to takes on heightened significance as the outlines of the modern French state begin to emerge. In the 1570s, the recourse of the monarchy to the *droit d'aubaine*, according to which the estates of foreigners residing in France could not be inherited by their descendants but were instead forfeited to the king, spurred requests for naturalization. As historian Peter Sahlins has shown, the fluctuating status of the foreigners, or *aubains*, was closely bound up with the process of state building and the formation of national identity.[3]

Given the importance of discussions of the French language in those very same processes, it is hardly surprising that the legal sense of *naturaliser* should have almost simultaneously evoked a linguistic sense. The first edition of the Academy dictionary in 1694 gives both (that is, *naturalize* in terms of citizenship and *naturalize* in terms of adoption or translation of foreign words). Later editions add a "botanical" sense, *naturaliser une plante*. Throughout, the linguistic sense is designated as figurative. The database of the Project for American and French Research on the Treasury of the French Language (ARTFL) reveals a number of figurative uses beginning in the first years of the seventeenth century, many of which relate to either the importation of foreign words or translation. In many instances, the legal and linguistic merge seamlessly. English usage closely follows French usage, from which it is derived, with both legal and figurative, including linguistic, uses appearing from the end of the sixteenth century onward.[4]

In both countries, the naturalization of foreign bodies was more problematic than the easy migration of vocabulary might imply. English naturalization laws were geared to encourage economic growth through the immigration of productive workers, but these plans ran counter to "ethnic and religious chauvinism." The General Naturalization Act of 1709, which allowed for the uncomplicated naturalization of foreign Protestants, was repealed within a few years because of hostility toward German immigrants. Immigrants to England had an option unavailable in France of applying for "denizen" status, an intermediate location between resident alien and naturalized citizen, for which some, though not all, of the legal disabilities incurred by aliens were lifted. Given the expense of both naturalization and denization, however, many immigrants remained aliens.[5]

In France, the absence of legislation meant that naturalization was granted to petitioners on an individual basis. As Peter Sahlins's study of these petitions shows, there is a tension between two conflicting notions of citizenship: on the one hand, as a "voluntary affiliation to king and kingdom" and, on the other, as "a 'natural' condition" anticipating later "essentialist" notions of citizenship based on cultural identity.[6] Under the absolute monarchy, the naturalization process produced various "legal fictions" regarding both the naturalized subjects, treated "as if" they were born French, and the body politic, treated "as if" it were uniformly Catholic.[7] Naturalization thus both maintains difference—naturalized aubains were not, in fact, treated exactly like naturels—and effaces it, by closing its eyes to the presence of Protestants and Jews. Initially, naturalization conferred only a seemingly limited and negatively conceived, if powerful, difference in status—the exemption from the droit d'aubaine—because there was no single status of "French citizen" in the society of orders. Over the course of the "citizenship revolution" of the mid-eighteenth century, however, to be "French" came to mean no longer simply "one status among a multiplicity of identities," as Daniel Gordon puts it, but rather a "common, overarching identity of individuals within a well-ordered community."[8] What of the status of imported words and translated texts?

Already the double linguistic usage—*naturaliser* referring (strictly) to the adoption of foreign words and (more loosely) to the translation/adaptation of texts—parallels the tension within the legal meaning whereby foreigners remain foreigners but are treated "as if" they were natural residents, and the more essentializing notion that one can truly become or be recognized as "naturally" a member of the community—this latter perhaps inflected by the botanical usage, in which the exotic species becomes indistinguishable from the native. Analogously, certain words may be treated "as if" they were French or English, while preserving their intrinsic foreignness; foreign texts, however, can be adapted so thoroughly as to produce the illusion that they have been originally written in the target language. Yet neither situation remains undisturbed: borrowed words can forget their origins, and authors who speak as if they were French or English occasionally manifest a slight accent.

THE TRANSLATORS OF THE QUIXOTE

Just as an individual's sense of belonging was modulated by evolving concepts of nation and citizenship, so the international literary field shifted its center of gravity in response to the rise of the novel. As recent critics have argued, the evolution of extended prose fiction in Europe is inextricably linked to translation and intercultural communication in general, and to the cross-Channel dialogue in particular.[9] Although it relates to a later period in the novel's development, Franco Moretti's notion of an Anglo-French "core" of novelistic production is equally applicable to the previous century.[10] Both national literatures, however, are nourished by what Moretti dubs the "first international bestseller," Miguel de Cervantes's *Don Quixote*, a work whose successive translations chart not only the changing views of translation and authorship that we have already observed but also the consolidation of a new notion, the vernacular literary "classic." One of the most thoroughly "naturalized" texts of all time, the *Quixote*'s many versions show us why translations do not entirely fade into their surroundings.

Let us first quickly survey the early European translations. Cervantes published part 1 of *El ingenioso hidalgo Don Quijote de la Mancha* in 1605; part 2 appeared in 1615, the year before his death. The earliest translation in any language was Thomas Shelton's 1612 English translation of part 1, *The Delightful Historie of the most Ingenious Knight Don Quixote of the Mancha*; Shelton then published a complete edition with both parts in 1620. Meanwhile, in 1616 lexicographer César Oudin brought out a French translation of part 1, *Le Valeureux Don Quixote de la Manche* (the conventional French spelling *Quichotte* would not appear until later), and François de Rosset translated part 2 into French in 1618; the two would be published together in 1625. Both the Shelton and Oudin-Rosset versions continue to be looked upon as remarkably faithful. An Italian translation by Lorenzo Franciosini appeared in 1622. Cervantes's works, especially the *Quixote*, but also the *Novelas exemplares*, were widely read, admired, and imitated in the seventeenth century, particularly in France, where the Oudin-Rosset version was reprinted many times. In 1678 a new French translation appeared, updated in the spirit of the *siècle classique* by François Filleau de Saint-Martin, a peripheral member of the Port-Royal circle. The English reception during this period remained largely superficial, treating the novel only in its most farcical sense, giving rise to parodies and light theatrical adaptations of various episodes.[11]

English appreciation for the novel's social and epistemological complexity deepened with the dawning of the eighteenth century, which saw a series of new translations: in 1700, John Stevens's revised and corrected edition of Shelton appeared, as well as a new translation by Huguenot émigré Peter Motteux and "several hands." Motteux's translation proved quite successful; following his death in 1718, the fourth edition (1719) appeared with revisions and corrections by the prolific translator John Ozell. In 1743—the year of his own death—Ozell published an expanded seventh edition, "revis'd a-new" and with copious "Explanatory Notes." Ozell's notes and revisions took advantage of the publication in 1742 of a completely new translation by Charles Jervas (or "Jarvis," as the name appears in print), portrait painter and friend of Alexander Pope. As Tobias Smollett set about his translation in the late 1740s, he was thus able to draw on the work of Shelton and Stevens, Motteux and Ozell, and Jervas, as well as Stevens's Spanish-English *Dictionary* of 1706. The remainder of the eighteenth century saw only undistinguished, recycled translations in English; a new French translation by Florian appeared in 1799.

The importance of the *Quixote* for the development of the European novel cannot be overstated and has been the object of much critical attention.[12] Recently, Franco Moretti's analysis of the "translation waves" of the *Quixote* has shed light on the role of variously configured reading publics in the constitution of European identity.[13] Like Moretti, I am interested in the ways in which the successive versions of the work reflect other shifts in the literary field. Unlike Moretti's quantitative approach, of course, I will be looking at what the translators themselves have to say about the work—and about each other—in their critical prefaces and notes, to find out what they can tell us about changing attitudes toward language, literature, authorship, and translation.

Thomas Shelton's 1612 translation of part 1 was made for one friend and published at the behest of others. An Irish Catholic living in exile in the Low Countries as a result of his involvement in Tyrone's rebellion, Shelton states in his dedicatory epistle to Lord Howard de Walden that he had made the translation in haste, "in the space of fortie dayes" for "a very deare friend" some five or six years previously, hence shortly after the text's initial publication.[14] Shelton explains that he had been under the mistaken impression that someone else was to correct his text; later editors and commentators have noted the text's numerous errors, apparently due to its speedy composition.[15] Faulty or not, Shelton's translation remained the principal English translation for a century.

Throughout the seventeenth century in England, stage adaptations, abridged versions, and pastiches, including one in Hudibrastic verse, continued to appear. Of these, John Phillips's 1687 version, "Now made English according to the Humour of our Modern language," deserves a moment of attention.[16] Phillips's penchant for amplification and low humor (for example, the passing mention of Don Quixote's niece among the members of the household becomes "He kept . . . a Niece of Twenty for private Recreation") suggests that the entire production is intended less as a translation than as a parody aimed at readers already familiar with either the original or Shelton's version, in the manner of the comic Virgil translations by Paul Scarron in France and Charles Cotton in England.[17] Such translations seek not to "replace" their originals, since they are best appreciated through comparison with the original or a strict translation. They offer their readers the pleasure of collusion and enhanced self-esteem from being complicit in the joke.[18] Educated by his uncle, the poet Milton, whom he served for some time as amanuensis, Phillips was a man of considerable letters, with a number of works and translations from French, Latin, and Greek already to his credit. His prefatory statements signal the dual nature of the novel—"no less pleasant than gravely Moral"—and evoke the liveliness of the literary marketplace. The dedication to the Earl of Yarmouth mentions the work's "frequent Translations" and celebrity throughout Europe. In a short, witty dialogue that stands in for a preface, Phillips describes the literary world as a cruel, dangerous environment, fueled by stimulants and economic competition: "Coffee has so inspir'd Men with Contradiction and ill Nature, that Readers are as hard to be pleas'd as Ladys in a Mercer's Shop." His work is a "Book-Errant" sent forth with shield and buckler to defend itself against a sea of critics and provide moral guidance "in a pleasing Mirrour" (A2r–v).

I mention Phillips's preface because the image of the "Book-Errant" is echoed in the preface to John Stevens's 1700 revised edition of Shelton: "This I think (to Speak in his own Language) may very well be call'd *Don Quixote's* third Sally amongst us, since he has twice before appear'd in English, and now comes abroad again to seek Adventures, somewhat more refin'd in Language than the first time, and much more like himself than the second."[19] Stevens develops at even greater length the analogy of the noble book under attack in a cruel world: "Thus the Adventurer in Print is in all respects equally expos'd, and finds much the same Entertainment as does the Knight in Armour: the base and meaner sort Persecute, but the wise and generous support him" (A4r). Unlike Phillips's short, spritely dialogue, Stevens offers a full-scale critical preface, a form of writing that, as we have seen, had been current in France and Italy since the Renaissance but less prevalent in England until the late seventeenth century.

Stevens's preface takes up first the question of his relationship to Shelton, explaining that the text is "partly Corrected and partly Translated anew" (A4r), then outlines the principles underlying his own approach to translation. Stevens is at some pains to emphasize the depth of his revisions and the extent of entirely new translation. Shelton's version, he tells us, was frequently incorrect and its English "so antiquated or corrupt" that he has translated much anew (A4r–v). He defends himself vigorously against any charge of secondhand translation ("Copying from a Copy") and underscores the fidelity of his version: "Choosing rather to be blam'd for adhering too servilly to my Author, as it is generally term'd, than to alter any thing of his Sense" (A4v).

Stevens's insistence on literality, while consistent with Shelton's approach, is at odds to a certain extent with much of his contemporaries' discussions of translation, which since midcentury had emphasized the translator's relative freedom and creativity: "the middle way," as Dryden and many others put it, between the extravagant license of adaptations such as Phillips's Cervantes and the "servile" approach here explicitly endorsed by Stevens. It may well be that the literalness of the Shelton translation was precisely what attracted Stevens, serving him as an anchor—a literal pretext—to ground his own version in response to the flurry of imitations and adaptations.[20] At the same time, Stevens's emphasis on his own contribution to the project and his shunning of secondhand translation from the French bespeak the need for self-authorization that also underpins much of the discourse of free translation.

In 1700, the same year as Stevens's revision of Shelton, there appeared a new translation by Peter Anthony Motteux. A French Huguenot whose family had settled in England following the revocation of the Edict of Nantes, this journalist and translator is probably best remembered for his revision and completion of Thomas Urquhart's translation of Rabelais (1694), a version still much appreciated for its colloquial energy and verve. Motteux brought the same talents to his translation of Cervantes; his version quickly dominated the market and it continues to be reprinted today in the Modern

Library edition. Like Stevens, Motteux sets his translation in the context of the international and multilingual circulation of the *Quixote*, observing that the novel had been "very happily patroniz'd in other Languages."[21]

Motteux's preface has been cited as representing something of a sea change in the English appreciation of the *Quixote*, the shift from seeing the main character as a purely extravagant, ridiculous figure to considering him in universal terms.[22] Motteux writes, "Every man has something of *Don Quixote* in his Humor, some darling *Dulcinea* of his thoughts, that sets him very often upon mad Adventures" (A5r). Motteux is unsparing in his judgments of his predecessors, criticizing Shelton's literal approach ("he translated word for word, and often as School-boys do their Exercises," A5v) and dismissing Stevens's version as "hastily furbish'd up" and Phillips's as "a Burlesque Imitation of the *French* Translation." Motteux claims that a literal translation "wou'd be to make the Book unintelligible, and not English," but still prides himself on maintaining the authenticity of the original: "Tho our Spaniard speaks English, he is still in his own Country, and preserves his native Gravity and Port" (A6r).

It is often averred that translators' statements do not always coincide with their actual practice, and Motteux may well fall into that category; his version would eventually be denounced as "a kind of loose paraphrase . . . taken wholly from the French" by Jervas and as "distinctly Franco-cockney . . . an absolute falsification of the spirit of the book" by Ormsby.[23] Prefaces such as Motteux's may provide imperfect road maps to the translations themselves, but they tell us a great deal about the world of discourse that sustains them, about the norms and expectations of the reading public, and about the translators' ideals, if not their reality—their "Dulcinea" as Motteux might have put it. Whether or not Motteux (a native speaker of French) based his version as much or more on a French translation than on a Spanish text, as Jervas claimed, it was necessary for him, as it was for Stevens, emphatically to state that he had not translated from an intermediate translation—even though we know that such "secondhand" translation continued to be a frequent practice among translators throughout the period. It is also significant that Motteux draws such a clear distinction between his version and that of John Phillips, a distinction that is largely lost on modern ears. One could frame two responses to his claim. On the one hand, for him to claim to be quite different from Phillips, he must have had some expectation of finding agreement among his readers, which suggests that we need to tune our twenty-first-century responses to these older translations more keenly.

On the other hand, Motteux's critique of Phillips may point to their very resemblance and the "narcissism of minor differences." In either case, what is more telling than Motteux's actual practice is his need to distance himself from the burlesque tradition as well as from secondhand translation, neither of which corresponded to the norms and expectations of "translation" among his audience.[24]

The opprobrium attached to secondhand translation is writ large in Charles Jervas's preface to his translation, published in 1742, a few years after his death. Whereas earlier translators had criticized Shelton's version as simply outdated, Jervas levied another accusation, claiming that it was "taken from the *Italian* of *Lorenzo Franciosini*" and going on to cite faulty emendations in Franciosini that are replicated in Shelton.[25] Given, however, that the Shelton translation of part 1 appeared in print fully twelve years before Franciosini's, the borrowing apparently took place in the other direction. Jervas entirely discounts Stevens's edition as a sorry patchwork of old and new diction (1:iv) and, as we have seen, judges the Motteux version to be based on the French, "which, by the way, was also from the *Italian*." Given the inaccuracy of Jervas's account of the origins of Shelton's translation, one is entitled to some doubts about his casual dismissal of the French translation, particularly inasmuch as it is not clear whether he was referring to the Oudin-Rosset version (which predates Franciosini) or Filleau de Saint-Martin's version, produced so long after Franciosini as to make derivation unlikely. Jervas's references to Franciosini thus appear gratuitous, serving simply to discount the earlier translators. His own translation—termed "wooden" by Ormsby and "lifeless" by Martin Battestin—is considered to be reasonably close to the text but lacking in literary value.[26]

Jervas's translation is generally acknowledged to have been an important resource for Tobias Smollett, who began working on his translation in the late 1740s. Before turning to Smollett, however, let us note one further contribution. In 1719, the year following Motteux's death, a fourth edition of his translation appeared, "*Carefully* Revised" by John Ozell. Ozell was one of the most prolific translators of the period, specializing in the work of recent and contemporary French writers (Corneille, Molière, Fénelon, Boileau, Montesquieu, Jean Le Clerc, and others); he contributed revisions to the Motteux-Urquhart Rabelais and produced a blank-verse rendition of Anne Dacier's *Iliad*, along with a translation of her preface. His brief "Avertisement" to the fourth edition of Motteux simply notes that he has complied with the bookseller's request to bring Motteux's translation in line with the more recent Madrid edition of the novel; a cursory examination of the 1719 edition suggests nothing more: emendations and corrections here and there, a few explanatory footnotes, some carried over from Motteux.[27] In 1743, the year following the publication of Jervas's translation, Ozell came out with a seventh edition of the Motteux-Ozell version, "Revis'd a-new" and with copious annotations based on Jervas and others.[28] In this edition, something new happens on the very first page: "In a certain Village in *La Mancha*,* which I shall not name, there liv'd not long ago one of those old-fashion'd Gentlemen who are never without a Lance upon a Rack, an old Target, a lean Horse, and a Greyhound. His Diet consisted more of Beef† than Mutton; and with minc'd Meat on most Nights, Lentils on *Fridays*, Eggs and Bacon‡ on *Saturdays*, and a Pigion extraordinary on *Sundays*, he consumed three Quarters of his revenue." While Ozell's first two footnotes appear in earlier editions and are of the ordinary explicative variety, noting the location of La Mancha and observing that beef is "cheaper in Spain than Mutton," his third note overwhelms the reader. "*Duelos y Quebrantos*; in *English, Gruntings and Groanings*," observes the translator, going on to claim that "He that can tell us what Sort of Edible the Author means by those Words, *Erit mihi magnus Apollo*." Ozell enlightens us with the readings of Oudin, Stevens, and Jarvis, and with observations from Spanish and French dictionaries, with numerous asides commenting on culinary traditions, and concluding, "After all these learned Disquisitions, who knows but the Author means a Dish of Nichils!" The meaning of the phrase *duelos y quebrantos* has caused much ink to spill, and not only among translators. Contemporary editors concur that the term refers to a meal of semiabstinence but point to a long tradition of vexed commentary among Cervantists; for some, the "gripes and grumblings" (as Smollett has it) inspired by the ham-and-egg dish suggest a "New Christian" subtext.[29]

Smollett's comic spirit is clearly inspired by Ozell's lead. "Gripes and grumblings on Saturday" launches a footnote even longer than Ozell's: "Gripes and grumblings, in Spanish *Duelos y Quebrantos*: the true meaning of which, the former translators have been at great pains to investigate, as the importance of the subject (no doubt) required. But their labours have, unhappily, ended in nothing else but conjectures, which, for the entertainment and instruction of our readers, we beg leave to repeat" (27n). Smollett proceeds on his gastronomic foray with *mucho gusto*, until at last, "Having considered this momentous affair with all the deliberation it deserves, we in our turn present the reader, with cucumbers, greens, or pease por-

ridge, as the fruit of our industrious researches . . . such eatables as gener-
ate and expel wind; qualities (as every body knows) eminently inherent in
those vegetables we have mentioned as our hero's saturday's repast" (28n).
Smollett's send-up of "the former translators" is a fine satire on translators'
notes—many more of which he will produce, both from his own reflections
as well as from earlier translators, especially Jervas. Smollett's careful reading
of his predecessors produces a wonderful palimpsest of versions and revisions that foreground Smollett's writerly verve and allow us insights into his
reading process.[30]

Smollett's translation went through nineteen editions and reprints before
the end of the century, while Jervas's and Motteux-Ozell's were reprinted
four times each. The critical tide began to turn against Smollett, however,
with the assessment of Alexander Tytler, Lord Woodhouselee, whose *Essay
on the Principles of Translation* (1791) included an entire chapter comparing
Smollett and Motteux, to the disadvantage of the former.

Tytler sums up the relative strengths of his two translators, finding in
Smollett "a strong sense of ridicule, a great fund of original humour, and
a happy versatility of talent" completely in keeping with the spirit of Cervantes. Motteux, however, while possessing "no great abilities as an original
writer," nevertheless has "a just discernment of the weaknesses and follies
of mankind" and, more important, "a great command of the various styles
which are accommodated to the expression both of grave burlesque, and
of low humour."[31] Despite his admiration for Smollett's talent as a writer,
Tytler ultimately finds Motteux's translation superior, arguing that Smollett relies too heavily on "the armour of Jarvis" (180), whose literality and
"studied rejection" of Motteux's version led him, and through him Smollett, to make poor choices in the use of colloquial speech and idiomatic
expressions. (Tytler's purpose in the chapter is precisely to underline the
difficulty of translating such language; it is the prominent place of proverbs and idiomatic expressions in the *Quixote* that spurs the comparison.)
Tytler's position throughout the *Essay* is to be sympathetic toward adaptative translations and critical of close or literal translations; in his scheme,
the freer Motteux version has every advantage over the literal Jervas version
to begin with, and the chapter on the *Quixote*, as an object lesson on idioms, the prime pitfall of literality, is set up to make that point. By yoking
Smollett to Jervas, Tytler set the stage for later critics to dismiss Smollett's
version as entirely derivative—indeed, as no translation at all. In the 1880s,
John Ormsby, while showing a renewed appreciation of Jervas's literalism

(which he termed "ascetic abstinence"), remarked that Smollett's translation gave "very little or probably no heed . . . to the original Spanish."[32] In the twentieth century, scholars would go so far as to deny Smollett any hand in the translation or indeed any knowledge of Spanish at all, charges that have been thoroughly refuted by Martin Battestin.[33] The recent critical edition thus allows us to savor the intricacies of Smollett's relationships with his predecessors and with Cervantes's text, plus the relationships among the other texts, almost as if we had all the books open before us at once. Jervas's high-minded seriousness and Ozell's humor become part of our conversation with Smollett.

Let us turn to France, where Filleau de Saint-Martin's translation continued to be the standard version throughout almost the entire eighteenth century. The contrasts in the presentation of his translation and the earlier one by his predecessors César Oudin and François de Rosset suggest why the French remained satisfied with one translation while the English reading public devoured one after another. A lexicographer, César Oudin would be accused by later commentators as having been overly literal; his attachment to the Spanish language is evident in his dedication to Louis XIII, where he encourages the king to "savor [*gouster*, or taste] the original language" and expresses his belief that the work would be better presented *de vive voix*— a phrase suggesting not just the original language but oral transmission— rather than translated.[34] But only a decade after the first joint edition of Oudin's part 1 and Rosset's part 2, translator Perrot d'Ablancourt and his circle of academicians called for a new style of translation, one that was attuned to national literary values and that would contribute to the perfection of the French language. Filleau's 1678 translation of the *Quixote* thus follows the temper of the times in seeking an approach freed from the constraints and the language of the older translation, whose "language is already old" and much too closely aligned with the original. "I have dispensed with being as exact," says Filleau, "because the taste of the French is completely different today than what it was fifty years ago."[35] Like many another neoclassical translator, Filleau tells us that he has sought local equivalents of the proverbs, shaped the poetry in conformity with French rules, and rendered Spanish manners of speech acceptable "au genie & au goust des François." As a reminder to us that the aims of the belles infidèles translators are more complex than they at first appear, however, Filleau promptly informs his reader that a good translation should retain "some scent of the original" and not stray too far from the "the character of its author." As in the case of

Motteux, what matters here is not whether Filleau's claims appear valid to our modern eyes but rather the function of those claims in his readers' horizon of expectations. His emphasis on the contemporaneity of "taste" and the progress of the French language, but also on the need for a subtle infusion of the original's presence, its *odeur*, would continue to resonate throughout the Enlightenment, when sensorial qualities linking translation and original would become one of the primary topoi of translators' prefaces, as we saw in d'Alembert's call for translations that provide a *goût de terroir*.[36]

In 1783, more than a century after Filleau's translation appeared, Jean-Pierre Claris de Florian, known primarily as a dramatist, fabulist, and poet, published a translation of Cervantes's *La Galatea*. In the preface he called for a new translation of the *Quixote*, claiming that the "only" existing translation was "too far from the original's elegance and finesse" and criticizing it for its literality.[37] Despite Filleau's stated rejection of a literal approach, it seems highly unlikely that Florian could have been speaking of any translation other than his, since editions of Filleau proliferated throughout the eighteenth century yet there had been no editions of Oudin-Rosset since 1665. The irony, then, is that Florian levels exactly the same criticisms at Filleau that Filleau had leveled at Oudin-Rosset. Florian's own translation of the *Quixote* would not appear until 1799, several years after his death.

Florian's translation stands at the crossroads. Published at the turn of a new century, in a post-revolutionary France, it bears the trappings of an earlier era. Like the eighteenth-century translators across the Channel, he emphasizes the hero's "philosophy" and his deeply felt humanity over his comic qualities: "Don Quixote is mad whenever he acts, and wise whenever he reasons; and because he is always good, we never cease caring about him."[38] He, too, has provided an impressive apparatus for his translation: preface, biography of the author, footnotes. Like neoclassical translators of an earlier age, however, he castigates his predecessor for awkward literality and freely admits that he has abridged the work and modified it in keeping with contemporary taste. The conversation between generations of translators—sometimes a *dialogue des morts*, sometimes a *dialogue des sourds*—continues.[39]

The generations of translations, from Shelton's to Edith Grossman's, are also part of that conversation. Like generations, translations age. As Ormsby observed of Shelton, however, this is not always to their disadvantage. Smollett's language is not so far from us as to seem alien, nor so close as to create jarring incongruities.[40] Language change becomes acutely visible in translation, which foregrounds the temporality of the act of reading. As we have seen in earlier chapters, the French translators of the period, keenly attuned to l'usage, are typically haunted by this realization. "Le langage est déja vieux," says Filleau de Saint-Martin of Oudin and Rosset; Motteux too claims that Shelton's language "falls short of the Purity of the English Tongue, even of that time" (A5v).

The successive versions of the *Quixote* also point toward changes in the concept of authorship throughout the period. It is not entirely the case, as George Steiner argued, that translators have only recently begun "emerging from a background of indistinct solitude."[41] While the translators of the *Quixote* from earlier centuries whom he cites—among them Motteux, Smollett, and Tieck—may no longer spark instant associations with Cervantes for today's readers, they certainly were visible to the readers of their own day. The neoclassical translators may have called for texts that made the author "speak" like a compatriot, but far from rendering the translator "invisible," such practice lent power and creative authority to the translator. Rival translations such as those by Stevens, Motteux, Jervas, and Smollett enhanced the status of individual translators through competition in the literary marketplace. So while it may be the case that during this period "increased authorial prestige . . . undermined the durable institution of literary imitation," as Joseph Loewenstein has argued, the equally durable institution of literary translation—whose boundary with imitation had long been mobile and indistinct—takes on new luster as it participates in the emergence of individual authorship.[42] Of course, translation and authorship never merge, however prominent particular translators, from Cowley to Smollett to Gregory Rabassa and Eliot Weinberger, may become. The continuing "difference" inherent in translation and retranslation, the knowledge that one is engaged in what Smollett termed "a task already performed" (20), and the unavoidable awareness that we have seen among all our translators of other versions, revisions, and languages point toward another understanding of writing—as repetition, revision, and rewriting—and hence a disenchanted notion of originality, often unacknowledged, but quietly present, an ongoing alternative to Romantic notions of textual production. "Several hands" are always present in the making of a translation—not only the author's and translator's but also those of previous translators, editors, and readers. For all the ease with which the *Quixote* was welcomed and naturalized into the local environment, as much in France as in England, the very multiplication of versions and adaptations prevents any construction of it as an unvarying monument; the "hostile dynasties" of successive translators remind us of the slippages and insecurities attendant on even the most fluent of translations.[43]

During the first 150 years of translations of the *Quixote*, we also see the rise of a new phenomenon, the "modern classic," which is concurrent with the emergence of the modern use of the word "literature" in both French and English over the course of the eighteenth century. Tytler's reliance on examples from translations from modern languages to justify his theoretical principles bespeaks a profound change. Prior to 1700, it would have been unheard of to consider such translations worthy of critical analysis or to see them accorded the sort of scholarly treatment reserved for the Greek and Latin classics or scripture: critical preface, author's biography, explanatory notes. Just as in earlier centuries the advent of moveable type consolidated vernacular culture and conferred an air of historicity and truthfulness on the printed word, so the production of elegant editions in the eighteenth century, with illustrations and editorial apparatus, lent to works from the living languages a kind of cultural authority that had previously belonged only to the ancients. The translator's footnote marks a small but telling step in this process, by denoting that the text cannot be instantly seized in the entirety of its meaning but instead requires—and merits—gloss and commentary.

THE ENGLISH CANON IN FRANCE

If among the distinguishing features of a "classic" work is the appearance of competing translations, accompanied by important theoretical prefaces, then one of the earliest works to receive clear canonization as a contemporary classic is not a novel but a work in the more traditional genre of poetry, Pope's *Essay on Man*, translated in prose by Etienne de Silhouette in 1736 and in verse by the abbé du Resnel in 1737. Then, because Resnel criticized Silhouette's approach in his preface, Silhouette published a new edition in 1737 with an extended theoretical essay, "Réflexions préliminaires du traducteur sur le goût des traductions," regarded as one of the major statements on translation from the period.[44] Even in the shorter preface published with the 1736 edition, Silhouette emphasizes translation's cultural work: "These sorts of translations are particularly useful in that they do not disguise the taste and character of the works of a nation. This work therefore asks the reader sometimes to transport himself in his mind to England for certain ideas, expressions, and comparisons that seem either too daring, or too low."[45] Both Resnel and Silhouette cite from earlier theoreticians. Resnel cites Bouhier against Anne Dacier on behalf of verse translation, and in his "Réflexions," Silhouette quotes extensively from Tourreil's final preface to the orations on the crown. Both cite Roscommon. Resnel recalls that "it is appropriate to choose one's author as one chooses a friend," and both he and Silhouette quote the comparison between English and French: "The weighty *Bullion* of *One Sterling Line*, / Drawn to *French Wire*, would thro' whole *Pages* shine." Despite Resnel's defense of verse translation, he makes no attempt at rhyme, citing Roscommon in prose, while Silhouette, in the 1736 preface to his version of the *Essay on Criticism*, is characteristically both closer to the original and more awkward than Resnel, further accentuating his punctilio with a laborious footnote on English and French currency.[46] Their agreement on the essential differences between English and French leads the two translators to opposite conclusions: whereas Resnel champions the freer approach necessitated by verse, Silhouette responds in his "Réflexions" by denouncing adaptative translation as "that interior complacency that never ceases bringing everything back to ourselves, to the taste of our nation and our age, in such manner that instead of making ourselves like others, we remake them like us."[47] Silhouette proceeds to take aim squarely at the familiar prosopopoeia of neoclassical translation, the "maxim" that "we should always make foreign authors speak our language as we assume they would have spoken it themselves." He goes on to observe that since language reflects ideas and ideas "vary according to the diversity of manners, usage, customs," an author would have different thoughts, depending on his cultural/linguistic context: "If Pope had written in French, I am sure that he would have said something quite different. . . . A translation should never disguise the taste and character of the works of a nation; it is imperfect if it does not allow the reader to know and to evaluate them" (8–9). It is not surprising that Silhouette's essay is typically cited as a turning point in French translation theory, a moment when Enlightenment respect for cultural otherness trumps the insistence on local norms. Such was already the judgment of a reviewer in the *Journal des sçavans*, who observed that the "foreignness" (*air étranger*) of Silhouette "might disturb some readers" but that "for the thinking man, the philosopher," the spectacle of historical and cultural diversity is a fine one indeed.[48]

As we have seen, however, the neoclassical discourse of adaptation is considerably more complex. It would be an error to imagine that Resnel—whose translation is anticipated, but not yet seen, by the *Journal*'s reviewer—is simply unaware, uninterested, or negatively predisposed toward Pope's "Englishness." Indeed, Resnel offers an extended discussion of the difference in the two nations' génie and goût, noting an English taste for ellipsis and the French preference for completed thoughts; the scrupulousness of English "imitation" and the French insistence on polite expression. What the English call "simple and familiar [*naïf et familier*] is almost always seen by us as low, vulgar, and trivial" (xxv–xxvi). Referring to Silhouette's supposedly more exact prose translation and to its review in the *Journal des sçavans*, Resnel remarks that nothing would be more useful than such a project, were it only possible: "Is not expressivity the soul of poetry? And can you ever let others know the poet, if you do not render his expressivity? . . . You give me the poet's skeleton, not the poet himself" (xlii–xliii). According to Resnel, then, it is Silhouette who in his concern for literalism has nevertheless "forgotten" poetic language; his insistence on *l'expression* oddly echoes Anne Dacier's. Even so, Resnel's version would be criticized for its "diffuseness" by the marquis de Fontanes, who in his own verse translation seeks to escape the regularity of Pope's couplets by varying the rhythm and the relationships among the lines of verse.[49]

Among the later translations of Pope, the marquis de Saint-Simon's volume of "litteral and energetic" translations of Pope and other writers, originally published in 1771, is of greatest philosophical interest. In Saint-Simon's preface, the specific writers to be translated are of less import than the theoretical premise, constructed on sensationist principles, that the Republic of Letters, by facilitating the communication of "sensations," would ultimately produce a new universal language. Unlike the seventeenth century's artificial, abstract proposals for universal languages, or even eighteenth-century claims, such as Rivarol's, that French itself was universal, Saint-Simon calls for a process of hybridization that turns its back on any form of linguistic purity: "Linguistic perfection or purity is an imaginary idea. . . . Different peoples have always aided one another and will continue to do so by reciprocally communicating the signs of their ideas and hence their feelings; they will continue to receive new sensations, new images, and new expressions."[50] While translator-philosophes like d'Alembert and Delille imagined language change via contact between literary traditions, Saint-Simon's proposal offers a utopian Babel—cacophonic, constantly on the move, and strikingly modern.

As we saw in the case of the *Quixote* translators, however, not all of the discourse on translation is "theoretical," concerned with overarching aesthetic, linguistic, political, or philosophical issues. The prefaces to the rival translations of Fénelon's *Télemacque* by Abel Boyer and John Ozell, for example, compete primarily in the number of errors that each translator can denounce in the other's work.[51] Like the British translators of Cervantes or the French translators of Pope, however, they direct the reader's attention to the presence of other versions, and to the fact of translation and the multilingual diffusion of texts. One 1762 edition of the *Essay on Man*, a sort of "polyglot Pope," makes this point literally.[52]

I focus here on critical or theoretical discussions of translation, but these texts represent only a small percentage of the material available in translation. Other genres, such as history and philosophy, frequently receive the "publication honors"—fine editions, prefaces, and notes—accorded to literary classics. The paratextual materials, however, usually focus on providing the reader with historical or conceptual background rather than discussing translation per se. The substantial prefaces of the preeminent philosophical translators of the day—such as John Lockman, the primary English translator of Voltaire, or Pierre Coste, the translator of Locke—do not, in general, contribute to the critical discourse on translation.[53] Lockman shifts to the domain of letters, however, in the preface to his translation of Voltaire's *Henriade*; while his defense of Miltonic blank verse is most notable for its contribution to the ongoing discussion of English prosody, he confirms the trends we have seen before in the constitution of a canon of critics, with prominent citations of Roscommon's *Essay* and Dryden's *Dedication of the Aeneis*, along with a reference to a more recent work, Henry Felton's *Dissertation on Reading the Classics*.[54] French novels, by contrast, while generating a great deal of discussion and imitation, only rarely merit any sort of preface—although as we saw in Chapter 5, Haywood and other women translators sometimes situate themselves with respect to these texts in interesting ways.[55] More often we see introductory comments that underscore the emotional or moral tenor of the narrative to come, as when Samuel Humphreys whets our interest in Crébillon's *Lettres de la marquise de ****** with descriptions of "the Progress of an unfortunate Passion, from its seducing birth, to its fatal Period" and "an amiable Mind variously agitated by the Impressions of Tenderness, and the Dictates of Duty."[56]

The sheer presence of many circulating, and often competing, translations, with or without critical apparatus, reinforces both a sense of connection with others and a sense of one's linguistic and cultural distance from them. The "Anglo-French core" is vividly present in the persistent—

and consistent—descriptions that English writers feel compelled to give of the French language. Many continue to cite Roscommon's lines on English "Bullion" versus "French Wire." Thomas Gordon criticizes the French language for "laxness and effeminacy"; William Guthrie terms it "flimsey"; and Charlotte Lennox, an accomplished translator from French, makes similar comparisons: "The French language, although agreeable and easy to read, is difficult and harsh to translate; smooth as ivory to the sight, rough as iron to the touch. . . . The French flutter in the air; the English walk majestically on the ground. The French have a great scope of language, but their expressions are seldom nervous, and scarce ever sublime."[57] Such comparisons might appear to be typical expressions of British Francophobia, but the situation is more complex. Lennox was no Francophobe. Rather, these comparisons reflect an enhanced *prise de conscience* of writers in English, mediated through their contacts not just with classical languages (both Gordon and Guthrie make their remarks in the context of translations from Latin) but with the most prominent and "present" contemporary neighbor—and its language. Awareness of France and of French, as of French literature and French cultural institutions, creates the environment through which English is apprehended and constituted. This individual national identity in turn enables dialogue and exchange. As Margaret Cohen and Carolyn Dever observe with respect to the Anglo-French evolution of the novel, "National identification does not precisely reinforce monolithic notions of national identity; rather, it confirms the existence of nongeneric universal humanity by showing how it can vary according to local contexts."[58] Francophobia and Francophilia, like Anglophobia and Anglophilia, represent multiple aspects of an intensely experienced relationship through which self, other, and world are brought into view.

We see this phenomenon even more dramatically in looking at French translations from English. The two most celebrated French translators of the period, Pierre Antoine de La Place and Pierre Le Tourneur, made their careers with translations of British writers, including the radically foreign plays of Shakespeare, of which I will have more to say later. In Le Tourneur especially, we encounter a translator manifestly committed to creating a coherent body of work—*faire oeuvre*—in which critical commentary plays a key role in maintaining the overall unity. An extremely self-reflective translator, he provided each of his major translations with a substantial preface elucidating not only the cultural and intellectual background of the source text but also his own translating practice and reasons for taking on the project.[59] Le Tourneur made a career of translating British writers, especially those whose work offered new directions for writing in French. Although he varied his genres and even occasionally translated from languages other than English, following the overwhelming success of his first translation, *Les Nuits d'Young* (1769), he quickly became identified with the "strange," melancholy English writers to whom French literary aesthetics was most resistant: Hervey, Gray, Ossian, and, of course, Shakespeare. He is credited with a major role in the diffusion of Young on the Continent, and the first Italian, Spanish, and Portuguese translations of *Night Thoughts* were based on *Les Nuits* rather than on the English original.[60]

Produced half a century before Le Tourneur's major works, the abbé Desfontaines's 1727 translation of *Gulliver's Travels* offers an early—if infamous—look at translation's role in the rise of *anglomanie*. The acid-tongued critic of the philosophes portrays himself in his preface as a trend-setting Anglophile, deciding to translate Swift's work in order to improve his skills in English, "which is beginning to be à la mode in Paris."[61] (A few years later, Riccoboni would claim a similar impetus for her translation of Fielding's *Amelia*.) It quickly becomes apparent that the subject of the preface is not Swift or his book but Desfontaines himself—his experience, tastes, and abilities. He is frank on the question of taste, finding the chapter on Lilliput "mediocre" (vii) and criticizing elsewhere the "impenetrable allegories, insipid allusions, childish details, trivial reflections, low thoughts, boring repetitions, vulgar humor and lame jokes: in brief, things that if they were rendered literally in French would have . . . been repugnant to French good taste" (ix–x). Desfontaines promises, however, to "make up for these defects." He defends the work's genre, situating *Gulliver's Travels* in a respectable line of fantastic works ranging from Plato's *Republic* to Cyrano de Bergerac's *Voyage dans la lune*. As for the translation itself, he makes cuts, softens the language, and changes the ending, giving us a Gulliver who ultimately reconciles himself to his family and society, although he remains "something of a misanthrope," as the narrator remarks at the end of his tale.[62] Desfontaines claims not to have entirely gallicized Swift, explaining that despite his adjustments to French taste, "a foreigner is always a foreigner" and "retains something of his accent and manners" (xviii). Etienne de Silhouette would single out Desfontaines's translation as a prime example of the arrogance lurking behind adaptative translation.[63]

Several things are going on at once in Desfontaines's translation. This is not just an act of national or cultural appropriation but also one of *personal*

appropriation: Desfontaines displays himself as "à la mode," a language vir-
tuoso (but not a pedant), and a known literary property (he expects that
people will recognize his prose style in the translation). He fiercely guards
his French turf against foreign competitors—not the English but rather Van
Effen and another anonymous Dutch translator, along with the publishers
in The Hague—maintaining the visibility of the competing translations even
as he dismisses them. As his excursus on *le genre fantastique* hints, translation would remain bound up with larger questions of literary criticism for
Desfontaines, whose critical preface to his translation of Virgil would be
admired by both friend and foe. He would return to novels at the end of his
career with a translation of *Joseph Andrews*, offering a preface written in the
persona of "an English lady" that says little on translation per se but provides a scathing overview of modern French and English novels.[64]

   There are many other examples, needless to say, of English texts being
reshaped to French taste, even in works where the translator's admiration
of the source text is less conflicted than Desfontaines's response to Swift.
Antoine de La Place is frank about the perceived need to provide "French
clothing" for, and *not* a literal translation of, Aphra Behn's *Oronooko*.[65]
While some scholars have criticized his attenuation of Behn's abolitionist
message, others have pointed to the significance of his intertextual weav-
ing of French and British novelistic techniques and to his valorization of
female writing.[66] La Place calls attention to his modifications by expressing
his hope that readers who know English and are aware of the changes "will
forgive my daring on account of my motives" (ix). Similarly, he prefaces
his 1750 translation of *Tom Jones, ou L'Enfant trouvé* with something resembling a fan letter to Henry Fielding but nevertheless goes on radically to
abridge the novel, cutting most notably all the "digressions" and authorial
interventions at the beginning of each book—suggesting that at some point
he might use these passages to create "a separate volume, as instructive as
it would be amusing." "French taste" is again responsible: La Place claims
that once his compatriots are caught up by a good plot, they regard "digressions, dissertations, or moral treatises" such as Fielding's authorial interventions "as so many obstacles to their pleasure." Hence, La Place argues, "I
have done what the author himself would probably have done."[67] La Place's
translations of Behn and Fielding went on to become best-sellers.

   The year following La Place's *Tom Jones* saw the publication of the abbé
Prévost's extremely popular and deeply abridged translation of Samuel
Richardson's *Clarissa*. Although Diderot and others would criticize Prévost's

cuts—Pierre Le Tourneur later speculated that the changes were due to "his haste to leave behind the humble role of translator, in order to create for himself"—Prévost's preface is not easily categorized in terms of "foreignizing" or "domesticating," as one might think.[68] As Prévost tells us, even if English literature requires "slight repairs" in order to be "naturalized" in France, "I made it my duty to preserve the national flavor of characters and customs. . . . And why not? A foreign air is not unwelcome in France."[69] Prévost would like to have it both ways, to "naturalize" his text and preserve its air étranger. Once again, whatever these statements may or may not say about the translator's practice, they speak volumes about his perception of his reading public.

Despite increasingly affirmative evocations of "foreignness," even the most progressive translators readily admit to textual modifications that would strike us as unacceptable. Le Tourneur would bring a distinctly different sensibility to his work as a translator, yet he too saw limits to the degree of alterity that he thought the French public could bear. In his translation of Young's *Night Thoughts*, he cuts and reorganizes the text in order to bring a degree of thematic unity to each *Nuit*: "My intention was to draw from the English Young a French Young who could please my countrymen, and whom they would read without worrying whether he was an original or a copy."[70] We find a similar reordering of another text wholeheartedly admired by its translator in the abbé Morellet's 1766 translation of Beccaria's *Dei delitti e delle pene*. Morellet claims that his editorial changes "render this work more useful to our nation" and that he furthermore has the right to make alterations "because a book that so eloquently pleads the cause of humanity belongs henceforth to the world."[71] Peter France expresses the view of many scholars in concluding that "the hegemony of polite culture" was too powerful for any authentically "foreign" voices to be heard or to have much effect.[72]

As the conventional account goes, the empire of the belles infidèles was nevertheless coming to an end in the second half of the eighteenth century through the efforts of such philosophes as d'Alembert and Diderot. There is real power in that account, which is intrinsically linked to the metanarrative of Enlightenment progressivism. We need to problematize this particular form of the metanarrative, however, by considering how multiple and sometimes contradictory subnarratives may be present in the same place. While it is the case that the Encyclopedists' reflections on language and translation open up the discussion in important ways, it would be an error to polarize "philosophic" and "polite" approaches to translation. Morellet is certainly a philosophe, and Prévost wants to respect Richardson's air étranger.

One way of demonstrating the complexity of these translations would be to go back to a couple of domesticating examples and show how they do, in fact, perform as *translations*, "displacing" their readers and offering them something quite new or foreign. Let us take La Place's *Tom Jones*, which bears every mark of strongly adaptative translation. La Place cuts nearly half the text, including Fielding's authorial interventions at the beginning of each book; such politically sensitive material as the discussion of politics and the "popish priest" in book 7, chapter 9; and some of the most famous scenes and "digressions" of the novel, such as the battle scene "sung by the Muse in the Homerican style, which none but the classical reader can taste" (book 4, chapter 8). La Place apparently felt that few of his readers were "classical." In general, he seems to take Fielding at his word each time that the author suggests that his text may appeal to a more "select" group, such as with the "metaphysical" discussion between Thwackum and Square that "some readers, perhaps may not relish." He also transposes numerous cultural references, bringing them home to France, as in his description of Sophia Western. The "true author of this story," we are told, has given a detailed portrait of the heroine, but because of the French impatience with such things, "I will simply say that *Sophia was beautiful, and furthermore amiable.*" For the benefit of readers whose imagination requires a bit more help, the first-person narrator, clearly identified as the translator, recommends that they pick up one of "our novels" and read the description of the first princess that they come across: "Let him find such a portrait in Cyrus or Clélie or elsewhere, it will be the image of our heroine and my job is done" (1:79–80). Even with the relocalized reference to *Clélie* or *Cyrus*, the passage is a far cry from, and considerably shorter than, Fielding's "short hint of what we can do in the sublime." As La Place indicates in his fan letter to Fielding, he views his French public as principally interested in plot, with little or no interest in digressions or "ornaments." His *Tom Jones* is amusing, we might say, but it is *très infidèle* to the original—deliberately and explicitly so in deference to "French taste."[73]

And yet one might want to pause a second over the reference in the Sophia passage to *le véridique auteur anglais*. It is only one of many. Consider another example: "It was about five o'clock (the eloquent English author tells us in a much more ample style)."[74] Indeed, despite the absence of his "digressions," *l'auteur anglais* is as much a presence in La Place's version as Fielding is in his own. There is even an additional figure of the translator, prominent in the chapter title "In Which the Translator Talks to Himself" ("Où le traducteur parle tout seul"; originally, "Jones arrives at Gloucester"). La Place might be a domesticating, hegemonizing translator in some respects, but he understands and renders something profoundly important in Fielding's novel: its theatricality, its wink to the reader, its self-reflexiveness. And La Place—here in the purest sense a "foreignizing" translator—*never* allows us to be lulled into thinking we are reading an "original work." The véridique auteur is absent, the text is elsewhere, and La Place strenuously resists the "translator's invisibility," no less than would any progressive twenty-first-century critic.

LA PLACE'S SHAKESPEARE:
NATURALIZING THE INTRUDER

In 1745, the same year as his *Oroonoko* translation, La Place embarked on a major project, his eight-volume anthology *Le Théâtre anglois*, which included, in addition to ten of Shakespeare's plays, works by Otway, Fletcher, Dryden, Rowe, Addison, and others. Fueled by best-selling translations of English novels, anglomanie was already well under way in France. As La Place observes, however, translations of works written for the stage had not kept pace with translations of poetry, philosophy, and prose fiction. Taking his cue from Père Brumoy's 1730 anthology of Greek drama, La Place proposes to fill the gap. Any such project, he tells us, must necessarily begin with Shakespeare, "the inventor of the art of drama in England." Shakespeare was a true original, having "neither models, nor rivals . . . [nor] any knowledge of the dramatic works of antiquity."[75] His inspiration came instead from "within his own genius, or rather within nature" (v).

In the long history of French translations of the Bard, more attention has been given to Pierre Le Tourneur, who gave the first complete translation of the plays; Jean-Pierre Ducis, who wrote the first versions performed on stage (adapted from Le Tourneur's translations); and of course Voltaire, who translated relatively little but whose early rendering of Hamlet's soliloquy in the *Lettres philosophiques* and subsequent highly conflicted attitude toward Shakespeare's work were very influential.[76] Despite the notoriety and proliferation of translations, François-Victor Hugo would nevertheless argue in the 1865 preface to his *Oeuvres complètes de W. Shakespeare* that no truly authentic translation had yet appeared: "For a literal translation of Shakespeare to be possible, it was necessary that the literary revolution of 1830 vanquish all opposition, that the liberties which triumphed in politics did so in literature, that the new language, the revolutionary language, the language of concrete words and images, be created once and for all. Now that a literal translation of Shakespeare has become possible, we have attempted it."[77] Yves Bonnefoy, arguably Shakespeare's greatest contemporary French translator, expresses similar sentiments, suggesting that Shakespeare has not been re-experienced (*revécu*) in France because his various translators "have not been able to establish from the start, as however one must, a rhythm, that fundamental rhythm that carries the poetic line" and provides "the logic of the text as well as the logic of existence."[78] In three hundred years of translations, Shakespeare is still a foreigner or, in Jean-Luc Nancy's more forceful term, an "intruder": "As long as he stays, instead of becoming 'naturalized,' his arrival never ceases: he continues to arrive and the arrival does not cease being in some way an intrusion . . . an intimate disturbance [*un trouble dans l'intimité*]."[79] Shakespeare, indeed, has never stopped arriving in France and thus has never become completely naturalized in the etymological sense of, as we might say, "going native." Yet this early "arrival" in La Place's *Théâtre anglois* does correspond to the complex and contradictory patterns we have seen in the concept of naturalization, as well as occasioning a profound rethinking of the status of French drama. La Place's extended formal introduction, the "Discours sur le théâtre anglois," aims to shape the reader's understanding not only of the plays but of the role of the theater in general, through an intercultural encounter available only in translation.

La Place's Shakespeare has been cited as a significant moment in the constitution of "pre-Romantic" aesthetics, but on the whole it has received much less attention than his translations of Behn and Fielding.[80] One of the few contemporary critics to attend to it criticizes the work for failing to live up to the aesthetic program described in the preface and dismisses the preface as internally flawed and incoherent.[81] Indeed, it is hard to see how the ambitious and daring program announced in the preface, in which La Place asks his readers to appreciate "the sublimity of the ideas, the grandeur of the images, the fire of enthusiasm, the singularity of new and daring features, the naturalness of the feelings," could possibly relate to the abridged, often bowdlerized, primarily prose versions of the plays that follow.[82] At the same time, I do not think that La Place's inadequacy or timidity as a translator (by today's standards) diminishes the force of the aesthetic vision

of the "Discours," or that the "Discours" fails because of perceived contradictions. In fairness, La Place's emendations should be set in the context of
contemporaneous British efforts to bring Shakespeare in line with "modern" standards of taste; over the course of the eighteenth century, the Bard
was transformed "from a brilliant but incorrect and inchoate dramatist to
nature's darling and the model of native genius."[83] La Place's "Discours" is
an attempt to come to terms with the foreign, with the strange, with "difference," and to make difference "understandable" at some level while maintaining its alterity on another—the impossible translator's task.

Delineating the cultural differences between France and England provides
the primary structuring device of the "Discours." La Place often proceeds
by analogy: gastronomy (viii); gardening, in a comparison of the "superb" if
irregular gardens at Versailles to the "boring symmetry" of the Tuileries (xvii–
xviii); architecture, via Pope's analogy of Gothic versus classical buildings to
describe Shakespeare (xxxii–xxxiii); and painting (xlv–xlvi). La Place situates
his exploration of the foreign as central to the Enlightenment project. A phil-
osophically inclined reader, he tells us, will seek clues to understanding "the
attributes of the soul of the nation for whom Shakespeare wrote." Such dis-
coveries are "precious" because they "extend one's sphere of ideas" and form
the basis for cultural comparisons. Thus "a reader who does not believe that
French thinking [*l'esprit François*] is necessarily the same as all other nations"
will take pleasure in a text that offers something truly new (xii–xiii). The de-
familiarization of taste offers an antidote to the most hegemonizing forms of
French universalism and provides experiences hitherto inaccessible. La Place
thus situates his discussion of Shakespeare and of English dramaturgy within
a larger search for new experiences and ways of viewing the world.

Like other descriptions of English and French national characters that
define one in opposition to the other, La Place contributes to the *production*
of national identity. Subjective identification with either identity, however,
is always open to the knowledge that there are other ways of construing
reality: *l'esprit François* is not *l'esprit tout court*. More important, the study
of the imbrication of the English character with English drama leads to
a new concept of truth. Whereas the French insist on verisimilitude (*le
vraisemblable*) in their theater, the English "rebel against verisimilitude" because of their "thorough study of the truth" (xxxix). "Truth" on the English
stage can be apprehended through a greater flexibility of register, tone, and
characterization (xlv). Ultimately, La Place identifies "truth" as the "essence
of tragedy" (lii), although he is speaking not of ordinary truth "of actions

and things" but rather of a "truth of sentiment" that speaks directly to the spectator (liv). The *vérité de sentiment*, if it could be realized on the French stage, would represent something quite new: not factual correspondence to events, nor verisimilitude's portrayal of what might be, but instead "a tableau that shows characters and events as they must be, in the moment of representation, in order to make an impression on the spectator in the present situation where he sees them," a tableau "drawn from nature and authorized by reason" (lv–lvi). The full analysis of La Place's proposal and its significance for dramatic aesthetics lies beyond the scope of this study, but a theater that rejects verisimilitude in the name of truth, that places the spectator at its center, and that presents itself as a "tableau" bears startling parallels to the innovative dramaturgy that Diderot would call for a decade later in his manifesto *Les Entretiens sur le Fils naturel*. Here, though, I want to emphasize the role of "difference": vérité de sentiment is more absolute than vraisemblance, but inasmuch as it is constituted for and through the spectator, it is also culturally relative. The "spectator" is not an abstract universal but is bound to time and place. The specificities of time and place open the door to the potential for change: the contact with other artistic forms will inspire creative genius to discover "new paths" and new rules of art (lxiv). In an extended reflection on change, La Place compares progress in the arts to progress in the sciences, citing the novel as an example of a genre that has been transformed into something radically different from the models of antiquity and noting developments and new freedoms on the French stage.

There are limits to freedom and limits to change. Despite his acknowledgment that the rules of art are constantly evolving (lxxi), La Place suddenly calls a halt to some forms of innovation represented by Shakespeare's "extreme" scenes, or the mixture of high and low elements such as we see in the gravediggers' scene in *Hamlet*. It is "contrary to reason, to nature, and to the vérité de sentiment" to fuse comic and tragic elements or modes of speech (lxxxi). With this proviso, La Place leaves room for Diderot to surpass his model by calling for mixed genres in the renewal of the theater in the following decade; for now, some part of Shakespeare remains entirely unassimilable.

The remainder of the preface returns to the differences between the English and the French, the role of court culture in the determination of popular taste (much more important in France than in England), and the role of love in the theater (also more important in France). Here as elsewhere, La Place is clearly offering the English model as an alternative, "a comparison piece," and suggesting that French customs are susceptible to change. Here, too, La Place plays the role of diplomat, refusing to pronounce in favor of one approach or the other but rather offering by way of conclusion a few remarks on his approach as translator: "It remains for me only to give an account of the precautions that I took lest I be guilty of imprudence, unfaithfulness, or neglect in the eyes of the two nations, the English and the French" (cviii). He comes back several times to this image of himself "in the eyes" of two countries, reminding us of his bilingual education by exiled English Jesuits in Calais and of his bi-confessional family background, his parents having abjured Protestantism at the time of the Revocation.[84] His double allegiance complicates his task: "If I wish to spare certain elements that would be repugnant to us, the English will say that I forced, perverted, or failed to render the meaning of their author. If I render it faithfully, the author will be the loser among us; and both nations will hold me responsible for what flatters neither the taste of one side nor the self-regard of the other" (cix). He resolves the dilemma through several techniques: he abridges, he adapts, and he mixes prose and verse. Although the last of these appears the least harmful to modern eyes—and even suggests a sensitivity to the variety of tone and the elusive quality of Shakespearean meter that Bonnefoy sees as crucial—the first two would hardly be appreciated today. Nevertheless, as André Lefevere once pointed out, we should not underestimate the powerful role of anthologizing abridgments and extracts in cultural transmission; La Place's *Théâtre anglois* was a best-seller and marked the beginning of a literary debate, the *Querelle de Shakespeare*.[85] But as we have seen elsewhere, La Place's very evident editorial presence in his work never lets his readers "assimilate" the text or forget that they are reading a translation.

To what extent, then, has Shakespeare been "naturalized"? As we have seen, both the legal and linguistic uses of the term involve a complex interplay of truth and fiction, homogeneity and difference. The naturalization of persons provides fictions of integration while both maintaining and obscuring real differences; and yet the practice may have enabled processes of integration and belonging to occur. The naturalization of words and texts refers, on the one hand, to words that retain the markers of their foreign origins and, on the other, to texts that have lost theirs; like the fiction of "Catholic France," the translation that sounds "as if the author had been born French" disguises national and cultural differences. La Place appears to head straight between the horns of this dilemma as well: adapting, shaping, and modifying his text but also calling attention to the process and, most important, never letting us forget that Shakespeare is, above all, "different." Indeed, the *representation* of Shakespeare as exotic other is critical to the French understanding of the native literary tradition: its past, present, and future. If Shakespeare did not exist, he would have to be invented.

Shakespeare is thus represented not merely as a foreigner, an aubain who might someday "pass" for a naturel, but rather as the intruder who permanently disrupts the order of things. He can be "naturalized" only inasmuch as we have understood naturalization to entail a complex process that obscures difference while maintaining it. La Place's preface leads us to expect a more disruptive text than we are actually given, but the text also constantly points out its own deficiencies, leading us to imagine—and hence indirectly to experience—the violence of disruption.

For Julia Kristeva, the eighteenth century marks a decisive moment in the West's coming to terms with the foreignness of the foreigner, through a cosmopolitanism stemming from an awareness of the strangeness of the self, a strangeness later to be theorized by Freud as the *unheimlich*, *l'inquiétante étrangeté*, the uncanny.[86] It is this identification that Nancy implicitly critiques in *L'Intrus*, observing, in effect, that Kristeva "naturalizes" l'étrangeté by assimilating it to the unconscious and hence, ultimately, locating it as a part of ourselves—to the detriment of the progressive political agenda of Kristeva's book *Etrangers à nous-mêmes*. Nancy's model for the intruder is his own transplanted heart—and all the attendant medical mysteries, technological interventions, immunosuppressant drugs, susceptibility to cancer and so on that lead him on a voyage to a place from whose bourn few travelers return: "The intruder is in me and I become a stranger to myself" (31). As there is really no way to close this *béance*, this open wound, the philosopher finds in the experience both the pain of total exposure—"The intruder exposes me excessively" (42)—and, through that exposure, with its Levinassian overtones, an enlarged capacity for openness, for identification with others in their ongoing otherness, as "the same that never stops changing" (45).

I will conclude with a final glance at Pierre Antoine de La Place. Unlike some of his contemporaries, La Place does not call for a change in translating *practice*, but his ultimate aims as a translator are nevertheless consonant with what Antoine Berman called translation's "ethical aim": encountering the other, allowing the self to be changed through that encounter. There is a "foreignizing" dimension in his "adaptative" practice. La Place depicts himself as "exposed" ("in the eyes of the two nations"), as a sort of double agent forced to operate in broad daylight with his dual allegiances on display. Thus exposed, the translator is the intruder, complicit with both sides, wholly trusted by neither. Nor should he be, if to be worthy of trust he is obligated to respect the status quo. As an agent of change, both with regard to the source text and to the target culture, his homeland is nowhere, which is to say *utopia*—but it is also very much in the here and now, in the ongoing, disruptive moment of translation.

Conclusion

Historicizing Translation

As we have seen, neoclassical translation is marked from its inception by historical consciousness: an awareness of the historicity of language—l'usage—and of translation practice. In France and England, the early neoclassical translators proclaim the "newness" of their endeavor, their break with past practices, the progress and triumph of the national language. As the "new and nobler way" becomes the standard for all, translation remains bound up in questions of temporality, of the entwinement of past and present. By the eighteenth century, translation is perceived as having its own history. What can neoclassical translation history tell us about neoclassical translation practice? In these final pages, I turn to three accounts, quite different in their aims and scope: the preliminary discourse and chapter on the history of translation theory from the abbé Goujet's *Bibliothèque françoise* (1740), Samuel Johnson's *Idler* essays on the history of translation (1759), and Alexander Tytler's *Essay on the Principles of Translation* (1791). While all three reflect mainstream neoclassical taste in translation, all call on us to view the movement in its complexity.

Claude-Pierre Goujet (1697–1767) was involved in a number of dictionary projects, historiographies, and compilations; his *Bibliothèque françoise, ou Histoire de la littérature françoise* relates to all three. This ambitious undertaking (eighteen volumes appearing over the course of fifteen years) claims on its title page to show "the use that may be gained from books published in French since the invention of the printing press, for understanding belles lettres, history, the sciences and the arts" as well as providing critical commentary on "the principal works in each genre written in that language."[1] The double emphasis on works "published" as well as "written" in French are the focus of much of the abbé's discussion of his project in his "Discours préliminaire." Let us examine Goujet's account of his overall project in order to comprehend his interest in translation. According to the "Discours," the *Bibliothèque* is meant to demonstrate and inform, "to make known what we possess" in every area of knowledge, and to answer the question of whether or not French suffices in providing a complete education to someone ignorant of Greek or Latin. There are several interrelated issues here. Goujet explains that his work is both a *bibliothèque*, or organized repository of knowledge (not a simple "catalogue"), and a history, or *histoire*, of the French language, literature, and culture (1:v). His chapters will thus not be mere alphabetical compilations of data but rational groupings of works, most of which he will discuss in some depth, and all of which he has read himself.[2] The systematic aspect of the project is balanced by its historical component, since each subject category (chapter) is organized chronologically. The abbé consecrates most of the "Discours," however, to the question of his intended reader. The work is aimed at two sorts of persons: those whose Latin and Greek are so poor as to force them to seek "notions of the arts and sciences in works written in the vernacular" and those who have never learned the languages of erudition but possess "a desire to learn" (1:xiii). Goujet explicitly includes women in this group, decrying their lack of educational opportunities (1:xx–xxi).

Indeed, Goujet's project, at least in this initial conception, is an extended defense of an education conducted entirely in the French language. Although he carefully distinguishes himself from the polemical "modernism" of a Perrault (1:iii, xxxvi–vii) and professes the greatest admiration for the works of the ancients, he argues that for practical pedagogical reasons, the study of ancient languages can be safely deferred till a period in life when one has either the desire or professional need to learn them (1:xv–xvii). The all-French curriculum contains a non-ethnocentric premise, since Goujet recognizes that there is knowledge to be obtained from works in other languages. Goujet takes for granted that "content" can be extracted and transferred from one language to another without significant loss, to the greater enrichment of the French *bibliothèque*. This assumption is linguistic, however, not cultural.

The reflection on translation is thus central to the enterprise. Goujet invokes the greater ease of reading in one's native language, based on two factors: that one need not pause in uncertainty over the meaning of words, and that—as he puts it delicately—"order and clarity" are not always the predominant features of ancient masterpieces (1:xvii–xviii). There is nothing worse, he tells us, than having to puzzle out a text, dictionary in hand, without any idea "if one has indeed seized upon his [the author's] meaning, if one has not imputed to him thoughts he did not have, if one has felt the same things as he" (1:xix). Translation obviates this inconvenience as well as furthering the advancement of enlightenment (*lumières*) by offering women the opportunity to give themselves an education equal to men's. One should note, however, the burden placed here on the work of *reading*, which must then be borne by translation: to produce within the reader the same thoughts, the identical feelings, harbored by the writer. For Goujet, language expresses an interior state. Only when readers have acceded to the original thoughts or impetus of the writer can they be said to have understood the text. His reasoning reminds us how the notion of a general grammar, according to which all languages represent lived reality through a set of determinable logical operations, could provide a powerful model for reading and for educational progress.

The reflection on the advantages of reading in translation leads Goujet to announce the second motivation for offering his project: "To honor our nation by displaying its literary riches; by demonstrating that there is no aspect of literature, science, history, or the arts that has not only been carefully cultivated in France, but treated in our language" (1:xxiii). Looking back to French literary glories of the previous century, Goujet proclaims that French has taken the place of Latin as "the universal language of Europe" (1:xliv).[3] French has incorporated the riches of other languages into itself, both through translation and through creative emulation, especially of ancient models. Goujet's guiding assumption throughout remains that French must be seen in relation to Greek and Latin; nowhere in the "Discours" does he discuss the other modern languages, although in later volumes of the *Bibliothèque* he will, in fact, study translations from Italian, Spanish, and, of course, English. Does the project represent ethnocentrism and exclusionary politics? Yes, to some extent. But it is also important to emphasize how new the French preeminence in the literary field is, only coming about in the previous century. For Goujet, French has only lately emerged from the domination of antiquity, both in the educational system and in a broader cultural sense. His repeated denials that he does not share Perrault's position that classical culture is actually inferior to modern culture exemplify the difficulty of his position, his desire for nuance.

The complexities of Goujet's stance explain why he devotes several chapters to the history of the French language, the development of dictionaries in French, and the history of reflection on translation. Strictly speaking, chapter 5 ("Des Traités sur la maniere de traduire") deals with "books containing rules for translating well" (194), but here as elsewhere, we encounter the intimate connection between the "rules" of translation and more general issues concerning language and understanding. Addressing the reader directly, he observes that even if "you are not able to translate into French the authors who wrote in learned languages that you do not know," critical reflection on the act of translation may nevertheless be of value because "these rules extend to all languages" (1:194). Here for the first time in the *Bibliothèque* we find an implicit reference to the other modern languages and the suggestion that the reader might indeed know them. Interestingly, Goujet feels obliged to point out that the critical reflection on translation (all of which, indeed, focuses on the relations between Latin and French) could also be relevant to modern languages. Clearly, "translation" does not automatically call "modern languages" to mind. We have perhaps been insufficiently attentive to this different perception of "foreignness" and relatedness among languages, the idea that, in some spheres at least, only the languages qualified as "learned" might appear to warrant a formal interpretative operation known as "translation."

For Goujet, it is indeed the case, but it is not self-evident, that critical reflection on translation might be applicable to the modern languages; and he further asserts that such reflection might enhance understanding of the reader's native French. Although it does not seem likely that Goujet would take as extreme a position as Diderot, who could find foreignness at the heart of his native language, we can see the potential for such a view in the awareness that the questions of style, transposition, and meaning open up possibilities for seeing one's own language in a new light, and that critical reflection on translation often, if not inevitably, entails a reflection on the current state of one's own language.

As he promised in the "Discours," Goujet gives us a chronological account. He sees the beginnings of French translation theory—as have many more-recent scholars—in the figure of Etienne Dolet. Goujet summarizes Dolet's short work, recommending that the reader consult it personally, and then moves on to another milestone in neoclassical translation theory, Gaspard de Tende's *Traité de la traduction* (1660), which he also summarizes. Goujet proceeds from there, alternating lists of some texts (including significant prefaces by a number of translators) with detailed accounts of others. Although his emphasis in this chapter is on the elaboration of "rules" for translation, the historical theme is always discreetly present; in addition to the chronological order of the presentation, the appearance of increasingly detailed reviews offers a figure of progress from Dolet to De Tende to Coustel, whose *Traité de l'éducation des enfants* (1687) is summarized in detail.

Goujet's historical consciousness is intimately linked to his desire to set forth rules and systems, which he sees in terms of their progressive development over the preceding two centuries, the period that corresponds to the rise of French as a national language. The gradual articulation of such rules indicates the arrival of French as an international language, as a machine through which everything may be translated, and as a means of communication between past and present. We shall see a similar emphasis on progress as the primary vehicle for understanding translation history in Samuel Johnson. "Progress" is the code for newly enabled "modern" subjectivity to give an account for its own sense of capacity and purposiveness. The historicizing process I've described here is analogous to Eric Méchoulan's description of modernity as the shift in the understanding of community from "collective memory" to "culture" through a concomitant shift in the subject's constitution via language. The global redistribution and redefinition of social roles prevents the subject either from "being spoken by" or "speaking" older roles; the alternative is to "make them speak" (*faire parler*): to acknowledge one's insertion in language and rhetoric, to open the way for new forms of personal mastery, as well as to the awareness of one's own situatedness, one's temporality.[4]

In addition to the topos of progress, another historicizing model is woven into much eighteenth-century writing on translation; indeed, Goujet confirms the significance of what I have called citation networks. Enlightenment literati were well aware of a tradition of writing on the theory of translation. In the previous century, translators' primary historical references were to Cicero's remarks on his (lost) translation of Demosthenes and the much-debated passage regarding the *fidus interpres* in Horace. An exception might be seen in Gaspard de Tende's references to contemporaries Le Maistre de Sacy and Vaugelas, except that his references are exclusively examples of practice, not theoretical statements. The eighteenth-century translators are concerned with a more recent tradition being constructed in the theoretical writings, especially the critical prefaces, of their own day. Sometimes the references are familiar to us now—Anne and André Dacier, for example—but not always, as Goujet's list of significant preface writers Dubois, Tourreil, Bouhier, and d'Olivet suggests. As we have seen, citation networks become increasingly "modern" in the eighteenth century. Even controversies would become important reference points, as evinced by Jacques Delille's contemptuous reference to "a time when . . . La Motte disfigured Homer in order to correct him."[5] Such references situate translators within a community and within a history that they are bringing into being through the references themselves. Citation becomes as much a performative act as a referential one, underscoring temporal and relational aspects of translation, in which a text is never final or definitive but always open to further commentary, further versions.

We see another approach to both these historicizing tactics—the chronological survey and the network of citations—in Samuel Johnson's 1759 *Idler* essays on "the history of translations." While Johnson's focus will ultimately be on English translators, he begins with a broad historical view designed to show that translation "may justly be claimed by the moderns as their own."[6] Goujet implied as much through his emphasis on French writers since the Renaissance; Johnson casts an eye at ancient civilizations in order to make his point. There are two aspects to the historical survey. On the one hand, Johnson offers a theory of linguistic development: "In the first ages of the world instruction was commonly oral and learning traditional, and what was not written could not be translated" (1:87). The insistence on *written* language as preliminary to translation suggests that the oral search for equivalencies between sign systems, whether spontaneous or carefully considered, would thus not constitute translation. Or Johnson may be suggesting that without a written language, exclusively oral forms of communication are simply not susceptible to a formalized, definite process. The corollary would be that writing stabilizes speech, makes it available as transmissible "content," as opposed to the evanescence of speech. Little would it matter whether one saw either speech or writing as more intrinsically "true"; in either event, translation is here classified as a discipline of writing, of written culture.

On the other hand, Johnson proposes a theory regarding the sorts of cultural practices that foster an interest in translation. Conquering nations imposed their own culture: "*Greece* considered herself as the Mistress if not as the Parent of Arts, her language contained all that was supposed to be known" (1:87). Educated Romans read the Greek classics in the original and "had no need of versions"; hence, despite the evidence of translations produced either for popular entertainment or for personal amusement, "it does not appear that any man grew eminent by interpreting another" (1:88). Strikingly, then, Johnson locates the first cultural impetus toward translation among the Arabs, who in the advance of Islam "found their captives wiser than themselves, and made haste to relieve their wants by imparted knowledge" (1:89). While there are clear cultural prejudices apparent in this description, given that the overall structure of the essay aims at demonstrating both the modernizing work of translation and the particular strengths of English translators, the positive values inherent in this link between Islamic and English translators should not go unnoticed. Johnson admits his own ignorance of the Islamic tradition in a sentence that also bespeaks his historical theory: "Whether they attempted the Poets is not known; their literary zeal was vehement, but it was short, and probably expired before they had time to add the arts of elegance to those of necessity" (1:89).

From "necessity" to "elegance"—such indeed is the trajectory written throughout Johnson's history of translation and structuring his account of the rise of translation in Europe following the Middle Ages. The movement is from practical knowledge (as when the Arabs focused on "medicine and philosophy") to the pleasures of literate, leisured culture: "To enquire after speculative truth, to enjoy the amusement of imaginary adventures, to know the history of former ages, or study the events of any other lives" (1:90). When Johnson turns to translation's role in "the progress of *English* literature" (1:91), we see an analogous trajectory, this time from the material, practical approach of scrupulous word-for-word translation to a method permitting "greater liberty" and "elegance." Unlike Goujet, whose history of translation was the history of translation theory, Johnson's chronological survey looks exclusively at the practice of translation. His only reference to translation theory or criticism is a brief echo of John Denham's poem in praise of Fanshaw; the other references are to the literary success or failure of translations by Ben Jonson, Thomas May, Barten Holyday, and others.

Johnson dismisses the early translations printed by Caxton "in which the original is so scrupulously followed, that they afford us little knowledge of our own language; tho' the words are *English*, the phrase is foreign" (1:92). His expression offers us insight into the meaning and purpose of neoclassical translation as an exploration of "our own language." Johnson here coincides with Goujet in seeing translation as a device for entering into a fuller understanding, and a better mastery, of one's native tongue. Hence his praise for Dryden at the end of the *Idler* essay for having given us the model of the translator "who when he translates changes nothing but the language" (1:95). Later, in both the "Life of Dryden" and the "Life of Pope," what matters is not the erasure of the cultural other but the work needing to be carried out within the English language itself. As Greg Clingham observes, Johnson's *Lives*—these two in particular—are themselves acts of "translation," articulating a relation between past and present.[7] Johnson credits Dryden with having transformed English poetry—"He found it brick, and he left it marble"—and Pope with having "tuned the English tongue."[8] It is also worth considering the political weight of the terms Johnson uses to describe Dryden's contribution to the history of translation (the overall account of which parallels that given in the *Idler* essays): "It was reserved for Dryden to fix the limits of poetical liberty, and give us just rules and examples of translation" (2:125). Given the centrality of "the limits of liberty" to natural-rights philosophy and Enlightenment social thought, the age-old meditation on the translator's liberty or servitude takes on a new light. Johnson further underscores the degree to which neoclassical translation, with its sensitivity to local canons of taste and nuance, nourishes a reflection on the present state of languages, on their distance from the past and from each other, and, ultimately, on eighteenth-century analysis of national culture and le génie de la langue: "Time and place will always enforce regard" (4:73).

Alexander Tytler's *Essay on the Principles of Translation*, originally published in 1791 and appearing in an expanded third edition in 1813, is often cited as a definitive statement of eighteenth-century translation theory. Lawrence Venuti turns to Tytler's work as the crowning moment of neoclassical "ethnocentric violence."[9] Venuti's reading of the unspoken social typologies and class values that underlie much of Tytler's discussion is useful for underscoring the relevance of poetical translation to larger questions of authorship, individual agency, and social life. But to proceed to claim, as Venuti does, that the desire for fidelity to both source-language text and target-language culture was both "clearly impossible and knowingly duplicitous" leaves far too many questions unasked and unanswered. I have been arguing that it requires an entirely different (or "foreign") epistemology, another view of language and meaning, in order to see the double fidelity of Dryden's and others' middle way as "impossible." The hegemony of neoclassical theory did not, as we have seen, prevent alternative critical reflections on the relationships among language, thought, and culture, especially in France, where ironically the omnipresence of neoclassical practice seems to have provoked a more multifaceted discussion on the theoretical level. I am not sure, however, that it would be appropriate to view the coexistence of these threads as "dominant," "residual," or "emergent," since they are all present from the outset. Neoclassical hegemony is always fissured, to say the least, and can actively produce and coexist with strains that from our twentieth-century perspective seem antithetical to it, as when the studied adherence to local taste nourishes the realization that there are, indeed, other locales and that they are not the same as ours.

Let us then consider the multiple threads that arise within Tytler's work, looking both at the general project sketched in his early chapters and at the historical account of "the Progress of Poetical Translation in England" given in chapter 4. Tytler begins the *Essay* with the bald assertion that there has been "no attempt to unfold the principles of this art, or to reduce it to rules."[10] Tytler's claim is all the more startling when one considers the remarkable breadth of his citation network, which includes both English and French examples of practice and critical reflections. But he dismisses the work of Charles Batteux, for example, on the grounds that he is more concerned with "what may be termed the Philosophy of Grammar" (4), and passes over d'Alembert's important theoretical preface to Tacitus, saying that its observations, "though extremely judicious, are too general to be considered as rules" (5). He clearly knows both texts well, however, and returns to them frequently in the opening chapters. In addition to Batteux and d'Alembert, other theoretical references will eventually include Tytler's acquaintance George Campbell, Pierre-Daniel Huet, Jacques Delille, Catherine Talbot (in a letter to Elizabeth Carter), John Denham (inevitably), and the Earl of Roscommon. But although the citation network contains an interesting range of "critics" (half of whom are French), the preponderance of references are to actual translations, "specimens," which are nearly all from English translators—Bourne, Sotheby, Jonson, Holyday, Sandys, May, Rowe, Dryden, Fanshawe, Pope, and Cowper—though Tytler also discusses examples from d'Alembert and Malherbe. In brief, Tytler finds some critics too broad, others too narrow, and ultimately prefers to develop his own approach, primarily commenting on existing translations.

Tytler thus positions himself as a reader—discerning, critical—whose judgments are based on his reactions to the texts he confronts. The reactions are conditioned by "taste." Venuti has pointed out Tytler's tendency to universalize this highly localized, class-based criterion.[11] Again, however, we need to recognize the complexity of this concept in its intellectual context. Tytler, a man of the Scottish Enlightenment, aims at establishing general precepts or rules drawn from experience; his approach to "taste," like that of David Hume, attempts to account for value through appeals to social norms and conventions—class-based, most certainly, but for the empiricists, knowledge and value judgments could only come from one's environment, itself a shaky construct, especially for Hume. Tytler's "common-sense" approach aims to avoid the skeptical aporia by remaining resolutely audience-centered in his attention to reader response. Tytler's prose is also subtly infused with medical discourse, a reminder that Edinburgh's major medical center played no small role in shaping the intellectual environment: "I would therefore describe a good translation to be, *That, in which the merit of the original work is so completely transfused into another language, as to be as distinctly apprehended, and as strongly felt, by a native of the country to which that language belongs, as it is by those who speak the language of the original work.*"[12] The first experiments on transfusion of the blood were recorded by the Royal Society in 1678, and Dryden also used the term as a metaphor for translation.[13] To "transfuse," with its etymological emphasis on the physical act of pouring a liquid, is more "material" a term than to "translate" and certainly by the late eighteenth century less arcane than another common metaphor, to "transmute." Strongly physiological in connotation as well is the phrase *"distinctly apprehended, and . . . strongly felt,"* which bespeaks Tytler's sensationist orientation. The discursive infrastructure underlines the importance of "examples." Although the expository structure of the *Essay* may not present the examples as sources for inductively derived rules, examples serve nevertheless as the guarantors and overwhelmingly present material textual instantiation of the rules.

What sort of a history of the "progress of Translation" does Tytler propose? A curious one in several ways, one that contains some surprising additions and one glaring omission. Like Johnson, Tytler sees the shift from a strict word-for-word approach to greater liberty as the hallmark of "progress," yet he takes issue with certain features of the general view and adheres less unequivocally to the freer approach than we might expect. Without being noticeably original, Tytler is nevertheless idiosyncratic. Chapter 4 addresses a general topic ("the Freedom allowed in Poetical Translation") from a historical perspective (the "Progress of Poetical Translation in England"). Other than a quotation from the "subtle spirit" passage in Denham's preface, all the examples are "specimens," as Tytler calls them, of good and bad translations from the past three hundred years. The historical narrative, shorn of its examples, is relatively simple. During the sixteenth and most of the seventeenth centuries, we are told, translators "placed their whole merit in presenting a literal and servile transcript of their original" (64). Other than the occasional exception, such as Sandys, few "manifested a better taste in poetical translation" (68):

> But it was to Dryden that poetical translation owed a complete emancipation from her fetters; and exulting in her new liberty, the danger now was, that she should run into the extreme of licentiousness. The followers of Dryden saw nothing so much to be emulated in his translations as the ease of his poetry: Fidelity was but a secondary object, and translation for a while was considered as synonymous with paraphrase. A judicious spirit of criticism was now wanting, to prescribe bounds to this increasing licence, and to determine to what precise degree a poetical translator might assume to himself the character of an original writer. In that design, Roscommon wrote his *Essay on Translated Verse*. (76–77)

Despite his longer format, Tytler thus produces a "history" that is even more concise than Johnson's short *Idler* essays. His examples do offer a few departures from the usual account, however. While following in the footsteps of both Dryden and Johnson in his criticisms of the literal translations of Jonson and Holyday, Tytler defends early translators May and Sandys, crediting them with having achieved the "ease of expression" of "original composition" (key words in his lexicon), and criticizes Denham for having over-rated Fanshawe at their expense. Most surprising, if one assumes that the neoclassical theorists inevitably held up contemporary aesthetic norms and standards, particularly in verse translation, is his critique of the dominance of the heroic couplet and concomitant praise for "the varied harmony of the measure" in May (71–72). Tytler does not reflect on the historical-cultural circumstances that might lead him to find heroic couplets irritatingly "uniform" and a varied meter "musical," yet surely his unintentional example of the mutability of "taste" ultimately makes a point about the inescapability of "taste"—his and our own—as we see so clearly the limits of another's aesthetic sensibilities yet remain blind to those that structure our own perceptions.

The primary idiosyncrasy in the account, however, is surely the ellipsis of Dryden in the passage cited above. Not only is his achievement as a translator reduced to his having opened the floodgates of free translations, but his work as "the father of English criticism" is neglected altogether, as if Roscommon's *Essay* were the only word on the matter from the late seventeenth century. To acknowledge Dryden's prefaces to Ovid, to the *Aeneid*, and to the *Fables* would perhaps engage Tytler in too complex a set of arguments, too labyrinthine a style, too multi-layered a personal-political-literary project, one that would overwhelm the concision and the surface simplicity of the *Essay*'s series of encounters with "specimens."

Even when Tytler quotes directly from another theoretician, however, he distorts the record. For example, he refers to Roscommon primarily in order to embark on a longer discussion of the translator's obligation to correct his original: "I consider it to be the duty of a poetical translator, never to suffer his original to fall" (78). In a footnote to the 1813 edition of the *Essay*, Tytler acknowledges a reviewer of the first edition who had criticized him for permitting translators too great a departure from "truth and fidelity of representation." At this point, Tytler calls the "respectable authority" of Jacques Delille to his side, citing Delille's preface to his translation of the *Georgics*: "One must sometimes be superior to one's original precisely because one is so very inferior" (79–80n).[14] Delille is an unlikely ally for Tytler, given his view of translation as a vehicle for enriching and enlarging the target culture with new ideas and turns of phrase. As we have seen, Delille argues not that the translator should "correct" the original when it "falls" but rather that we should recognize that apparently equivalent terms do not necessarily belong to the same register in their different languages. Delille is interested in the links between language and culture, and in the social and political institutions that inflect register—for example, he valorizes agriculture in Roman culture but not in the France of his day. His approach to the problem is thus considerably more nuanced than the simple injunction, quoted by Tytler, to "raise [the author] on his own pinions."[15] This sentence indeed comes from another context altogether, Delille's discussion of *harmonie imitative* and the need for the translator to compensate for lost rhetorical or metrical flourishes with others in order to maintain a certain poetic tone. "Historical consciousness" in Tytler thus seems beset by the problems attendant on individual consciousness— privacy, idiosyncrasy, a tendency to read the other as oneself. Even in his summaries and references to other critics, Tytler performs the same operations that he recommends to the translator: emendation, correction, modernization. "Fidelity in representation" is clearly no easier for the critic than for the translator; the distortions are not reserved for cultural others who speak other languages but represent more general forms of misreading and misprision.

Goujet, Johnson, and Tytler look at the history of translation from different perspectives and in very different contexts. All concur nonetheless on the merit of adaptive translation and view the evolution in translating styles from the early seventeenth century onward in terms of progress, the gradual perfecting of technique and "elegance." All operate within a view of language as separable from thought, as the representation of thought, the classical episteme. Within that general consensus, a number of individual projects and emphases emerge: Goujet sees the development of translation theory, whereas Johnson and Tytler (despite the latter's wide reading in theory) are mainly interested in practice. Johnson emphasizes a connection between translation and literacy, Tytler's language is inflected by the discourse of sympathy and sensation, and Goujet surreptitiously inserts radical educational reform.

For each writer, the reflection on translation is an important mode for reflecting on the historicity of his own discourse. Each writes with an awareness that the language in which he writes has undergone profound changes within the past two centuries. It is one thing to acknowledge one's temporal distance from Greece and Rome, and another to see one's own culture slipping back in time, part of one's own national past definitively separated from modernity. Hence the recurring theme of translation as an exploration, exemplification, and elaboration of the national language, and the realization that current norms are of recent vintage. We habitually credit the nineteenth century with the dawning of modern historical consciousness; here we already see some of the modalities, particularly in the association between language and culture, by which it could develop.

What has happened between the *Huit oraisons* volume, published in 1638, and Tytler's *Essay*, published during the early years of the French Revolution? Everything has changed in the political and social world. The literary field is similarly transformed—indeed, it is during this period that the "literary field" as such comes into being. It includes women as both readers and writers, and it includes men and women who write for a living and whose books find their way to a wider, more socially diverse public than d'Ablancourt could have imagined for the *Huit oraisons*.

What has changed in the discourse on translation during these years? Both the politicization of translation in seventeenth-century England and its poeticization in absolutist France point to the lack of a clearly demarcated public sphere—in both contexts, translation becomes a means for reflecting on the basis for human relations, communities. The explicit ideological coding of work by a Denham or a Harrington can distract us from the subtler ways in which the French reflection on translation, like other literary *querelles* of the day, also contributes to the expansion of a space for debate and critique that will flourish in the Enlightenment to come. The emergence of the literary field and of literary criticism generally reinforces the sense of a "public" with a vested interest in a participatory society. We've also seen large shifts in the ways in which translators position their work intellectually: from rivaling the Ancients in an effort to prove the modern vernacular equal to the classical languages in beauty and eloquence to opening up those modern languages to strange new sounds and turns of phrase, and from seeing Cicero and Horace as mentors and interlocutors on the nature of translation to engaging in dialogue with contemporary critics such as Anne Dacier and John Dryden. As the interlocutors change and intellectual energies formerly channeled into analysis of the classics are poured into the modern languages, the field of translation undergoes a shift similar to that described by Marco Cipolloni in his discussion of the emergence of anthropological thinking during the eighteenth century, resulting in a "double intellectual framework" wherein an earlier dichotomy of Ancients and Moderns intersects with a differently articulated distinction between Old World and New World.[16] Translators, whose work is entwined with the rise of anthropology, see themselves in a changed temporal configuration in which, as we have seen, the distant past is recoded as "foreign" and the privileged metaphors have less to do with making the dead speak than with travel and commerce.

There are significant continuities from d'Ablancourt and Sacy to Elizabeth Griffith and Pierre-Antoine de La Place, though these are not only the commonalities supposed in conventional accounts of the belles infidèles. I am referring to the recurring subterranean thread suggesting an emotive, expressive, nonvehicular dimension of language, a form of linguistic embodiment described variously as eloquence, transubstantiation, obscurity, génie, and goût de terroir. This "corporeal" dimension runs counter to accounts of neoclassical theories of language as a noiseless vehicle of intact, unproblematic meaning. I hope to have shown that such accounts do not begin to do justice to the complexity of linguistic thinking that infuses the discourse on translation in this period.

The translating practices recommended by the neoclassical translators would be condemned by the Romantic generation. From Schlegel's perspective, "It is almost as if they expected foreigners to conform their dress and behavior to the local customs; as a result they never really get to know a foreigner."[17] What is clear in reading the eighteenth-century critics, however, is that "getting to know a foreigner" is not the only goal. Encountering that "foreigner" could be a significant element of translation for some—Delille comes to mind, but one can go back at least as far as Anne Dacier's preface to Homer to find a discussion of translation's role in mediating cultural otherness. But the "foreigner" is but one instantiation of the multiple forms of otherness that neoclassical translation attempts to understand. The "utterly other" is infused into language itself: as eloquence for d'Ablancourt and via eucharistic participation for Sacy. Derek Attridge's "singularity"— which is not only compatible with, but productive of, translation—is perhaps a better term. As all translators from this period make clear, the work of translation takes place on an infinite number of other levels as well. It is the richness and variety of that discursive field that we should seek to recover. Like the "curious perspective" of Fanshawe's version of *Il Pastor Fido*, translation deconstructs and reconstructs the world, setting its own artificiality in high relief, offering a perfect image that is nevertheless subject to ongoing critique.

Notes

Introduction

1. D'Ablancourt: "Let the reader not be surprised, if my weakness and [my author's] Eloquence forced me to take some occasional liberties." D'Ablancourt et al., *Huit oraisons de Ciceron*, 137.

2. Recent scholarship on "the Channel zone" emphasizes the significance of the Anglo-French dialogue in this period. See the essays in M. Cohen and C. Dever, *Literary Channel*; see also Falvey and Brooks, *Channel in the Eighteenth Century*. Franco Moretti charts the ongoing relationship of France and Britain as the "narrative super powers" of the nineteenth century (*Atlas of the European Novel*).

3. Linda Colley discusses Francophobia as a manifestation of anti-Catholicism and a prime factor in the consolidation of British national consciousness in *Britons*, a view that has been nuanced to a certain extent by Robin Eagles in *Francophilia in English Society*. Both Francophobia and Francophilia point to the inextricability of political, social, and economic encounters between the two nations, as well as to the "mixed feelings" attendant on encounters and exchanges in the cultural sphere. David Bell discusses similarly shifting and conflicted accounts of Britain in the French context in *Cult of the Nation in France*, esp. 43–49 and 78–106; Edmond Dziembowski argues that the *anglomanie* of the *philosophes* fails to extend to a broader public in *Un nouveau patriotisme français*, esp. 11–166.

4. George Steiner sees a single "first period" in translation history that extends "from Cicero's famous precept not to translate *verbum pro verbo* . . . to Hölderlin's enigmatic commentary on his own translation of Sophocles." *After Babel*, 248. Louis G. Kelly, while subdividing Steiner's "first period" somewhat, concurs that the largely "pre-theoretical" period is marred by an "empiricist" emphasis. *True Interpreter*, 223–24. For Frederick Rener, classical and early modern writing on translation qualifies as "theory," but he concludes that it "remained basically unaltered during the period between Cicero and Tytler." *Interpretatio*, 336.

5. See Robinson, *Translator's Turn* and *Translation and Taboo*. While not historical studies as such, Robinson's books offer provocative readings of translation's "ascetic tradition" in a wide range of historical contexts.

6. See Copeland, *Rhetoric*, 33–34; see also her discussion of Jerome's "misappropriation" of Cicero and Horace, 46–52.

7. On the history of readings of the lines from Horace, see Copeland, *Rhetoric*, 170–78; Norton, *Ideology and Language*, 57–90; DeLater, *Translation Theory*, 114–15n.

8. D'Ablancourt et al., *Huit oraisons de Ciceron*, 228. On the importance of the *Huit oraisons* as a statement on translation, see Zuber, *Belles infidèles*, 54–60. See also his discussion of Pierre-Daniel Huet's and others' criticism of the (mis-)quotation of Horace, 141–43.

9. Du Bellay, *La Deffence*, book 1, ch. 5. Scholars have continued to sort out the nuances in Du Bellay's position: see Norton, *Ideology and Language*, 292–300; Wells, "What Did Du Bellay Mean," 175–85.

10. Cave, *Cornucopian Text*, 35–77; Berman, "De la translation à la traduction," and "Tradition—Translation—Traduction."

11. See Norton, *Ideology and Language*, 203–17, for a valuable close reading of the "rules." Valerie Worth discusses the *Maniere* in the context of a full investigation of Dolet's practice as translator and as neo-Latin writer in *Practising Translation*, 50–60.

12. Guillerm, *Sujet de l'écriture*, 457–77, 550.

13. Meziriac, *De la traduction*, 5.

14. See d'Ablancourt's defense of the style in his preface to Thucydides. D'Ablancourt, *Lettres et préfaces critiques*, 203. On Furetière's military allegory, see Zuber, *Belles infidèles*, 141.

15. On Ménage's joke, see Zuber, *Belles infidèles*, 195. More generally, see Georges Mounin, *Belles infidèles*; Ballard, *De Ciceron à Benjamin*, 147–97. Lori Chamberlain offers a feminist critique of the phrase in "Gender and Metaphorics"; see also S. Simon, *Gender in Translation*, 10–12.

16. The chief study of d'Ablancourt's relationship to French neoclassicism remains Zuber, *Belles infidèles*. On Conrart's circle and its influence, see Fumaroli, *Le Poète et le roi*, 130–35, 142–43, 150.

17. "One must not do as the French, giving one's own coloration to all that one translates." Staël, "De l'esprit des traductions," 2:294.

18. See, for example, Balibar, *L'Institution du français*; Sorenson, *Grammar of Empire*. Specifically on translation, see Cheyfitz, *Poetics of Imperialism*; Niranjana, *Siting Translation*.

19. Genette, *Seuils*, 150–81. Genette gives relatively little attention to the generic peculiarities of the translator's preface, although in his earlier work he discusses translation as one of several forms of "hypertextuality" linking text to text. *Palimpsestes*, 238–43.

20. Norton, *Ideology and Language*, 234–35.

21. G. Steiner, *After Babel*, 248–49.

22. See Ballard, *De Cicéron à Benjamin*; D'Hulst, "Unité et diversité." One should note the careful attention given to early modern critical prefaces in studies such as Norton, *Ideology and Language*; Dunn, *Pretexts of Authority*; Wall, *Imprint*

of Gender. Useful anthologies of translators' prefaces include T. Steiner, *English Translation Theory*; Horguelin, *Anthologie*; D'Hulst, *Cent ans de théorie française de traduction*; Robinson, *Western Translation Theory*.

23. Séguin, *French Works in English Translation*; Rochedieu, *Bibliography of French Translations of English Works*. Both emphasize literary translations, although Séguin includes other genres of writing as well. Rochedieu only lists some 250 translations, organized by each original author (or "anon."); Séguin proceeds year by year in a more exhaustive listing, providing an index of authors and translators at the end of his last volume. For a genre-based study, see Streeter, *Eighteenth-Century English Novel*. An ambitious project based at the Université de Metz proposes a database of all eighteenth-century French translations of English novels; unfortunately, the publicly accessible version (online at http://www.lettres.univ-metz.fr/UFR/centre/reche_f.htm) offers only sets of "fiches" organized by original author that cannot be manipulated in any way. Working with this database, however, Alain Lautel has published some interesting charts tracing the publishing fortunes of six English novelists in French translation (in Ballard and D'Hulst, *La Traduction en France*, 135–54); see also Cointre, "Bibliographie commentée des traductions de romans anglais."

24. McMurran, "National or Transnational?" 53.

25. In addition to the works cited in note 2 above, see the articles on England and France in Porter and Teich, *Enlightenment in National Context*.

26. On the translators of the Huguenot diaspora, see Häseler and McKenna, *La Vie intellectuelle*; Rumbold, *Traducteur huguenot*; Flagg, "Abel Boyer"; DeJean, "Transnationalism."

27. Pym, *Method in Translation History*, 11.

28. See Toury, *Theory of Translation*, as well as numerous issues of *Poetics Today*, in particular the special issues on "Translation Theory and Intercultural Relations" (edited by Even-Zohar and Toury) and "Polysystem Studies" (edited by and featuring a collection of a number of important pieces by Even-Zohar). See also the essays in Hermans, *Manipulation of Literature*.

29. Viala, *Naissance de l'écrivain*; Brown, *Field of Honor*. Part of Columbia University Press's "Gutenberg-e" project, Brown's book is available electronically to subscribers at http://www.gutenberg-e.org/brg01/. More broadly, see Dorleijn and Van Rees, *Eighteenth-Century Literary Field*. On the relation of polysystem theory to Bourdieu's work, see Codde, "Polysystem Theory Revisited."

30. Bourdieu, *Règles de l'art*, 381; citation from *Rules of Art*, 232.

31. Nineteenth-century critics of d'Ablancourt and his followers include both Romantics such as Staël, Schlegel, and Schleiermacher and academics such as Frédéric Hennebert, whose 1858 study included a strongly worded dismissal of d'Ablancourt's "system of translation, or rather travesty" (*Histoire des traductions françaises*, 163).

32. Antoine Berman, *L'Epreuve de l'étranger*; citation from *Experience of the Foreign*, 2.

33. For a series of articles assessing the impact of Berman's work on translation studies, see Nouss, "Antoine Berman aujourd'hui."

34. Venuti, *Translator's Invisibility*, 43. Berman later attenuated his critique of d'Ablancourt, taking into account the explicitness of the latter's translating strategies and his clear desire to "faire oeuvre" (*Pour une critique des traductions*, 92–94; see also Venuti, *Scandals*, 81). Neither, however, substantially departs from the position that adaptative translations are to some degree damaging to "otherness" and hence at variance with an "ethical" approach.

35. Friedrich Schleiermacher, "On the Different Methods of Translating (1813)," trans. Douglas Robinson, in Robinson, *Western Translation Theory*, 229. Schleiermacher's approach has been critiqued in turn on the basis of its own form of nationalism. See Venuti, *Translator's Invisibility*, 100–118; Pym, *Pour une éthique du traducteur*, 33–38.

36. Renken, *Représentation de l'étranger*, 96.

37. Dacier, "Préface à l'Iliade," in *L'Iliade d'Homère*, 1:xlii.

38. Derrida, *Le Toucher*.

39. Attridge, *Singularity of Literature*, 33.

40. See Harpham, *Getting It Right* and *Shadows of Ethics*; Buell, "In Pursuit of Ethics."

41. Lévinas, *Autrement qu'être*, 264–65; citations from *Otherwise Than Being*.

42. Nancy, *Etre singulier pluriel*, 50; citations from *Being Singular Plural*, 30.

43. Webb, "Rhetoric of Ethics."

44. Graham, *Difference in Translation*.

45. Derrida, *Politiques de l'amitié*, 235–37; citations from *Politics of Friendship*, 208–11.

46. I am following the move made by J. Hillis Miller in *Others*.

47. Derrida, *Monolinguisme*, 103; citations from *Monolingualism*, 57.

48. Nancy, *Corpus*.

Chapter 1

An earlier version of part of this chapter appeared as "Translation's Temporal Rhetoric: Pierre Du Ryer and *Le Quinte-Curce de Vaugelas*," *Mediaevalia* 26.2 (2006): 77–94.

1. See the classic study by Lucien Goldmann, *Le Dieu caché*.

2. Baillet, *Jugemens*, 3:105. See his discussions of translations by Malherbe (122–23), Vaugelas (125), d'Ablancourt (129–32), and Port-Royal (133–59).

3. Derrida, *Monolinguisme*, 99; citation from *Monolingualism*, 56.

4. See Chédozeau, *Le Baroque*. In addition to Chédozeau's theologically inflected understanding of the baroque, I also have in mind recent accounts of the baroque as a libidinal resistance to classical order: Greenberg, *Detours of Desire* and *Baroque Bodies*. On the "postmodern Baroque," see the essays in Hampton, "Baroque Topographies," or those from the 1976 Colloque de Cérisy, in Benoist, *Figures du baroque*. Didier Soulier likewise underlines the "modernity" of the baroque in the conclusion to *La Littérature baroque en Europe*, 263.

5. Giry, *Des Causes de la corruption*. On the *Dialogus de oratoribus* and its place in early modern rhetoric, see Fumaroli, *L'Age de l'éloquence*, 63–70. See also Mathieu-Castellani, *La Rhétorique des passions*, 38–39. Zuber discusses Giry's translation and Godeau's preface in *Belles infidèles*, 45–52. For opinions on Giry, see Baillet, *Jugemens*, 3:132.

6. Zuber, *Belles infidèles*, 47, 54.

7. Originally published as part of a collective volume, *Recueil de lettres, harangues et discours differens*, Godeau's essay on Malherbe would be republished and more widely circulated in the much-reprinted edition of Malherbe's collected works. See Ballard, *De Ciceron à Benjamin*, 156–60, as well as Zuber, *Belles infidèles*, 45.

8. On the political relevance of the *Dialogue on Orators* for Montaigne and other sixteenth- and seventeenth-century figures, see Fumaroli, *L'Age de l'éloquence*, 69–70.

9. Amyot would remain an important model for d'Ablancourt and his friends, albeit an increasingly controversial one after the attack on his inaccuracies by Claude-Gaspard de Bachet, sieur de Meziriac, presented to the Academy in 1635. Bachet, "Discours de la traduction." See Zuber, *Belles infidèles*, 56–57. Ballard shows considerably more sympathy for the theoretical import of Meziriac's work in *De Ciceron à Benjamin*, 161–70.

10. D'Ablancourt, *Lettres et préfaces critiques*, 105.

11. Luce Guillerm situates d'Ablancourt with respect to earlier translators, arguing that a vividly personal concept of the "author" underpins Renaissance and seventeenth-century topoi of "clothing the author in French dress," "making the author speak," etc. While my reading of the latter topos is somewhat different, her analysis has the merit of reexamining the notion of "fidelity" so often taken for granted in historical translation studies. Guillerm, "Belles infidèles."

12. Hennebert, *Histoire des traductions françaises*, 148; Meschonnic, *Poétique du traduire*, 44.

13. On the rabbinic traditions of *midrash* (extreme literalism) and *peshat* (contextual and philological study), see Kasher, "Interpretation of Scripture."

14. Venuti, *Scandals*, 82.

15. Berman, *Pour une critique des traductions*, 92, 94; Venuti, *Scandals*, 81.

16. On adaptative translation as a positive strategy for emerging literatures, see Brisset, *Sociocritique de la traduction*; Cronin, *Translating Ireland*, as well as his "Changing Sides: The Case of Ireland."

17. Little is known with certainty of d'Ablancourt's religious views; see Zuber, *Belles infidèles*, 255–65, 272–73. In a brief but moving biography of his friend, Olivier Patru says the impressions of d'Ablancourt's early religious training "had never entirely left him" ("La Vie de Monsieur d'Ablancourt," in Zuber, *Belles infidèles*, 426).

18. Zuber, *Belles infidèles*, 128, 133–34, 140. For contemporary approaches to Du Ryer, see the special issue of *Littératures classiques* edited by Dominique Moncond'huy, "Pierre Du Ryer: Dramaturge et traducteur." For a biographical study, see Lancaster, *Pierre Du Ryer, Dramatist*.

19. Pierre Du Ryer, preface to Vaugelas, *Quinte-Curce*, 1:*2r.

20. Baillet, *Jugemens*, on Du Ryer, 3:128; on d'Ablancourt, 3:129–32. Even so, he cites the authority of Boileau, Bouhours, and Guez de Balzac in qualifying the *Quinte-Curce* as an "inimitable" model of style (3:125).

21. The process left its traces in other materials Vaugelas left at the time of his death: comments on usage, with alternatives and comparisons, that once gathered up by Louis-Auguste Alemand proved sufficient to make a new book, the *Nouvelles remarques sur la langue françoise*.

22. Sorel, *Bibliothèque*, 240.

23. Petit, *Lettres de S. Jerôme*, E8r.

24. Arnauld, *Regles*, 112.

25. Arnauld's reflections on Vaugelas are critical to the extent that they broaden his definition and grounding of "le bon usage," but they do not fundamentally contest the importance of *usage* itself. Vaugelas had in fact been co-opted to a certain extent to serve the aims of the Port-Royal translators and their circle in Gaspard de Tende's *De la traduction* (Zuber, *Belles infidèles*, 150–51). As for Vaugelas himself, as Wendy Ayres-Bennet notes, his understanding of *usage* was hardly antithetical to notions of universal reason. Ayres-Bennet, "Usage and Reason."

26. Ballard, *De Ciceron à Benjamin*, 161–70. See also Ballard's substantial preface to his facsimile edition of Merziriac, *De la traduction*.

27. Meziriac, *De la traduction*, 5.

28. Ayres-Bennet and Caron, *Remarques de l'Académie française*. See Caron, "Une traduction relue à l'Académie française" and "*Quinte Curce* de Vaugelas."

29. De Man, "The Rhetoric of Temporality," in *Blindness and Insight*, 190–91.

30. Enders, "Memory, Allegory."

31. Blanchot, *L'Amitié*, 69.

32. Derrida, *Donner le temps*, 23–26; *Given Time*, 11–15. Further page references are to the English version.

33. Although ostensibly a critique of Derrida's account of the gift, John Milbank's analysis offers a structurally similar solution in a Christian framework, a form of open-ended "participatory giving" constituted through non-identical repetition and delay. Milbank, "Can a Gift Be Given?" See also Billings, "John Milbank's Theology."

34. René Descartes, *Les Passions de l'âme* § 193, in *Oeuvres*, 11:473–74.

35. My vocabulary derives from Abraham and Torok, *L'Ecorce et le noyau*.

36. Derrida, *Monolinguisme*, 101; *Monolingualism*, 56.

37. On the subversion of classical style by a persistence of the baroque, see Cronk, "Metaphor and Metamorphosis" and "Singular Voice." On the ubiquity of allegory in seventeenth-century culture, see Couton, *Ecritures codées*.

38. Baillet, *Jugemens*, 3:134–58.

39. See Sedgwick, *Travails of Conscience*. On the political tensions surrounding Jansenism, see his *Jansenism*; see also Van Kley, *Religious Origins*, 58–72. On Jansenist theology, see Laporte, *La Doctrine de Port-Royal*; and Hildesheimer's narrative history *Le Jansénisme en France*.

40. Fumaroli, *L'Age d'éloquence*, 623–46; Zuber, *Belles infidèles*, 109–18, 149–58. This tendency is most manifest in Gaspard de Tende, *De la Traduction*. Zuber sees the frequency of Tende's examples drawn from the Port-Royal translators as well as from Vaugelas as indicative of a "recuperation" of the latter on the part of the Solitaires.

41. Munteano, "Port Royal." See also Zuber on the "differend" in *Belles infidèles*, 111–15. The manuscripts were later published by a group of scholars working with Luigi Nardis as *Regole della traduzione: Testi inediti di Port-Royal e del "Cercle" di Miramion (metà del XVII secolo)*. See also Sacy, *Choix de lettres inédites*.

42. Zuber, *Belles infidèles*, 111. Zuber speculates that as a late "memorial" to his earlier translation, Arnauld d'Andilly had "deuxième édition" printed on the earliest known edition, *Les Confessions de S. Augustin* (Paris: la Veuve Jean Camusat et Pierre Le Petit, 1649). This translation was re-edited in 1993 (with modernized spelling and without the translator's preface) by Philippe Sellier.

43. For Le Maistre's original set of rules, *Règles de la traduction françoise*, see Nardis et al., *Regole*, 215–16, and see in the same volume Arnauld d'Andilly's *Remarques sur la traduction françoise*, 59–72, and Le Maistre's revised and extended text, *Règles de la traduction*, 31–47. Occasional divergences between the two show Arnauld d'Andilly somewhat more inclined to advocate the "freedoms" of the d'Ablancourt circle than Le Maistre.

44. In Nardis et al., *Regole*, 59.

45. See Jonathan Culler's well-known discussion of apostrophe in *Pursuit of Signs*, 153.

46. Schroeder, *Canons and Decrees*. The Fourth Session declared the Latin Vulgate to be the "authentic" text of the Catholic Church and banned any "interpretation"—which could be taken as a reading or as a translation—"contrary to that sense which holy mother Church, to whom it belongs to judge of their true sense and interpretation, has held and holds" (18–19). See also Rules 3 and 4 of the "Rules Concerning Prohibited Books" (ibid., 274–75).

47. Despite a sentimentalizing tone, D. Lortsch offers a thorough survey of French translations in *Histoire de la Bible*. See also B. Chambers, *Seventeenth Century French-Language Editions*.

48. On the history of the Port-Royal Bible, see Wetsel, *L'Ecriture*, 45–70; Delassault, *Le Maistre de Sacy*, 151–66; Ballard, *De Ciceron à Benjamin*, 173–84; Sellier, preface to *La Bible*, x–liii.

49. Scholarly interest in Sacy has rarely extended beyond his correspondence with Barcos, the New Testament preface, and (more rarely) his preface to Genesis. The only modern editions available to scholars are Delassault's and Goldmann's editions of his and Barcos's letters (Sacy, *Choix de lettres inédites*; Barcos, *Correspondance*) and the Nardis edition of Le Maistre's *Règles* and related documents (Nardis et al., *Regole*), which includes three of Sacy's nonbiblical prefaces. The complete original edition of the 1667 Bible de Mons is available online via the Bibliothèque Nationale's Gallica site (http://gallica.bnf.fr/), along with early editions of his *Lettres chrestiennes* and several other works.

50. Guyot, *Les Fleurs morales*, 16.

51. Sacy, "Avant-propos," in *Poème de Saint Prosper*, a4v. The Avant-propos is reprinted in Nardis et al., *Regole*, 201–14, along with Sacy's prefaces to Phaedrus and Terence.

52. Sacy [Le Sieur de Saint Aubin, pseud.], "Au Lecteur," in *Les Fables de Phedre*, a3r.

53. See the classic essay by Markus, "Saint Augustine on Signs."

54. Sacy, preface to *Poëme contenant la tradition de l'Eglise*, a4v.

55. Sacy, preface to *Le Nouveau Testament*, 5r.

56. Barcos, *Correspondance*, 373–74. For Louis Marin, Sacy's exchange with the uncompromising Barcos fuels his restless questioning of the status of representation and a constant oscillation between *lettre* and *sens*. Marin, "Critique."

57. Although Sacy and his collaborators claimed their version was based on the Vulgate, they also relied on other versions, particularly the Septuagint, indicating in the notes which readings were based on the Latin, the Greek, or the Hebrew. Richard Simon was critical of this practice, which he regarded as a translation of a nonexistent original. See Certeau, "L'Idée de traduction." On Arnauld's response to Simon, see Martine Pécharman, "Question des 'règles de la critique.'"

58. Certeau, "L'Idée de traduction," 84–85.

59. Marin refers to Sacy's "écriture-lecture" as a "generalized Eucharist" ("Critique," 573). Marin comes to this notion by setting Sacy's textual-sacramental parallels in the light of Barcos's metaphor of instruction with "nourishment." Indeed, these parallels resonate more deeply and more literally than Marin implies. Marin also takes up, brilliantly, the entwinement of Port-Royal linguistics and theology in *La Critique du discours* (74–77, 203–5, 360–63) and *La Parole mangée* (11–35). Throughout, however, his interest is in the semiotization of the Eucharist rather than the corporalization of language.

60. Sacy did not live to see the full publication of his translation; Thomas Du Fossé was charged with editing his manuscripts and is presumed to have written the posthumous commentaries in whole or in part. The status of the prefaces is less clear; in style, tone, and philosophical orientation, the posthumous Old Testament prefaces correspond to those we know to be by Sacy, and I will be referring to them as his. The later New Testament prefaces, however, mark a distinct departure; I assume them to have been written by Charles Huré and others. In any case, the "Bible de Sacy," like the other Port-Royal translations, is a collective endeavor; it is no detraction from the pivotal role of the individual Sacy to recognize that "Sacy" is often multivoiced, plural.

61. Sacy, preface to *Les Proverbes de Salomon*, *5v.

62. See Sacy, prefaces to *La Genese*, ***7r; *Les Nombres*, a3v; *Le Deuteronome*, a3v; *Job*, c4v; *Les Paralipomenes*, a3r; *Tobie, Judith & Esther* (see the "Avertissement" to *Judith*); *Jérémie*, b7v.

63. Sacy, preface to *La Genese*, ***9r. Sacy also cites Augustine's musical analogy in the prefaces to *Paralipomenes*, a3r; *Les Nombres*, a5r–a5v.

64. Sacy, preface to *Isaïe*, a6r.

65. Sacy admits that the distinction does not always hold; when the literal meaning was exceptionally "obscure and defective," the spiritual meaning might serve to enlighten it, and vice versa. Preface to *Douze petits prophetes*, e1r–e1v.

66. Sacy's successors took a rather different view. In the New Testament prefaces published after his death, particularly the "Préface générale sur l'explication litterale de toutes les epistres de Saint Paul," the literal interpretation is given preeminence and spiritual interpretation is downplayed, presumably in reaction to the accusations confounding Jansenists with Protestants in the 1680s and 1690s. Charles Huré is generally credited with completing the new edition of the New Testament after the deaths of Sacy and Du Fossé.

67. Sacy, preface to *Ezechiel*, *4r. Similarly, the "sens propre" of the *Song of Songs* is "in reality spiritual and divine, but enveloped by metaphorical expressions" (Sacy, preface to *Cantique des cantiques*, a7r).

68. Sacy, preface to *Daniel*, a5r.

69. Van Kley, *Religious Origins*, 92–98. For Patrick Coleman, figurism also subtends certain reading practices of the eighteenth-century *philosophes*; see his "Figure in the *Encyclopédie*."

70. Sacy, preface to *L'Exode et le Levitique*, lvi.

71. Auerbach, "Figura," in *Drama of European Literature*, 53.

72. Arnauld and Nicole, *La Logique*, 80.

73. Ndiaye, *Philosophie d'Antoine Arnauld*, 39.

74. On the fifth edition of the *Logique* (1683), see Marin, *La Parole mangée*, 11–35; see also Robinet, *Langage à l'âge classique*, 40–51.

75. Herbert McCabe has offered what in some ways is the opposite of Sacy's approach: seeing the Eucharist as language rather than language as eucharistic ("The body of Christ is present in the Eucharist as meaning is present in a word"). For McCabe, language and Eucharist find their common ground precisely through "commonality," whether in the shared social habitus that gives rise to language or in the *agape* of the Lord's Supper. For Sacy, however, it is semiosis itself that becomes, at its deepest level, eucharistic. McCabe, "Eucharist as Language."

76. In a recent reading, Andrea Frisch explores the representational function of the Calvinist concept of the Eucharist. Predictably quite different from the post-Tridentine account, the Calvinist sacrament functions via "attestation" and "testimony." Frisch, "In a Sacramental Mode."

77. See Robinet, *Langage à l'âge classique*, 57. Robinet's study is one of several tracing variations and evolutions in general grammar in the seventeenth and eighteenth centuries. See also Droixhe, *Linguistique et l'appel*; Ricken, *Linguistics, Anthropology and Philosophy*.

78. I am thinking of Sylvain Auroux's explication of the "hypothèse langue-traduction" of eighteenth-century general grammar. Auroux, *La Sémiotique des Encyclopédistes*, 69–70.

79. Nancy, *Corpus*, 29. See also Ward, *Cities of God*, 81–96, for a contemporary theological reflection on "transcorporeality."

80. See also Antoine Le Maistre, *Règles de la traduction* (extended version), in Nardis et al., *Regole*, 40–44.

81. Giry, preface to *S. Augustin*, [iii].

82. Boileau, preface to the "Traité du sublime," in *Oeuvres complètes*, 336. Boileau obscures any distinction between author and translator, telling us that he sought less to translate Longinus than "to give the Public a treatise on the sublime" (337).

83. Baillet, *Jugemens*, 3:1–204; Sorel, *Bibliothèque*, 216–40; Goujet, *Bibliothèque françoise*, 1:194–208.

84. Morvan de Bellegarde, "Des règles de la Traduction," in *Réflexions*, 425–37.

85. On the circumstances under which Arnauld composed this text, see Jacques, *Années d'exil*, 674–76.

86. Consider the eighth rule as a demonstration of Arnauld's feistiness: "We need not respect criticism that is based on a faulty example." Arnauld cites Bouhours as his prime example (*Regles*, 70).

87. Arnauld, *Regles*, 109–18. Although Vaugelas was held up by Gaspard de Tende and the Port-Royal translators as a model translator (and a foil to d'Ablancourt), scholars have tended to see him at the opposite end of the spectrum from the general grammarians. Arnauld's engagement with the *Remarques* in this essay, however, suggests a more nuanced relation. On Vaugelas's approach to "doubtful usage," see Ayres-Bennet, "Usage and Reason," 233–46.

88. In addition to his brother's translation, seventeenth-century translations of the *Confessions* include those by René de Cerisiers and Philippe Goibaud Du Bois.

89. See, for example, Morvan de Bellegarde, "Des règles," 434, as well as the criticisms leveled at Du Ryer and Jean Baudoin by Gabriel Guéret in *Le Parnasse réformée*. Du Ryer, whose numerous translations were often produced under financial pressure, is said to have lamented that much of his work was a repackaging of translations by Michel de Marolles (Zuber, *Belles infidèles*, 128).

90. D'Ablancourt, *Lettres et préfaces critiques*, 190.

91. The argument for the *Pro Archias* (translated by Patru) and that for the *Pro Ligario* (translated by d'Ablancourt) make a special point of underscoring the transformative power of eloquence (D'Ablancourt, *Huit oraisons*, 113, 155).

92. Le Maistre, *Règles de la traduction* (extended version), in Nardis et al., *Regole*, 31. For Guyot, whose prefaces always contain pedagogical considerations, translation teaches both grammar and eloquence (see the "Avis au lecteur" of his *Nouvelle traduction des Captifs de Plaute*, in Nardis et al., *Regole*, 239). See Guyot's repeated references to "force" in his preface to *Bucoliques de Virgile*, [xi–xiii].

93. Bouhours, *Vérité de la religion chrétienne*, A8r.

94. Lamy, *La Rhétorique*, 229.

95. De Man, "Autobiography as De-facement," in *Rhetoric of Romanticism*, 78.

96. See Sacy, preface to *Poème de S. Prosper*, ã3v–ã4r.

97. Le Maistre, *Règles de la traduction*, in Nardis et al., 36.

98. The living/dead topos is present in many prefaces of the period; for a striking reversal (the translator offers a dead translation), see Anne Dacier's preface to the *Iliad*, in which she compares her work to the mummy of Helen of Troy.

99. Contrast with Pascal's "Prosopopée" from the "A.P.R." fragment in the *Pensées*, in which Divine Wisdom meditates on human splendor and misery. Wetsel, *L'Ecriture*, 140–45.

100. Chase, *Decomposing Figures*, 69; Clymer, "Graved in Tropes," 372.

101. Lévinas, *Autrement qu'être*, 264; *Otherwise Than Being*, 170. Lévinas makes his point with regard to the "discussion I am elaborating at this very moment," providing another example of an unsettling voice from beyond the grave.

Chapter 2

1. John Denham, "To the Author of this Translation," in Fanshawe, *Il Pastor Fido*, a4r. Denham's commendatory poem appeared with the initial publication in 1647 as well as in all subsequent editions and has been frequently anthologized and published with Denham's works.

2. N. Smith, *Literature and Revolution*, 318. See also Hardacre, "Royalists in Exile," esp. 363–64; C. Smith, "French Philosophy."

3. T. Steiner, *English Translation Theory*, 18–25.

4. On the influence of the French critics, see Clark, *Boileau*.

5. F. Saunders, "To the Reader," A4r–A4v.

6. Potter, *Secret Rites*, 52; Venuti, *Translator's Invisibility*, 48.

7. Webbe, preface to *Familiar Epistles*, A8v–A9r.

8. Vicars, "To the courteous not curious Reader," in *Aeneids*, A3r.

9. Stapylton, *Dido and Aeneas*, A2r.

10. The first poem is by Thomas Drant, the second by "W. Sq." In Vicars, *Aeneids*, A4r–A4v.

11. Hermans, "Literary Translation."

12. Denham, *Poems and Translations*, 26–27. The original edition of *The Destruction of Troy*, printed by the Royalist printer Humphrey Moseley, contains the same preface.

13. Sandys, "Dedication," in *Ovid's Metamorphosis*.

14. See Lyne, *Ovid's Changing Worlds*, 198–258; Pearcy, *Mediated Muse*, 37–70.

15. Dryden, preface to *Examen Poeticum*, in *Works*, vol. 4, ed. A. B. Chambers and William Frost, 370.

16. Sharpe, *Remapping Early Modern England*, 118.

17. On the "Tacitean vision," see Pocock, *Machiavellian Moment*, 351–52. See also Salmon, "Stoicism and Roman Example." On the function of classical historians in the evolution of English historiography, see Hicks, *Neoclassical History*.

18. May, dedication to the earl of Devonshire, in *Pharsalia*, A3r–A3v.

19. Norbrook, *Writing the English Republic*, 47–48.

20. Hobbes, *Eight Bookes*, [2]. On May's *Pharsalia* and the English republican tradition, see N. Smith, *Literature and Revolution*, 204; Norbrook, *Writing the English Republic*, 23–62. See also Norbrook's comment on Hobbes's Thucydides, ibid., 59.

21. Patterson, *Censorship and Interpretation*; Potter, *Secret Rites*. Patterson and Potter have been criticized by N. Smith (*Literature and Revolution*, 24) for telling

only "half the story" and neglecting the need for coding and secrecy among non-Royalists; and Patterson has been criticized by David Saunders and Ian Hunter ("Lessons from the 'Literatory'") for relying on what they view as an insufficiently rigorous notion of language as "transgressive." Neither of these criticisms speaks to the central insights of Patterson's and Potter's books regarding the codes and associations affecting writing and interpretation during the seventeenth century.

22. Fanshawe, "Dedication," in *Il Pastor Fido*, A3r.

23. On the relationship between Fanshawe's poem on Strafford and his translation, see Potter, *Secret Rites*, 87–90.

24. Baltrušaitis, *Anamorphoses*, 125–60.

25. Lyons, "Speaking in Pictures," 186.

26. Baltrušaitis, *Anamorphoses*, 100.

27. Peter Davidson, ed., in Fanshawe, *Poems and Translations*, 1:368.

28. Dryden, preface to *Ovid's Epistles*, in *Poems, 1649–1680*, in *Works*, 1:117.

29. "If I suffer and am held unadvised [in so speaking], so be it" (Patterson's translation). Patterson, *Censorship and Interpretation*, 144.

30. Norbrook, *Writing the English Republic*, 159–60.

31. N. Smith, *Literature and Revolution*, 227–28.

32. The political tract in question is Sherburne's *Character of an Agitator*.

33. Sherburne, "To the Reader," in *Medea*, A2v.

34. Sherburne, "Dedication," in *Seneca's Answer*, A2r–A3r.

35. James I, *Meditation*.

36. Freeman, trans., *L. A. Seneca*.

37. Corns, *Uncloistered Virtue*, 253.

38. Cowley, preface to *Poems*, A5r. See Corns, *Uncloistered Virtue*, 250–59; Patterson, *Censorship and Interpretation*, 144–58; Zwicker, *Lines of Authority*, 26–30. On Cowley's poetic legacy, see Hammond, *John Oldham*, 21–29.

39. Patterson, *Censorship and Interpretation*, 150–51.

40. Zwicker, *Lines of Authority*, 27.

41. The anonymous author of *Essayes upon Several Subjects* (1651) internalizes public debate in calling for readers to pass "an Act of oblivion in our own brests," procuring "the generall peace of the nation" with "our own peace" (34). Decades after the Restoration, Dryden recommended "an Act of *Oblivion*" as a remedy for the "Distemper'd" body politic in his 1684 preface to *Absalom and Achitophel* ("To the Reader," in *Works*, 2:5).

42. On the history of legislated oblivion, see Loraux, *La Cité divisée*. For David Norbrook, the "cost" involved is the voluntary erasure of an English republican tradition (*Writing the English Republic*, 1–22). I will be arguing for a more generalized psychological trauma as well.

43. On *Davideis* as "Royalist fantasy," see Corns, *Uncloistered Virtue*, 265–68.

44. Norbrook, *Writing the English Republic*, 71. Even at the height of Augustanism, the couplet proves intractable to essentializing interpretations. See Hunter, "Form as Meaning," on the resistance to resolution in Pope's couplets. See also Ross, "Rules of the Game."

45. Venuti, *Translator's Invisibility*, 44–65.

46. See Hugh de Quehen, "Editor's Introduction," in Hutchinson, *Translation of Lucretius*, 1–20.

47. Waller and Godolphin, *Passion of Dido*. On the Waller-Godolphin translation, the politics of Virgil translation in the 1650s, and Hutchinson's attack on Waller, see Norbrook, *Writing the English Republic*, 310–16.

48. Harrington, "The Translator to the Author," in *Virgil's Aeneis*, A5r.

49. Scarron, *Virgile travesty*; Lalli, *L'Eneide travestita*. Charles Cotton's version (*Scarronides*), inspired by Scarron and published shortly after Harrington's translation, begins irreverently: "I *sing the man*, (read it who list, / A *Trojan*, true, as ever pist)" (1).

50. On the "political unconscious" of Harrington's translation, see Norbrook, *Writing the English Republic*, 375–78.

51. Boys cites as predecessors Sandys, Denham, Waller, and Godolphin in "Dedication," in *Aeneas His Errours*, A3r. Dropping Sandys from the list in his second translation, he refers obliquely but unmistakably to Denham, Waller, and Godolphin, whom he praises. Preface to *Aeneas His Descent*. Boys ignores John Vicars's 1632 complete *Aeneid*, Robert Stapylton's *Aeneid* IV, and John Ogilby's *Aeneid* of 1654.

52. Brome, "Dedication," in *Poems of Horace*, A5v, A6v.

53. Denham, *On Mr. Abraham Cowley*, 3.

54. Denham, *Cato Major*, A1r–A1v.

55. For example, query 10: "Whether all innovating Rebels must not of necessity, if they invade the regall power, destroy the *liberty* they pretended to assert" (Boys, *Aeneas His Descent*, 159).

56. Calle, *Patriae Parricida*.

57. Sallust, *All the Works*.

58. T. Gordon, *Conspirators*.

59. The first English translation of the Qu'rān was a translation from the French version by André Du Ryer, a diplomat and Arabist. Du Ryer's translation offers a preface ("Au Lecteur") denouncing "ces absurditez," but that text is followed by a "Sommaire de la religion des Turcs," which offers a positive account of Muslim customs and morals. The translation itself reproduces the Arabic initials of each chapter and includes references to the principal Islamic commentators in the margins (and no other commentary). The English version contains the same materials, plus "A needfull Caveat or Admonition," which condemns the Qu'rān's "errors," yet argues that reading the text is no more "dangerous" than reading the accounts of the errors and superstitions of certain peoples of the Old Testament. The writer also finds occasion to remark on the "devotion, piety, and charity" of Muslims. Du Ryer, *L'Alcoran de Mahomet*; *The Alcoran of Mahomet*.

60. See John Evelyn, *An Essay on the First Book of T. Lucretius Carus, De Rerum natura* (London: Gabriel Bedle and Thomas Collins, 1656), 7; Creech, *Epicurean Philosopher*. On the diffusion and influence of Lucretius during the period, see Kroll, *Material Word*, 140–79.

61. Sherburne, *Troades*, 50.

62. For a variety of methodological viewpoints on the response of translators to discursive control, see Merkle, "Censure et traduction."

63. See Kupersmith, *Roman Satirists*.

64. For a reading of the gender politics in Juvenal translations, see Wahrman, "How the English Wrote."

65. Stapylton, *Mores Hominum*, B2r.

66. Holyday, *Decimus Junius Juvenalis*.

67. Higden, "To the Reader," in *Thirteenth Satyr of Juvenal*, B2r.

68. Higden, "The Preface to the Reader," in *Tenth Satyr of Juvenal*, n.p. Thomas Shadwell, mocked in Higden's preface, defends himself against Higden and Dryden—and attacks adaptative translations—in his own Juvenal preface (*Tenth Satyr of Juvenal*, A3r–A3v).

69. Echard, preface to *Plautus's Comedies*, B2r.

70. Rowe, "Some Account."

71. Weinbrot, *Formal Strain*, 22–30.

72. I will be looking primarily at the following of L'Estrange's translations: *Aristotle's Treatise of Poesie*; *Dom Francisco de Quevedo Villegas*; *Twenty Select Colloquies*; *Tully's Offices*; *Seneca's Morals*; *Fables*; *Spanish Decameron*; *Works of Flavius Josephus*.

73. On L'Estrange's *Fables*, see Patterson, *Fables of Power*, 139–46; Lewis, *English Fable*, 24–28, 44–45. See also Turner, "L'Estrange's Deferential Politics"; Hinds, "Roger L'Estrange."

74. See Zwicker and Bywaters, "Politics and Translation."

75. Johnson, *English Poets*, 2:118.

76. Roscommon, *Essay on Translated Verse*, 4. Frequently anthologized, the poem can be found in both T. Steiner, *English Translation Theory*, and Womersley, *Augustan Critical Writing*, 108–20. The lines would be cited on both sides of the 1736–37 debate between Etienne de Silhouette and the abbé de Resnel over their rival translations of Pope's *Essay on Man*; they were well enough known to be gently parodied in Walter Harte's *An Essay on Satire*; Harte claims that English satire is but a pale imitation of Boileau, who "Drawn to our Tinsel, thro' whole Pages shines!" with a marginal quip: "Roscommon, Revers'd" (19).

77. Dryden, preface to *Sylvae*, in *Works*, 3:3.

78. Johnson, *English Poets*, 2:21.

79. T. Steiner, *English Translation Theory*, 88; Venuti, *Translator's Invisibility*, 274.

80. On the relationship of Johnson's "Life of Roscommon" to his "Life of Dryden," see Clingham, "Roscommon's 'Academy,'" 20.

81. Boileau, *L'Art poétique*, Chant IV, in *Oeuvres complètes*, 180.

82. The eighteenth-century poet and translator Christopher Pitt interrupts his own translation of Virgil to comment on Roscommon's handling of the lines from *Aeneid* VI and the failure of the Lauderdale and Dryden versions to capture the movement of the text. Pitt, *Works of Virgil*, 3:172–73n.

83. On Roscommon's quotations and references, see H. Mason, "Clique Puffery," 296.

84. Winn, *John Dryden*, 387–88.

85. Clingham, "Roscommon's 'Academy.'" See also Clingham, "Knightly Chetwood."

86. Roscommon, "On Mr. Dryden's Religio Laici," in *Poems*, 115.

87. On Roscommon and the seventeenth-century Anglo-Irish milieu, see Vance, *Irish Literature*, 17–63.

88. Cronin, *Translating Ireland*, 70–71; see also 47–48.

89. Dryden, preface to *Ovid's Epistles*, in *Works* 1:114–15.

90. Caldwell, "John Dryden and John Denham."

91. Derrida, *Politiques de l'amitié*, 252; *Politics of Friendship*, 224 (translation modified).

92. On seventeenth-century Latin-English bilingualism and the curriculum of the Latin grammar school, see Hammond, *John Oldham*, 2, 4–20.

93. See Hale, *Milton's Languages*, esp. 68–74.

94. Womersley, introduction to *Augustan Critical Writing*, xi–xliv. For a critique of "Whig history," see Sharpe, *Remapping Early Modern England*, 3–37.

95. Blackmore, preface to *Paraphrase*, lxxv–lxxvii.

96. N. Smith, *Literature and Revolution*, 25.

97. The recent bibliography on the search for a "Universal Characteristic" is immense. For a discussion of universal language theory in the immediate political context of the 1640s, see Achinstein, "Politics of Babel"; on the larger "political semiotics" of the language reform movements, see Markeley, *Fallen Languages*, esp. 63–94.

98. Wilkins, *Essay*, 18.

99. Sprat, *History of the Royal Society*, 43.

100. Derrida, *Donner la mort*, 124–25; *Gift of Death*, 90.

101. Loraux, *La Cité divisée*, 146–72.

102. I. Chambers, *Migrancy, Culture, Identity*, 6.

103. Descartes, *Discours de la méthode*, in *Oeuvres*, 6:6.

104. Sherburne, *Tragedies*, A3v.

Chapter 3

An earlier version of this chapter appeared as "Temporality, Subjectivity, and Neoclassical Translation Theory: Dryden's 'Dedication of the Aeneis,'" *Restoration* 26 (2002): 97–118.

1. Dryden, "Dedication of the Aeneis," in *Works*, 5:326. All Dryden references are to *Works*.

2. On the social and biographical context of Dryden's translations, see Winn, *John Dryden*. Dryden's translations have been the object of a substantial amount of critical work, from William Frost's *Dryden and the Art of Translation* (1955) through the 2001 special issue of the journal *Translation and Literature*, "John Dryden: Classicist and Translator," edited by Stuart Gillespie. On translation as one of the modes by which Dryden engaged the past, see Hammond, *Dryden*.

3. Kevin Dunn discusses Dryden's prefaces in the consolidation of the discourse of literary criticism, in *Pretexts of Authority*, 138–45.

4. Coleman, *Reparative Realism*, 17.

5. See Fujimura, "Dryden's Virgil"; Zwicker, *Politics and Language*, 177–205; Reverand, *Dryden's Final Poetic Mode*, 146–47; Caldwell, *Time to Begin Anew*, 91–104.

6. Sloman, *Dryden*, 36. See also Morton, "'Bringing *Virgil*'"; Corse, *Dryden's Aeneid*. On the significance of Virgil for Dryden's age, see Lefevere, "Translation Practice(s)."

7. I do not altogether agree with David Bruce Kramer, who reads "abjection" and acceptance of "second-class citizenship in the republic of letters" in the "Dedication," although his larger point, that the works of Dryden's late period abandon the aggressivity and will to conquer of his earlier writings, in favor of a new melding of voices, is certainly well taken. See *Imperial Dryden*, 128–31.

8. Similar claims to steer between the competing requirements of sound and sense can be found in translators considered to be quite different from one another, from the literalist Barten Holyday (*Horace*, A2) to the free-imitator John Denham, in his preface to "The Destruction of Troy" (*Poems and Translations*, 27–28).

9. Segrais, preface to *Traduction de l'Enéide*, 1:65.

10. On "reconciliation" in Dryden's work, see Winn, *John Dryden*, esp. 352–53, 377. See also Oscar Kenshur on Dryden's *via media*, in *Dilemmas of Enlightenment*, 49–76.

11. Segrais, preface to *Traduction de l'Enéide*, 1:65–66.

12. Denham, *Poems and Translations*, 28. On Denham's influence on Dryden, see Caldwell, "John Dryden and John Denham."

13. Denham, *Poems and Translations*, i.

14. See the anonymous "Vie de Monsieur de Segrais," in Segrais, *Oeuvres*, 1:i–xii. On the nature of his collaborations with Montpensier and Lafayette, see DeJean, *Tender Geographies*, 52–55, 65–66.

15. Segrais, *Memoires anecdotes*, in *Oeuvres*, 2:7.

16. Segrais, preface to *Traduction de l'Enéide*, 1:62–63. Hereafter, all Segrais references are to this source.

17. In addition to their critical schemes, it is interesting to note that both Dryden and Segrais forgo a lengthy discussion on prosodics, promising a separate, deferred treatise. See Segrais, 1:73; Dryden, 5:321–22.

18. Dryden's various editors and commentators permit one to trace the quotations and borrowings with precision. The references to Segrais, Ruaeus, André Dacier, Saint-Evremond, and Rapin are so numerous that W. P. Ker finds the "Dedication" to be "one of the less original of Dryden's Essays." Only the discussion of prosody in the final pages, we are told, is "completely free from the depressing influence of the French authors." Ker, introduction to the "Dedication of the Aeneas," 1:lxix–lxx.

19. Paul Davis argues that the biblical allusion (the "vineyard slave") provides Dryden with a covert form of authority. Davis, "'But slaves we are.'"

20. See Miner, "Poetics," as well as the essays in Miner and Brady, *Literary Transmission*.

21. Dryden refers approvingly to Roscommon's own translations in the "Dedication" (5:325) and in the preface to *Ovid's Epistles* (1:115).

22. Hammond, *Dryden*, 147.

23. Morris, "Writing/Reading/Remembering," 166.

24. Yates, *Art of Memory*.

25. Hobbes ends the preface to his translation of Homer with a wry question: "Why then did I write it? Because I had nothing else to do. Why publish it? Because I thought it might take off my Adversaries from shewing their folly upon my more serious Writings, and set them upon my Verses to shew their Wisdom." *Iliads and Odysses of Homer*, [18].

26. Hobbes, *Leviathan*, pt. 1, chap. 2, 88.

27. Benjamin, "Task of the Translator."

28. Jayne Lewis makes a similar comment on Dryden's translation of Aesop, in *English Fable*, 130.

29. Freud, "Mourning and Melancholia," 252.

30. Abraham and Torok, *L'Ecorce et le noyau*, 238.

31. See Derrida on the "unnatural" structure of the crypt, in "Fors."

32. Abraham and Torok, *L'Ecorce et le noyau*, 268.

33. See Timothy Murray on the affinities between translation and incorporation in Florio's translation of Montaigne. "Translating Montaigne's Crypts," 48.

34. Greg Clingham comments on Dryden's sense of "a reality that is also always outside and other," in "Translating Difference," 48.

35. Colletet, *Discours contre la traduction*, 2:207.

36. For example, Anthony Horneck's claim to "enter the Lists against so many Champions, and even Horace himself upon occasion." Horneck, *Short Dissertation*, 8. On such remarks, see Weinbrot, "'An Ambition to Excell,'" 133.

37. Derrida, "Moi—la psychanalyse," in *Psyché*, 150–51.

38. Gifford, preface to *Satires*, xvii.

39. Gifford, *Examination of the Strictures*.

Chapter 4

An earlier version of portions of this chapter appeared as "Of Meaning and Modernity: Anne Dacier and the Homer Debate," *EMF: Studies in Early Modern France* 8 (2002): 173–95.

1. Dacier's translations prior to Homer include *Florus* (1674), *Callimaque* (1675), *Dictys et Darès* (1680), *Aurélien Victor* (1681), *Anacréon et Sapho* (1681), *Eutrope* (1683), *Plaute* (1683), *Aristophane* (1684), *Térence* (1688), and *Marc-Aurèle* (1691).

2. Scott Bryson points out the importance of Ancients such as Rapin and Boileau to the later generation of *philosophes*, particularly Diderot. "Rules and Transgression," 133.

3. Rigault, *Histoire de la querelle*, 515–16.

4. Hepp, *Homère en France*.

5. DeJean, *Ancients against Moderns*. While I am sympathetic to much of DeJean's project, my reading of the Dacier–La Motte debate differs sharply from hers, as the discussion below will show. Because the Homer debate in France was fol-

lowed closely in England, where it intersected with the Battle of the Books, it has been an object of recent studies in British literature and culture. See J. Levine, *Battle of the Books*, 121–47; Weinbrot, *Britannia's Issue*, 193–236.

6. Perrault, *Parallèle*, 1:49; see also 2:29.

7. La Motte, *Oeuvres*, 2:146 (original pagination).

8. Pons, *Lettre*, 24.

9. Assaf, "La Deuxième querelle."

10. Cary, *Les Grands traducteurs français*, 32–34.

11. Pons, *Lettre*, 29.

12. J. Levine, *Battle of the Books*, 131.

13. Dacier, preface to *L'Iliade d'Homere*, 1:xviii.

14. La Motte, *Discours sur Homere*, in *Oeuvres*, 2:113.

15. Pons, *Lettre*, 19.

16. Dacier, *Des Causes*, 331.

17. La Motte, *Réflexions*, in *Oeuvres*, 3:181–82.

18. See Ricken, *Grammaire et philosophie*.

19. La Motte, *Discours*, 2:86–87.

20. La Motte, *Réflexions*, 3:155–56.

21. Pons, "Dissertation sur les langues en général, & sur la Langue Françoise en particulier," in *Oeuvres*, 182–83.

22. While it might seem counterintuitive to suppose that a member of the urban upper class could have a more detailed understanding of cowherding than the cowherd (*vacher*) himself, Pons argues that although ignorant peasants believe that life and labor in the countryside have always been exactly the same, educated elites possess knowledge of history and literature ("those ingenious fictions in which are depicted the gentle and tranquil manners of former ages"); pastoral fictions present "shepherds" (*bergers*) who have nothing in common with "rustic men made brutal by servitude and misery" known as *vachers* ("Dissertation," 168–70).

23. Fourmont, *Examen pacifique*, 262–320.

24. La Motte, *Réflexions*, 3:155–56.

25. Fern Farnham argues that she was, in *Madame Dacier*, 175. See also Pieretti, "Women Writers and Translation," 105.

26. Pons, *Lettre*, 16–17.

27. Saint-Hyacinthe, *Lettre à Madame Dacier*, 1.

28. Pons, "Dissertation sur le poeme epique, contre la doctrine de M. D. . . . ," in *Oeuvres*, 145.

29. Excerpts from Dacier's preface can be found in Horguelin, *Anthologie*, 113–14; Lefevere, *Translation/History/Culture*, 10–13 (English translation); Robinson, *Western Translation Theory*, 186–90 (English translation).

30. DeJean, *Ancients against Moderns*, 98.

31. Dacier, preface to *L'Iliade d'Homere*, 1:vi. Hereafter, all Dacier references are to this source unless otherwise indicated.

32. Dacier returns to this issue in her brief discussion of novels in the preface's conclusion. While underscoring her admiration for Madeleine de Scudéry ("this

illustrious woman who honors her century by the extent, the suppleness, and the fecundity of her mind," lxiv–lxv), she criticizes her novel *Cyrus* for having an anachronistic love plot incompatible with the manners of antiquity (lxii).

33. On Aristotle's place in seventeenth-century poetics, see Montgomery, *Terms of Response*, 13–16.

34. La Motte would respond with the claim that such a mixed composition *was* possible in French, but that writers chose not to attempt it (*Discours*, 2:116). Dacier came back in *Des Causes* to point out that there is a difference—or should be—between "base words" and "common words" and that Homer uses the latter.

35. See Mazon, *Madame Dacier*, 4, 18.

36. Derrida, *Monolinguisme*; *Monolingualism* (the epigraph to this section appears on page 1).

37. Cf. La Motte's comment on Homer's "particules sonores": "We admit no sound unless it contributes to sense." *Discours*, 2:116.

38. Rivarol, "Discours sur l'universalité de la langue française," in *Pensées diverses*, 129.

39. Diderot, *Lettre sur les sourds et les muets*, in *Oeuvres complètes*, 4:164.

40. It is in this respect that DeJean finds Dacier most retrograde. And yet Dacier's view that other emotions are more "noble" than romantic love is hardly uncommon among the *philosophes*—Diderot and Rousseau, to name the most obvious. What DeJean calls "the new affectivity" is not at all trivial, but neither is it the *sole* harbinger of the Enlightenment.

41. Delille, "Discours préliminaire," in *Les Georgiques de Virgile*, 7.

42. La Motte, *Discours*, 2:26–27; Dacier, *Des Causes*, 108; La Motte, *Réflexions*, 3:117–18.

43. D'Ablancourt was among the correspondents of the great humanist and scholar Tanneguy Le Fèvre, Anne Dacier's father, whose work he admired and cited (Zuber, *Belles infidèles*, 194).

44. On Dacier and Huet, see Moore, "Homer Revisited."

45. Her originality is cast into relief by the abbé d'Olivet's claim that "rhetoric and poetry are the same for all nations and all times." Pellisson-Fontanier and d'Olivet, *Histoire de l'Académie française*, 2:69.

46. On the Dacier-Pope exchange, see Farnham, *Madame Dacier*, 180–84; Weinbrot, "Alexander Pope"; Weinbrot, "Annotating a Career." For a more critical account of Pope's conflicted view of Dacier, see Williams, *Pope, Homer, and Manliness*.

47. "The affair being thus amicably settled, these two celebrated translators of Homer maintained, ever after, towards each other the most perfect appearance of esteem and regard." "Life of Alexander Pope," 8:383.

48. Philips, preface to *Compendious Way*, 16.

49. Beattie, *Essays*, 368, 407, 410, 563n; Greene, *Argonautic expedition*, 1:10–11; Burton, *Lectures on female education*, 1:166.

50. Goujet, *Bibliothèque françoise*, 1:23–24.

51. See Zinsser, "Entrepreneur," 599.

52. Richardson, *Sir Charles Grandison*, 1:49.

53. Edgeworth, *Letters for Literary Ladies*, 33.

54. Dacier's and La Fosse's prefaces and translations would be published in a combined edition (Dacier, *Les Poésies*).

55. Thomas More makes extensive comparisons between his verse translation and both Dacier's and La Fosse's versions in his *Odes of Anacreon*. For the Bouhier quotation, see *Poeme de Petrone*, v. See also Bouhier's preface to *Les Amours*, viii.

56. On the prose-verse debate, see Moore, *Prose Poems*.

57. Rollin, *De la maniere*, 1:86–87.

58. Desfontaines, *Les Oeuvres de Virgile*.

59. From *Observations sur quelques écrits de ce temps* (30:228), included in a period anthology of Desfontaines's writings, *L'Esprit de l'abbé Des Fontaines*, 1:283–84.

60. Lambert, letter to P. Bussier, in *Oeuvres*, 363.

Chapter 5

1. For example, Krontiris, *Oppositional Voices*; S. Simon, *Gender in Translation*. For an engaging series of short biographies, see Delisle, *Portraits de traductrices*.

2. On contemporary feminist translation practice, see Lotbinière-Harwood, *Re-belle et infidèle*; S. Levine, *Subversive Scribe*; Maier and Massardier-Kenney, "Gender"; Massardier-Kenney, "Towards a Redefinition."

3. Du Châtelet, "Préface du traducteur," 135.

4. Griffith, "The Life and Character of Ninon de l'Enclos," in *Ninon de l'Enclos*, 1:62n.

5. Ezell, "'By a Lady'"; Griffin, "Anonymity and Authorship."

6. Haywood, preface to *Virtuous Villager*, 1:ix–x.

7. Puisieux, "Avertissement du traducteur," in *Amélie*, xii.

8. See Kayman, "Lawful Writing."

9. See Rosenthal, *Playwrights and Plagiarists*.

10. Gallagher, *Nobody's Story*. See also McFarland, "Originality Paradox."

11. C. Thomas, *Alexander Pope*.

12. Robinson, "Theorizing Translation."

13. Margaret Tyler, "Epistle to the Reader," from *The First Part of the Mirrour of Princely deedes and Knyghthood* (1578), in Ferguson, *First Feminists*, 56.

14. Hutchinson, "Letter to Lord Anglesey," in *Translation of Lucretius*, 23–24.

15. Rosenthal, *Playwrights and Plagiarists*, 42.

16. Dacier, preface to *Anacreon et Sappho*, i.

17. Behn, "To the Unknown Daphnis on his Excellent Translation of Lucretius," in *Poems*, in *Works*, 1:25.

18. Haywood, dedicatory epistle, in *La Belle Assemblée*, vii.

19. Behn, "The Translator's Preface," in *Seneca Unmasked and Other Prose Translations*, in *Works*, 4:73.

20. Lennox, "Dedication," in *Memoirs*, 1:[1].

21. Lotbinière-Harwood, *Re-Belle et infidèle*, 156–57.

22. Dacier, *Anacreon et Sappho*, A2r–A2v.

23. Aubin, "To the learned and ingenious Dr. Smithson," in *Illustrious French Lovers*, 2; Du Boccage, "A Messieurs de l'Académie des sciences, belles lettres et arts de Rouen," in *Le Paradis terrestre*, [i]; Guizot, "Préface de l'auteur ou imitateur," in *La Chapelle d'Ayton*, 1:1.

24. On Aubin's translation of Challe, see Anne de Sola's introduction (in Aubin, *Illustrious French Lovers*, xi–xlii); on Guizot, see Sol, "French Reading."

25. Octavie Belot, "Avertissement," in *Histoire*, 1:[1].

26. Du Châtelet, "Préface du traducteur," 131.

27. The *Institutions de physique* continues the theme of self-education as well as that of "secondariness" inasmuch as Du Châtelet claims to be presenting the ideas of other thinkers. I have argued elsewhere, however, that within her presentation of Leibniz and Newton, Du Châtelet configures an original writer's voice. See Hayes, *Reading the French Enlightenment*, 86–110.

28. On Du Châtelet's translation of Mandeville, see Zinsser, "Entrepreneur"; A. Mason, "'L'air du climat'"; Emch-Dériaz and Emch, "On Newton's French Translator." See also Iverson and Pieretti, "Une gloire réfléchie."

29. Janet Todd, "Introduction," in Behn, *Works*, 4:ix. See also Irwin Primer's introduction and notes to Behn, *Seneca Unmasqued*; Dhuicq, "Aphra Behn." Mary Helen McMurran discusses the role of translation in Behn's *Oroonoko*, in "Aphra Behn."

30. It should be noted that the "Author's Preface" attributed to Behn in Ferguson, *First Feminists*, is actually Behn's translation of Fontenelle's own preface. See Behn, *Works*, for Behn's preface, as well as annotations concerning her modifications of Fontenelle's "Author's Preface."

31. Behn, *Works*, 4:77.

32. On Du Châtelet's reaction to Algarotti, see Harth, *Cartesian Women*, 199–201; Zinsser, "Emilie Du Châtelet," 182–85.

33. On Carter, see Agorni, *Translating Italy*, 56–89. On Behn and Carter, see Knellwolf, "Women Translators."

34. Collyer, preface to *Virtuous Orphan*, 4–5.

35. Dobson, "Conclusion," in *Life of Petrarch*, 2:400.

36. Brooke, preface to *Memoirs*, 1:x–xii.

37. Gallagher, *Nobody's Story*, 147.

38. See deJean, *Tender Geographies*.

39. Carter, introduction to *Works of Epictetus*, xxv, xxviii.

40. C. Thomas, "'Th' Insructive Moral,'" 166; see also Williams, "Poetry, Puddings, and Epictetus."

41. Belot, *Histoire*, v.

42. Haywood, preface to *Letters from a Lady*, v–vi.

43. Haywood, *Virtuous Villager*, vii–viii.

44. Riccoboni, "Lettre à M. Humblot, libraire," in *Amélie*, 3–6. On the place of translation in the oeuvre of Riccoboni, as well as a number of other figures discussed here, see Pieretti, "Women Writers."

45. Puisieux, *Amélie*, v. For a comparison, see Rivara, "*Amelia* de Fielding."

46. Thiroux d'Arconville, "Epître à ma nièce," in *Avis d'un Père*, i.

47. Thiroux d'Arconville, "Dedication" and "Avertissement," in *Méditations*, iii–xix.

48. Pieretti, "Veiled Presence."

49. Thiroux d'Arconville, "Avertissement," in *Avis d'un Père*, x–xii.

50. Floyd, "To the Honourable John Laws, Esq," in *Fatal Gallantry*, iv–v.

51. Keralio, *Fables de M. Gay*, iii–iv.

52. Sarah Fielding, preface to *Xenophon's Memoirs*, i–ii.

53. Although the numbers remain small, there appears to be an increase in the practice of woman-to-woman dedications during the eighteenth century. Rogers, "Book Dedications," 225.

54. Griffith, "The Character of the Princess of Cleves," in *Collection of Novels*, 2:4n.

55. Montolieu, *Raison et Sensibilité*.

56. Brooke, *Memoirs*, xii.

57. S. Simon, *Gender in Translation*, 83.

58. The L'Enclos materials are in vols. 4–5 of the *Petit réservoir*, both dated 1751.

59. See Voltaire, *Oeuvres*, 23:497–500.

60. The anecdote relates Ninon's response to her lover's question as to why she had deferred his happiness so long: "I must confess, replied she, it proceeded from a remain of vanity: I piqued myself upon having a lover at fourscore, and it was but yesterday that I was eighty compleat" (1:x–xi).

61. Demurral aside, Griffith has a keen enough sense of French idioms to criticize the previous translator's clumsy literality (1:147–51). She is particularly sensitive to the difficulty of translating the French *galanterie*, which she describes as "a *liberal art*, by no means synonymous with intrigue" (1:135), proposing a neologism, "galantry" (with one *l*), in order "to distinguish the character of a lover from that of a soldier" (1:152). The term continues to frustrate translators; see the animadversions of F.-N. Thomas, "Recent English Translations."

62. Derrida, *Marges de la philosophie*, 9; citation from *Margins of Philosophy*, 9.

63. Pecora, "Ethics, Politics." See Benveniste, "Actif et moyen dans le verbe," in *Problèmes de linguistique générale*, 1:168–75.

64. See Chamberlain, "Gender and Metaphorics."

65. Montolieu, preface to *Caroline de Litchfield*, viii.

66. Carroll, "Politics of 'Originality.'"

67. Griffith, preface to *Memoirs, Anecdotes, and Characters*, 1:vi, viii.

68. Griffith and Griffith, *Series of Genuine Letters*. Griffith's reference is to 4:6–7.

Chapter 6

1. Pope, preface to *Iliad of Homer*, in *Works*, 7:14.

2. M. Cohen, *Sensible Words*; Land, *Philosophy of Language*.

3. Ross, "Translation," 8.

4. Johnson, "The Life of Pope," in *English Poets*, 4:74.

5. Cowper, "Preface," in *Iliad and Odyssey*, v.

6. Knight, "Pope's *Iliad* Preface," 237.

7. On the centrality of imagination in Pope, see, among others, Fairer, *Pope's Imagination*; L. Damrosch, *Imaginative World*; Brower, *Alexander Pope*, 85–141.

8. Connelly, "Pope's *Iliad*."

9. Francklin, *Translation*, 9n. T. Steiner includes Francklin's poem in his anthology, but unfortunately without the footnotes.

10. T. Gordon, "Dedication," in *Conspirators*, iii.

11. Gordon is not a proponent of "exact" translation as such. In his translation of Sallust, he criticizes literal translation, comparing André Dacier's Plutarch to Amyot's: "*D'Acier*'s is an exact Translation of *Plutarch*'s Words: *Amyot* is a Copy of *Plutarch* himself; resembles his Author, and writes as well. *Amyot* is a Genius: *D'Acier* is a learned man." Introduction to *Works of Sallust*, xiii.

12. Guthrie, preface to *Orations*, 1:iii.

13. Colman, preface to *Comedies of Terence*, xxx–xxxi.

14. Francis, *Poetical Translation*, viii.

15. Alexander Strahan, preface to *First Six Books*, A6r–a2r.

16. Cowper, *Iliad and Odyssey*, vi.

17. Joseph Warton, "Dedication," in J. Warton, C. Pitt, et al., *Works of Virgil*, 1:vii.

18. Cowper, *Iliad and Odyssey*, xv.

19. Priestley, "Of the Revolutions of Language and of Translation," in *Lectures*, 233.

20. W. Smith, *Peloponnesian War*, b3r.

21. Guthrie, preface to *Cicero's Epistles to Atticus*, 1:xiv.

22. Bladen, "To the Reader," in *Caesar's Commentaries*, [2–3].

23. T. Warton, *Fairy Queen of Spenser*, 1:196.

24. Weinbrot, *Britannia's Issue*, 526–56.

25. On theories of the divine origins of Hebrew, see Paxman, *Voyage into Language*, 42–43; Bono, *Word of God*, 73–75.

26. R. Simon, *Histoire critique*, 363.

27. Le Clerc, *Sentimens*, 341–42. See Pitassi, *Entre croire et savoir*.

28. Le Clerc, *Twelve Dissertations*, 53–69. Le Clerc's Latin text was published in 1693.

29. Blackmore, *Paraphrase*, xlii.

30. Priestley, "Of Derivation and Syntax," in *Lectures*, 142, 157.

31. Lowth, *Lectures*, 72. Lowth's *De sacra poesi Hebraeorum* appeared originally in 1753.

32. Blackmore, *Paraphrase*, lxxv; Lowth, *Isaiah*, lii. On Lowth's context, see Hitchin, "Politics"; Sheehan, *Enlightenment Bible*.

33. On Tytler, Campbell, and their intellectual milieu, see Jeffrey Huntsman, "Introduction," in Tytler, *Essay*, 3rd ed., ix–xlix.

34. Tytler, *Essay*, 3rd ed., 4n.

35. Campbell, *Four Gospels*, 446.

36. Venuti, *Translator's Invisibility*, 72, 76. Venuti's accusation of anti-Semitism comes in response to Campbell's reference to the "slavish attachment to the letter," which he links to "the superstition, not of the Church, but of the synagogue" (cited

by Venuti, 76). Without denying the anti-Semitic dimension of the letter/spirit to-pos, which as we have seen had been part of translation discourse at least since the Renaissance, I would argue that the complexity of the topos, which points toward an alternative understanding of language as material, embodied, deserves closer study.

37. Campbell, *Four Gospels*, xvi–xvii.

38. Contrast Campbell's account, with its multidimensional analysis of "form" and "spirit," with Priestley's straightforward discussion of language change as a function of shifting political relations ("Of the Revolutions of Language and Trans-lation," in *Lectures*, 219–36).

39. Girard, *Justesse*.

40. The tension in Campbell is perhaps reflective of the larger tension within biblical exegetics of the period, as the traditional affiliation of literal and figural meanings—which we have seen active in Lowth—began to break down, sapping the credibility of the figural reading but also the innate meaningfulness of the bibli-cal narrative. See Frei, *Eclipse of Biblical Narrative*.

41. Lowth, *Lectures*, 72.

42. Campbell, *Philosophy of Rhetoric*, 2:16–17.

43. Campbell, *Four Gospels*, 60.

44. Huntsman, "Introduction," xxv.

45. Campbell, *Four Gospels*, 446.

46. See Grell, *Dix-huitième siècle*; Volpilhac-Auger, *Tacite en France*; Debailly, "Juvénal en France"; Bernier, *Parallèle*.

47. Rollin, *De la maniere*. Rollin discusses translation on pages 1:83–119.

48. Desfontaines, "Discours sur la traduction des poëtes," in *Les Oeuvres de Virgile*, xvii.

49. See Mercier, "Problématique," and especially his *L'Epreuve*.

50. Brumoy, *Le Théâtre des Grecs*, 1:ii.

51. Auroux, *La Sémiotique des encyclopédistes*, esp. 102–13. See also Robinet, *Langage à l'âge classique*; Droixhe, *Linguistique et l'appel*.

52. Buffier, *Examen*, 155–238.

53. Girard, *Justesse*, vii–liv.

54. I cite the edition of Maupertuis's *Réflexions* included with Turgot's response in Turgot, "Remarques critiques," 2:710.

55. Turgot, "Remarques critiques," 2:710.

56. Maupertuis, cited in Turgot, "Remarques critiques," 2:718.

57. Turgot, "Réflexions sur les langues."

58. See Ricken, *Grammaire et philosophie*.

59. Batteux, "Principes de la traduction," in *Cours de belles-lettres*, 4:290.

60. L. G. Kelly credits Batteux with articulating "the principle of dynamic struc-tural equivalence," in *True Interpreter*, 165–67.

61. I discuss Beauzée, the inversion controversy, and the role of translation in the *Encyclopédie* in my article "Translation, (In)version."

62. Diderot, *Lettre sur les sourds et les muets*, in *Oeuvres complètes*, 4:165.

63. On Diderot's approach to general grammar and translation, see Brewer,

"Language and Grammar"; Hobson, *Lettre sur les sourds*. I discuss translation and language theory in Diderot in Hayes, *Reading the French Enlightenment* and "Around 1740."

64. D'Alembert, "Observations sur l'art," 3:3–32.

65. Diderot, *Lettre sur les aveugles*, in *Oeuvres complètes*, 4:42.

66. Buffier, *Examen*, 166–67.

67. Vauvilliers, *Essai sur Pindare*, 25–27.

68. La Harpe, "Discours préliminaire," in *Les Douze Césars*, x.

69. Arnaud, "Discours sur les langues."

70. Clément, *Nouvelles observations critiques*, 137.

71. Dureau de la Malle, "Discours sur la traduction," in *Traité des bienfaits*, vii.

72. Pellisson-Fontanier and d'Olivet, *Histoire de l'Académie française*, 2:124.

73. Brissot, *Bibliothèque philosophique*, 185. On Brissot, see Darnton, *Literary Underground*, 44–48.

74. Silhouette, "Sur le goût des traductions," in *Essais sur la critique et sur l'homme*, 3.

75. D'Olivet, preface to *Philippiques de Démosthene*, 19.

76. Millot, preface to *Harangues d'Eschine*, xvi–xviii.

77. Tourreil, preface to *Harangues de Demosthene*, [ii].

78. Cicero, "The Best Kind of Orator," trans. H. M. Hubbell, in Robinson, *Western Translation Theory*, 9.

79. English translations of Tourreil's preface include Somers, *Several orations*; Leland, *Orations of Demosthenes*.

80. Tourreil, "Préface historique," in *Oeuvres*, 1:173. The preface first appeared in 1701; I cite the 1721 edition.

81. Friedrich Schleiermacher, "On the Different Methods of Translating," trans. D. Robinson, in Robinson, *Western Translation Theory*, 225–38.

82. Tourreil, "Préface," *Essais de jurisprudence*, in *Oeuvres*, 1:60.

83. Tourreil, "Si la torture est une bonne voie pour découvrir la vérité," in *Oeuvres*, 1:105; all subsequent references are to this edition.

84. Brissot, *Bibliothèque philosophique*, 184.

85. Massieu, "Préface de l'éditeur," in Tourreil, *Oeuvres*, 1:ii–iii.

86. Tourreil, "Préface sur les deux Harangues," in *Oeuvres*, 2:3.

87. One might note that each time Tourreil cites the passage from Cicero in French, it becomes longer: 83 words in 1691, 108 words in 1701, and 113 words in 1721.

88. On the interrelation of early modern exploration and language theory, see Paxman, *Voyage into Language*.

89. For a biography of Delille, see Guitton, *Jacques Delille*; see also the essay collection edited by Fabre, Ehrard, and Mauzi, *Delille est-il mort?*

90. Jacques Delille, "Discours préliminaire," in *Les Géorgiques de Virgile*, 1.

91. Delille's ambivalence, in spite of very real political commitments, bespeaks the lack of a strong pastoral tradition in French literature, in contrast to the role that such writing played in the British context. See Goodman, *Georgic Modernity*.

92. Turgot, "Réflexions sur les langues," 2:752.

93. Paxman, *Voyage into Language*, 243.

Chapter 7

An earlier version of part of this chapter appeared as "Tobias Smollett and the Translators of the *Quixote*," *Huntington Library Quarterly* 67 (2004): 651–68.

1. See David Damrosch on Goethe's coinage of *Weltliteratur*, in *What Is World Literature?* 1–36.

2. In seventeenth- and eighteenth-century French, *natif* bears an etymological relation to *naître* ("to be born") and corresponds to the literal place, the city, where one was born. The early Academy dictionaries cite a more general use but look on it with disfavor. *Naturel*, by contrast, refers (among other things) to a larger kind of belonging to one's *pays* ("Habitant originaire d'un pays," *Dictionnaire de l'Académie française*, first edition [1694]).

3. Sahlins, "Fictions"; see also his more recent book, *Unnaturally French*.

4. The linguistic sense of *naturalize* and *naturalization* appears to be rarer in English than in French. The *OED* cites Johnson's *Plan of a Dictionary* (1747) as the first such use of *naturalization*, but a cursory word search on the EEBO and ECCO databases turns up several instances of figurative uses of the verb *to naturalize* extending back to the late sixteenth century, though fewer overall than ARTFL.

5. D. Gordon, "Citizenship"; Statt, *Foreigners and Englishmen*.

6. Sahlins, *Unnaturally French*, 130–31.

7. Sahlins, "Fictions," 93–95.

8. Gordon, "Citizenship," 1:245.

9. See M. Cohen and C. Dever, *Literary Channel*. On French translations of English novels, see Lautel, "Fortune française"; Cointre, Lautel, and Rivara, *La Traduction romanesque*, 7–10.

10. Moretti, *Atlas*, 173–74.

11. See Edwin B. Knowles, "Cervantes and English Literature," 267–93, and Esther J. Crooks, "Translations of Cervantes into French," 294–304, both in Flores and Benardete, *Cervantes across the Centuries*. As the Flores and Benardete volume makes clear, the German and Russian reception initially took place through the French translations. The most thorough examination of the French context in this period remains Bardon, *'Don Quichotte.'* Needless to say, the literature on *Quixote*'s reception is immense. See Drake, *Don Quijote*.

12. See Paulson, *Don Quixote in England*; Motooka, *Age of Reasons*; Ter Horst, "Cervantes." In France, Cervantes's influence is less visible but remains deeply felt, particularly in the novels of Marivaux. See Bardon, *'Don Quichotte'*; for a contemporary study, see Sermain, *Singe de don Quichotte*.

13. Moretti, *Atlas*, 171–74.

14. Shelton, *History of Don-Quichote*, sig. 2r. See Knowles, "Thomas Shelton."

15. See Gerhard, *Don Quixote*.

16. Phillips, *History*.

17. See the discussion in Chapter 2.

18. See Howard Weinbrot on the "recognition of the original" in parody, in *Formal Strain*, 22–30.

19. Stevens, preface to *History*, A3r.

20. Victorian Cervantist John Ormsby's translation project also began with a return to Shelton. Ormsby argues that Shelton's "racy old version" had "a vitality that only a contemporary could feel . . . he put the Spanish of Cervantes into the English of Shakespeare." Introduction to *Ingenious Gentleman*, v.

21. Motteux, *History*, 1:A2r–A3v.

22. Knowles, "Cervantes and English Literature," 280–81.

23. Jervas, preface to *Life and Exploits*, 1:iv; Ormsby, introduction, vii–viii.

24. One critic decries secondhand translation as "the Adulteration of the noblest Wines." Felton, *Dissertation*, 126.

25. Jervas, preface, 1:iii.

26. Battestin attributes Jervas's accuracy to his "dependence on Shelton." Introduction to Smollett, *Life and Adventures*, xxxv.

27. Ozell, "Avertisement," in *History*.

28. Ozell, *History*. Ozell died in October 1743; the extent of his use of Jervas in the new *Quixote* edition suggests that this project occupied him intensely in the last year of his life.

29. For an overview, see Wardropper, "*Duelos y Quebrantos*." According to Cervantes's recent editors, "Los *duelos y quebrantos* eran un plato que no rompía la abstinencia de carnes selectas que en el reino de Castilla se observaba los sábados; podría tratarse de 'huevos con tocino.'" Cervantes, *Don Quijote*, 1:36n.

30. The Battestin-Brack edition is particularly valuable in this regard, as the editors offer meticulous comparisons of Smollett's version and notes with those of his predecessors, making visible the successive readings of the text and reminding us that the translation springs from a complex conjunction of text and commentary, reading and rereading.

31. Tytler, *Essay* (1791), 178–79.

32. Ormsby, introduction, x.

33. See Battestin, introduction, xxxiv; and Battestin, "Authorship." For a general account of Smollett's career as a translator, see Leslie A. Chilton, introduction to Smollett, *Adventures of Telemachus*, xvii–xxxv.

34. Oudin, "Au Roy," in Oudin and Rosset, *Valeureux Dom Quixote*, 1:ā2r–ā2v.

35. Filleau de Saint-Martin, "Avertissement," in *Histoire*, [v].

36. D'Alembert, "Observations sur l'Art," 3:19. See Chapter 6.

37. Florian, preface to *Galatée*, 19.

38. Florian, "Avertissement du traducteur," in *Don Quichotte de la Manche*, 6 vols. (Paris: Didot l'aîné, An VII [i.e., 1798–99]), 1:2–3.

39. On the significance of French translations as the basis for secondhand translations in Germany and elsewhere, with particular attention to the diffusion of the *Quixote*, see Stackelberg, "Traduction."

40. Twentieth-century French critics had a similar response to the Oudin-Rosset

translation, a revised version of which appears in the Pléiade edition of Cervantes. See Jean Cassou, introduction to *L'Ingénieux Hidalgo Don Quichotte de la Manche et Nouvelles exemplaires* (Paris: Gallimard, 1949), 12–13.

41. G. Steiner, *After Babel*, 285.

42. Loewenstein, *Author's Due*, 87.

43. Jorge Luis Borges: "Lane translated against Galland, Burton against Lane; to understand Burton we must understand this hostile dynasty." "The Translators of *The Thousand and One Nights*," trans. Esther Allen, in *Selected Non-Fictions*, 92.

44. Resnel, "Discours préliminaire du traducteur," in *Principes*; Silhouette, "Réflexions préliminaires sur le goût des traductions," in *Essais sur la critique et sur l'homme* (1737). On French translations of Pope, see Audra, *Traductions françaises*. On the French reception of the *Essay on Man*, see Knapp, *Fortunes*; France, "Translating the British," in *Politeness and Its Discontents*, 151–72. See also France, "French Pope." I discuss the role of the Silhouette and Resnel translations in the shaping of Diderot's thoughts on translation in my article "Around 1740."

45. Silhouette, "Préface du traducteur," in *Essai sur l'homme* (1736 version*)*, xxviii.

46. Resnel, "Discours," xviii; Silhouette, "Préface du traducteur," in *Essai sur la critique*, ix.

47. Silhouette, "Réflexions" (6). The phrase about "interior complacency" comes from Tourreil, whom Silhouette cites at length.

48. Anonymous reviewer, *Journal des sçavans* (avril 1736): 235–40.

49. Fontanes, "Discours préliminaire," in *Nouvelle traduction*, 1–46. Fontanes sees Silhouette's translation as precise, but lacking elegance. Interestingly, Fontanes speaks of a translation-in-progress of the *Essay* by Jacques Delille but seeks to diminish any rivalry: "If his translation appears, I will not hesitate to recognize its superiority" (46). To my knowledge, Delille never published this translation.

50. Saint-Simon, preface to *Essai de traduction*, viii–xi. See Gillet, "Approche sensualiste."

51. Boyer, "Advertisement," in *Adventures of Telemachus*, 1:iii–xx; Ozell, "The Translator's Advertisement Concerning this New Edition of the Adventures of Telemachus," in *Adventures of Telemachus*, i–v.

52. Pope, *Essai sur l'homme*. The volume contains both the Resnel and Silhouette translations, the one "for the poetry" and the other because it is supposedly closer to the original.

53. This can also be the case in a literary context: the translations of Milton by Dupré de Saint-Maur, Louis Racine, Jean-Baptiste Mosneron-Delauney, and Anne-Marie Le Page Du Boccage contain notes and other paratextual apparatus but little discussion of translation as such. The apparatus itself bespeaks the canonicity of the work.

54. See John Lockman, preface to *Henriade*, 18 pp. (unnumbered). Felton discusses the "Rules of Translation" in *Dissertation*, 116–66.

55. French novels figure prominently in the earliest accounts of the origins of the genre, such as Pierre-Daniel Huet's *Traité de l'origine des romans*, translated and widely read in England, and critical prefaces by Delariviere Manley and Letitia

Barbauld. See, among many recent critical discussions, McKeon, *Origins*, 54–63; Corman, "Early Women Novelists"; McMurran, "Taking Liberties"; and a cluster of essays edited by E. McMorran, "La Traduction au XVIIIe siècle." See also sources cited in the Introduction, note 2.

56. Humphreys, "The Translator's Preface," in *Letters from the Marchioness de M****, 1.

57. T. Gordon, "A Conjecture concerning the modern languages," section 13 from discourse 2, in *Works of Tacitus*, 1:30; Guthrie, preface to *Cicero's Epistles*, 1:xi; Lennox, preface to *Greek*, 1:i.

58. M. Cohen and C. Dever, "Introduction," in *Literary Channel*, 18.

59. For an extended analysis of Le Tourneur's project, see my article "Translation as Original Composition." Le Tourneur is often discussed in commentaries on French translations of Shakespeare; see note 76.

60. On the diffusion of Young and the graveyard poets, see Van Tieghem, *La Poésie de la nuit et des tombeaux*, in *Le Préromantisme*, 2:1–203.

61. Desfontaines, preface to *Voyages de Gulliver*, 1:viii. For an account of Desfontaines's and others' translations of Swift, see Goulding, *Swift en France*.

62. See Weil, "L'Abbé Desfontaines"; Léger, "Notes du traducteur."

63. Silhouette, "Réflexions," 6.

64. Desfontaines gives high marks to *Joseph Andrews* but has only scorn for contemporary French novels, especially those of Marivaux. See "Lettre d'une dame angloise," in *Avantures de Joseph Andrews*, ii. On Desfontaines's female pseudonym, see Léger, "Desfontaines travesti."

65. La Place, preface to *Oroonoko*, viii.

66. Jürgen von Stackelberg argues that an abolitionist interpretation of La Place's translation is "impossible" ("*Oroonoko*"). Others take a different view; see Rivara, "*Oroonoko ou le Prince Nègre*"; Kadish, "Translation in Context: Translating *Oronooko*," in Kadish and Massardier-Kenney, *Translating Slavery*.

67. La Place, preface to *Tom Jones*, 1:9.

68. Le Tourneur, preface to *Clarisse Harlowe*, ix.

69. Prévost, "Introduction," in *Lettres angloises*, [1:ii–iii]. See Shelly Charles's editor's introduction on the relationship between the Richardson translation and Prévost's narrative experimentation in his own novels (ibid., 1:7–42).

70. Le Tourneur, "Discours préliminaire," in *Oeuvres diverses*, 1:xlii.

71. Morellet, preface to *Traité des délits*, viii–ix. See Medlin, "André Morellet."

72. France, *Politeness and Its Discontents*, 172.

73. On the influence of La Place's *Tom Jones*, see Charles, "*Tom Jones* de La Place"; McMorran, "Fielding in France."

74. La Place, *Tom Jones*, 2:25. Compare the opening of Fielding's bk. 8, chap. 9.

75. La Place, "Discours sur le théâtre anglois," in *Théâtre anglois*, 1:iv.

76. See Cranston, "'Rome en anglais.'" The bibliography on Shakespeare in France is immense. On Ducis, see McMahon, "Ducis: Unkindest Cutter?" and, more recently, Golder, *Shakespeare*. On Le Tourneur, see Genuist, *Théâtre de Shakespeare*. On staged versions, see Heylen, *Translation, Poetics*. Michelucci

compares passages in versions by La Place and later translators in "Shakespeare traduit."

77. Hugo, "Avertissement," in *Oeuvres complètes de W. Shakespeare*, 1:34.

78. Bonnefoy, interview with Robert Kopp, 27. See Bonnefoy's reflections on poetic meter in Shakespeare in "Comment traduire Shakespeare?" and *La Communauté des traducteurs*.

79. Nancy, *L'Intrus*, 11–12.

80. On La Place's Shakespeare and "pre-Romantic" aesthetics, see Van Tieghem, *Le Préromantisme*.

81. Rand, "Translator."

82. La Place, "Discours," vii.

83. Weinbrot, *Britannia's Issue*, 115; on British alterations, see Marsden, *Re-Imagined Text*.

84. See Cobb, *Pierre-Antoine La Place*.

85. Lefevere, "The Extract."

86. Kristeva, *Etrangers à nous-mêmes*; *Strangers to Ourselves*.

Conclusion

1. Goujet, *Bibliothèque françoise*.

2. With regard to the authoritativeness of his judgments, Goujet manages to have it both ways—he both speaks from the personal experience of reading the works and promises to cite the opinions of experts ("les jugemens des Savans") (ibid., 1:vii).

3. It is interesting to compare Goujet's praise for the universality of French with the better-known 1783 essay by Rivarol. Rivarol's argument, although given a similar historical presentation (in a survey of the "rise and fall" of other European languages from antiquity to the present), is marked by linguistic philosophy, in particular the inversion controversy, in its claim that French achieved its preeminence through its reliance on its "natural order." (See Rivarol, *Pensées diverses*.) Goujet, by contrast, bases his argument principally on the literary value and richness of the French "bibliothèque."

4. Méchoulan, *Livre avalé*, 245–46.

5. Delille, "Discours préliminaire," in *Les Georgiques de Virgile*, 7.

6. Johnson, nos. 68 and 69, in *The Idler*, 1:87.

7. Clingham, *Johnson, Writing, and Memory*, 112–57.

8. Johnson, *English Poets*, 2:155, 4:73.

9. Venuti, *Translator's Invisibility*, 68.

10. Tytler, *Essay*, 3rd ed., 1.

11. Venuti, *Translator's Invisibility*, 71–73.

12. Tytler, *Essay*, 3rd ed., 15–16.

13. "I grant, that something must be lost in all Transfusion, that is, in all Translation." Dryden, preface to the *Fables Ancient and Modern*, in *Works*, 7:41. As Venuti points out (*Translator's Invisibility*, 49), the term is used in its alchemical connota-

tion in Denham ("if a new spirit is not added in the transfusion, there will remain nothing but a *caput mortuum*"). It is not clear whether Dryden is echoing his predecessor or the latest scientific jargon of his own day, but the discursive field had clearly shifted by Tytler's day, particularly given his milieu.

14. Delille, "Discours préliminaire," 43.

15. Tytler, *Essay*, 3rd ed., 79.

16. Cipolloni, "The Old Wor(l)d and the New Wor(l)ds: A Discursive Survey from Discovery to Early Anthropology," in Wolff and Cipolloni, *Anthropology of the Enlightenment*, 325–26.

17. August Wilhelm von Schlegel, "History of Classical Literature" (excerpt), in Robinson, *Western Translation Theory*, 219.

Bibliography

Translated works are generally listed under the name of the translator, not the author. Although the translator's name does not appear on the title page of many older texts, the attributions are not in doubt; I have therefore not put brackets around their names.

Aarsleff, Hans, et al., eds. *Papers in the History of Linguistics*. Amsterdam: John Benjamins, 1985.

Ablancourt, Nicolas Perrot d'. *Lettres et préfaces critiques*. Ed. R. Zuber. Paris: Didier, 1972.

Ablancourt, Nicolas Perrot d', et al., trans. *Huit oraisons de Ciceron*. Paris: J. Camusat, 1638.

Abraham, Nicolas, and Maria Torok. *L'Ecorce et le noyau*. Paris: Aubier-Flammarion, 1987.

Achinstein, Sharon. "The Politics of Babel in the English Revolution." In *Pamphlet Wars: Prose in the English Revolution*, ed. James Holstun, 14–44. London: Frank Cass, 1992.

Agorni, Mirella. *Translating Italy for the Eighteenth Century: British Women, Translation, and Travel Writing, 1739–1797*. Manchester: St. Jerome, 2002.

The Alcoran of Mahomet, translated out of Arabique into French; by the Sieur Du Ryer . . . And newly Englished, for the satisfaction of all that desire to look into the Turkish vanities. English translator unknown. London: n.p., 1649.

Alembert, Jean le Rond d'. "Observations sur l'art de traduire en général, et sur cet Essai de Traduction en particulier." In *Mélanges de littérature, d'histoire, et de philosophie, nouvelle édition, augmentée de plusieurs Notes sur la Traduction de quelques morceaux de Tacite*, 3:3–32. Amsterdam: Zacharie Chatelain et fils, 1763.

Arnaud, François, abbé. "Discours sur les langues." *Variétés littéraires* 1 (1768): 1–25.

Arnauld, Antoine. *Regles pour discerner les bonnes et les mauvaises critiques des traductions de l'Ecriture-Sainte en François, pour ce qui regarde la langue. Avec Des Reflexions sur cette Maxime: Que l'usage est la regle & le tyran des Langues vivantes*. Paris: Charles Huguier, 1707.

Arnauld, Antoine, and Pierre Nicole. *La Logique ou l'art de penser.* Paris: Flammarion, 1970.

Arnauld d'Andilly, Robert, trans. *Les Confessions de S. Augustin. Traduites en François, par Monsieur Arnaud d'Andilly.* 2nd ed. Paris: la Veuve Jean Camusat et Pierre Le Petit, 1649. Re-edited by Philippe Sellier as *Confessions,* trans. Arnauld d'Andilly. Paris: Gallimard, 1993.

———. For other works by this author, see Nardis et al., *Regole della Traduzione.*

Assaf, Francis. "La Deuxième querelle." In *D'un siècle à l'autre: Anciens et modernes,* ed. Godard de Donville, 277–92. Marseille: CMR, 1987.

Attridge, Derrick. *The Singularity of Literature.* London: Routledge, 2004.

Aubin, Penelope, trans. *The Illustrious French Lovers.* Ed. Anne de Sola. Amsterdam, 1727; repr. Lewiston, ME: Edwin Mellen Press, 2000.

Audra, E. *Les Traductions françaises de Pope (1717–1825), étude de bibliographie.* Paris: Librairie ancienne Honoré Champion, 1931.

Auerbach, Erich. *Scenes from the Drama of European Literature.* Minneapolis: Univ. of Minnesota Press, 1984.

Auroux, Sylvain. *La Sémiotique des encyclopédistes.* Paris: Payot, 1979.

Ayres-Bennet, Wendy. "Usage and Reason in Seventeenth-Century French Grammar: A Fresh Look at Vaugelas." In Aarsleff et al., *Papers in the History of Linguistics,* 233–46.

Ayres-Bennet, Wendy, and Philippe Caron, eds. *Les Remarques de l'Académie française sur le Quinte-Curce de Vaugelas, 1719–1720: Contribution à une histoire de la norme grammaticale et rhétorique en France.* Paris: Presses de l'Ecole Normale Supérieure, 1996.

Bachet, Claude-Gaspard de, sieur de Meziriac. "Discours de la traduction, à l'Académie françoise." In *Commentaire sur les epistres d'Ovide. Nouvelle edition, avec plusieurs autres Ouvrages du même Auteur, dont quelques uns paroissent pour la premiere fois,* 1:23–56. La Haye: Henri du Sauzet, 1716. For a modern edition of this work, see *De la traduction* (1635). Ed. M. Ballard. Artois, France: Artois presses universitaires; Ottawa: Presses de l'université d'Ottawa, 1988.

Baillet, Adrien. *Jugemens des savans sur les principaux ouvrages des auteurs. Revûs, corrigés & augmentés par M. De la Monnoye de l'Academie Françoise.* 8 vols. Paris: Charles Moette et al., 1722.

Balibar, Renée. *L'Institution du français.* Paris: PUF, 1985.

Ballard, Michel. *De Ciceron à Benjamin: Traducteurs, traductions, réflexions.* Lille: Presses universitaires de Lille, 1992.

Ballard, Michel, and Lieven D'Hulst, eds. *La Traduction en France à l'âge classique.* Villeneuve d'Ascq: Presses universitaires du septentrion, 1996.

Baltrušaitis, Jurgis. *Anamorphoses ou Thaumaturgus opticus.* 1984; repr. Paris: Flammarion, 1996.

Barcos, Martin, abbé de Saint Cyran. *Correspondance.* Ed. Lucien Goldmann. Paris: PUF, 1956.

Bardon, Maurice. *'Don Quichotte' en France au XVIIe et au XVIIIe siècle, 1605–1815.* 2 vols. Paris: Honoré Champion, 1931.

Battestin, Martin. "The Authorship of Smollett's *Don Quixote*." *Studies in Bibliography* 50 (1997): 295–321.

Batteux, Charles. *Cours de belles-lettres, ou Principes de la littérature, nouvelle édition.* 4 vols. Paris: Durand, 1763.

Beattie, James. *Essays on the nature and immutability of truth . . . on poetry and music, . . . on laughter, and ludicrous composition; on the utility of classical learning.* Edinburgh: printed for the author, 1777.

Beebee, Thomas O. *Clarissa on the Continent: Translation and Seduction.* University Park, PA: Penn State Univ. Press, 1990.

Behn, Aphra. *Seneca Unmasqued.* Ed. Irwin Primer. New York: AMS Press, 2001.

———. *The Works of Aphra Behn.* Ed. Janet Todd. 7 vols. Columbus: Ohio State Univ. Press, 1992–96.

Bell, David. *The Cult of the Nation in France: Inventing Nationalism, 1680–1800.* Cambridge, MA: Harvard Univ. Press, 2001.

Belot, Octavie, trans. *Histoire de la maison de Tudor sur le trône d'Angleterre, par M. David Hume.* 2 vols. Amsterdam: n.p., 1763.

Benjamin, Walter. "The Task of the Translator," trans. Harry Zohn. In *Illuminations*, ed. Hannah Arendt, 69–82. New York: Schocken Books, 1968.

Benoist, J.-M., ed. *Figures du baroque.* Paris: PUF, 1983.

Benveniste, Emile. *Problèmes de linguistique générale.* 2 vols. Paris: Gallimard, 1966.

Berman, Antoine. "De la translation à la traduction." *TTR: Traduction, Terminologie, Rédaction* 1 (1988): 23–40.

———. *L'Epreuve de l'étranger.* Paris: Gallimard, 1984. *The Experience of the Foreign.* Trans. S. Heyvaert. Albany: SUNY Press, 1992.

———. *Pour une critique des traductions: John Donne.* Paris: Gallimard, 1995.

———. "Tradition—Translation—Traduction," *Po&Sie* 47 (1988): 85–98.

Bernier, Marc André, ed. *Parallèle des anciens et des modernes: Rhétorique, histoire et esthétique au siècle des Lumières.* Laval: Presses de l'université Laval, 2006.

Billings, J. Todd. "John Milbank's Theology of the 'Gift' and Calvin's Theology of Grace: A Critical Comparison." *Modern Theology* 21, no. 1 (2005): 87–105.

Bissi, Claude de Thyard, comte de, trans. "Traduction de la premiere nuit de Young, précédée de quelques reflexions sur le caractere & les poésies de cet auteur." *Variétés littéraires* 2 (1768): 38–62.

Blackmore, Richard, trans. *A Paraphrase on the Book of Job: As likewise on the Songs of Moses, Deborah, David, on Six Select Psalms, Some Chapters of Isaiah, and the Third Chapter of Habakkuk.* 2nd ed. London: Jacob Tonson, 1716.

Bladen, Martin. *C. Julius Caesar's Commentaries of his Wars in Gaul, and Civil War with Pompey.* London: Richard Smith, 1705.

Blanchot, Maurice. *L'Amitié.* Paris: Gallimard, 1971.

Boileau, Nicolas. *Oeuvres complètes.* Ed. Françoise Escal. Paris: Gallimard, coll. Pléiade, 1966.

Bonnefoy, Yves. "Comment traduire Shakespeare?" *Etudes anglaises* 17, no. 4 (1964): 341–51.

————. *La Communauté des traducteurs.* Strasbourg: Presses universitaires de Strasbourg, 2000.

————. Interview with Robert Kopp. *Magazine littéraire* 421 (June 2003): 22–27.

Bono, James J. *The Word of God and the Languages of Man.* Madison: Univ. of Wisconsin Press, 1995.

Borges, Jorge Luis. *Selected Non-fictions.* Ed. E. Weinberger. New York: Viking, 1999.

Bouhier, Jean, trans. *Les Amours d'Enée et de Didon, poëme traduit de Virgile. Avec diverses autres Imitations d'anciens Poëtes Grecs & Latins.* Paris: J. B. Coignard, 1742.

————, trans. *Poeme de Petrone sur la guerre civile entre Cesar et Pompée; avec deux epitres d'Ovide: le tout traduit en vers françois avec des remarques: et des conjectures sur le poeme intitulé Pervigilium Veneris.* Amsterdam: François Changuion, 1737.

Bouhours, Dominique, trans. *La Vérité de la religion chrétienne. De l'italien de M. le Marquis de Piannesse.* Paris: Sébastien Mabre-Cramoisy, 1672.

Bourdieu, Pierre. *Les Règles de l'art: Genèse et structure du champ littéraire.* 2nd ed. Paris: Seuil, 1998. *The Rules of Art: Genesis and Structure of the Literary Field.* Trans. Susan Emanuel. Stanford: Stanford Univ. Press, 1995.

Boyer, Abel, trans. *The Adventures of Telemachus, son of Ulysses.* 11th ed. 2 vols. London: printed for M. Matthews et al., 1721.

Boys, John, trans. *Aeneas His Descent into Hell: As it is inimitably described by the Prince of Poets in the sixth of his Aeneis.* London: Henry Brome, 1661.

————, trans. *Aeneas His Errours, or his Voyage from Troy into Italy. An Essay upon the Third Book of Virgils Aeneis.* London: Henry Brome, 1661.

Brewer, Daniel. "Language and Grammar: Diderot and the Discourse of Encyclopedism." *Eighteenth-Century Studies* 13 (1979): 1–19.

Brisset, Annie. *Sociocritique de la traduction: Théâtre et alterité au Québec, 1968–1988.* Montreal: Balzac, 1990.

Brissot de Warville, Jean-Pierre. *Bibliothèque philosophique du Législateur, du politique, du jurisconsulte; ou Choix des meilleurs discours, dissertations, essais, fragments, composés sur la Législation criminelle par les plus célebres Ecrivains, en françois, anglois, italien, allemand, espagnol, &c. pour parvenir à la réforme des Loix pénales dans tous les pays, traduits & accompagnés de notes & d'observations historiques.* 10 vols. Berlin and Paris: Desauges, 1783.

Brome, Alexander, ed. *The Poems of Horace, Consisting of Odes, Satyres, and Epistles, Rendred in English Verse By Several Persons.* London: printed by E. Cotes for Henry Brome, 1666.

Brooke, Frances, trans. *Memoirs of the Marquis de St. Forlaix. Translated from the French of Mons. Framery. By Mrs. Brooke.* 4 vols. London: J. Dodsley, 1770.

Brower, Reuben. *Alexander Pope: The Poetry of Allusion.* Oxford: Clarendon Press, 1959.

Brown, Gregory S. *A Field of Honor: Writers, Court Culture, and Public Theatre in French Literary Life from Racine to the Revolution.* New York: Columbia Univ. Press, 2003.

Brumoy, Pierre, père. *Le Théâtre des Grecs.* 3 vols. Paris: Rollin Pere, 1730.

Bryson, Scott. "Rules and Transgression: *Imitatio naturae* and the Quarrel of the Ancients and the Moderns." *EMF: Studies in Early Modern France* 3 (1997): 121–48.

Buell, Lawrence. "In Pursuit of Ethics." *PMLA* 114 (1999): 7–19.

Buffier, Claude, père. *Examen des préjugez vulgaires, pour disposer l'esprit à juger sainement de tout.* Paris: J. Mariette, 1704.

Burton, John. *Lectures on female education and manners.* 2 vols. Rochester, UK: printed for the author, by Gilman and Etherington, 1793.

Caldwell, Tanya. "John Dryden and John Denham." *Texas Studies in Literature and Language* 46, no. 1 (2004): 49–72.

———. *Time to Begin Anew: Dryden's Georgics and Aeneis.* Lewisburg, PA: Bucknell Univ. Press, 2000.

Calle, Caleb. *Patriae Parricida; or, The History of the Horrid Conspiracy of Catiline against the Commonwealth of Rome.* London: printed by J.C. and F.C. for James Norris, 1683.

Campbell, George. *The Four Gospels, translated from the Greek. With Preliminary Dissertations and Notes Critical and Explanatory.* 2 vols. London: A. Strahan and T. Cadell, 1789.

———. *The Philosophy of Rhetoric.* 2 vols. London: W. Strahan and T. Cadell, 1776.

Caron, Philippe. "Le *Quinte Curce* de Vaugelas à l'épreuve: Une relecture critique à l'Académie française." In Ballard and D'Hulst, *La Traduction en France*, 123–33.

———. "Une traduction relue à l'Académie française, ou Vaugelas à l'épreuve de Vaugelas." *Littératures classiques* 13 (1990): 89–107.

Carroll, Berenice A. "The Politics of 'Originality': Women and the Class System of the Intellect." *Journal of Women's History* 2, no. 2 (1990): 136–63.

Carter, Elizabeth, trans. *All the Works of Epictetus, which are now Extant; Consisting of His Discourses, preserved by Arrian, In Four Books, The Enchiridion, and Fragments.* London: printed by S. Richardson, 1758.

Cary, Edmond. *Les Grands traducteurs français.* Geneva: Georg, 1963.

Cave, Terence. *The Cornucopian Text: Problems of Writing in the French Renaissance.* Oxford: Clarendon Press, 1979.

Certeau, Michel de. "L'Idée de traduction de la Bible au XVIIe siècle: Sacy et Simon." *Recherches de science religieuse* 66, no. 1 (1978): 73–92.

Cervantes Saavedra, Miguel de. *Don Quijote de la Mancha.* Ed. Francisco Rico and Joaquín Forradellas. 2 vols. Barcelona: Instituto Cervantes, 1998.

Chamberlain, Lori. "Gender and the Metaphorics of Translation." *Signs: Journal of Women in Culture and Society* 13 (1988): 454–72.

Chambers, Bettye Thomas. *Seventeenth Century French-Language Editions of the Scriptures.* Vol. 2 of *Bibliography of French Bibles.* Geneva: Droz, 1994.

Chambers, Iain. *Migrancy, Culture, Identity.* London: Routledge, 1994.

Charles, Shelly. "Le *Tom Jones* de La Place ou la fabrique d'un roman français." *RHLF* 94 (1994): 931–58.

Chase, Cynthia. *Decomposing Figures: Rhetorical Readings in the Romantic Tradition.* Baltimore: Johns Hopkins Univ. Press, 1986.

Chédozeau, Bernard. *Le Baroque.* Paris: Nathan, 1989.

Cheyfitz, Eric. *The Poetics of Imperialism.* Philadelphia: Univ. of Pennsylvania Press, 1991.

Clark, A. F. B. *Boileau and the French Classical Critics in England, 1660–1830.* 1925; repr. New York: Russell and Russell, 1965.

Clément, Jean-Marie-Bernard. *Nouvelles observations critiques, sur différens sujets de littérature.* Amsterdam: Moutard, 1772.

Clingham, Greg. *Johnson, Writing, and Memory.* Cambridge: Cambridge Univ. Press, 2002.

———. "Knightly Chetwood's *A Short Account of Some Passages of the Life & Death of Wentworth late Earle of Roscommon*: A Transcription and Introduction." *Restoration* 25 (2001): 117–70.

———. "Roscommon's 'Academy,' Chetwood's Manuscript 'Life of Roscommon,' and Dryden's Translation Project." *Restoration* 26 (2002): 15–26.

———. "Translating Difference: The Example of Dryden's 'Last Parting of Hector and Andromache.'" *Studies in the Literary Imagination* 33, no. 2 (2000): 45–70.

Clymer, Lorna. "Graved in Tropes: The Figural Logic of Epitaphs and Elegies in Blair, Gray, Cowper, and Wordsworth." *ELH* 62 (1995): 347–86.

Cobb, Lillian. *Pierre-Antoine de La Place: Sa vie et son oeuvre (1707–1793).* Paris: Editions de Broccard, 1928.

Codde, Philippe. "Polysystem Theory Revisited: A New Comparative Approach." *Poetics Today* 24, no. 1 (2003): 91–126.

Cohen, Margaret, and Carolyn Dever, eds. *The Literary Channel: The International Invention of the Novel.* Princeton, NJ: Princeton Univ. Press, 2002.

Cohen, Murray. *Sensible Words: Linguistic Practice in England, 1640–1785.* Baltimore: Johns Hopkins Univ. Press, 1977.

Cointre, Annie. "Bibliographie commentée des traductions de romans anglais du VIIIe siècle." In Rivara, *La Traduction des langues modernes,* 17–29.

Cointre, Annie, Alain Lautel, and Annie Rivara, eds. *La Traduction romanesque au XVIIIe siècle.* Arras, France: Artois Presses Université, 2003.

Coleman, Patrick. "Figure in the *Encyclopédie*: Discovery or Discipline?" In *Using the Encyclopédie: Ways of Reading, Ways of Knowing,* ed. D. Brewer and J. Hayes, 63–79. Oxford: Voltaire Foundation, 2002.

———. *Reparative Realism: Mourning and Modernity in the French Novel, 1730–1830.* Geneva: Droz, 1998.

Colletet, Guillaume. "Discours contre la traduction." In *Traitté de la poésie morale et sentencieuse,* 2:207–12. Paris: Antoine de Sommaville, 1658.

Colley, Linda. *Britons: Forging the Nation, 1707–1837.* New Haven, CT: Yale Univ. Press, 1992.

Collyer, Mary, trans. *The Virtuous Orphan, or The Life of Marianne, Countess of *****.* Ed. William Harlin McBurney and Michael Francis Shugrue. Carbondale: Southern Illinois Univ. Press, 1965.

Colman, George. *The Comedies of Terence, Translated into Familiar Blank Verse.* London: T. Becket [et al.], 1765.

Connelly, Peter J. "Pope's *Iliad*: *Ut Pictura Translatio*." *SEL* 21 (1981): 439–55.

Copeland, Rita. *Rhetoric, Hermeneutics, and Translation in the Middle Ages: Academic Traditions and Vernacular Texts*. Cambridge: Cambridge Univ. Press, 1995.

Corman, Brian. "Early Women Novelists, the Canon, and the History of the British Novel." In *Eighteenth-Century Contexts*, ed. Howard Weinbrot et al., 232–46. Madison: Univ. of Wisconsin Press, 2001.

Corns, Thomas N. *Uncloistered Virtue: English Political Literature, 1640–1660*. Oxford: Clarendon Press, 1992.

Corse, Taylor. *Dryden's Aeneid: The English Virgil*. Newark: Univ. of Delaware Press, 1991.

Cotton, Charles, trans. *Scarronides, or Virgile Travestie. A Mock-Poem. Being the First Book of Virgils Aeneis in English, Burlésque*. London: Henry Brome, 1664.

Couton, Georges. *Ecritures codées: Essais sur l'allégorie au XVIIe siècle*. Paris: Klincksieck, 1991.

Cowley, Abraham. *Poems*. London: Humphrey Moseley, 1656.

Cowper, William. *The Iliad and Odyssey of Homer, translated into English Blank Verse*. 2 vols. London: J. Johnson, 1791.

Cranston, Philip E. "'Rome en anglais se prononce Roum . . .': Shakespeare Versions by Voltaire." *MLN* 90 (1975): 809–37.

Creech, Thomas, trans. *The Epicurean Philosopher, His Six Books De Natura Rerum Done into English Vers, with Notes*. Oxford: printed by L. Lichfield for Anthony Stephens, 1682.

Cronin, Michael. "Changing Sides: The Case of Ireland." In Delisle and Woodsworth, *Translators through History*, 79–83.

———. *Translating Ireland: Translation, Languages, Cultures*. Cork, Ireland: Cork Univ. Press, 1996.

Cronk, Nicholas. "Metaphor and Metamorphosis." *Seventeenth-Century French Studies* 6 (1984): 179–98.

———. "The Singular Voice: Monologism and French Classical Discourse." *Continuum* 1 (1989): 175–202.

Culler, Jonathan. *The Pursuit of Signs*. Ithaca, NY: Cornell Univ. Press, 1981.

Cushing, Mary Gertrude. *Pierre Le Tourneur*. New York: Columbia Univ. Press, 1908.

———. "Unité et diversité de la réflexion traductologique." In Ballard and D'Hulst, *La Traduction en France*, 83–100.

Dacier, Anne. *Des Causes de la corruption du goust*. Paris, 1714; repr. Geneva: Slatkine, 1970.

———, trans. *L'Iliade d'Homere, traduite en françois, avec des remarques. Nouvelle édition. Avec quelques reflexions sur la préface angloise de M. Pope*. 4 vols. Paris: du fonds des Messieurs Rigaud & Anisson, Gabriel Marin, Jean-Baptiste Coignard et les Frères Guerin, 1741.

———, trans. *Les Oeuvres d'Homere*. 4th ed. 7 vols. Amsterdam: Wetsteins & Smith, 1731.

————, trans. *Les Poésies d'Anacréon et de Sapho, traduites en François, avec des Remarques par Madame Dacier. Nouvelle Edition, augmentée des Notes Latines de Mr. Le Fevre, & de la Traduction en vers François de Mr. De la Fosse.* Amsterdam: la veuve de Paul Marret, 1716.

Damrosch, David. *What Is World Literature?* Princeton, NJ: Princeton Univ. Press, 2003.

Damrosch, Leopold. *The Imaginative World of Alexander Pope.* Berkeley: Univ. of California Press, 1987.

Darnton, Robert. *The Literary Underground of the Old Regime.* Cambridge, MA: Harvard Univ. Press, 1982.

Davis, Paul. "'But slaves we are': Dryden and Virgil, Translation and the 'Gyant Race.'" In Gillespie, "John Dryden," 110–27.

De Man, Paul. *Blindness and Insight.* Minneapolis: Univ. of Minnesota Press, 1983.

————. *The Rhetoric of Romanticism.* New York: Columbia Univ. Press, 1984.

Debailly, Pascal. "Juvénal en France au XVIe et au XVIIe siècle." *Littératures classiques* 24 (1995): 29–47.

DeJean, Joan. *Ancients against Moderns: Culture Wars and the Making of a Fin de Siècle.* Chicago: Univ. of Chicago Press, 1997.

————. *Tender Geographies: Women and the Origins of the Novel in France.* New York: Columbia Univ. Press, 1991.

————. "Transnationalism and the Origins of the (French) Novel." In M. Cohen and C. Dever, *Literary Channel,* 37–49.

Delassault, Geneviève. *Le Maistre de Sacy et son temps.* Paris: Nizet, 1957.

DeLater, James Albert. *Translation Theory in the Age of Louis XIV: The 1683 De optimo genere interpretandi of Pierre-Daniel Huet.* Manchester, UK: St. Jerome, 2002.

Delille, Jacques, trans. *Les Georgiques de Virgile.* Paris: Claude Bleuet, 1770.

————. *Oeuvres.* Ed. A. V. Arnault. 6 vols. Paris: Edouard Leroi, 1835.

Delisle, Jean, ed. *Portraits de traductrices.* Ottawa: Presses de l'université d'Ottawa, 1997.

Delisle, Jean, and Judith Woodsworth, eds. *Translators through History.* Amsterdam and Philadelphia: John Benjamins, 1995.

Denham, John, trans. *Cato Major Of Old Age.* London: H. Herringman, 1669.

————. *On Mr. Abraham Cowley His Death, and Burial Amongst the Ancient Poets.* London: H. Herringman, 1667.

————. *Poems and Translations, with the Sophy.* London: H. Herringman, 1668.

Derrida, Jacques. "Des tours de Babel." In Graham, *Difference in Translation,* 209–48.

————. *Donner la mort.* Paris: Galilée, 1999. *The Gift of Death.* Trans. David Wills. Chicago: Univ. of Chicago Press, 1995.

————. *Donner le temps.* Paris: Galilée, 1991. *Given Time.* Trans. Peggy Kamuf. Chicago: Univ. of Chicago Press, 1992.

————. "Fors: Les Mots anglés de Nicolas Abraham et Maria Torok." Preface to

Cryptonomie: Le Verbier de l'Homme aux loups, by Nicolas Abraham and Maria Torok, 7–73. Paris: Aubier Flammarion, 1976.

———. *Marges de la philosophie*. Paris: Minuit, 1972. *Margins of Philosophy*. Trans. Alan Bass. Chicago: Univ. of Chicago Press, 1982.

———. *Le Monolinguisme de l'autre*. Paris: Galilée, 1996. *Monolingualism of the Other*. Trans. Patrick Mensah. Stanford: Stanford Univ. Press, 1998.

———. *Politiques de l'amitié*. Paris: Galilée, 1994. *Politics of Friendship*. Trans. George Collins. London: Verso, 1997.

———. *Psyché: Inventions de l'autre*. Paris: Galilée, 1987.

———. *Le Toucher, Jean-Luc Nancy*. Paris: Galilée, 2000. *On Touching—Jean-Luc Nancy*. Trans. Christine Irizarry. Stanford: Stanford Univ. Press, 2005.

Descartes, René. *Oeuvres*. 13 vols. Ed. Charles Adam and Paul Tannery. Paris: L. Cerf, 1897–1913.

Desfontaines, Pierre François Guyot, abbé, trans. *Avantures de Joseph Andrews et de son ami Abraham Adams. Ecrites dans le goût des Avantures de Don-Quichotte . . . Et traduites en François, à Londres, par une Dame Angloise*. 2 vols. Amsterdam: Au dépens de la compagnie, 1744.

———. *L'Esprit de l'abbé Des Fontaines, ou Reflexions sur différens genres de science et de littérature: Avec des Jugemens sur quelques Auteurs & sur quelques Ouvrages tant Anciens que Modernes*. 3 vols. London: Clément, 1757.

———, trans. *Les Oeuvres de Virgile traduites en françois, avec des remarques*. 4 vols. Paris: Quillau Pere, 1743.

———, trans. *Voyages de Gulliver, nouvelle éd.* 2 vols. Paris: Jean-Baptiste-Guillaume Musier, fils, 1772.

Dhuicq, Bernard. "Aphra Behn: Théorie et pratique de la traduction au XVIIème siècle." *Franco-British Studies* 10 (1990): 75–98.

D'Hulst, Lieven. *Cent ans de théorie française de traduction de Batteux à Littré (1748–1847)*. Arras, France: Presses universitaires de Lille, 1990.

Diderot, Denis. *Oeuvres complètes*. Ed. Herbert Dieckmann et al. 33 vols. Paris: Hermann, 1975–.

Dobson, Susanah, trans. *The Life of Petrarch. Collected from Memoires pour la vie de Petrarch*. 6th ed. 2 vols. London: n.p., 1805.

Dorleijn, G. J., and Keith van Rees, eds. *The Eighteenth-Century Literary Field in Western Europe: The Interdependence of Material and Symbolic Production and Consumption*. Amsterdam: Elsevier, 2001.

Drake, Dana B., ed. *Don Quijote in World Literature: A Selective, Annotated Bibliography*. New York: Garland, 1980.

Droixhe, Daniel. *La Linguistique et l'appel de l'histoire (1688–1800)*. Geneva: Droz, 1978.

Dryden, John. *The Works of John Dryden*. 20 vols. Berkeley: Univ. of California Press, 1956–2000.

Du Bellay, Joachim. *La Deffence et illustration de la Langue Francoyse*. Paris: n.p., 1549.

Du Boccage, Marie-Anne Le Page, trans. *Le Paradis terrestre, poeme imité de Milton, nouvelle édition.* Amsterdam: n.p., 1748.

Du Châtelet, Emilie. "Préface du traducteur" to *The Fable of the Bees*, by Bernard Mandeville. In *Studies on Voltaire: With Some Unpublished papers of Mme Du Châtelet*, ed. Ira O. Wade. Princeton, NJ: Princeton Univ. Press, 1947.

Du Ryer, André, trans. *L'Alcoran de Mahomet.* Paris: Antoine de Sommaville, 1647.

Dunn, Kevin. *Pretexts of Authority: The Rhetoric of Authorship in the Renaissance Preface.* Stanford: Stanford Univ. Press, 1994.

Dureau de la Malle, Jean-Baptiste-Joseph-René, trans. *Traité des bienfaits, de Séneque.* Paris: Pissot, 1776.

Dziembowski, Edmond. *Un nouveau patriotisme français, 1750–1770.* Oxford: Voltaire Foundation, 1998.

Eagles, Robin. *Francophilia in English Society, 1748–1815.* New York: St. Martin's Press, 2000.

Echard, Laurence, trans. *Plautus's Comedies, Amphitryon, Epidicus, and Rudens, Made English: With Critical Remarks upon Each Play.* London: Abel Swalle and T. Child, 1694.

Edgeworth, Maria. *Letters for Literary Ladies. To Which is added, an Essay on the Noble Science of Self-Justification.* London: J. Johnson, 1795.

Emch-Dériaz, Antoinette, and Gérard G. Emch. "On Newton's French Translator: How Faithful Was Madame Du Châtelet?" In *Emilie Du Châtelet: Rewriting Enlightenment Philosophy and Science*, ed. J. P. Zinsser and J. Hayes, 225–50. Oxford: Voltaire Foundation, 2006.

Enders, Jody. "Memory, Allegory, and the Romance of Rhetoric." *Yale French Studies* 95 (1999): 49–64.

Essayes upon Several Subjects: Not unworthy consideration in these times. Communicated by Letters to private Friends, and at their request to the Public. London: printed by Richard Cotes for Edward Husband, 1651.

Evelyn, John. *An Essay on the First Book of T. Lucretius Carus, De Rerum natura.* London: Gabriel Bedle and Thomas Collins, 1656.

Even-Zohar, Itamar. "Polysystem Studies." Special issue, *Poetics Today* 11, no. 1 (1990).

Even-Zohar, Itamar, and Gideon Toury, eds. "Translation Theory and Intercultural Relations." Special issue, *Poetics Today* 2, no. 4 (1981).

Ezell, Margaret J. M. "'By a Lady': The Mask of the Feminine in Restoration, Early Eighteenth-Century Print Culture." In *The Faces of Anonymity: Anonymous and Pseudonymous Publication from the Sixteenth to the Twentieth Century*, ed. Robert J. Griffin, 63–79. New York: Palgrave Macmillan, 2003.

Fabre, Jean, Jean Ehrard, and Robert Mauzi, eds. *Delille est-il mort?* Clermont-Ferrand: G. de Bussac, 1967.

Fairer, David. *Pope's Imagination.* Manchester, UK: Manchester Univ. Press, 1984.

Falvey, John, and William Brooks, eds. *The Channel in the Eighteenth Century: Bridge, Barrier, and Gateway.* Oxford: Voltaire Foundation, 1991.

Fanshawe, Richard, trans. *Il Pastor Fido, The faithfull Shepherd. A Pastorall written in Italian by Baptista Guarini, a Knight of Italie. And now Newly Translated out of the Originall.* London: R. Raworth, 1647.

———. *The Poems and Translations of Sir Richard Fanshawe.* Ed. Peter Davidson. 2 vols. Oxford: Clarendon Press, 1997.

Farnham, Fern. *Madame Dacier: Scholar and Humanist.* Monterey, CA: Angel Press, 1976.

Felton, Henry. *A Dissertation on reading the classics, written in the year 1709.* 4th ed. London: B. Motte, 1730.

Ferguson, Moira, ed. *First Feminists: British Women Writers, 1578–1799.* Bloomington: Indiana Univ. Press, 1985.

Fielding, Sarah, trans. *Xenophon's Memoirs of Socrates. With the Defence of Socrates, before his Judges.* Bath, UK: C. Pope, 1762.

Filleau de Saint-Martin, François, trans. *Histoire de l'admirable Don Quixotte de la Manche.* 5 vols. Amsterdam: Pierre Mortier, 1696.

Flagg, James. "Abel Boyer: A Huguenot Intermediary." *SVEC* 242 (1986): 1–73.

Flores, A., and Benardete, M. J., eds. *Cervantes across the Centuries.* New York: Dryden Press, 1947.

Florian, Jean-Pierre Claris de, trans. *Don Quichotte de la Manche.* 6 vols. Paris: Didot l'aîné, An VII [i.e., 1798–99].

———, trans. *Galatée.* Paris: A. A. Renouard, 1820.

Floyd, Ann, trans. *Fatal Gallantry, or The Secret History of Henrietta of England . . . Writ by the Countess de la Fayette.* London: E. Clay, 1722.

Fontanes, Louis Jean Pierre, marquis de, trans. *Nouvelle traduction de l'Essai su l'homme de Pope, en vers François.* Paris: A. Jombert jeune, 1783.

Fourmont, Etienne de. *Examen pacifique de la querelle de Madame Dacier et de Monsieur de la Motte sur Homère.* Paris, 1716; repr. Geneva: Slatkine, 1971.

France, Peter. "The French Pope." In *Alexander Pope: Essays for the Tercentenary*, ed. C. Nicholson, 117–29. Aberdeen, Scotland: Aberdeen Univ. Press, 1988.

———. *Politeness and Its Discontents: Essays in French Classical Culture.* Cambridge: Cambridge Univ. Press, 1992.

Francis, Philip, trans. *A Poetical Translation of the Works of Horace.* London: A. Millar, 1749.

Francklin, Thomas. *Translation; A Poem.* 2nd ed. London: R. Francklin . . . sold by R. Dodsley, 1754.

Freeman, Sir Ralph, trans. *L. A. Seneca the philosopher, his booke of consolation to Marcia. Translated into an English poem.* London: printed by E.P. for Henry Seile, 1635.

Frei, Hans W. *The Eclipse of Biblical Narrative: A Study in Eighteenth-Century Hermeneutics.* New Haven, CT: Yale Univ. Press, 1974.

Freud, Sigmund. "Mourning and Melancholia." In *The Standard Edition*, ed. James Strachey, vol. 14. London: Hogarth Press, 1957.

Frisch, Andrea. "In a Sacramental Mode: Jean de Léry's Calvinist Ethnography." *Representations* 77 (2002): 82–106.

Frost, William. *Dryden and the Art of Translation*. New Haven, CT: Yale Univ. Press, 1955.

Fujimura, Thomas H. "Dryden's Virgil: Translation as Autobiography." *Studies in Philology* 80 (1982): 67–83.

Fumaroli, Marc. *L'Âge de l'éloquence*. 1980; repr. Paris: Albin Michel, 1994.

———. *Le Poète et le roi: Jean de la Fontaine et son siècle*. Paris: Editions de Fallois, 1997.

Gallagher, Catherine. *Nobody's Story: Vanishing Acts of Women Writers in the Marketplace, 1670–1820*. Berkeley: Univ. of California Press, 1994.

Gaskill, Howard. "Ossian in Europe." *Canadian Review of Comparative Literature* 21 (1994): 643–78.

Genette, Gérard. *Palimpsestes: La Littérature au second degré*. Paris: Seuil, 1982.

———. *Seuils*. Paris: Seuil, 1987.

Genlis, Stéphanie Félicité de. *Les Veillées du château, ou Cours de morale à l'usage des enfans*. 3 vols. Dublin: Wogan et Jones, 1795.

Genuist, André. *Le Théâtre de Shakespeare dans l'oeuvre de Pierre Le Tourneur*. Rennes, France: Presses de l'université de Rennes, 1971.

Gerhard, Sandra Forbes. *Don Quixote and the Shelton Translation*. Madrid: Ediciones José Porrúa Turanzas, 1982.

Gifford, William. *An Examination of the Strictures of the Critical Reviewers on the Translation of Juvenal*. London: printed for J. Hatchard, 1803.

———, trans. *The Satires of Decimus Junius Juvenalis*. London: printed by W. Bulmer for G. and W. Nicol and R. Evans, 1802.

Gillespie, Stuart. "A Checklist of Restoration English Translations and Adaptations of Classical Greek and Latin Poetry, 1660–1700." *Translation and Literature* 1 (1992): 52–97.

———, ed. "John Dryden: Classicist and Translator." Special issue, *Translation and Literature* 10, no. 1 (2001).

Gillet, Jean. "Une approche sensualiste de la traduction: Le Marquis de Saint-Simon." *Revue de littérature comparée* 63, no. 2 (1989): 155–64.

Girard, Gabriel, abbé. *La Justesse de la langue françoise, ou les différentes significations des mots qui passent pour synonimes*. Paris: Laurent d'Houry, 1718.

Giry, Louis, trans. *Des Causes de la corruption de l'eloquence, dialogue. Attribué par quelques uns à Tacite, & par d'autres à Quintilien*. Paris: Charles Chappellain, 1630.

———, trans. *S. Augustin, De la cité de Dieu*. Paris: Pierre le Petit, 1665.

Golder, John. *Shakespeare for the Age of Reason: The Earliest Stage Adaptations of Jean-François Ducis, 1769–1792*. Oxford: Voltaire Foundation, 1992.

Goldmann, Lucien. *Le Dieu caché*. Paris: Gallimard, 1955.

Goodman, Kevis. *Georgic Modernity and British Romanticism*. Cambridge: Cambridge Univ. Press, 2004.

Gordon, Daniel. "Citizenship." In *The Encyclopedia of Enlightenment*, ed. Alan Kors. Oxford: Oxford Univ. Press, 2003.

Gordon, Thomas. *The Conspirators, or The Case of Catiline, As Collected from the best Historians, impartialy examin'd; with respect to his declared and covert Abettors;*

and the Artifices used to skreen the Conspirators from Punishment. 3rd ed. London:
J. Roberts, 1721.

———, trans. *The Works of Sallust.* London: Thomas Woodward and John Peele,
1744.

———, trans. *The Works of Tacitus.* 2 vols. London: Thomas Woodward and John
Peele, 1728.

Goujet, Claude-Pierre, abbé. *Bibliothèque françoise, ou Histoire de la littérature
françoise.* 18 vols. Paris: Mariette, Guerin, 1740–56.

Goulding, Sybil. *Swift en France au XVIIIe siècle.* Paris: Champion, 1924.

Graham, Joseph F., ed. *Difference in Translation.* Ithaca, NY: Cornell Univ. Press,
1985.

Greenberg, Mitchell. *Baroque Bodies: Psychoanalysis and the Culture of French
Absolutism.* Ithaca, NY: Cornell Univ. Press, 2001.

———. *Detours of Desire: Readings in the French Baroque.* Columbus: Ohio State
Univ. Press, 1985.

Greene, Edward Burnaby, trans. *The Argonautic expedition. Translated from the
Greek of Apollonius Rhodius.* 2 vols. London: Thomas Payne and Son, and
Robert Faulder, 1780.

Grell, Chantal. *Le Dix-huitième siècle et l'antiquité en France, 1680–1789.* 2 vols.
Oxford: Voltaire Foundation, 1995.

Griffin, Robert J. "Anonymity and Authorship." *New Literary History* 30 (1999):
877–95.

Griffith, Elizabeth, ed. *A Collection of Novels, Selected and Revised by Mrs. Griffith.*
3 vols. London: G. Kearsly, 1777.

———, trans. *Memoirs, Anecdotes, and Characters of the court of Lewis XIV: Translated from Les Souvenirs, or Recollections of Madame de Caylus, Niece to Madame
de Maintenon: By the Translator of the Life and Writings of Ninon de l'Enclos.*
2 vols. London: J. Dodsley, 1770.

———, trans. *The Memoirs of Ninon de l'Enclos, with her Letters to Monsr de St
Evremond and to the Marquis de Sevigné.* 2 vols. London: R. and J. Dodsley, 1761.

———, trans. *Select Moral Tales.* Glocester: R. Raikes, 1763.

Griffith, Elizabeth, and Richard Griffith. *A Series of Genuine Letters, Between
Henry and Frances.* 5 vols. London: J. Bew, 1786.

Guéret, Gabriel. *Le Parnasse réformée.* Paris, 1671; repr. Geneva: Slatkine, 1968.

Guillerm, Luce. "Les Belles infidèles, ou l'auteur respecté (de Claude de Seyssel à
Perrot d'Ablancourt)." In Ballard and D'Hulst, *La Traduction en France,* 23–42.

———. *Sujet de l'écriture et traduction autour de 1540.* Paris: Aux amateurs de
livres, 1988.

Guitton, Edouard. *Jacques Delille (1738–1813) et le poème de la nature en France de
1750–1820.* Paris: Klincksieck, 1974.

Guizot, Elisabeth Charlotte Pauline, trans. *La Chapelle d'Ayton, ou Emma Courtney.*
5 vols. Paris: Maradan, An VII [i.e., 1798–99].

Guthrie, William, trans. *Cicero's Epistles to Atticus.* 2 vols. London: T. Waller, 1752.

———, trans. *The Orations of Marcus Tullius Cicero.* 3 vols. London: T. Waller, 1745.

Guyot, Thomas, trans. *Les Fleurs morales et épigrammatiques tant anciens que des nouveaux autheurs*. Paris: la veuve de Claude Thiboust, 1669.

———, trans. *Nouvelle traduction des Bucoliques de Virgile*. Paris: Claude Thiboust, 1666.

Hale, John K. *Milton's Languages: The Impact of Multilingualism on Style*. Cambridge: Cambridge Univ. Press, 1997.

Hammond, Paul. *Dryden and the Traces of Classical Rome*. Oxford: Oxford Univ. Press, 1999.

———. *John Oldham and the Renewal of Classical Culture*. Cambridge: Cambridge Univ. Press, 1983.

Hampton, Timothy, ed. "Baroque Topographies." Special issue, *Yale French Studies* 80 (1991).

Hardacre, P. H. "The Royalists in Exile during the Puritan Revolution, 1642–1660." *Huntington Library Quarterly* 16 (1953): 353–70.

Harpham, Geoffrey Galt. *Getting It Right: Language, Literature, and Ethics*. Chicago: Univ. of Chicago Press, 1992.

———. *Shadows of Ethics: Criticism and the Just Society*. Durham, NC: Duke Univ. Press, 1999.

Harrington, James, trans. *Virgil's Aeneis: The Third, Fourth, Fifth, and Sixth Books*. London: printed by J. Cottrel for Henry Fletchers, 1659.

Harte, Walter. *An Essay on Satire*. London: Lawton Gilliver, 1730.

Harth, Erica. *Cartesian Women: Versions and Subversions of Rational Discourse in the Old Regime*. Ithaca, NY: Cornell Univ. Press, 1992.

Häseler, Jens, and Anthony McKenna, eds. *La Vie intellectuelle aux refuges protestants*. Paris: Champion, 2002.

Hayes, Julie Candler. "Around 1740: Diderot and the Subject of Translation." In *Diderot and European Culture*, ed. A. Strugnell and F. Ogée, 129–44. Oxford: Voltaire Foundation, 2006.

———. *Reading the French Enlightenment: System and Subversion*. Cambridge: Cambridge Univ. Press, 1999.

———. "Translation, (In)version, and the Encyclopedic Network." In *Using the Encyclopédie: Ways of Reading, Ways of Knowing*, ed. D. Brewer and J. Hayes, 99–118. Oxford: Voltaire Foundation, 2002.

———. "Translation as Original Composition: Reading the Work of Pierre Le Tourneur." In *Ritual, Routine, and Regime: Repetition in Early Modern British and European Culture*, ed. Lorna Clymer, 201–23. Toronto: Univ. of Toronto Press, 2006.

Haywood, Eliza, trans. *La Belle Assemblée, or The Adventures of Six Days . . . by Madam de Gomez*. London: D. Browne, 1724.

———, trans. *Letters from a Lady of Quality to a Cavalier. Translated from the French By Mrs. Haywood*. London: n.p., 1721.

———, trans. *The Virtuous Villager, or Virgin's Victory, being the Memoirs of a Very Great Lady at the Court of France, Written by Herself*. 2 vols. London: Francis Cogan, 1742.

Hennebert, Frédéric. *Histoire des traductions françaises d'auteurs grecs et latins pendant le XVIe et XVIIe siècles.* Brussels: Imprimerie de Th. Lesigne, 1861.

Hepp, Noémi. *Homère en France au XVIIIe siècle.* Paris: Klinksieck, 1968.

Hermans, Theo. "Literary Translation: The Birth of a Concept." *New Comparison: A Journal of Comparative and General Literary Studies* 1 (1986): 28–42.

———, ed. *The Manipulation of Literature: Studies in Literary Translation.* New York: St. Martin's Press, 1985.

Heurtematte, François, ed. *Fragments de poésie ancienne: Traduction de Diderot, Turgot, Suard.* Paris: José Corti, 1990.

Heylen, Romy. *Translation, Poetics, and the Stage: Six French Hamlets.* London: Routledge, 1993.

Hicks, Philip. *Neoclassical History and English Culture from Clarendon to Hume.* London: MacMillan, 1996.

Higden, Henry, trans. *A Modern Essay on the Tenth Satyr of Juvenal.* London: printed by T.M., 1687.

———, trans. *A Modern Essay on the Thirteenth Satyr of Juvenal.* London: Jacob Tonson, 1686.

Hildesheimer, Françoise. *Le Jansénisme en France au XVIIe et XVIIIe siècles.* Paris: Publisud, 1991.

Hinds, Peter. "Roger L'Estrange, the Rye House Plot, and the Regulation of Political Discourse in Late Seventeenth-Century London." *Library*, 7th ser., vol. 3, no. 1 (2002): 3–31.

Hitchin, Neil W. "The Politics of English Bible Translation in Georgian Britain." *Transactions of the Royal Historical Society*, 6th ser., vol. 9 (1999): 67–92.

Hobbes, Thomas, trans. *Eight Bookes of the Peloponnesian Warre.* London: imprinted for Hen. Seile, 1629.

———, trans. *The Iliads and Odysses of Homer.* 2nd ed. London: Will Crook, 1677.

———. *Leviathan.* Ed. C. B. MacPherson. London: Penguin, 1985.

Hobson, Marion. "*La Lettre sur les sourds et les muets* de Diderot: Labyrinthe et langage." *Semiotica* 16, no. 4 (1976): 291–327.

Holyday, Barten, trans. *Decimus Junius Juvenalis, and Aulus Persius Flaccus Translated and Illustrated, As well with Sculpture as Notes.* Oxford: printed by W. Downing, 1673.

———, trans. *Horace: The Best of Lyrick Poets. Containing much morality, and Sweetnesse. Together with Aulus Persius Flaccus, His Satyres.* London: W. Webb, 1652.

Horguelin, Paul, ed. *Anthologie de la manière de traduire: Domaine français.* Montreal: Linguatech, 1981.

Horneck, Anthony, trans. *A Short Dissertation upon Horace, with the Fifth Ode.* London: n.p., 1708.

Hugo, François-Victor, trans. *Oeuvres complètes de W. Shakespeare.* 16 vols. Paris: Pagnerre, 1865.

Humphreys, Samuel, trans. *Letters from the Marchioness de M***, to the Count de R***,* by Crébillon fils. London: J. Wilford, 1735.

Hunter, J. Paul. "Form as Meaning: Pope and the Ideology of the Couplet." In *Ideology and Form in Eighteenth-Century Literature*, ed. Daniel Richter, 147–62. Lubbock: Texas Tech Univ. Press, 1999.

Hutchinson, Lucy, trans. *Lucy Hutchinson's Translation of Lucretius: De rerum natura.* Ed. Hugh de Quehen. Ann Arbor: Univ. of Michigan Press, 1996.

Iverson, John, and Marie-Pascale Pieretti. "Une gloire réfléchie: Du Châtelet et les stratégies de la traductrice." In *Dans les miroirs de l'écriture: La Réflexivité chez les femmes de l'Ancien Régime*, ed. Jean-Philippe Beaulieu and Diane Desrosiers-Bonin, 135–44. Montreal: Publications du département d'études française de l'université de Montréal, 1998.

Jacques, Emile. *Les Années d'exil d'Antoine Arnauld (1679–1694).* Louvain, Belgium: Editions Nauwelaerts, 1976.

James I. *A Meditation upon the 27, 28, 29, Verses of the XXVII. Chapter of St. Matthew, or A paterne for a Kings inauguration.* London: printed by John Bill, 1620.

Jervas, Charles, trans. *The Life and Exploits of the ingenious gentleman Don Quixote de la Mancha. Translated from the Original Spanish of Miguel Cervantes de Saavedra.* 2nd ed. 2 vols. London: Tonson and Dodsley, 1749.

Johnson, Samuel. *The Idler.* 2 vols. London: J. Newbery, 1761.

———. *The Lives of the Most Eminent English Poets.* Ed. Roger Lonsdale. 4 vols. Oxford: Clarendon Press, 2006.

Kadish, Doris, and Françoise Massardier-Kenney, eds. *Translating Slavery: Gender and Race in French Women's Writing, 1783–1823.* Kent, OH: Kent State Univ. Press, 1994.

Kasher, Rimon. "The Interpretation of Scripture in Rabbinic Literature." In *Mikra: Text, Translating, Reading, and Interpretation of the Hebrew Bible in Ancient Judaism and Early Christianity*, ed. Martin Jan Mulder, 547–94. Assen, Netherlands: Van Gorcum, 1988.

Kayman, Martin A. "Lawful Writing: Common Law, Statute and the Properties of Literature." *New Literary History* 27 (1996): 761–83.

Keith, Jennifer. "'Pre-Romanticism' and the Ends of Eighteenth-Century Poetry." In *The Cambridge Companion to Eighteenth-Century Poetry*, 271–90. Cambridge: Cambridge Univ. Press, 2001.

Kelly, Louis G. *The True Interpreter: A History of Translation in the West.* New York: St. Martin's Press, 1979.

Kenshur, Oscar. *Dilemmas of Enlightenment: Studies in the Rhetoric and Logic of Ideology.* Berkeley: Univ. of California Press, 1993.

Ker, W. P. Introduction to the "Dedication of the Aeneas." In *Essays of John Dryden,* ed. W. P. Ker. 2 vols. New York: Russell and Russell, 1961.

Keralio, Marie-Françoise Abeille de, trans. *Fables de M. Gay, suivies du poëme de l'Eventail.* Paris: Duchesne, 1754.

Knapp, Richard Gilbert. *The Fortunes of Pope's "Essay on Man" in Eighteenth-Century France.* Geneva: Institut et musée Voltaire, 1971.

Knellwolf, Christa. "Women Translators, Gender and the Cultural Context of the Scientific Revolution." In *Translation and Nation: Towards a Cultural Politics of Englishness,* ed. Roger Ellis and Liz Oakley-Brown, 85–119. Clevedon, UK: Multilingual Matters, 2001. ← OUR BOOK!

Knight, Douglas. "The Development of Pope's *Iliad* Preface: A Study of the Manuscript." *Modern Language Quarterly* 16 (1955): 237–46.

———. "Thomas Shelton, Translator of Don Quixote." *Studies in the Renaissance* 5 (1958): 160–75.

Kramer, David Bruce. *The Imperial Dryden: The Poetics of Appropriation in Seventeenth-Century England.* Athens: Univ. of Georgia Press, 1994.

Kristeva, Julia. *Etrangers à nous-mêmes.* Paris: Arthème Fayard, 1988. *Strangers to Ourselves.* Trans. L. Roudiez. New York: Columbia Univ. Press, 1991.

Kroll, Richard W. F. *The Material Word: Literate Culture in the Restoration and Early Eighteenth Century.* Baltimore: Johns Hopkins Univ. Press, 1991.

Krontiris, Tina. *Oppositional Voices: Women as Writers and Translators of Literature in the English Renaissance.* London: Routledge, 1992.

Kupersmith, William. *Roman Satirists in Seventeenth-Century England.* Lincoln: Univ. of Nebraska Press, 1985.

La Harpe, Jean-François de, trans. *Les Douze Césars.* 2 vols. Paris: Lacombe & Didot l'aîné, 1770.

La Motte, Antoine Houdar de. *Oeuvres.* 11 vols. Paris, 1754; repr. Geneva: Slatkine, 1970.

La Place, Pierre Antoine de, trans. *Oroonoko traduit de l'anglois de Madame Behn.* Amsterdam: Aux dépens de la Compagnie, 1745.

———, trans. *Le Théâtre anglois.* 8 vols. Paris: la Veuve Pissot, Jorry, Prault, Guillyn, 1745.

———, trans. *Tom Jones, ou L'Enfant trouvé. Imitation de l'anglois de M. Fielding.* 6th ed. 2 vols. Paris: Bauche, 1783.

Lalli, Giovanni Battista, trans. *L'Eneide travestita.* Venetia: Giacomo Sarzina, 1635.

Lambert, Anne-Thérèse de Marguenat de Courcelles, marquise de. *Oeuvres.* Paris: Léopold Collin, 1808.

Lamy, Bernard. *La Rhétorique, ou L'Art de parler.* Ed. C. Hoille Clauzade. Paris: Champion, 1998.

Lancaster, H. C. *Pierre Du Ryer, Dramatist.* Washington, D.C.: Carnegie Institute, 1912.

Land, Stephen K. *The Philosophy of Language in Britain: Major Theories from Hobbes to Reid.* New York: AMS Press, 1986.

Laporte, Jean. *La Doctrine de Port-Royal.* 2 vols. Paris: PUF, 1923.

Lautel, Alain. "La Fortune française de six auteurs anglais du XVIIIe siècle fondée sur des appréciations numériques." In Ballard and D'Hulst, *La Traduction en France,* 135–54.

Le Clerc, Jean. *Sentimens de quelques théologiens de Hollande sur l'Histoire critique du Vieux Testament.* Amsterdam: Henri Desbordes, 1685.

———. *Twelve Dissertations out of Monsieur Le Clerk's Genesis. Done out of the Latin by Mr. Brown.* London: R. Baldwin, 1696.

Le Maistre, Antoine. See Nardis et al., *Regole della Traduzione.*

Le Maistre de Sacy, Isaac-Louis, trans. *Cantique des cantiques*. 1693; repr. Paris: Guillaume Desprez, 1694.

———. *Choix de lettres inédites*. Ed. G. Delassault. Paris: Nizet, 1959.

———, trans. *Daniel*. Paris: Guillaume Desprez, 1691.

———, trans. *Le Deuteronome*. 2nd ed. 1685; repr. Paris: Guillaume Desprez, 1686.

———, trans. *Les Douze petits prophetes*. Paris: Guillaume Desprez, 1679.

———, trans. *L'Exode et le Levitique*. 1682; repr. Lyon: Leonard Plaignard, 1683.

———, trans. *Ezechiel*. Paris: Guillaume Desprez, 1692.

———, trans. *La Genese*. 1682; repr. Paris: Guillaume Desprez, 1698.

———, trans. *Isaïe*. Paris: Guillaume Desprez, 1675.

———, trans. *Jérémie*. Paris: Guillaume Desprez, 1690.

———, trans. *Job*. Paris: Guillaume Desprez, 1688.

———, trans. *Les Nombres*. Paris: Guillaume Desprez, 1685.

———, trans. *Le Nouveau Testament de Nostre Seigneur Jesus Christ, traduit en François selon l'édition Vulgate, avec les differences du Grec*. Mons, Belgium: Gaspard Migeot, 1667.

———, trans. *Les Paralipomenes*. Paris: Guillaume Desprez, 1693.

———. *Poëme contenant la tradition de l'Eglise sur le tres-saint Eucharistie*. Paris: Guillaume Desprez, 1695.

———, trans. *Poème de Saint Prosper contre les ingrats. Ou la doctrine catholique de la Grace est excellemment expliquée, & soustenuë contre les erreurs des Pelagiens des Semipelagiens*. Paris: la Veuve Martin Durand, 1667.

———, trans. *Les Proverbes de Salomon, traduits en françois. Avec les differences de l'Hebreu*. Brussels: Lambert Marchant, 1672.

———, trans. *Tobie, Judith & Esther*. Paris: Guillaume Desprez, 1688.

———, trans. [Le Sieur de Saint Aubin, pseud.] *Les Fables de Phedre, affranchy d'Auguste*. Paris: la Veuve Martin Durand, 1647.

Le Tourneur, Pierre, trans. *Clarisse Harlowe. Traduction nouvelle et seule complète*. 10 vols. Geneva: Paul Barde; Paris: Moutard, Merigot le jeune, 1785.

———, trans. *Méditations d'Hervey, traduites de l'anglois, par M. Le Tourneur*. 2 vols. Paris: Le Jay, 1771.

———, trans. *Les Nuits d'Young, traduites de l'anglois par M. Le Tourneur. Nouvelle édition*. 2 vols. Paris: Cailleau, 1783.

———, trans. *Oeuvres diverses du docteur Young*. 4 vols. Amsterdam: E. van Harrevelt, 1772.

———, trans. *Ossian, fils de Fingal, barde du troisième siècle: Poésies galliques, traduites sur l'Anglois de M. MacPherson, par M. Le Tourneur*. 2 vols. Paris: Musier fils, 1777.

———. *Préface du Shakespeare traduit de l'anglois*. Ed. J. Gury. Geneva: Droz, 1990.

———, trans. *Shakespeare traduit de l'Anglois*. 20 vols. Paris: la Veuve Duchesne [et al.], 1776–83.

Lefevere, André. "The Extract: Literary Guerilla as Literary Interchange." In Ballard and D'Hulst, *La Traduction en France*, 275–90.

———, ed. *Translation/History/Culture: A Sourcebook*. London: Routledge, 1992.

———. "Translation Practice(s) and the Circulation of Cultural Capital: Some Aeneids in English." In *Constructing Cultures: Essays on Literary Translation*, ed. S. Bassnett and A. Lefevere, 41–56. Clevedon, UK: Multilingual Matters, 1998.

Léger, Benoit. "Desfontaines travesti: Une 'Dame angloise' traduit les *Avantures de Joseph Andrews* de Fielding." *TTR: Traduction, Terminologie, Rédaction* 15, no. 2 (2002): 19–48.

———. "Les Notes du traducteur des *Voyages de Gulliver*: Détonation et 'déton-nement.'" *Lumen* 21 (2002): 179–98.

Leland, Thomas, trans. *The Orations of Demosthenes*. London: W. Johnston, 1771.

Lennox, Charlotte, trans. *The Greek Theatre of Father Brumoy*. 3 vols. London: Millar, Vaillant, Baldwin, et al., 1754.

———, trans. *Memoirs for the History of Madame de Maintenon and of the Last Age. Translated from the French, by the Author of the Female Quixote*. 5 vols. London: A. Millar, J. Nourse, R. and J. Dodsley, L. Davis, and C. Reymer, 1757.

L'Estrange, Roger, trans. *Fables, of Aesop and Other Eminent Mythologists: With Morals and Reflections*. 3rd ed. London: R. Sare, B. Took, M. Gillyflower, A. and J. Churchil, G. Sawbridge, and H. Hindmarsh, 1699.

———, trans. *Reflections on Aristotle's Treatise of Poesie. Containing the Necessary, Rational, and Universal Rules for epick, Dramatick, and the other forms of Poetry. With Reflections on the Works of the ancient and Modern Poets, And their Faults Noted. By R. Rapin*. London: printed by T.N. for H., 1674.

———, trans. *Seneca's Morals by Way of Abstract. To which is added, A Discourse under the Title of An After-Thought*. 13th ed. London: G. Strahan, A. Bettes-worth, J. Tonson, B. Lintot, B. Motte, and D. Browne, 1729.

———, trans. *The Spanish Decameron, or Ten Novels*, by Miguel de Cervantes. 3rd ed. London: printed by E.P. for George Harris, 1712.

———, trans. *Tully's Offices, in Three Books*. 5th ed. London: printed by M.B. for J. Tonson, R. Knaplock, and H. Hindmarch, 1699.

———, trans. *Twenty Select Colloquies, out of Erasmus Roterodamus; Pleasantly rep-resenting Several Superstitious Levities That were crept into the Church of Rome in his Days*. London: printed by Thomas Newcomb, for Henry Brome, 1680.

———, trans. *The Visions of Dom Francisco de Quevedo Villegas, Knight of the Order of St. James*. 6th ed. London: H. Herringman, 1678.

———, trans. *The Works of Flavius Josephus*. London: Richard Sare, 1702.

Lévinas, Emmanuel. *Autrement qu'être ou au-delà de l'essence*. Paris: Livre de poche, 1978. *Otherwise Than Being or Beyond Essence*. Trans. Alphonso Lingis. Pittsburgh: Duquesne Univ. Press, 1998.

Levine, Joseph. *The Battle of the Books: History and Literature in the Augustan Age*. Ithaca, NY: Cornell Univ. Press, 1991.

Levine, Suzanne Jill. *The Subversive Scribe: Translating Latin American Fiction*. St. Paul, MN: Gray Wolf Press, 1991.

Lewis, Jayne. *The English Fable: Aesop and Literary Culture, 1651–1740*. Cambridge: Cambridge Univ. Press, 1996.

"The Life of Alexander Pope." In vol. 8 of *British Biography, or An Accurate and Impartial Account of the Lives and Writings of Eminent Persons in Great Britain and Ireland*. 10 vols. London [Sherborne]: R. Goadby, 1778–80.

Lockman, John, trans. *Henriade. An epick Poem*. London: C. Davis, 1732.

Loewenstein, Joseph. *The Author's Due: Printing and the Prehistory of Copyright*. Chicago: Univ. of Chicago Press, 2002.

Loraux, Nicole. *La Cité divisée: L'Oublie dans la mémoire d'Athènes*. Paris: Payot, 1997.

Lortsch, D. *Histoire de la Bible en France*. Paris: Agence de la Société Biblique britannique et étrangère, 1910.

Lotbinière-Harwood, Suzanne de. *Re-belle et infidèle/The Body Bilingual*. Montreal: Les Editions du remue-ménage, 1991.

Lowth, Robert, trans. *Isaiah, A New Translation* . . . 2nd ed. London: printed by J. Nichols for J. Dodsley and T. Cadell, 1779.

———. *Lectures on the Sacred Poetry of the Hebrews*. Trans. G. Gregory. 2 vols. London: J. Johnson, 1787.

Lu, Jin. "La Traduction de romans anglais dans le *Journal étranger*." In Cointre, Lautel, and Rivara, *La Traduction romanesque*, 187–202.

Lyne, Raphael. *Ovid's Changing Worlds: English Metamorphoses, 1567–1632*. Oxford: Oxford Univ. Press, 2001.

Lyons, John D. "Speaking in Pictures, Speaking of Pictures: Problems of Representation in the Seventeenth Century." In *Mimesis: From Mirror to Method, Augustine to Descartes*, ed. John D. Lyons and Stephen Nichols, 166–87. Hanover, NH: Univ. Press of New England, 1982.

Maier, Carol S., and Françoise Massardier-Kenney. "Gender in/and Literary Translation." In *Translation Horizons*, ed. Marilyn Gaddis Rose, 225–42. Binghamton, UK: Center for Research in Translation, 1996.

Marin, Louis. "La Critique de la représentation classique: La Traduction de la Bible à Port-Royal." In *Savoir, faire, espérer: Les Limites de la raison*, ed. Daniel Coppieters de Gibson, 2:549–75. Brussels: Facultés Universitaires Saint-Louis, 1976. Repr. in Marin, *Pascal et Port-Royal*, ed. Alain Cantillon, 169–96. Paris: PUF, 1997.

———. *La Critique du discours*. Paris: Minuit, 1965.

———. *La Parole mangée*. Paris: Klincksieck, 1986.

Markeley, Robert. *Fallen Languages: Crises of Representation in Newtonian England, 1660–1740*. Ithaca, NY: Cornell Univ. Press, 1993.

Markus, R. A. "Saint Augustine on Signs." *Phronesis* 2 (1957): 60–83.

Marsden, Jean. *The Re-imagined Text: Shakespeare, Adaptation, and Eighteenth-Century Literary Theory*. Lexington: Univ. Press of Kentucky, 1995.

Mason, Adrienne. "'L'air du climat et le goût du terroir': Translation as Cultural Capital in the Writings of Madame Du Châtelet." In *Emilie Du Châtelet: Rewriting Enlightenment Philosophy and Science*, ed. J. P. Zinsser and J. Hayes, 123–40. Oxford: Voltaire Foundation, 2006.

Mason, H. A. "Clique Puffery in Roscommon's *Essay on Translated Verse*?" *Notes and Queries* 37, no. 3 (1990): 296.

Massardier-Kenney, Françoise. "Towards a Redefinition of Feminist Translation Practice." *The Translator* 3, no. 1 (1997): 55–69.

Mathieu-Castellani, Gisèle. *La Rhétorique des passions.* Paris: PUF, 2000.

May, Thomas, trans. *Lucan's Pharsalia, or The Civill Warres of Rome, between Pompey the Great and Julius Caesar.* London: Thomas Jones and John Marriott, 1627.

Mazon, Paul. *Madame Dacier et les traductions d'Homère en France.* Oxford: Clarendon Press, 1936.

McCabe, Herbert. "The Eucharist as Language." *Modern Theology* 15, no. 2 (1999): 131–41.

McFarland, Thomas. "The Originality Paradox." *New Literary History* 5, no. 3 (1974): 447–76.

McKeon, Michael. *The Origins of the English Novel, 1600–1740.* Baltimore: Johns Hopkins Univ. Press, 1987.

McMahon, Joseph H. "Ducis: Unkindest Cutter?" *Yale French Studies* 33 (1964): 14–25.

McMorran, Edith, ed. "La Traduction au XVIIIe siècle." *SVEC* 4 (2001): 269–318.

McMorran, Will. "Fielding in France: La Place's *Tom Jones*." *SVEC* 4 (2001): 285–90.

McMurran, Mary Helen. "Aphra Behn from Both Sides: Translation in the Atlantic World." *Studies in Eighteenth-Century Culture* 34 (2005): 1–23.

———. "National or Transnational? The Eighteenth-Century Novel." In M. Cohen and C. Dever, *Literary Channel*, 50–72.

———. "Taking Liberties: Translation and the Development of the Eighteenth-Century Novel." *The Translator* 6, no. 1 (2000): 87–108.

Méchoulan, Eric. *Le Livre avalé: De la littérature entre mémoire et culture.* Montreal: Presses de l'université de Montréal, 2004.

Medlin, Dorothy. "André Morellet, Translator of Liberal Thought." *SVEC* 174 (1978): 189–201.

———. "André Morellet's 'Observations' on the Translation of *Othello* by Le Tourneur." *Actes de langue française et de linguistique* 10–11 (1997–98): 89–106.

Mercier, Daniel. *L'Epreuve de la représentation: L'Enseignement des langues étrangères et la pratique de la traduction en France au XVIIe et XVIIIe siècles.* Paris: Les Belles lettres, 1995.

———. "La Problématique de l'équivalence des langues aux XVIIe et XVIIIe siècles." In Ballard and D'Hulst, *La Traduction en France*, 63–81.

Merkle, Denise, ed. "Censure et traduction." Special issue, *TTR: Traduction, Terminologie, Rédaction* 15, no. 2 (2002).

Meschonnic, Henri. *Poétique du traduire.* Paris: Verdier, 1999.

Meziriac, Claude-Gaspar Bachet de. *See* Bachet, Claude-Gaspard de, sieur de Meziriac.

Michelucci, Pascal. "Shakespeare traduit devant le tribunal du goût: *Macbeth* et *Othello* (1746–1829)." *Actes de langue française et de linguistique* 10–11 (1997–98): 75–88.

Milbank, John. "Can a Gift Be Given? Prolegomena to a Future Trinitarian Metaphysic." *Modern Theology* 11, no. 1 (1995): 119–61.

Miller, J. Hillis. *Others*. Princeton, NJ: Princeton Univ. Press, ~~2001~~. *[2001]*

Millot, Claude François Xavier, abbé, trans. *Harangues d'Eschine et de Démosthene sur la couronne*. Lyon: Benoit Duplain, 1764.

Miner, Earl. "The Poetics of the Critical Act: Dryden's Dealings with Rivals and Predecessors." In *Critical Essays on John Dryden*, ed. James Winn, 33–47. New York: G. K. Hall, 1997.

Miner, Earl, and Jennifer Brady, eds. *Literary Transmission and Literary Authority: Dryden and Other Writers*. Cambridge: Cambridge Univ. Press, 1993.

Moncond'huy, Dominique, ed. "Pierre Du Ryer: Dramaturge et traducteur." Special issue, *Littératures classiques* 42 (Spring 2001). *[2001]*

Montgomery, Robert L. *Terms of Response: Language and Audience in Seventeenth- and Eighteenth-Century Theory*. University Park, PA: Penn State Univ. Press, 1992.

Montolieu, Isabelle de. *Caroline de Litchfield, ou Mémoires d'une Famille Prussienne*. 3rd ed. Paris: Arthus-Bertrand, 1815.

———, trans. *Raison et Sensibilité, ou Les Deux Manières d'Aimer*, by Jane Austen. Paris: Arthus-Bertrand, 1815.

Moore, Fabienne. "Homer Revisited: Anne Le Fèvre Dacier's Preface to Her Prose Translation of the *Iliad* in Early Eighteenth-Century France." *Studies in the Literary Imagination* 33, no. 2 (2000): 87–107.

———. *Prose Poems of the French Enlightenment: Re-placing a Genre*. Aldershot, UK: Ashgate, forthcoming. *[forthcoming]*

More, Thomas, trans. *Odes of Anacreon*. London: John Stockdale, 1800.

Morellet, André, trans. *Traité des délits et des peines, traduit de l'italien, d'après la troisieme Edition, revue, corrigée et augmentée par l'Auteur. Avec des Additions de l'Auteur, qui n'ont pas encore paru en Italien*, by Beccaria. Lausanne: n.p., 1766.

Moretti, Franco. *Atlas of the European Novel, 1800–1900*. London: Verso, 1998.

Morris, David B. "Writing/Reading/Remembering: Dryden and the Poetics of Memory." In *Critical Essays on John Dryden*, ed. James Winn, 161–80. New York: G. K. Hall, 1997.

Morton, Richard. "'Bringing *Virgil* over into *Britain*': John Dryden Refigures *Aeneid* 1–5." *Studies in Eighteenth-Century Culture* 27 (1998): 147–67.

Morvan de Bellegarde, Jean-Baptiste. *Réflexions sur l'élégance et la politesse du style*. Paris, 1695; repr. Geneva: Slatkine, 1971.

Motooka, Wendy. *The Age of Reasons: Quixotism, Sentimentalism and Political Economy in Eighteenth-Century Britain*. London: Routledge, 1998.

Motteux, Peter Anthony, trans. *The History of the Renown'd Don Quixote De la Mancha. Written in Spanish by Miguel de Cervantes Saavedra. Translated from the Original by several Hands: and publish'd by Peter Motteux, Servant to his Majesty*. 2 vols. London: Sam Buckley, 1700.

Mounin, Georges. *Les Belles infidèles*. Paris: Cahiers du sud, 1955.

Munteano, Basil. "Port Royal et la stylistique de la traduction." *C.A.I.E.F.* 8 (1956): 157–72.

Murray, Timothy. "Translating Montaigne's Crypts: Melancholic Relations and the Sites of Altarbiography." In *Repossessions: Psychoanalysis and the Phantasms of Early Modern Culture*, ed. Timothy Murray and Alan K. Smith, 47–77. Minneapolis: Univ. of Minnesota Press, 1998.

Nancy, Jean-Luc. *Corpus*. Paris: Métailié, 2000.

———. *Etre singulier pluriel*. Paris: Galilée, 1996. *Being Singular Plural*. Trans. Robert D. Richardson and Anne E. O'Byrne. Stanford: Stanford Univ. Press, 2000.

———. *L'Intrus*. Paris: Galilée, 2000.

Nardis, Luigi, et al., eds. *Regole della Traduzione: Testi inediti di Port-Royal e del "Cercle" di Miramion (metà del XVII secolo)*. Napoli: Bibliopolis, 1991. (Includes works by Antoine Le Maistre, Robert Arnauld d'Andilly, and other members of the Port Royal circle. French texts with Italian apparatus.)

Ndiaye, Aloyse Raymond. *La Philosophie d'Antoine Arnauld*. Paris: Vrin, 1991.

Niranjana, Tejaswini. *Siting Translation: History, Post-structuralism, and the Colonial Context*. Berkeley: Univ. of California Press, 1992.

Norbrook, David. *Writing the English Republic: Poetry, Rhetoric, and Politics, 1627–1660*. Cambridge: Cambridge Univ. Press, 1999.

Norton, Glyn P. *The Ideology and Language of Translation in Renaissance France and Their Humanist Antecedents*. Geneva: Droz, 1984.

Nouss, Alexis, ed. "Antoine Berman aujourd'hui." Special issue, *TTR: Traduction, Terminologie, Rédaction* 14, no. 2 (2001).

Olivet, Pierre-Joseph Thoulier, abbé d', trans. *Philippes de Démosthene, et Catilinaires de Ciceron*. 3rd ed. Paris: Piget, 1744.

Ormsby, John, trans. *The Ingenious Gentleman Don Quixote of La Mancha*. 2 vols. London, 1883; New York: Century, 1907.

Oudin, César, and François de Rosset, trans. *Le Valeureux Dom Quixote de La Manche ou L'Histoire de ses grands exploicts d'armes, fideles Amours, & Adventures estranges*. 2 vols. Rouen: Jacques Cailloué, 1646. Re-edited as *L'Ingénieux Hidalgo Don Quichotte de la Manche et nouvelles exemplaires*. Paris: Gallimard, 1949.

Ozell, John, trans. *The Adventures of Telemachus, the Son of Ulysses*, by Fénelon. 2 vols. London, 1735.

———, trans. *The History of the Renowned Don Quixote de la Mancha. Written in Spanish by Miguel de Cervantes Saavedra. Translated by Several Hands: and published by the Late Mr. Motteux. Revis'd a-new from the best Spanish Edition, By Mr. Ozell: Who has likewise added Explanatory Notes from Jarvis, Oudin, Sobrino, Pineda, Gregorio, and the Royal Academy dictionary of Madrid*. 2 vols. Glasgow: Robert and Andrew Foulis, 1771.

Ozell, John, and Peter Motteux, trans. *The History of the Renowned Don Quixote de la Mancha*. 4th ed. 4 vols. London: Knaplock, Midwinter, Tonson, Churchill, 1719.

Patterson, Annabel. *Censorship and Interpretation: The Conditions of Writing and Reading in Early Modern England*. Madison: Univ. of Wisconsin Press, 1984.

———. *Fables of Power: Aesopian Writing and Political History*. Durham, NC: Duke Univ. Press, 1991.

Paulson, Ronald. *Don Quixote in England: The Aesthetics of Laughter.* Baltimore: Johns Hopkins Univ. Press, 1998.

Paxman, David B. *Voyage into Language: Space and the Linguistic Encounter, 1500–1800.* Aldershot, UK: Ashgate, 2003.

Pearcy, Lee T. *The Mediated Muse: English Translations of Ovid, 1560–1700.* Hamden, CT: Archon Books, 1984.

Pécharman, Martine. "La Question des 'règles de la critique' à Port-Royal." *Revue de métaphysique et de morale* 4 (1999): 463–87.

Pecora, Vincent P. "Ethics, Politics, and the Middle Voice." *Yale French Studies* 79 (1991): 203–30.

Pellisson-Fontanier, Paul, and Pierre-Joseph Thoulier, abbé d'Olivet. *Histoire de l'Académie française.* 3rd ed. 2 vols. Paris: J.-B. Coignard, 1743.

Perrault, Charles. *Parallèle des anciens et des modernes en ce qui concerne les arts et les sciences.* 4 vols. Paris, 1692–1697; repr. Geneva: Slatkine, 1979.

Petit, Jean, abbé, trans. *Lettres de S. Jerôme. Traduction nouvelle, derniere edition, corrigée & augmentée.* Paris: Jean Couterot, 1679.

Petit réservoir, contenant une Variété de faits Historiques et Critiques, de Litterature, de Morale et de Poësies, etc. Et quelques fois de Petites Avantures Romanesques et Galantes, ouvrage périodique. 5 vols. Berlin: J. Neaulme, 1750–51.

Philips, Jenkin Thomas, trans. *A Compendious Way of Teaching Ancient and Modern Languages,* by Tanneguy le Fèvre. London, 1723; repr. Menston, UK: Scolar Press, 1972.

Phillips, John, trans. *The History of the most Renowned Don Quixote of Mancha: and his Trusty Squire Sancho Pancha.* London: printed by Thomas Hodgkin, 1687.

Pieretti, Marie-Pascale. "Veiled Presence in the Diffusion of English Letters: Mme Thiroux d'Arconville's Translations in the 1770s." In *These Women Who Want to Be Authors . . . ,* ed. Mihaela Mudisre, 123–39. Cluj-Napoca, Romania: Editura Motiv, 2001.

———. "Women Writers and Translation in 18th-Century France." PhD diss., New York Univ., 1998.

———. "Women Writers in Eighteenth-Century France." *French Review* 75 (2002): 474–88.

Pitassi, Maria Cristina. *Entre croire et savoir: Le Problème de la méthode critique chez Jean Le Clerc.* Leiden, Netherlands: E. J. Brill, 1987.

Pitt, Christopher, trans. *The Works of Virgil.* 4 vols. London: R. Dodsley, 1753.

Pocock, J. G. A. *The Machiavellian Moment: Florentine Political Thought and the Atlantic Republican Tradition.* Princeton, NJ: Princeton Univ. Press, 1975.

Pons, Jean-François, abbé de. *Lettre à Monsieur *** sur l'Iliade de M. de la Motte.* Paris: Laurent Seneuze, 1714.

———. *Oeuvres de Monsieur l'abbé de Pons.* Paris: Prault, 1738.

Pope, Alexander. *Essai sur l'homme, Poëme philosophique par Alexandre Pope, en cinq langues, savoir: Anglais, Latin, Italien, François & Allemand.* Polyglot edition with English original followed by translations by Johan Joachim Gottlob

Am-Ende (Latin), Giovanni Castiglioni (Italian), Etienne de Silhouette, the abbé du Resnel (French), and Heinrich Christian Kretsch (German). Strasbourg: Armand König, 1762.

———, trans. *The Iliad of Homer*. Vols. 7–8 of *The Works of Alexander Pope*, ed. Maynard Mack et al. London: Methuen, 1967.

———, trans. *The Odyssey of Homer*. Vols. 9–10 of *The Works of Alexander Pope*, ed. Maynard Mack et al. London: Methuen, 1967.

Porter, Roy, and Mikuláš Teich, eds. *The Enlightenment in National Context*. Cambridge: Cambridge Univ. Press, 1981.

Potter, Lois. *Secret Rites and Secret Writing: Royalist Literature, 1641–1660*. Cambridge: Cambridge Univ. Press, 1989.

Prévost, Antoine François, abbé, trans. *Lettres angloises, ou Histoire de Miss Clarisse Harlove*. 6 vols. London: Nourse, 1751; repr. Paris: Desjonquères, 1999.

Priestley, Joseph. *A Course of Lectures on the Theory of Language and Universal Grammar*. Warrington, UK: W. Eyres, 1765.

Puisieux, P. F. de, trans. *Amélie, histoire angloise. Traduite fidèlement de l'anglois de M. Fielding*. London [Paris?]: Charpentier, 1762.

Pym, Anthony. *Method in Translation History*. Manchester, UK: St. Jerome, 1998.

———. *Pour une éthique du traducteur*. Artois: Artois presses université; Ottawa: Presses de l'université d'Ottawa, 1997.

Radnóti, Sándor. *The Fake: Forgery and Its Place in Art*. Trans. Ervin Dunai. Lanham, MD: Rowman and Littlefield, 1999.

Rand, Nicholas. "The Translator and the Myth of the Public: 'Introductory Remarks' to the First French Translations of Swift, Young, and Shakespeare." *MLN* 100 (1985): 1092–1102.

Rener, Frederick. *Interpretatio: Language and Translation from Cicero to Tytler*. Amsterdam and Atlanta: Rodopi, 1989.

Renken, Arno. *La Représentation de l'étranger: Une réflexion hermeneutique sur la notion de traduction*. Lausanne: Centre de traduction littéraire, 2002.

Resnel, Jean François du Bellay, abbé de, trans. *Les Principes de la morale et du goût, traduits de l'anglois de M. Pope . . . Nouvelle edition*. 1737; repr. London: n.p., 1750.

Reverand, Cedric D. *Dryden's Final Poetic Mode: The Fables*. Philadelphia: Univ. of Pennsylvania Press, 1988.

Riccoboni, Marie-Jeanne, trans. *Amélie, roman de Mr. Fielding, traduit de l'Anglois par Madame Riccoboni*. Paris: J. F. Bassompierre, 1763.

Richardson, Samuel. *The History of Sir Charles Grandison*. Ed. Jocelyn Harris. 3 vols. London: Oxford Univ. Press, 1972.

Ricken, Ulrich. *Grammaire et philosophie au siècle des Lumières: Controverses sur l'ordre naturel et la clarté du français*. Villeneuve d'Ascq, France: Publications de l'université de Lille, 1978.

———. *Linguistics, Anthropology and Philosophy in the French Enlightenment*. Trans. R. E. Norton. London: Routledge, 1994.

Rigault, Hyppolite. *Histoire de la querelle des anciens et des modernes*. Paris, 1859; repr. New York: Burt Franklin, n.d.

Rivara, Annie. "*Amelia* de Fielding en 'habit françois,' Puisieux et Mme Ricco-boni." In Cointre, Lautel, and Rivara, *La Traduction romanesque*, 221–46.

———. "*Oroonoko ou le Prince Nègre*: La Traduction du *Royal Slave* d'A. Behn par La Place." In Rivara, *La Traduction des langues modernes*, 109–35.

———, ed. *La Traduction des langues modernes au XVIIIe siècle*. Paris: Honoré Champion, 2002.

Rivarol, Antoine de. *Pensées diverses, suivi de discours sur l'universalité de la langue française*. Ed. S. Menant. Paris: Desjonquères, 1998.

Robinet, André. *Le Langage à l'âge classique*. Paris: Klincksieck, 1978.

Robinson, Douglas. "Theorizing Translation in a Woman's Voice: Subverting the Rhetoric of Patronage, Courtly Love, and Morality." *The Translator* 1 (1995): 153–75.

———. *Translation and Taboo*. DeKalb: Northern Illinois Univ. Press, 1996.

———. *The Translator's Turn*. Baltimore: Johns Hopkins Univ. Press, 1991.

———, ed. *Western Translation Theory from Herodotus to Nietzsche*. 2nd ed. Manchester, UK: St. Jerome, 2002.

Rochedieu, Charles. *Bibliography of French Translations of English Works*. Chicago: Univ. of Chicago Press, 1948.

Rogers, Pat. "Book Dedications in Britain, 1700–1799: A Preliminary Survey." *British Journal for 18th-Century Studies* 16, no. 2 (1993): 213–33.

Rollin, Charles. *De la maniere d'enseigner et d'étudier les belles-lettres, par raport à l'esprit & au coeur*. 2 vols. Paris: la Veuve Estienne, 1740.

Roscommon, Wentworth Dillon, earl of. *An Essay on Translated Verse*. 2nd ed. London: Jacob Tonson, 1685.

———. *Poems*. London: J. Tonson, 1717.

Rosenthal, Laura. *Playwrights and Plagiarists in Early Modern England: Gender, Authorship, Literary Property*. Ithaca, NY: Cornell Univ. Press, 1996.

Ross, Trevor. "The Rules of the Game, or Why Neoclassicism Was Never an Ideology." In *Ideology and Form in Eighteenth-Century Literature*, ed. Daniel Richter. Lubbock: Texas Tech Univ. Press, 1999.

———. "Translation and the Canonical Text." *Studies in the Literary Imagination* 33, no. 2 (2000): 1–21.

Rowe, Nicholas. "Some Account of Boileau's Writings, And this Translation." Preface to *Boileau's Lutrin: A Mock-heroic Poem*. Trans. John Ozell. London: E. Sanger and E. Curll, 1708.

Rumbold, Margaret. *Traducteur huguenot: Pierre Coste*. New York: Peter Lang, 1991.

Sacy, Isaac-Louis le Maistre de. *See* Le Maistre de Sacy, Isaac-Louis de.

Sahlins, Peter. "Fictions of a Catholic France: The Naturalization of Foreigners, 1685–1787." *Representations* 47 (1994): 85–110.

———. *Unnaturally French: Foreign Citizens in the Old Regime and After*. Ithaca, NY: Cornell Univ. Press, 2004.

Saint-Hyacinthe, Thémiseul de. *Lettre à Madame Dacier, Sur son Livre des Causes de la Corruption du goust*. n.p.: n.p., 1715.

Saint-Simon, Maximilien-Henri, marquis de, trans. *Essai de traduction littérale et énergique, nouvelle edition.* Amsterdam: D. J. Changuion, 1787. Translation of Pope, *Essay on Man.*

Sallust. *All the Works of that Famous Historian Caius Salustius Crispus . . .* Translator unknown. London: printed by T.B. for Richard Wild, 1687.

Salmon, J. H. M. "Stoicism and Roman Example: Seneca and Tacitus in Jacobean England." *Journal of the History of Ideas* 50 (1989): 199–225.

Sandys, George, trans. *Ovid's Metamorphosis Englished, Mythologiz'd, and Represented in Figures. An Essay to the translation of Virgil's Aeneis.* Oxford: printed by John Lichfield, 1632.

Saunders, David, and Ian Hunter. "Lessons from the 'Literatory': How to Historicise Authorship." *Critical Inquiry* 17 (1991): 479–509.

Saunders, Francis. "The Publisher to the Reader." In *The Temple of Death, a Poem . . . With several other Excellent Poems . . .* 2nd ed. London: printed by Tho. Warren for Francis Saunders, 1695.

Scarron, Paul, trans. *Le Virgile travesty en vers burlesques.* Paris: T. Quinet, 1648.

Schroeder, H. J., O.P., trans. *Canons and Decrees of the Council of Trent.* London: B. Herder, 1941.

Schulte, Rainer, and John Biguenet, eds. *Theories of Translation: An Anthology of Essays from Dryden to Derrida.* Chicago: Univ. of Chicago Press, 1992.

Sedgwick, Alexander. *Jansenism in Seventeenth-Century France: Voices in the Wilderness.* Charlottesville: Univ. Press of Virginia, 1977.

———. *The Travails of Conscience: The Arnauld Family and the Ancien Régime.* Cambridge, MA: Harvard Univ. Press, 1998.

Segrais, Jean Regnault de. *Oeuvres, nouvelle édition revue et corrigée.* 2 vols. Paris, 1755; repr. Geneva: Slatkine, 1968.

———, trans. *Traduction de l'Enéide de Virgile.* 2 vols. Paris: Denys Thierry [et] Claude Barbin, 1668.

Séguin, J.-A.-R. *French Works in English Translation, 1731–1799.* 6 vols. Jersey City, NJ: Ross Paxton, 1965–1970.

Sellier, Philippe. Preface to *La Bible,* trans. Le Maistre de Sacy, x–liii. Paris: Robert Laffont, 1990.

Sermain, Jean-Paul. *Le Singe de don Quichotte: Marivaux, Cervantes et le roman postcritique.* Oxford: Voltaire Foundation, 1999.

Shadwell, Thomas, trans. *The Tenth Satyr of Juvenal, English and Latin.* London: printed by D. Mallet, for Gabriel Collins, 1687.

Sharpe, Kevin. *Remapping Early Modern England: The Culture of Seventeenth-Century Politics.* Cambridge: Cambridge Univ. Press, 2000.

Sheehan, Jonathan. *The Enlightenment Bible.* Princeton, NJ: Princeton Univ. Press, 2005.

Shelton, Thomas. *The History of Don-Quichote.* n.p.: n.p., 1620.

Sherburne, Edward. *The Character of an Agitator.* n.p.: n.p., 1647.

———, trans. *Medea: A Tragedy.* London: Humphrey Moseley, 1648.

————, trans. *Seneca's Answer, to Lucilius His Quaere; Why Good Men suffer misfortunes seeing there is a Divine Providence? Written Originally in Latin Prose, and Now Translated into English Verse.* London: Humphrey Moseley, 1648.

————, trans. *The Tragedies of L. Annaeus Seneca the Philosopher; viz. Medea, Phaedra and Hyppolitus, Troades, or the Royal Captives, and the Rape of Helen, out of the Greek of Coluthus . . .* London: S. Smith and B. Walford, 1702.

————, trans. *Troades, or The Royal Captives. A Tragedy. Written Originally in Latin, By Lucius Annaeus Seneca, The Philosopher.* London: printed by Anne Godbid and John Playford for Samuel Carr, 1679.

Silhouette, Etienne de, trans. *Essai sur la critique. Par M. Pope. Traduit de l'Anglois en François par M.D.S.* Paris: chez Alix, 1736.

————, trans. *Essai sur l'homme. Par M. Pope. Traduit de l'Anglois en François par M.D.S.* [Paris]: n.p., [1736].

————, trans. *Essais sur la critique et sur l'homme, par M. Pope, nouvelle édition.* London: n.p., 1737. This is Silhouette's second edition, containing the first appearance of his "Réflexions préliminaires du traducteur sur le goût des traductions" (3–16).

Simon, Richard. *Histoire critique du vieux testament . . . Nouvelle edition.* Rotterdam: Reinier Leers, 1685.

Simon, Sherry. *Gender in Translation: Cultural Identity and the Politics of Transmission.* London: Routledge, 1996.

Sloman, Judith. *Dryden: The Poetics of Translation.* Toronto: Univ. of Toronto Press, 1985.

Smith, Charles Kay. "French Philosophy and English Politics in Interregnum Poetry." In *The Stuart Court and Europe: Essays in Politics and Political Culture,* ed. R. Malcolm Smuts, 177–209. Cambridge: Cambridge Univ. Press, 1996.

Smith, Nigel. *Literature and Revolution in England, 1640–1660.* New Haven, CT: Yale Univ. Press, 1994.

Smith, William, trans. *The History of the Peloponnesian War, translated from the Greek of Thucydides.* 2 vols. London: printed by John Watts, 1753.

Smollett, Tobias, trans. *The Adventures of Telemachus, the Son of Ulysses,* by Fénelon. Ed. Leslie A. Chilton and O. M. Brack. Jr. Athens: Univ. of Georgia Press, 1997.

————, trans. *The Life and Adventures of the Renowned Don Quixote.* Ed. Martin C. Battestin and O. M. Brack Jr. Athens: Univ. of Georgia Press, 2003.

Sol, Antoinette. "A French Reading and Critical Rewriting of Mary Hays's *Memoirs of Emma Courtney*." *EMF: Studies in Early Modern France* 8 (2002): 226–43.

Somers, John, ed. *Several orations of Demosthenes . . . To which is prefix'd the historical preface of Monsieur Toureil.* London: Tonson, 1702.

Sorel, Charles. *La Bibliothèque françoise.* 2nd ed. 1667; repr. Geneva: Slatkine, 1970.

Sorenson, Janet. *The Grammar of Empire in Eighteenth-Century British Writing.* Cambridge: Cambridge Univ. Press, 2000.

Soulier, Didier. *La Littérature baroque en Europe.* Paris: PUF, 1988.

Sprat, Thomas. *The History of the Royal Society of London, For the Improving of Natural Knowledge*. London: printed by T.R. for J. Martyn, 1667.

Stackelberg, Jürgen von. "*Oroonoko* et l'abolition de l'esclavage: Le Rôle du traducteur." *Revue de littérature comparée* 63, no. 2 (1989): 237–48.

———. "La Traduction dans l'Europe française (1680–1760)." In *L'Aube de la modernité, 1680–1760*, ed. Peter-Eckhard Knabe et al., 47–61. Amsterdam: John Benjamins, 2002.

Staël, Germaine de. "De l'esprit de traductions" (1816). In *Oeuvres completes*, 2: 294–97. 1861; repr. Geneva: Slatkine, 1967.

Stapylton, Robert, trans. *Dido and Aeneas. The Fourth Book of Virgils Aeneas*. n.p.: William Cooke, [1634].

———, trans. *Mores Hominum. The Manners of Men, described in sixteen Satyrs, by Juvenal*. London: R. Hodgkinsonne, 1660.

Statt, Daniel. *Foreigners and Englishmen: The Controversy over Immigration and Population, 1660–1760*. Newark: Univ. of Delaware Press, 1995.

Steiner, George. *After Babel: Aspects of Language and Translation*. 2nd ed. Oxford: Oxford Univ. Press, 1992.

Steiner, T. R. *English Translation Theory, 1650–1800*. Assen, Netherlands: Van Gorcum, 1975.

Stevens, John, trans. *The History of the most Ingenious Knight Don Quixote de la Mancha. Written in Spanish by Michael de Cervantes Saavedra. Formerly made English by Thomas Shelton; now Revis'd, corrected, and partly new Translated from the Original, by Capt. John Stevens*. 2nd ed. London: printed for R. Chiswell, S. and J. Sprint, R. Battersby, S. Smith, and B. Walford, M. Wotton, and G. Conyers, 1706.

Strahan, Alexander, trans. *The First Six Books of the Aeneid, translated into Blank Verse*. London: T. Payne and A. Strahan, 1753.

Streeter, Harold Wade. *The Eighteenth-Century English Novel in French Translation: A Bibliographic Study*. 1936; repr. New York: Benjamin Blom, 1970.

Tende, Gaspard de. *De la Traduction, ou Regles pour apprendre a traduire la langue latine en la langue françoise. Tirées de quelques-unes des meilleures Traductions du Temps. Par le Sr. de L'Estang*. Paris: Jean le Mire, 1660.

Ter Horst, Robert. "Cervantes and the Paternity of the English Novel." In *Cultural Authority in Golden Age Spain*, ed. M. S. Brownlee and H. U. Gumbrecht. Baltimore: Johns Hopkins Univ. Press, 1995.

Thiroux d'Arconville, Marie-Geneviève-Charlotte, trans. *Avis d'un Père à sa Fille. Par le marquis d'Hallifax*. London: n.p., 1756.

———, trans. *Méditations sur les tombeaux, par Hervey; traduites de l'Anglois*. Paris: Lacombe, 1771.

Thomas, Claudia. *Alexander Pope and His Eighteenth-Century Women Readers*. Carbondale: Southern Illinois Univ. Press, 1994.

———. "'Th' Instructive Moral, and Important Thought': Elizabeth Carter Reads Pope, Johnson, and Epictetus." *The Age of Johnson* 4 (1991): 137–69.

Thomas, Francis-Noël. "Recent English Translations of *La Princesse de Clèves*." *EMF: Studies in Early Modern France* 8 (2002): 268–83.

Tourreil, Jacques de, trans. *Harangues de Demosthene. Avec des remarques.* Paris: Antoine Dezallier, 1691.

———. *Oeuvres.* 2 vols. Paris: Brunet, 1721.

Toury, Gideon. *In Search of a Theory of Translation.* Tel Aviv: Porter Institute, 1980.

Turgot, Anne-Robert-Jacques. "Réflexions sur les langues," In *Oeuvres*, 2:752–56. 1844; repr. Osnabrük, Germany: Otto Zeller, 1966.

———. "Remarques critiques sur les Réflexions de M. de Maupertuis, sur l'origine des langues et la signification des mots." In *Oeuvres*, 2:709–24. 1844; repr. Osnabrük, Germany: Otto Zeller, 1966.

Turner, Dorothy. "Roger L'Estrange's Deferential Politics in the Public Sphere." *Seventeenth Century* 13, no. 1 (1998): 85–101.

Tytler, Alexander. *Essay on the Principles of Translation.* London: T. Cadell and W. Creech, 1791.

———. *Essay on the Principles of Translation.* 3rd ed. 1813; repr. Amsterdam: John Benjamins, 1978.

Van Kley, Dale. *The Religious Origins of the French Revolution.* New Haven, CT: Yale Univ. Press, 1996.

Van Tieghem, Paul. *L'Année littéraire (1754–1790) comme intermédiaire en France des littératures étrangères.* Paris: F. Rieder & Cie., 1917.

———. *Le Préromantisme: Etudes d'histoire littéraire européenne.* 3 vols. 1924–47; repr. Geneva: Slatkine, 1973.

Vance, Norman. *Irish Literature: A Social History.* 2nd ed. Dublin: Four Courts Press, 1999.

Vaugelas, Claude Favre de. *Nouvelles remarques sur la langue françoise.* Ed. Louis-Auguste Alemand. Paris: G. Desprez, 1697.

———, trans. *Quinte-Curce, De la vie et des actions d'Alexandre le Grand. De la traduction de Mr. De Vaugelas. Avec les supplemens de Freinshemius traduits par Monsieur Durier.* 2 vols. The Hague: Alberts & Vander Kloot, 1727.

Vauvilliers, Jean-François de, trans. *Essai sur Pindare, contenant une Traduction de quelques Odes de ce Poëte, avec une Analyse raisonnée & des Notes historiques, poétiques, & grammaticales; le tout précédé d'un Discours sur Pindare & sur la vraie maniere de le traduire.* Paris: Paul-Denis Brocas, 1772.

Venuti, Lawrence. *The Scandals of Translation.* London: Routledge, 1998.

———. *The Translator's Invisibility: A History of Translation.* London: Routledge, 1995.

Viala, Alain. *Naissance de l'écrivain: Sociologie de la littérature à l'âge classique.* Paris: Minuit, 1985.

Vicars, John, trans. *The XII Aeneids of Virgil, the most renowned Laureat-Prince of Latine-Poets; translated into English deca-syllables.* [London]: Alsop, 1632.

Volpilhac-Auger, Catherine. *Tacite en France de Montesquieu à Chateaubriand.* Oxford: Voltaire Foundation, 1993.

Voltaire. *Oeuvres.* Ed. Louis Moland. 52 vols. Paris: Garnier, 1877–85.

Wahrman, Dror. "How the English Wrote Their Juvenal, 1644–1815." *Representations* 65 (1999): 1–41.

Wall, Wendy. *The Imprint of Gender: Authorship and Publication in the English Renaissance*. Ithaca, NY: Cornell Univ. Press, 1993.

Waller, Edmund, and Sidney Godolphin, trans. *The Passion of Dido for Aeneas. As it is Incomparably exprest in the Fourth Book of Virgil.* London: Humphrey Moseley, 1658.

Ward, Graham. *Cities of God*. London: Routledge, 2000.

Wardropper, Bruce W. "*Duelos y Quebrantos*, Once Again." *Romance Notes* 20 (1980): 413–16.

Warton, Joseph, Christopher Pitt, et al., trans. *The Works of Virgil*. 4 vols. London: R. Dodsley, 1753.

Warton, Thomas. *Observations on the Fairy Queen of Spenser*. 2 vols. London: R. and J. Dodsley, 1762.

Webb, Stephen H. "The Rhetoric of Ethics as Excess: A Christian Theological Response to Emmanuel Levinas." *Modern Theology* 15, no. 1 (1999): 1–16.

Webbe, Joseph, trans. *The Familiar Epistles of M. T. Cicero. Englished and Conferred with the French and Italian and Other Translations*. London: Edward Griffin, [1620].

Weil, Françoise. "L'Abbé Desfontaines traducteur: Des *Voyages de Gulliver* (1727) aux *Avantures de Joseph Andrews* (1744)." In Rivara, *La Traduction des langues modernes*, 49–55.

Weinbrot, Howard. "Alexander Pope and Madame Dacier's *Homer*: Conjectures Concerning Cardinal Dubois, Sir Luke Schaub, and Samuel Buckley." *Huntington Library Quarterly* 62, no. 1–2 (1999): 1–23.

———. "'An Ambition to Excell': The Aesthetics of Emulation in the Seventeenth and Eighteenth Centuries." *Huntington Library Quarterly* 48 (1985): 121–39.

———. "Annotating a Career: From Pope's Homer to the Dunciad: From Madame Dacier to Madame Dacier by Way of Swift." *Philological Quarterly* 79 (2000): 459–83.

———. *Britannia's Issue: The Rise of British Literature from Dryden to Ossian*. Cambridge: Cambridge Univ. Press, 1993.

———. "Enlightenment Canon Wars: Anglo-French Views of Literary Greatness." *ELH* 60 (1993): 79–100.

———. *The Formal Strain: Studies in Augustan Imitation and Satire*. Chicago: Chicago Univ. Press, 1969.

Wells, Margaret B. "What Did Du Bellay Mean by 'Translation'?" *Forum for Modern Language Studies* 16 (1980): 175–85.

Wetsel, David. *L'Ecriture et le Reste: The Pensées of Pascal in the Exegetical Tradition of Port-Royal*. Columbus: Ohio State Univ. Press, 1991.

Wilkins, John. *An Essay towards a Real Character, and a Philosophical Language*. London: printed for S. Gellibrand and John Martyn, 1668.

Williams, Carolyn D. "Poetry, Puddings, and Epictetus: The Consistency of Elizabeth Carter." In *Tradition in Transition: Women Writers, Marginal Texts, and the Eighteenth-Century Canon*, ed. Alvaro Ribeiro and James G. Basker, 3–24. Oxford: Clarendon Press, 1996.

————. *Pope, Homer, and Manliness: Some Aspects of Eighteenth-Century Classical Learning.* London: Routledge, 1993.

Winn, James. *John Dryden and His World.* New Haven, CT: Yale Univ. Press, 1987.

Wolff, Larry, and Marco Cipolloni, eds. *The Anthropology of the Enlightenment.* Stanford: Stanford Univ. Press, 2007.

Womersley, David, ed. *Augustan Critical Writing.* London: Penguin, 1997.

Worth, Valerie. *Practising Translation in Renaissance France: The Example of Etienne Dolet.* Oxford: Clarendon Press, 1989.

Yates, Frances A. *The Art of Memory.* Chicago: Univ. of Chicago Press, 1966.

Young, Edward. *Conjectures on Original Composition.* 1759; repr. Leeds: Scolar Press, 1966.

————. *Night Thoughts.* Ed. Stephen Cornford. Cambridge: Cambridge Univ. Press, 1989.

Zinsser, Judith P. "Emilie Du Châtelet: Genius, Gender, and Intellectual Authority." In *Women Writers and the Early Modern British Political Tradition*, ed. Hilda L. Smith, 168–90. Cambridge: Cambridge Univ. Press, 1998.

————. "Entrepreneur of the 'Republic of Letters': Emilie de Breteuil, marquise du Châtelet, and Bernard Mandeville's *Fable of the Bees*." *French Historical Studies* 25 (2002): 595–624.

Zuber, Roger. *Les Belles infidèles et la formation du goût classique.* 2nd ed. Paris: Albin Michel, 1995.

Zwicker, Steven. *Lines of Authority: Politics and English Literary Culture, 1649–1689.* Ithaca, NY: Cornell Univ. Press, 1993.

————. *Politics and Language in Dryden's Poetry: The Arts of Disguise.* Princeton, NJ: Princeton Univ. Press, 1984.

Zwicker, Steven, and David Bywaters. "Politics and Translation: The English Tacitus of 1698." *Huntington Library Quarterly* 52 (1989): 319–46.

Index